*Karl Marx and the
Radical Critique of Judaism*

THE LITTMAN LIBRARY OF JEWISH CIVILIZATION

Karl Marx and the
Radical Critique of Judaism

JULIUS CARLEBACH

ROUTLEDGE & KEGAN PAUL
LONDON, HENLEY AND BOSTON

First published in 1978
by Routledge & Kegan Paul Ltd
39 Store Street,
London WC1E 7DD,
Reading Road,
Henley-on-Thames,
Oxon RG9 1EN and
9 Park Street,
Boston, Mass. 02108, USA
Set in Monotype Bembo
Printed in Great Britain by
Morrison & Gibb Ltd, London and Edinburgh

British Library Cataloguing in Publication Data

Carlebach, Julius
    Karl Marx and the radical critique of Judaism.
    —(The Littman library of Jewish civilization).
    1. Marx, Karl   2. Jews—Political and social
    conditions
    I. Title   II. Series
    301.45′19′24   HN40.J5   77–30188

    ISBN 0 7100 8279 7

To my parents
Chief Rabbi Dr Joseph Zvi Carlebach and
Charlotte Carlebach, née Preuss

They lived as Jews . . .
Loved Judaism . . .
And died because they were Jews . . .
in a concentration camp outside Riga,
26 March 1942—8 Nissan 5702

Contents

Acknowledgments

I would not have attempted this venture into the complex world of Marx studies but for the fortuitous circumstance of Professor T. B. Bottomore occupying the chair of sociology in the University of Sussex at the time that I took up my appointment there. I am very grateful to him for his patience, encouragement and guidance, which enabled me to complete the project. Long discussions and occasional exchanges of letters with Professors Chimen Abramsky, Shlomo Avineri, Zev Barbu, Sir Isaiah Berlin and Helmut Hirsch have also been most valuable in helping me to clarify my ideas.

I am greatly indebted to the Memorial Foundation for Jewish Culture in New York and the Norman Angell Fund of the University of Sussex for assisting me with grants to go in search of archival and other inaccessible materials in Europe and Israel and to Dr A. Maimon, literary executor of Dr Jona Fink, for making some of the latter's unpublished material available.

It is also with gratitude and appreciation that I acknowledge the tremendous help and constant co-operation I have received from the German Institute of the Embassy of West Germany in London, the Wiener Library, the Institute for Social History in Amsterdam, the Germania Judaica Library in Cologne, the National and University Library of the Hebrew University in Jerusalem and last, but certainly not least, the Inter-Library loan section of the University of Sussex.

These expressions of thanks are not a mere formality, but a sincere recognition that the help I have received, so readily given in the face of constant demands over several years, has been at all times more than I had a right to expect and absolutely essential for the completion of the task.

The section on Moses Hess in chapter VI first appeared as a paper in vol. 18 (1973) of the *Year Book* of the Leo Baeck Institute, and chapter XIX was originally published in *Soviet Jewish Affairs*, 2 (2), 1972; I am grateful to the respective publishers for permission to reproduce them here. Hans Liebeschütz has kindly allowed me to quote extensively from his essay, 'German radicalism and the formation of Jewish political attitudes during the earlier part of the 19th century'. Finally I would like to thank Mrs Camilla Raab of Routledge & Kegan Paul for the interest and effort she has invested in helping me to complete the task.

MAIN ABBREVIATIONS

AZJ   *Allgemeine Zeitung des Judentums*
DFJB   *Deutsch-Französische Jahrbücher*, Paris, 1844
LBIYB *Leo Baeck Institute Year Book*
MEW   *Marx-Engels Werke*, Dietz Verlag, (East) Berlin, 1961 *et·seq.*

TRANSLATIONS

Unless otherwise stated, translations used in this study are my own.

Preface

Some four years have passed since this book was completed, but technical difficulties beyond my control have delayed its publication. A number of books and articles relevant to my main topic have since appeared and these have been briefly outlined in a short Epilogue which has been appended to the text in order to avoid the complex and costly task of altering the printed proofs. I have also taken the opportunity, with sadness rather than pleasure, to draw attention once more to the topicality of the theme of this study, which ought properly to have been a relic of a bygone age.

It would be appropriate here to explain my deviation from accepted academic practice, in allowing some of my views and evaluations to appear in parts of the text with the very personal pronoun 'I'. The reason for this reflects the reality that most additions to the seemingly endless literature on Marx, including my own, tend to be varieties of personal interpretations rather than reports of new discoveries. It seemed to me appropriate to emphasise this where conflicting interpretations are presented.

Throughout the text I have used 'Marxian' to denote all matters pertaining to Karl Marx, and 'Marxist' for everything pertaining to the intellectual and ideological adherents of Marxism.

University of Sussex,   J.C.
July 1977

Introduction

In 1844 Karl Marx published two review essays in the *Deutsch-Französische Jahrbücher* under a general heading, 'On the Jewish Question'. These articles remained virtually unknown until the end of the nineteenth century, but since then they have attracted a great deal of attention and have been the subject of a prolific array of different interpretations which tend to leave one both puzzled and confused. The essays themselves, no less than the various interpretations of them, seem to raise more questions than they answer, not least because many writers attempt to provide perspectives for the essays by drawing on their antecedents in a few bold strokes, which, like the proverbial rumours, are liable to a degree of distortion that can, in the end, leave one with the precise opposite of what was originally stated.

What, for example, did Bruno Bauer write to provoke Marx's response? Was it his view that Jewish emancipation was 'incomplete',[1] or was it 'Bauer's contention that the social emancipation of the Jews was dependent upon their religious emancipation'?[2] Was it 'Bauer's position . . . [that] . . . Judaism, being confined to one race, was inferior to Christianity' and that Jews 'would find emancipation more difficult since it involved two steps for them as opposed to one for Christians',[3] or did Bauer argue 'for full equality for all religious groups and for a religiously neutral state based on human rights'?[4] Is it true that Marx's articles were written to refute 'Bruno Bauer's plea for the

emancipation of the Jews and their elevation to political membership as Jews'?[25]

It is well known that, particularly in the second of Marx's
two essays, there are some pungent comments on Jews and
Judaism—how are these to be interpreted? Should we follow
Mehring who thought that 'any comment would only weaken
this fundamental investigation. These few pages obviate the
mountain of literature that has since appeared',[6] or should we
follow Isaiah Berlin, who described the articles as 'a dull and
shallow composition'?[7] Do we agree that 'the tragic events of the
Nazi era neither invalidate the classic Marxist analysis of the
Jewish question, nor call for its revision',[8] or should we accept
that in writing these articles, Marx was not concerned with Jews
at all?[9] Did Marx write as a Jew,[10] or was he trying to emancipate
himself from his Jewishness?[11] Was Marx right in principle, but
wrong in detail,[12] or was he fundamentally and factually wrong?[13]

The essays themselves also raise many questions which are not
satisfactorily dealt with in the substantial literature that has grown
up around them. Why, for example, did Marx write two separate
articles on the subject of the Jews and why did he virtually
rewrite both articles in *The Holy Family*, where he also admitted
error in the earlier version and ambiguity arising from his own
use of 'philosophical phraseology'? Marx stated that he was
writing about the emancipation of German Jews. Did he really
mean German Jews or was he mainly concerned with Prussian
Jews? Who were the Jews who clamoured for emancipation, and
who was preventing them from achieving it? What was so special
about the years 1842–3 that inspired so many protagonists and
opponents of Jewish emancipation to concern themselves with
that issue at that particular time?

Marx was of Jewish origin, and many writers have assigned
great significance to this fact, but how relevant was it to the
Marxian approach to the Jewish question and what influence has
it exercised? Is the importance of Marx's essays to be sought in
the fact that it was Marx who wrote them, or in the intrinsic
contribution they have made to the solution of a problem?
Perhaps the most original contribution of Marx in relation to the

Jewish question was his attempt to convert flesh and blood people into a socioeconomic category. How valid is such an interpretation, and what effect has it had on the emergence of political anti-semitism in the latter years of the nineteenth century?

In an attempt to answer these questions, I have tried to re-create the several social contexts in which both the problem and the Marxian solution have emerged. These can be summarised under four headings. First, to outline briefly the empirical reality of the Jews, more particularly the Jews of Prussia, and their efforts to achieve emancipation up to the time Marx wrote. Second, I have tried to convey the wide spectrum of views on Jews which were current at that time and which are likely to have influenced Marx because we know he was aware of them. Third, I have looked in some detail at the radical's image of the Jews, partly because this is the proper framework for the Marxian contribution and partly because the contributions of several radical writers have been, as I have indicated, summarised to a degree that makes their actual positions well-nigh unintelligible. This has meant the adoption of a somewhat pedestrian approach, which, one hopes, will be acceptable precisely because it endeavours to avoid the facile distortions which sometimes creep into the more erudite summations by more skilful writers. Finally, I have attempted to follow the essays into the various camps in which they have been studied, judged and commented upon.

It will be apparent that in adopting such an approach I have been guided by Karl Mannheim in that I have accepted that 'the approach to a problem, the level on which the problem happens to be formulated, the stage of abstraction and the stage of concreteness that one hopes to attain, are all and in the same way bound up with social existence'.[14] Equally, in looking at the very diverse interpretations which the Jewish question has given rise to, I have assumed that, 'For each of the participants, the "object" has a more or less different meaning because it grows out of the whole of their respective frames of reference, as a result of which the meaning of the object in the perspective of the other person remains, at least in part, obscure.'[15]

Hence, one of my aims throughout has been to try to understand the several contributions to the radical and Marxist debate on the Jews by trying to understand their perspectives and by seeing these as functions of their respective social positions. To the extent that I have been successful, this study should however be seen only as 'illustrative material'[16] in the sociology of knowledge, rather than as substantive theoretical analyses which would in any event be premature with such a multiplicity of theoretical models and the social contexts which moulded them.

The critical stance I have adopted towards Marx's and Marxist analyses of Jews and Judaism has been determined by two factors. The first and essentially impersonal factor is the brilliant critical approach of Sartre, which seemed to me to be the most incisive, even though I have been unable to comprehend why he appears to exclude Marx's own work. If it is true that Lukács and other Marxists employed a method which 'does not derive its concepts from experience . . . [because] it has already formed its concepts; it is already certain of their truth . . . its sole purpose is to force the events, the persons, or the acts considered into prefabricated moulds',[17] then this is also true, in our case, of Marx. Were Marxists 'able to reject and condemn more precisely, to refute more triumphantly, exactly in so far as they first know what it is they are damning and refuting',[18] then that also applies to Marx's critique of Judaism. Not only Marxists, but Marx himself 'ought to study real men in depth, not dissolve them in a bath of sulphuric acid', and it could fairly be argued that the tenor of Marx's critique of Judaism shows that 'if one totalizes too quickly, if one transforms—without evidence—signification into intention, and result into an objective deliberately aimed at, then the real is lost'.[19] There would be equal justice in arguing against Marx, as Sartre did against Marxists, that 'when he dissolves the particular in the universal, he has the satisfaction of believing that he is reducing appearance to truth. Actually, by defining his *subjective* concept of reality, he has only defined himself'. Sartre described as 'lazy Marxism' the attempt to turn 'real men into the symbols of its myths',[20] but this is precisely the problem we have to face here.

The second factor arises from my subjective attitude, as a

committed Jew, to the varieties of critiques of Jews and Judaism I have described. I have been conscious of the problem of bias and have tried to guard against its deliberate intrusion into my reading and recording of the views of critics. To the extent that they have been unknowledgeable and ill informed about Judaism and Jewish history, this has not been difficult, since one can demonstrate lack of substance based on lack of knowledge without becoming defensive. Thus, while I have tried to report as faithfully as I can the many views on Jews which are found in the literature, I have enjoyed 'debating' the interpretations of Jewish history and religion with Max Weber, but found it difficult to develop a sense of empathy with such distortions of Jewish history as those, for example, of Leon and Heller. In the case of Marx, the problem has been more difficult. He displayed on the one hand such a complete lack of knowledge of Jews and Judaism that his critique hardly warrants serious attention. As a contribution to a critique of social conditions, however, he offers a serious challenge to the 'particularistic' attitude of Judaism which he rejected as narrow and alienating. At that level I have chosen to differ from Marx and to adhere to the traditional Jewish view that the ultimate hope of improving relations between men lies in the affirmation of a strong cultural identity as an imperative mediator between the constraints imposed on natural man and his more malleable needs as social man. As a Jew, I do not believe, but accept as an arguable alternative, that man has the psychosocial capacity to transform himself into a social being by electing to identify himself with such obtusely heterogeneous reference groups as 'workers of the world' or 'mankind'.[21]

Accordingly, no further justification is required for another aim of this study, namely to place 'the Jews' and Judaism squarely into the centre of my research. In spite of the frequent assertions that in writing about Jews, Marx was really writing about capitalism or commercialism or the bourgeoisie, I have rejected this view, that this same Marx, master of the written word, manipulator of several European languages, journalist and author, the man who devoted his entire life to shaping and expressing thoughts, ideas and observations, was not capable of finding the right terminology for his arguments. Marx consistently used the terms 'Jews' and 'Judaism', in addition to commercialism and capitalism; hence I have considered it right to retain the distinction between them and have assumed that Jews and Judaism mean what they are generally understood to mean.

A further problem arising from my own subjectivity lies in the application of the term 'anti-Jewish' to various writers, some of whom would have defined themselves in this way, while others would have utterly rejected it. Bruno Bauer, for example, strongly denied any prejudice against Jews and wanted to draw a sharp distinction between criticising and hating them. Although I accept the distinction made by Bauer, I would, however, make this reservation. If criticism leads to a denial of the right of the Jew to exist as a Jew, then the critic has become anti-Jewish, and it is in this sense that I have used the term.

If in spite of these explanations it is still argued that I place too great an emphasis on Jews instead of concentrating more attention on such problems as Hegel's influence on Marx and the current debates about the nature of the state, then I would reply with Max Weber that, since 'all knowledge of cultural reality . . . is always knowledge from particular points of view',[22] the approach I have chosen is legitimate and the aims I have set myself will have been fulfilled if this study is regarded as a contribution towards a better understanding of social processes because it adds a further dimension to a plurality of other, equally one-sided, explanations of the meaning of cultural reality.

Finally I ought to add that, in looking at the many contributors to the debate on the Jews, I have always inquired, though not necessarily written, about their personal backgrounds. In this I have been guided by Marx, who recognised very early in his career that 'philosophers do not rise out of the ground like mushrooms, they are the fruits of their time, of their people, whose subtlest, most precious and least apparent essences are manifested in philosophical ideas'.[23]

PART ONE

*Citizen Jews in a
Christian State*

CHAPTER I

The Struggle for Jewish Emancipation

Karl Marx set the scene for his essays 'On the Jewish Question' which are to be the focus of our study, with a simple statement: 'The German Jews seek emancipation.'[1] Neither Marx, nor Bruno Bauer whom he is reviewing, said anything about the real nature of the problem: i.e. who were 'the German Jews', how many were there and what caused them to seek emancipation at just that time. Our first task therefore must be to present the context in which the Jewish struggle for emancipation and the great debate surrounding it took place.[2] Since Marx and Bauer were primarily concerned with the Jews of Prussia, and because conditions under which Jews lived in different German states varied markedly and, in terms of their emancipation, significantly, we will focus here on the Jews of Prussia, albeit within a general Jewish framework of the time.

Both Marx and Bauer were puzzled by the Jewish desire to be emancipated, i.e. to achieve civil and political equality in an absolutist state. To Bauer the demand was perverse and, in his view, improper because the very nature of the Prussian state left its citizenry unemancipated. Marx thought that, to the extent that the state offered political emancipation, the Jews had a right to demand it, though it would solve no problems for them or the state since both had failed to recognise the fundamental problem which Marx described as the achievement of human emancipation. If the Marx–Bauer assumptions were logical and objectively true,

9

they nevertheless missed the sociological reality of the Jewish position and the underlying issues which motivated the Jews and the state to work towards a systematic change in the socio-political approach to Prussia's Jewish minority.

The nineteenth century was the period of the greatest expansion in numbers of the Jews in their long history. According to Ruppin there were 4.5 million Jews in 70 CE at the time the Romans destroyed their political independence. By the twelfth century this number had shrunk to 1.5 million, but rose again slowly from the seventeenth century to reach a total of 2.5 million by 1800. The Jewish population nearly doubled during the next forty years to 4.5 million and more than redoubled in the second half of the nineteenth century to 10.5 million. Thus if we take a baseline of 100 for the total populations of a number of European countries in 1800, the increase by 1920 was as follows:[3]

France	139	Norway	300
Spain	203	Scotland	336
Portugal	206	England & Wales	426
Sweden	251	Jews	640

The distribution of the world's Jews in 1840 was also substantially different from that of our own day in that nearly 90 per cent of them lived in Europe, the vast majority in Russia and under the Habsburg monarchy.[4] Z. Rudy has given the following figures for the world distribution of the Jews in 1840:[5]

Europe	3,950,000	(87.8%)			
America	50,000	(1.1%)			
Asia	300,000	(6.7%)			
Africa	198,000	(4.4%)			
Australia	2,000	(—)	Total	4,500,000	(100%)

If Western Europe was in the forefront of commercial and industrial development during the nineteenth century, it also had the smallest Jewish populations. In Prussia the number of Jews fluctuated in the century 1825 to 1925 between 1.25 and 1.06 per cent of the population. For Germany as a whole the figure was slightly less. Between 1880 and 1921 the Jews represented between 0.38 and 0.4 per cent of the population of France,[6] and Roth has quoted a figure of 20,000–30,000 Jews in England in 1815.[7] In 1843 Prussia, with a total population of some 15 million, had 206,527 Jews, the largest group in Germany, representing about 5 per cent of the Jewish population of the world and about two-thirds of the Jewish population of Germany. Although the fear of an unchecked growth of the Jewish population is a common theme in German anti-semitic literature, the steady decline of the Jewish birthrate after 1864 and the vigorous control over Jewish immigration from Eastern Europe kept the Jews as a numerically insignificant group, even during the period of their fastest natural increase. This can be illustrated by the following table which gives the percentage of Jews in the total population of Prussia in various census years:[8]

1816	1.19	1864	1.36
1825	1.22	1875	1.32
1834	1.30	1885	1.29
1843	1.33	1895	1.19
1852	1.34	1905	1.09
1861	1.37	1925	1.05

To understand how a numerically insignificant group could cause so much debate, involve so many partisans on one side or the other and stir so many emotions at a time when the emancipation of the serfs took place with very little repercussion, it will be necessary to try to draw together a multiplicity of interacting ideas, events and personalities; for the emancipation of the Jews owed as much to developments within the community as to the forces acting upon it. It was not a simple consequence of a direct, linear progression of ideas or events or legal enactments, but a complex see-saw in which planned action, unexpected events and unpredictable personalities moved in confusing patterns until a series of forces had been generated which not only carried the Jews to complete emancipation but in the last analysis also gave rise to the movements which led to their ultimate destruction. For the sake of clarity, we will divide the subject into a number of separate areas, although it must be stressed that their real significance lies in their constant and total interplay with each other.[9]

THE BACKGROUND

Although Jews are generally described as living in 'ghettos' prior to their emancipation, this is a political rather than a geographic description. There were specific areas in some large cities to which Jews were confined and which were known as 'ghettos', but there were also many scattered and rural communities in Germany unified as *Landesgemeinden*[10] which were treated as single units for tax purposes and which, like the true city-ghettos, were administered by almost completely independent Jewish civil authorities.[11] The reasons for the extent of internal autonomy granted to Jewish communities by central governments lay partly in the nature of medieval social structures in which socially defined groups exercised sharply delineated autonomous functions, and partly in the fact that, as Wirth expressed it, in most countries, Jews 'were not citizens—not even men—in the eyes of the law, but rather were taxable property'.[12] Although there was considerable social diversity and stratification within the Jewish community, this was not identical with the usual class structures, to some extent because of the essentially democratic tradition of Jewish communities, the elitist role of the intellectual (i.e. rabbinic) as well as the economically dominant sections, and the unstructured social mobility between upper and lower levels in the community. Thus, for example, education was universal and exclusively religious, but it was not allocative in the accepted sense in that outstanding performance was not necessarily seen as a means of access to positions of power in the social elite, but was its own reward. The scholar even without an institutionalised position exercised power by virtue of his scholarship alone, and was often reinforced in this position because wealthy Jews would seek learned Jews for their daughters to marry. In this way wealth and learning tended to combine to form ruling elites, access to which, however, always remained open to both the newly wealthy and the rising scholar. Jewish communities were very different therefore from other estates, guilds and corporations in the middle ages because in the classic medieval group position was determined by birth, democratic government unknown and social mobility virtually non-existent. But like other medieval groups Jews were seen as a single socioeconomic unit in the social structure. Their internal composition was unknown, their scholars largely isolated and their function seen and defined exclusively in terms of the dominant area of contact they had with the external world—trade. Wirth has described trade as an 'abstract relationship',[13] but it seems to me that such a concept should not be applied without further refinement. It is certainly true that to central church or state authorities, Jews as a trading entity was an adequate concept and their position was determined by purely economic considerations. Originally they tended to be seen predominantly as a source of revenue, and a very useful one, because Jews relied almost entirely on cash transactions in their commercial activities and had access to international trade links; taxes were imposed communally so that there were not even the problem and expense of tax collection. The implicit power this vested in the communal administration did not become an issue until the late eighteenth century. The Prussian monarchs, however, expected a greater return than mere taxes from the Jews they permitted to reside in Prussia. They defined the value of Jews as entrepreneurs and industrial innovators. They wanted economic expansion, foreign trade and currency and industrial investments. To this end Prussia's Great Elector (later Friedrich Wilhelm I) permitted not only Jews, but also some 20,000 Huguenots to settle in Prussia and, if anything, would have regarded the protests of Christian traders—that Jews used innovatory, aggressive trading methods as opposed to their own sedate and settled methods—as a full vindication of his intentions.[14]

Before we go on to consider the influence of Friedrich II (der Grosse), let us return briefly to the problem posed by Wirth's description of trade as an abstract relationship. Peter Burke once described some of the conflicts of the Renaissance as a conflict between its great (social and philosophical) and little (folkways and customs) traditions.[15] Let us stipulate that there was a great tradition in eighteenth-century Prussia, i.e. the enlightenment, the Prussian state, etc., and a little tradition, the ways and customs of the period. The Jewish community also had its great tradition in its religion, biblical and talmudic law and history, and a little tradition in its folktales, customs, etc. In the ghetto period, the two great traditions were in the main isolated from each other and dominated the lives of their respective adherents. However, at the level of the little traditions, there was a constant interchange which not only created a link between the different groups but was also destined to play an important part in the subsequent struggle for emancipation. The fact that Jews had to wear a distinguishing mark on their clothes makes it clear that fashion-modes passed from one group to the other. Glückel of Hameln, writing in the seventeenth century, tells us how she sent her daughter to a local inn for safety during an outbreak of the plague: 'They reached the small village and found lodgings in a peasant's house, for they had money with them and as long as one has money use can be made of it. The peasant said, "Today is your festival: why are you not among Jews?" '[16] Similarly, Schwab tells of peasants visiting the synagogues on Yom Kippur (which *they* called 'the long day'), helping to decorate the huts used for the Feast of Tabernacles, hanging a Matza (used on Passover) under the roof to protect them from lightning and of village inns keeping a special saucepan with the Hebrew word 'Kasher' written on it, to be used by Jewish travellers who were bound by their dietary laws.[17] In his *German Ideology*, Marx quoted a medieval German folksong which has an almost exact parallel in the Passover Haggada song 'Chad Gadya'. Such examples could be multiplied endlessly and are supported by ecclesiastical dicta of the early middle ages designed to protect Christians who might be 'infected with the superstitions and depraved morals of the Jews living among them'.[18]

The trading process then, at grass-roots levels, was much more than an abstract relationship. It was a meeting-point for little traditions, sometimes even an arena for the interchange of little traditions, a process essential if a confluence of great traditions was to take place. Inevitably the little tradition of the Jews would make itself felt mainly and most of the time only in small rural communities. In large urban areas it was the little tradition of the majority which filtered through to the isolated minority. Hence in German cities such as Berlin and Hamburg it was the German little tradition which made itself felt among the Jewish communities and conveyed to them the norms and mores of the larger society, its attractions and excitements. It was for many Jews the first glimpse of a world whose great tradition remained beyond their reach until they had liberated themselves in one way or another from the internal autonomy which confined them to their own great tradition. Thus, for example, although in terms of restrictions and lack of personal freedoms the position of Jews in eighteenth-century Prussia was closest to that of its peasants, there were important differences between the two groups which illustrate the complexity of the internal problems raised by the emancipation process. Just as among Jews there were 'protected' and unprotected groups and later on Jews with and Jews without civil rights,[19] so there were true serfs (*Leibeigene*) amongst the peasants, while the majority were *Erbuntertanen*, peasants bound to the land and its owners. Like Jews, peasants did not have freedom of movement and could not marry without their lord's consent. While Jews were legally restricted to a family of one child, with a special tax payable on a second, peasants had to present their children for domestic service in the lord's household. Whereas Jews were subject to the laws and whims of the monarch, serfs were subjects not of the king but of their lord.[20] Like the Jews, the peasants were offered some protection by the state (*Bavernschutz*), until a decree (11 November 1810) declared all peasants to be free men and all land available to all men. A similar decree, introduced by Hardenberg in March 1812 proclaiming civil rights for Jews, met violent external and internal opposition and was effectively nullified by the Prussian state itself. The conflict it engendered was not resolved until 1869, when complete *de jure* (if not *de facto*) emancipation was granted to the Jews.

Emancipation[21] for the Prussian peasant was the road from a little tradition to a great tradition. Access to it may have been limited or too restricted, but henceforth conflict would be over the nature of access to it, not over the principle of its quality or desirability. In the case of the Jews, the very access it offered to the 'other' great tradition engendered intense conflicts of loyalty, choice and comparison within the community, conflicts which were constantly increased and reinforced by external challenges to the Jews to modify, abandon or adapt their great tradition to the standards and values of the dominant majority. These challenges were not directed merely at the civil and rabbinic authorities within the community, but were aimed at Jewish law itself, a law that for centuries had derived its authority and legitimation from divine revelation.

There was another and perhaps even more fundamental difference between the emancipation of Jews and peasants which would explain the relative simplicity of peasant emancipation and the turbulent history of Jewish emancipation. For all its significance as a precursor of social revolution,[22] the emancipation of peasants did not appear to the landowning aristocracy as a serious threat to the existing social order. Not the freedom of the peasant, but the rights of Jews to purchase land was seen by them as the greatest threat, because it changed the nature of land-ownership from 'the surest anchorage of the nation's stability' to its crude use as an income-yielding investment, with the result that 'our venerable old Brandenburg-Prussia will become a new-fangled Jew-state'.[23] Underlying this complaint was the acute recognition that the emancipated peasant would essentially remain at a social level which would not challenge the distance maintained by the aristocracy, while the emancipation of the Jews with their wholly alien traditional stratification would seek to intrude new forces into all social classes. It was not so much a question of Jews occupying 'interstitial roles' in social structures as Bauer and Marx were to argue, or Jews being 'interlopers' between social classes (Klasseneinschiebsel) as Jacob Lestschinsky argued,[24] but that Jews would move unpredictably into all social classes, most of which at that time of transition from feudal to capitalist society were unwilling to grant Jews membership of their groups. This applied particularly to the highest and lowest

social strata and in varying degrees to the middle classes—the
broad 'bourgeoisie'—who, though for Marx almost synonymous
with Jews, nevertheless had strong elements within it who
vigorously opposed Jewish emancipation. Such opposition was
most marked amongst civil servants, shop-keepers and salaried
officials (e.g. teachers and academics), and least manifest in the
independent professions and higher merchant groups.[25] Indeed
the apparently irrational list of restrictions applicable to Jews in
Prussia in the early 1840s[26] acquires a semblance of meaning when
they are viewed as state-sponsored responses to class prejudices in
the Prussian population.[27] The dilemma was not of course one-
sided. The Jews themselves, unacquainted with and perplexed by
the rigid and highly structured class system in Prussian society,
were at a loss to know how they could fit into such a closely-knit
system which made no concessions to newcomers and tended to
obliterate any vestige of 'other-group identity' of those it
eventually accepted.

CHAPTER II

The Quiet Revolution

The democratic tradition of Jewish communal life, manifested as it was in secret ballots for communal government, publicly financed education and social welfare and the use of the synagogue service as a forum for complaints and protests, was subject to rabbinic law, which in the course of time acquired an authority as awesome as biblical law itself. Throughout the middle ages, therefore, rabbinic law was the instrument of legitimation for accommodation to changing social and economic pressures on the communities. If this provided stability and security, it also led to considerable conflict between the communities (*Kehilloth*) and individual rabbis mainly because the multiplicity of autonomous communities posed an insoluble problem of uniformly maintaining the authority of the rabbi's office, while at the same time restricting that authority so that rabbinic dictates emerging in given social situations would not become binding on communities or individuals living in or transferring to others. Though damaging at times, the very persistence of these conflicts tended to maintain the democratic tradition and to vitalise its participants.[1]

The first major change in this situation was the emergence of the 'court Jew', the economically powerful Jew whose close association with external authority usually meant a disproportionate degree of power and influence also within the community. Thus the way was prepared for a ruling elite which through its influence on the selection of rabbis also exercised considerable influence on religious and social developments. The second factor was the changing role of the Jew in late medieval Central Europe when, as in the case of Prussia, the emphasis changed from the Jew as a source of revenue to the Jew as an instrument for promoting trade and industry. The high premium the Prussian rulers placed on economic achievement gave rise to implicit shifts in values and norms within the community. Its freedom was reduced in terms of determining its own internal composition, and the wealthy Jew was less able to protect the unsuccessful sections of the community by simply accepting a greater share of the communal tax burden. Rabbinic authority, to the extent that it protected traditional values, was increasingly seen as a handicap to economic expansion, and the democratic tradition was eroded because the dominant groups in the community considered it to be detrimental to their interests. The third factor, and one which stood in direct conflict with the previous one, was the growing state intervention in communal affairs, both in its efforts to wrest control from communal organisations in order to exercise a greater control over an economically important sector of the population, and in its attempts to bolster rabbinic authority in order to prevent the economic rise of Prussian Jewry from spilling over into social unrest. Short of conversion to Christianity, an economically vigorous community controlled by rabbinic authority was the ideal the Prussian government strove for. Indeed, state intervention in internal religious affairs of Jewish communities was prevalent throughout Germany. Thus the Prussian government forbade 'Reform' services in Berlin in 1823, the government of Württemberg enacted legislation on the role and function of the rabbi, while in Bavaria at the same time, talmudic colleges were closed by order of the state to force the Jewish communities to select rabbis with secular education.[2]

MOSES MENDELSSOHN

Although these changes were slow and gradual and did not always become explicit until the first quarter of the nineteenth century,

19

they began to manifest themselves throughout the later part of the eighteenth century when education and conversion to Christianity started to impinge on communal unity. The underlying issues were first expressed openly by Moses Mendelssohn (1729–86), the most important and most controversial figure in the movement for Jewish emancipation, the man hailed by Heine as the Luther of the Jews who freed the Jews from the Talmud,[3] and by F. H. Heinemann as the man who failed in his efforts on behalf of the Jews.[4] Whereas 'the old Moses gave the Jews a religion but failed to enter the promised land, the new Moses entered the promised land but failed to give the Jews an appropriate religion for it'.[5] From our point of view, the significance of Mendelssohn lies in his unique position as the first Jew since Spinoza to master the German great tradition so completely that he in fact became a part of it.[6] A classic representative of German enlightenment, he gained his reputation as a philosopher and might never have taken a stand on the conflict between the two great traditions had the Christian world not challenged him to live up to the logical consequences of his own position as a recognised constituent part of the German great tradition by rejecting the Jewish great tradition. In 1769 the Swiss theologian John Caspar Lavater publicly challenged him to accept Christianity or defend his adherence to Judaism in the context of his philosophical position. Mendelssohn rose to this and similar challenges by publishing *Jerusalem oder über religiöse Macht und Judentum* (1783), the first German philosophical treatise to plead for the separation of church and state and for freedom of belief and conscience. Like Spinoza before him, he argued from an acceptance of the idea that in its original, i.e. biblical, form, Judaism represented the perfect fusion of church and state, but, unlike Spinoza, Mendelssohn found it possible to redefine a function for biblical law outside the boundaries of a Jewish state. Like Marx, he divided his essay into two parts, the first being a general discussion of the relationship between state and religion, and the second a more specific discussion of Judaism.[7] Mendelssohn affirmed absolutely his belief in God and the immortality of the soul, but also insisted on the supremacy of reason, 'no less divine' than revealed religion.[8] His defence of Judaism was not so much an assertion of the integrity of the Jewish great tradition as a restatement of the Jewish great tradition in terms of the German enlightenment. Hence he saw no conflict or tension between them. He proclaimed himself an adherent of Judaism because he subscribed to the German great tradition, not in spite of it or in an 'as well as' sense. For all that, Mendelssohn clearly recognised the central issues that would generate the conflicts of the future. If he insisted on a complete separation of church and state or, in other words, rejected the right of the state to control its citizens through religious coercion or discrimination, he was equally strongly opposed to the exercise of civil power by religious authorities. Thus, at a time when temporary or permanent excommunication was a primary sanction to enforce Jewish communal authority, Mendelssohn vigorously opposed this. If this indicated a rejection of rabbinic authority, he was nevertheless conservative enough to want to retain rabbinic teaching. Equally, he recognised the centrality of law in Judaism and sought to align his enlightenment-oriented concept of religion with his loyalty to traditional Judaism by stipulating Judaism not as a revealed religion but as revealed law. As a meticulous student of Spinoza, however, he recognised that this law had to be given a context appropriate to a Jewish religious autonomy in a secular, civil state. It could no longer be even a quasi-political constitutional law, and so he redefined it as *ceremonial* law, as a moral instrument, 'a link between thought and action, between theory and practice'.[9] Yet in the result, while Mendelssohn's philosophy was rational, his religion was rationalisation. By converting rabbinic law into rabbinic philosophy and biblical, constitutional law into rationalised ceremonial law, he emasculated the intellectual core of his religion, turning it into an appendage of the German great tradition which brought him an inner peace that those who knew him envied and admired, but left nothing for his descendants except total dissolution. Only those who took issue with the critical themes he identified but did not resolve survived to perpetuate their great tradition.[10]

The inadequacy of the Mendelssohnian solution to the Jewish

problem was not readily apparent in his own lifetime, first, because of the sheer weight of his own position and the deference paid to him by Jew and Gentile alike as a philosopher and a 'cultured' Jew. Second, because he raised fundamental issues which were at that time of little significance to the broad masses of Prussia's Jews, and third, because as a manager of a manufacturing firm he did not either represent or challenge any particular social group or class. He stood on and by his own performance as a gifted individual. His friend and disciple David Friedländer (1750–1834), who took over the leadership of Prussia's Jewish population, was an altogether different personality. A wealthy Jew, Friedländer moved in upper-class circles, knew mainly Jews of similar social background and displayed a certain contempt for his lesser brethren, whom he referred to in 1790 as 'the great mass of the Jews . . . characterised by a babbling array of their prayers, conscientious observance of religious ceremonies and . . . outward piety, just like the riff-raff of other religious groups'.[11] He drew logical conclusions from the analysis of Judaism which Mendelssohn had offered. If Jewish law is in fact only a ceremonial law, and if one accepted, as Friedländer appeared to do, the constant assertions of Christian clergymen that the principles of Judaism corrupted its adherents and led them into usury and dishonesty, then the solution to the problem of the Jews was the abolition of Jewish law on the one hand and the grant of full citizenship on the other. Thus only those Jews who insisted on retaining their traditional Judaism would be deprived of full citizenship. Judaism in the Friedländer vision would become a deistic ethic, unencumbered by any laws; in 1799 he sent a letter to the theologian Teller in which he offered to become a Christian on condition that he need not accept Christian dogma,[12] an offer contemptuously rejected by Friedrich Schleiermacher, who responded by writing that Jews as enlightened as the proposers of that offer 'had a greater obligation to help other Jews than to help themselves'.[13] The unfavourable reaction from both Christians and Jews led Friedländer to abandon this line of thought and turn his attention to ways and means of 'reforming' Judaism, which, in his own terms, meant making it more acceptable to his social and cultural peers or, in our terms, adapting it to the dominant great tradition.

Although the social currents of the late eighteenth and early nineteenth centuries which aimed at or strove for emancipation in one form or another were concentrated on the *content* of the Jewish religion, patterns of differentiation began to emerge which were based much more on social, intellectual and economic than on genuinely religious factors. Among the Jewish upper classes, the Berlin 'salons' made their appearance, the first genuine meeting-points of two great traditions, where wealthy and cultured Jews met liberal and secularised members of the German intelligentsia and aristocracy. In this type of forum Henrietta Herz and her friends formed a 'Society of Virtue' in which 'members agreed to bare their souls to one another and hold back no secrets. Jew or Gentile was of no consequence in their rebellious but chaste fraternity. The aim was to make one another happy through love'.[14] If they met on equal terms, the members of this and similar groups were equal only at the social level or at any rate pursued only an ideal of a social equality which would adequately reflect the similarity of their economic status and cultural aspirations. Judaism, at that time seen only as a religion and devoid of cultural content, had perforce to be a very poor second best and most of the Jewish participants eventually married Gentiles and/or converted to Christianity. There was, however, yet another attempt originating in the same social circles to bring about a synthesis of the two great traditions.

THE KULTURVEREIN

With the advent of the second decade of the nineteenth century, the Jews had to adjust to a host of complex events. Prussia had suffered humiliating defeats at the hands of the French and had enjoyed the benefits of the strong administrations of Stein and Hardenberg. The Jews had an exhilarating experience of almost complete civil emancipation through the Edict of 1812, had participated fully and bravely in the wars of liberation as citizens and soldiers of Prussia, had paid with their blood for the privilege

23

of citizenship and had simultaneously watched with dismay the
flood of anti-Jewish polemic which accompanied the emergence
of the romantic movement and the emergence of nationalism.
They suffered in silence the contemptuous regulation of the
Prussian administration which provided for all wounded veterans
of the Wars of Liberation but pointedly excluded those who were
Jewish, and finally they witnessed the anti-Jewish riots of 1818 and
1819. Enlightenment, equality and reason were seen in many
circles as sterile prescriptions. Perhaps, however, the most important result of these events and many that preceded them was
the discovery made by many educated, enlightened, learned and
cultured Jews that, no matter how deeply they engrossed themselves in the pleasures and challenges of the German great
tradition, there remained a Jewish consciousness, a sense of
awareness, an emotional attachment which appeared to defy
both reason and intellect.

This sense of Jewish identity was strongly reinforced by the
sad spectacle of the 'Hep Hep' riots in Germany which were
sparked off by an attack by students in August 1819 on the
Jewish quarter in Würzburg which followed severe restrictions
on nationalist student movements after a student's assassination of
the poet Kotzebue. There were a number of casualties in the
ensuing fighting and the Jews, because they offered resistance to
the students, were expelled from the town. The riots spread
rapidly throughout the Upper Rhine region and were named
after the mocking call, 'Hep Hep', which was used by the mobs.[15]
As an expression of this identity, a group of young Jewish
intellectuals came together under the leadership of Eduard Gans,
then twenty-one and a brilliant jurist, to found the Verein für
Kultur und Wissenschaft der Juden in November 1819. In
analysing the problems of the Jews, Gans, a student and subsequent
editor of Hegel, described the Jews of the pre-enlightenment
era as 'half oriental, half medieval', immersed in an alien culture.
Following the impact of European culture,[16]

> The subjective spirit, freed of its fetters, had long to persist in the
> individual in his detachment and his negative condition in order to

gain that strength which could move him to a voluntary return, not a forced one. This return is what matters . . . The break with the intimacy of the old existence has indeed occurred, but the deeper return to this intimacy has not taken place.

In true Hegelian fashion Gans called for a new synthesis to displace the 'empty abstraction' of the enlightenment, but had no concrete suggestions as to how this might be achieved. He drew the attention of the group to the futility of responding to attacks on the Jews by counter-arguments which endeavoured to prove their good qualities. Another member, Joel List, argued: 'If we feel the inner necessity of our continued existence, then its inner existence is undeniable.' His solution was the creation among Jews of a new consciousness which would be neither religious nor traditional, but would approach a romantic notion of *Volk*, albeit without political connotations. Moses Moser suggested a consciousness built on a concept of culture—a culture brought into harmony with European culture. The source material for this cultural revival would be precisely those aspects of the Jewish faith which were least acceptable to the 'modern' Jew and subjects of the greatest hostility both inside and outside the community—the Old Testament and the Talmud. Moser wanted to identify them not as instruments of religious legitimation but as monuments of Jewish social and intellectual development. Immanuel Wolf added yet another ingredient to the creation of a new synthesis— history. If Moses Mendelssohn had a blind spot, it was in the field of history, to which he remained impervious and indifferent all his life. But these young men, imbued with the spirit of a Hegelian approach to history, saw its significance in relation to the Jews. In a memorandum submitted to the Verein in 1822, Wolf argued that[17]

An idea such as Judaism, which has developed and remained in existence for so many centuries, which has been alive and productive for such a long period in the history of the world, must, for this very reason, be founded on the essence of humanity itself and thus be of the greatest significance and importance for the thinking spirit.

Thus the 'science of Judaism', destined to play an important part in the history of German Jewry, was born. The Verein as a movement was a total failure. Faced with the insuperable obstacles posed by their Jewishness in Prussia, Gans and several other members including Heine converted to Christianity and were absorbed by, but also contributed to, the German great tradition. Others such as J. M. Jost and Leopold Zunz laid the foundations of Jewish scholarship and historiography, confining themselves to the history and culture of the Jews, but yielding nothing in methods and standards to the intellectual demands of their time. As a social movement the Verein collapsed, but not before it had added a new and lasting dimension to the Jewish great tradition, or, as Heine described it, 'a mediation between historical Judaism and modern science'.[18]

If the Verein gave rise to a 'science of Judaism' and provided a forum in which some crucial ideas could germinate and even be fulfilled, it also exposed the absolute dissonance between the two great traditions and, indeed, the wide gap between the mass of the Jews and their europeanised intellectual elite. For these intellectuals the new movement appeared as a magnificent link bridging two great traditions, but the Jewish masses were looking for a *modus vivendi* with their Gentile neighbours, seeking means to preserve their tradition while at the same time exercising their rights and duties as citizens of a secular state. To them, these young intellectuals perhaps appeared like native dancers performing before tourists—the choreography may have been right, but the cultural and above all religious meaning had been abstracted— Jewish scholarship designed to impress Gentile intellectuals was no substitute for Jewish scholarship offered in the service of God and the community. Nor did European intellectuals respond to the attempts of Jews to make the Jewish great tradition accessible to them on their terms. The critique of Jews and Judaism did not change its tone, its purpose or its sources. The debate over the rights of Jews to be emancipated remained constant in that the content of their religion continued to be seen as a primary obstacle.

EDUCATION

In their concern to foster education, however, Moses Mendelssohn and the members of the Verein had correctly identified an area in which change was most likely to occur and to be effective in its results. The idea of educating children as a means of transmitting the cultural and religious heritage goes back to biblical law,[19] but since, as we have already noted, a direct link between education and subsequent socioeconomic performance was only marginally operative,[20] the trend over the centuries, and particularly after restrictions on Jewish participation in trades, industry and agriculture had become established in Europe, was increasingly to separate the idea of education from vocation. Whereas the former was seen almost exclusively as a function of religious development, the latter was regarded as incidental and of little consequence beyond satisfying the immediate economic needs of the individual.[21] From the mid-eighteenth century onwards, Moses Mendelssohn and his disciples began to advocate secular education as the best means of facilitating the access of Jews to the wider society in which they lived. Like many non-Jewish observers, they regarded secular education as a prerequisite of emancipation. Conversely, rabbinic opposition to such education was partly due to its utilitarian approach which was regarded as contrary to the spirit and purpose of education, and partly because they recognised correctly that the challenge to rabbinic authority, already inherent in the economic expansion and elevation of Jewish elites, would lead to a more generalised dissatisfaction within the community and thus undermine its already threatened cohesion. Although the question of Jewish education had been a subject of continuous debate in Jewish circles, a sharp distinction was made between the aims and methods of education. Most of the argument and innovation in education was concerned with method, since the aims were generally accepted as being divinely ordained.[22] Mendelssohn approached the problem from two angles. On the one hand he actively encouraged the establishment of Jewish schools which would divide their teaching between religious and secular subjects,[23] and on the other he began to translate the Old Testament into a pure, literary German, which was at first printed in Hebrew letters on an assumption that, once the masses of the people mastered the German language, they would gain access to its literature and thought, an expectation that was certainly fulfilled.[24] A theoretical discussion which provided the rationale for the new approach to education was provided by another friend of Mendelssohn, Naphtaly Herz Wessely, whose *Divrei Shalom Ve-Emeth* (*Words of Peace and Truth*)[25] set out revised aims for Jewish education in which secular education was justified as an appropriate means for creating for the new generation a meaningful synthesis of the two great traditions they were to inherit. Like Mendelssohn's translation of the Pentateuch, Wessely's book came under fierce attack from many rabbinic authorities and he was in danger of excommunication, which would also have meant his expulsion from Berlin, until Mendelssohn intervened with the Prussian state authorities to protect him.

While the motivation for educational reform can thus be linked with the names of a small group of Jewish innovators, its explosive spread and success was due to deeper and more far-reaching factors. The whole of Western European Jewry had been profoundly affected by the Edict of Toleration in 1782 of Emperor Joseph II of Austria which explicitly called for Jewish children to receive secular education and opened trades and agriculture to Jews, though with a proviso that they could not join guilds or own land.[26] Another factor was the spontaneous spread of secular education, which Jewish and civil authorities recognised. If they intended to control it, they would have to involve themselves in its institutionalisation. Briefly, this spontaneous spread had three main sources. Those Jews whose economic position induced ever-increasing aspirations to find acceptance and status in non-Jewish society engaged private tutors for their children, whose primary task was to equip them with the social and cultural skills to enable them to participate on equal terms in the cultural activities of their socioeconomic peers. The second group, at the other end of the social pyramid, were the destitute, deprived and orphaned children. As Jews they were the responsibility of the community. Unless they could be prepared for some useful social role within the community they were liable to become a permanent drain on community resources, since tax burdens were imposed in relation to size of community and had to be paid irrespective of *per capita* income. Hence the strong emphasis on orphanages, free schools and foster care for needy children. It was poor children, perhaps more than an immediate recognition of the abnormal occupational structure of the Jews, which also led to the growth of Jewish vocational associations that aimed to provide training for Jews in handicrafts and trades. Although such schools spread fairly quickly, their graduates could not gain access to appropriate guilds.[27] The third group were a growing number of young men (Mendelssohn, H. Graetz and Solomon Maimon were typical examples) who roamed from place to place and from teacher to teacher in search of education and learning. They supported themselves partly by acting as private tutors to children of the wealthy and partly by making use of the following traditional Jewish custom. In many communities, young students were assigned for meals to different families on different days of the week (*Freitisch*). This practice not only sustained the young scholars but must also have had an effect in spreading their ideas and aspirations amongst the younger members of many ordinary families.

That non-sectarian schools should have made their appearance as early as 1801 and the admission of Jewish pupils to a number of non-Jewish schools at a time when Jewish teachers were debarred from teaching in such schools is a reflection of the simultaneous emergence of middle classes in the Jewish and Gentile sections of the population. Whilst the new Gentile middle class was free of the anti-Jewish tradition of the established social groups who had their origins in the feudal structure of society,[28] the new Jewish middle class was strongly motivated to find acceptance in the Gentile world by educating their children alongside non-Jews. Finally we may note that here, as in other important cultural manifestations, the general trend for educational reform and innovation found its echo in the Jewish community. The revolution in Jewish education owed as much to the influential work of

Basedow and Pestalozzi, and more indirectly to the writings of John Locke and Rousseau, as it did to the other factors outlined above.[29] Michael Hess, for almost half a century the headmaster of the Philanthropin in Frankfurt am Main, has suggested one other reason for the early success of Jewish schools offering secular education. In a report on this school, Hess recounted how it had started as a charitable institution for destitute children. In July 1804 it held its first public examination, attended by leading figures from the community and the city's educational experts as well as many parents. The performance of the children and the verdict of the experts was such that, within a month, the school was admitting fee-paying pupils and was granted provisional recognition by the city in December of that year. The next public examination in 1805 was equally successful and led to a formal certification of the school by the Senate of Frankfurt.[30]

It is not surprising therefore that by the time Friedrich Wilhelm IV ascended the throne of Prussia in 1840 the Jews of his kingdom had developed a comprehensive educational system which ranged from simple religious schools to high schools and teacher-training colleges. Where there were no Jewish schools, children increasingly found their way into existing high schools, and a growing number of Jewish youths entered universities.[31] The struggle begun by Moses Mendelssohn to introduce secular subjects into a closed religious education system ended some sixty years later with equally desperate attempts to maintain religious education for children preoccupied with secular studies.

CONVERSION AND EMIGRATION

Education and economic advancement created the unrest which led to rebellious attitudes. Education meant awareness of the great ideals of the enlightenment, the longing for freedom, equality and brotherhood for all men, the supremacy of reason and the rule of love. For the Jew at the end of the eighteenth century, there were two insurmountable barriers between the utopia of the enlightenment and his immediate reality: the constraints imposed on him as a member of an autonomous religious community and the restrictions imposed upon him as a Jew by the state. While the former represented a continuous deprivation of personal freedom and arbitrary taxation, the latter meant a permanent denial of choice of residence, occupation and freedom of association. The weakening of religious authority, which reached an unprecedented peak in this period,[32] and the rise of a bourgeoisie so much less entangled in the rigid hostilities of feudal groups offered the Jews a unique opportunity to resolve their difficulties by a single act of rebellion—baptism. At a time when Christian dogma was itself so much under attack that few enlightened Christians took it very seriously, when Christianity was nevertheless the dominant social power in the state, when being a Jew meant extra taxes and being a Christian meant total freedom—at such a time, baptism represented a perfect opportunity for breaking away altogether from the confines of the Jewish community as well as from the onerous controls exercised by the state. Many Jews at the turn of the eighteenth century did just that. Their baptism was a social rather than a religious act, it was a personal revolution, a form of rebellion sanctioned by the authority of church and state, and rewarded by an instant acceptance into the wider community, coupled with immediate relief from special Jewish taxes and responsibility for communal taxes. This first wave of conversions attracted attention mainly because it was, proportionately, extensive and because it offered a serious challenge to Christian and Jewish leaders as well as to the state.[33] In Vienna, conversion was an important mode of entry into the lower nobility and began earlier than in Prussia,[34] where the first great wave of conversions took place at the turn of the eighteenth century. Certainly by 1800 it had reached such proportions that Rachel Varnhagen estimated it at half the Jewish population of Berlin. Friedländer reported to Hardenberg in 1811 that thirty-two Jewish families and eighteen single Jews he knew had converted, and a Prussian minister, Friedrich L. von Schrötter, estimated that, if the conversion rate of 1800 were to be maintained, there would be no more Jews by 1820.[35] It was reported that

Prussia was showing concern over loss of revenue from Jewish taxes, and there was certainly concern among theologians about the nature of the conversions. While Knigge complained in 1805 that 'most of those that renounce their national prejudices and manners, differ from the rest of their brethren in very little else than in exchanging the simplicity and rigour of their customs for Christian vices and follies',[36] *Sulamith* thundered against 'the blasphemers who, without thinking, have thrown off the yoke of the Jewish religion'.[37] Although the controversy over conversion was liveliest during the first wave, it was the second wave which followed the withdrawal of civil rights after 1812 and the anti-Jewish riots of 1819 which was the more important, even though proportionately it was probably smaller.[38] This second wave began in the early 1820s and was much cruder in its origins and purpose. Most Jews who now converted to Christianity did so simply as a mode of qualifying for social and professional positions in society, with little interest in Christianity *per se* and, as often as not, without really relinquishing their family and social ties with the Jewish community.[39] This wave was of special importance however for a number of reasons. It brought many famous Jewish names into the Christian fold (e.g. Marx, Gans, Heine, Börne), contributed as much to discrediting Christianity, or, more particularly the Christian state, as did the radical critique of it, greatly strengthened the Jewish claims for emancipation and exposed, perhaps for the first time, the depth of hostility towards Jews in Germany, because it affected the lower as well as the upper social strata and precipitated the shift from religious to economic and racial hostility to the Jews.

The Prussian state supported and encouraged such conversions as much as possible. Any convert who asked Friedrich Wilhelm III to be his 'godfather' (*Pathenschaft*) would receive 10 ducats as a baptismal gift. Since there were many poor Jews, this gift itself induced many to convert. Cases were recorded of converts who had never received instruction in the new faith, had never attended communion and did not know the Lord's Prayer. Some clergymen in Berlin turned baptism into an industry, charging heavy fees for certifying that they had 'instructed' the rich or demanding from the poor a substantial portion of the royal gift as their fee. To the Jews of Berlin this industry of rapid conversion was known as '*fix bleichen*'.[40] Some converts, of course, were genuine and sincere and were often drawn into missionary activities.[41] Such converts also drew attention to themselves for their exceptional hostility towards Jews, their desire to be 'more Christian than the Christians'[42] and for their opposition to equality for Jews. Thus the convert Julius Stahl, father of German conservatism and professor in the University of Berlin (where he occupied the chair held by another famous convert, Eduard Gans), rejected the suggestion of admitting Jews to public office on the grounds that 'it is one thing to grant equality to a person who is in error concerning religion and another to cultivate religious error in the public domain'.[43] The reputation of some former Jews as opponents of their erstwhile co-religionists went so far that a Hungarian deputy pointed out in a parliamentary debate on Jewish emancipation that 'evidence of a baptised Jew does not deserve attention because it is usually the apostates who slander their former religion'.[44] Converts, whether genuine or opportunist, were also subject to considerable satire and contempt. Heine claimed a vitriolic conversation with Börne on baptised Jews in which they agreed that it was impossible to change lice into fleas by pouring water over them, and Börne was said to have expressed his disgust at such lice, still bearing traces of their Egyptian origins, imagining themselves to be fleas and 'commencing to jump in truly Christian fashion'. Börne was also said to have complained of 'aged daughters of Israel' wearing crosses longer than their noses.[45] On the other hand, the anti-Jewish statistician J. G. Hoffmann could see no difference between Jews and converts. In his *Zur Judenfrage* (1842) he complained that 'Jews or newly baptised Christians' had provided 15 per cent of Prussia's physicians.

More significant factors emerging from the trend to convert were, first, the tremendous impetus it gave to the movement for the reform of Judaism. Although traditional Judaism remained fairly indifferent to the series of defections from its ranks on the grounds that this was a type of weeding-out process in which

33

those without a well-founded sense of identity would disappear, thus leaving a smaller but very much stronger remnant with a better chance of survival, others were considerably alarmed and saw the reform movement as the only real method of stemming the tide of desertions. Nor were the state and church authorities concerned about the difficulties which arose from the cynical processes. Their attitude appeared to be that, even if those who converted did so for purely material reasons and even if they continued to associate with the Jewish community, even if they became the butt of everyone's jokes or made fools of themselves in their determination to appear as real Christians, what mattered was that within two or three generations their Jewish origins would have been forgotten, their children would know nothing of Judaism and their descendants would be indistinguishable from the rest of the population. In short, the Jewish 'problem' would quietly disappear, provided the conversion process could be maintained.[46]

Among the most important consequences of the conversion movement was the evidence it produced concerning the inability of the Jews to alter their occupational structure independently. Resentment at being exclusively classified as, and restricted to, commercial roles was felt throughout the community. We have already noted that, from the beginning of the nineteenth century, attempts had been made to establish vocational training centres, to educate the poorer and less able children as artisans and crafts-men. Michael Hess described what happened in his Philanthropin in the period 1806–9:[47]

> Education heightened the boys' self-respect and they were repelled by petty trade; the lads grew but no one knew how to place them. We were delighted therefore to receive provisional permission from the government for Jewish boys to train as artisans. The community contributed funds to establish a vocational training class and con-tributions were so substantial that ten lads were immediately apprenticed to local master craftsmen, who were very keen to take them.

A long footnote told of the outcome of this experiment. A few of those trained found an outlet for their skills abroad; the rest, after completing their travels and training as journeymen, returned, but were debarred from following their trades and therefore turned to commerce. Twenty years later the problem had not only not been resolved, but in some instances had even been exacerbated. Immanuel Wohlwill, a member of the Kultur Verein and a friend of Heine, was a teacher at the Hamburg Israelitische Freischule in 1830 when he reported to his friend Moser that, while it had been the intention of the founders of his school 'to divert poor youngsters . . . from retailing and peddling . . . to the acquisition of useful crafts and trades', their plan failed because local artisan guilds refused to accept Jewish boys as apprentices.[48] Support for this also came from Löwenstein, who observed that while the Jewish apprentice managed to become a journeyman and even acquire the rank of master in a craft, he would find it so difficult to gain access to a guild and practise his craft that he would be forced to revert to peddling for a livelihood.[49] It is not surprising therefore to find that Menes, who carefully analysed the archives of the Prussian Statistical Office where a special section on *Judentaufen* was kept, discovered that a significant proportion of recorded baptisms relate to apprentices, journeymen, masters and servants in domestic service.[50] It seems fairly clear that those who opted to become artisans would lose contact with Jewish religious life, which made apprenticeship with a Christian master virtually impossible anyway. The road into the ranks of the Germans proletariat meant the abandonment of both Jewish traditions, the acceptance of a lifestyle determined by the German little tradition and, from there, probably quite naturally, a transition to Christianity, the dominant manifestation of the German great tradition. The extent to which access to the working class was dependent on conversion was, however, mitigated in two ways by alternatives mentioned by Hess and Wohlwill. The frustrated artisan could revert to traditional petty trading or, from the 1830s onwards, there was yet another alternative open to him—emigration.

Before we briefly consider emigration, we might look at another aspect of the distribution of conversions which has some bearing on the determinants of some emigration patterns. The *Jewish Encyclopedia* lists 103 prominent Jews born between 1754 and 1839 who converted to Christianity.[51] Their professional and national distribution was as follows:

Profession			Nationality		
academics	..	53	German ..	..	66
artists	.. ..	12	English ..	..	9
writers	.. ..	11	Austrian ..	..	3
politics	.. ..	8	French	..	3
medicine★	..	4	Hungarian	..	3
theology★	..	4	Dutch	.. ..	2
law★..	.. ..	3	Swedish ..	..	2
finance	.. ..	1	Danish	.. ..	1
others	.. ..	8	Italian	.. ..	1
★Excluding university			Russian ..	..	1
professors in these			Not known	..	12
fields who have been					
listed as academics.					

Of these 103, 33 were born in the eighteenth century and 57 in the nineteenth, with 13 whose year of birth is not stated. These figures tend to support three observations. First, the intellectual force of German Jewry, second, the significance of occupational interests as a determinant of conversion, and third, the relatively unique position of Germany as a factor in conditioning Jewish responses. For Germany, and more particularly Prussia, was the land which made a fetish of the Jew in commerce, which nurtured and hunted him as a trader, which challenged him with visions of the good life and threats of oblivion. From the gentle philosopher Kant to the liberal historian Mommsen it beckoned to him to relinquish his faith, to accept Christianity as 'the only bond which can unite the cultures and societies of Europe'.[52] In the final analysis, however, it was those whose economic condition was more exposed than their social situation who succumbed and accepted either harsh reality or gentle persuasion. Intellectuals and artisans, those who were faced by insurmountable class barriers and who yet strove to conquer them, were the ones who paid the price, not so much for an 'entrance-ticket to European culture' as Heine would have it, but rather an entrance ticket to European society.[53] For the majority, some degree of entrenchment in the ancestral faith sufficed to enable them to enjoy the fruits of both cultures, to search for a synthesis of two great traditions which ultimately led them to success culminating in their own destruction.

It is not at all clear from available sources why the trend to emigrate took so long to emerge and why it was mainly the poor and those who felt that they could no longer tolerate the burdens of life in Prussia who chose to leave. They were, in the main, not the radicals or the intellectuals in search of freedom but rather those whose livelihood depended on trade or manual skills, who appeared to lack the ability to rise socially and the incentive to transform their way of life.

The movement of German Jews began with a slump in trade in Bavaria in 1836. By 1840 this had developed into a massive movement, mainly to the United States of America, the land of no restrictions, no special taxes, no discrimination. In the decade 1840–50 some 35,000 German Jews went to America.[54] Most of those who left Prussia were petty traders, small merchants and frustrated artisans who spread rapidly across the length and breadth of the United States. By 1880 the number had risen to almost a quarter of a million, so that the United States had proportionately more Jews than Gentiles from Germany by the end of the century.[55] The success of those who went undoubtedly encouraged many others to follow. It also threw into stark relief the senselessness of the petty restrictions to which Jews were subjected in German states, including Prussia. The influential positions which German Jews achieved in American life, and more especially in the American Jewish communities, left little doubt about the wisdom of their decision to leave 'the fatherland'. Although the extent of Jewish emigration quickly achieved significant proportions (between 1826 and 1848 the Jewish population of America rose from 6,000 to 50,000), it did not give rise to communal comment or anxiety, partly because geographic mobility among Jews was too common to warrant

CITIZEN JEWS IN A CHRISTIAN STATE

special mention, and partly because many, even of those who only toyed with the idea of emigrating,[56] would have recognised its obvious advantages as a mode of escape for those who found the pressures to convert too irksome and the penalties for not converting too great. For those remaining behind in Prussia there was probably also the comforting thought that, no matter how large the emigration from Germany might become, there was in Eastern Europe a vast reservoir of Jews, many of whom were only too eager to move westward and take up the positions and opportunities vacated by those who had left.[57] For the Jews of Eastern Europe, Prussia would appear as a haven of refuge and a land of opportunities compared with the squalid brutality and abject poverty which was their lot in Russia. As far as the Prussian authorities were concerned, the emigration of Jews could only have been welcome, for even in the late 1840s most of Prussia's rulers and aristocrats still regarded some form of elimination—i.e. conversion, expulsion or emigration—as the most desirable solution to the Jewish question, hence it is unlikely that they would have expressed concern about, or obstructed in any way, those who were about to leave.[58]

Nevertheless the progress towards emancipation which gathered momentum in the 1830s and 1840s would probably have been slower in emerging and considerably more difficult but for the active and constant initiatives of Prussia's rulers and civil servants. The road towards emancipation for the Jews was a revolution, a searing disruption of everything they held dear, a process which transformed the very roots of their social being— but it was the Prussian state which challenged, guided and, as often as not, coerced them, to move forward into the nineteenth century.

RELIGIOUS CONFLICTS

Once the Prussian administration had embarked on a policy of involving the Jews in the economic development of the country, it had, however reluctantly and unwillingly, assigned them a role which would involve them increasingly in a process of identification with the dominant concerns, interests and welfare of the state. The growing expansion of Prussia also meant a greater likelihood of progress for its Jewish population. On the other hand, where the economic position of Jews improved, communal bonds were weakened, religious consciousness declined and Jews tended to turn more and more to state authority for protection, guidance and support. The result of this was a gradual streaming of religious attitudes. While the majority of the Jews represented increasingly religiously ill-informed but conservative traditionalists—that is to say, Jews adhering more or less consistently to the Jewish little tradition without having, or indeed aspiring towards, knowledge and interest in their great tradition—a polarisation was taking place at the extremes between 'rigidity and an attitude of indifference';[59] those determined to maintain the classic patterns of Jewish medieval communal and religious life, and those drifting steadily into a wholly secularised position in which both great and little tradition ceased to have meaning or function. Between these polarisations stood the intellectuals, imbued with ideals of enlightenment, too progressive to resort to simple traditionalism and too conscious of the still powerful influence of rational religion to opt for a secular stance. These intellectuals, of whom the members of the Berlin Verein were good examples, were looking for a compromise to free them of the shackles of traditional Judaism and allow them to meet their Gentile neighbours on equal terms.

Israel Jacobson (1768–1828) was typical of this group and is generally regarded as the originator of the Reform movement in Germany.[60] Significantly he was not a rabbi but a banker and philanthropist, the founder of the first non-sectarian school in Germany,[61] in which he introduced the first changes in the synagogue ritual. These were based not so much on any theological considerations of Jewish dogma, but were pragmatic in nature and designed to make Jewish worship more like a church service: he introduced an organ to 'harmonise' musical content, he replaced Hebrew with German prayers and generally changed the atmosphere from the informal and seemingly irreverent synagogue tradition[62] to the formalised, high decorum atmosphere of the church. Jacobson also introduced sermons in German during the service,[63] which were appeals as much to his non-Jewish pupils to learn to accept and respect their Jewish fellows as they were to his Jewish pupils to familiarise themselves with, and to adopt, the great tradition of the Gentile environment. Jacobson transferred his Reform practices to Berlin in 1815 and established his new style of religious service in a private house.

His success in attracting Jewish worshippers away from traditional synagogues and even bringing many who had drifted away from religion to his services led to intense opposition from rabbinic and communal authorities, who appealed to the government to intervene. The Prussian state responded at first by forbidding religious assemblies in private houses in 1817, but when this proved inadequate to stop the Reform services, the Cabinet issued a decree on 9 December 1823 which directed that 'the divine services of the Jews must be conducted in accordance with the traditional ritual and without the slightest innovation in language, ceremonies, prayers or songs'.[64] By that time, however, the spirit of Reform, the idea of creating a new Jewish ritual which would be less susceptible to the biting mockery of critical philosophers, the contemptuous denigration of Christian theologians, and above all to the frigid incomprehension of well-disposed and liberal fellow-citizens, had gathered too much momentum to be stopped in its tracks by either a hostile rabbinate or an imperious government decree. In other parts of Germany, notably in Hamburg, similar attempts at reform were made. Like Jacobson's, they tended to be sponsored by the laity, were experimental, piecemeal and pragmatic, or perhaps, more correctly, were inspired by the ideals of Mendelssohn, in that they were, an attempt to preserve the Jewish great tradition by giving it an outward guise which was comprehensible in terms of the German great tradition. Thus the earliest religious conflicts were centred on relatively petty issues such as the language used in worship, the garb to be worn by the clergy, the omission of medieval liturgy in the prayer-book and the argument over the meaning of references to a '*Goel*' in prayer.[65] Such changes were in part little more than adaptations to real situations, as in the case of Jacobson's innovation in using German as the language of prayer simply because most of his fellow-worshippers no longer understood Hebrew,[66] but other new practices were clearly modelled on church services.

Reform Judaism as a coherent intellectual revolt owed its origins to a variety of factors. Not only did the need for a rational religion link up with the growing resentment against rabbinic authority and communal autonomy, which was recognised as an effective barrier against emancipation, but the rapid growth of education also played an important part though in a somewhat unexpected direction. The formal and informal means of access to secular and higher education which, as we have outlined, developed steadily from the mid-eighteenth century onwards, produced a substantial group of young Jewish intellectuals, most of whom, apart from those choosing medicine, found no outlets for their energies and skills unless they opted for conversion to Christianity, emigration or service within the Jewish community as rabbis or teachers. Thus by their discriminatory legislation the German states were nullifying their own policies of persuading the Jews to resolve the Jewish question by relinquishing Judaism. The Jews were considerably strengthened and reinforced in their religious position by receiving into their communal services streams of able and ambitious young men who in other situations and conditions would have sought outlets appropriate to their abilities in academic and professional fields. It was among these intellectuals that young rabbis emerged who, equipped with a dual education in both the Jewish and the German great traditions, were able to formulate intellectually coherent alternative concepts of Judaism which were to shake the entire community to its foundations in their radicalism and impact. Abraham Geiger (1810–74) was one of the pioneers of this group and soon became a focus of interest and conflict. He postulated the idea of an 'inner core' of Judaism, which was timeless, but which must also be subject to constant evolution. Hence all traditional legal and customary practices should be subject to continuous searching criticism. To do this it would be necessary to be scrupulously honest and to have a substantial knowledge of the historical developments of revelation and the alien influences which have acted upon it. Geiger's aim was to restore 'the true meaning of Judaism', to defend it against the attacks of Christian theologians, to demonstrate the compatibility of Judaism with full civil rights, to divert Jewish scholars from perpetuating a now meaningless tradition of semantic acrobatics with biblical and talmudic texts and to encourage them to concern themselves with 'live' issues. Geiger regarded extreme Jewish orthodoxy as a useful but outdated mode of living for Jews totally isolated in ghettos.[67]

Geiger's critical-evolutionary approach to Judaism did not go far enough for some Jewish radicals, particularly a group formed by Michael Creizenach (1789–1842), a teacher at the Philanthropin in Frankfurt, who formed the 'Frankfurt Society of the Friends of Reform' in 1842 and whose members were required to sign a declaration signifying their agreement with the following principles:[68]

That 'Mosaismus' can develop without restriction;
That the Talmud is unacceptable in dogma and practice;
That all Jewish-talmudic ceremonies and ordinances should be abolished;
That circumcision as a religious or civil act is rejected;
That the Messiah is neither expected nor desired because he is considered to have been realised in the German fatherland.

Dr Moritz Abraham Stern (1807–94), a famous mathematician and another founder member of the society, went further. He described Judaism as 'a dead, old faith' and the final objective of Reform as 'the destruction of positive belief in revelation'. He was aware that challenging the Bible would bring 'howls of mutiny from Christian and Jewish state and church priests', that the Talmud turned its adherents into 'jelly' and that Jews must free themselves from this 'slavery'. He therefore advocated an extension of the principles of the Frankfurt Society to ensure that the Reform movement did not degenerate into 'a stupid Bible faith'. First he demanded that modern philosophy must determine progress in Judaism, second, that the authority of the rabbis must be abolished, and third, that 'we owe it to our Christian fellow-citizens' to reject the very notion of a Messiah altogether.[69]

As the Reform movement gathered momentum, traditional or orthodox Judaism also found advocates amongst the new intelligentsia. Some, such as Solomon Plessner (1797–1883), defended their position by demagogy and charismatic leadership. In Posen, for example, Plessner began a simple campaign of anti-Reform preaching which attracted great attention and drew fearful and caustic comments in the Jewish press of 'a new Moses' leading his audiences back to 'rigid rabbinism' by using 'sinister passages of the Kabbalah' (Jewish mystical literature). While he was credited with making positive inroads into the scourge of the period, an attitude of 'indifference', he threatened to engulf his listeners in 'Polish-Russian Hasidism' and to push them back into 'a particularism of earlier centuries'.[70] Ironically, the Reform movement appealed to the police to stop Plessner from preaching against the introduction of the organ into the synagogue.

The most serious and consistent response to Geiger's approach to Reform, however, came from Samson Raphael Hirsch (1808–88), a fellow-student of Geiger and the most vigorous defender of traditional Judaism in his time. He published his first response to the Reform movement in 1837 when his *Nineteen Letters* appeared,[71] in which he proposed a new synthesis for the Jews, combining absolute loyalty to Jewish law with an equal loyalty towards the state in which the Jews lived, provided that that state accorded full and equal rights. He defined emancipation as 'the natural rights of men to live as equals amongst equals', which should be 'freely extended without force or compulsion'.[72] Geiger's criticism of Jewish law as 'rigid formalism' would apply only where observance is mechanical. Hence the law must be retained, but its observance must be informed, it must be imbued with the living spirit of Judaism. Rejection of the law was tantamount to rejection of Judaism. Hirsch demanded emancipation to enable Jews to practise their religion in freedom, but totally rejected any change or abolition of ritual to meet external demands. He opposed reductions of ritual obligations which

43

would make life easier for the Jew, but was equally opposed to any 'false pietism', by which he meant a voluntary withdrawal from civil obligations and 'Kabbalistic castles in the air'.[73] If emancipation held any dangers, these would not lie in any conflict it would generate between a Jew's religious and civil obligations, but only in that it would entice him away from his religion so that he would devote himself entirely to 'those passions which are degrading to humanity, namely, greed for gain and narrow selfishness'.[74]

From a religious point of view, the debates which developed within Judaism between 1828 and 1846,[75] the most fundamental for some seven hundred years, proved to be a revitalising force; Jost described a number of the positive effects they generated: first, they awakened a new interest among rabbis and teachers and thus gave rise to new scholarly interest and popular literature. Second, they stirred public interest in religious questions and halted the growing apathy and indifference, and third, this new interest and awareness spilled over into the political field and heightened the demands not only for religious reform but also for civil rights.[76]

In addition, the debates also created three clear rabbinic approaches to their tasks which were to have profound long-term implications. Modern knowledge was clearly destined to play a major role in the evolution of Judaism. Those who followed S. R. Hirsch utilised secular knowledge for the support and furtherance of obedience to Jewish law. Those who followed Leopold Zunz's approach used modern methodologies to apply standards of critical scholarship to Jewish subjects without involving themselves in problems of theology. They accepted Judaism as they found it and pursued their researches mainly in historical and literary fields. The third group, which followed Geiger, thought to combine their knowledge of modern science and Judaism to create a new theology.[77]

If Marx thought that social questions also had religious implications, then we have to note that religious questions also have political implications. The radicalism of the Frankfurt Society was regarded by many Jews as especially politically dangerous because it ignored the reality of the Jewish position and might therefore detract from the rising demands for civil rights. When the Frankfurt Society published its declaration, Ludwig Philippson (1811–89), the famous founder and editor of the *Allgemeine Zeitung des Judentums* (1837), published a scathing attack on their entire programme, concentrating particularly on the notion of a German fatherland as the realisation of the Jews' messianic hopes. He presented his credentials as a patriot by explaining that three members of his family had fought in the War of Liberation of 1815, of whom one had been wounded and awarded an Iron Cross. Nevertheless, he challenged:[78]

> How many Germans will recognise Germany as the fatherland of the Jew? A nice Messiah that, if the Jew of Bavaria still has to pay *Judengänsegelder*, and cannot settle until he has acquired registration. A nice Messiah that, if the Jew of Hanover must pay protection tax and cannot pursue a trade even in the smallest village. A nice Messiah that, if the Jew of Saxony is restricted to two areas which he cannot even use alternately. A nice Messiah that, if the Jew in Prussia is subject to twenty-one special laws, and cannot live on the right bank of the Elbe if he was born on the left bank. A nice Messiah that, if the Jew of Anhalt-Dessau can be a master craftsman, but cannot have an apprentice or journeyman.
>
> I wish the originator of this idea would go two miles beyond the boundaries of Frankfurt to look for his Messiah, and that the police would deport him back to Frankfurt to enjoy his Messiah, because a Frankfurt Jew may not live anywhere else. Or that the Jewish Realschule at which he is a teacher would become German, and Dr Creizenach could not teach there because no Jew may teach in a German school. Would he still think then that the Messiah came with the German fatherland? No! We can love our German fatherland with all our hearts . . . but we must not hide our lack of freedom . . . with emotive phrases.

Philippson went on to offer yet another telling argument against Creizenach. Had the Jews of Germany full civil rights, he maintained, the Messiah idea would still be a nonsensical claim. The Jewish concept of the Messiah, the only universalistic concept in Judaism, visualised an era of peace and justice for all men. If that idea were now to be restricted to Germany, Jews would be lost in a meaningless particularism, which could be justified only so long as it served to teach mankind the idea of universal peace. Hence Creizenach's claim was hollow, meaningless, a form of 'Jewish suicide'. Philippson described Creizenach and Stern as 'the Sancho Panzas of Bauer and Feuerbach'. Those two at least had the courage to say that they did not want any form of Christianity, while the Jewish reformers spoke of Reform but really intended to abolish Judaism.[79]

In reply the Frankfurters tried to enrol the support of Germany's most respected and admired Jew—Gabriel Riesser. But he was not to be won over. In a statement in *Der Orient* he explained his position:

Dr Stern and Dr Creizenach had tried to involve him in the leadership of a new Reform movement and had used his name in a number of publications. He strongly objected to this, partly because he did not entirely agree with the movement and partly because he was concerned with fighting for the freedom of religion, but he did not regard himself as theologian enough to express opinions on details of Jewish ceremonial observance.

The specific subject was circumcision, which the Reformers wanted to abolish. Riesser took the view that, although he regarded circumcision as 'an innocent though meaningless ceremony', he was violently opposed to any move either to enforce or to forbid it. He thought that while a Jew had a right to reject it, an orthodox Jew had an equal right to declare an uncircumcised Jew as not Jewish on purely religious grounds. But neither had any right to try to use the law to establish his position.

Time and again he stressed that his concern was a *Freiheitsprinzip* and nothing else. He thus regarded religious controversy as perfectly legitimate, provided no coercion was applied. He went so far as to say that, since he no longer observed religious ceremonies, the orthodox had a right to deny his Jewishness.[80]

The approach was typical of Riesser, the man who electrified the Jewish fight for emancipation and gave the Jews of Germany a new self-respect, for lack of which the community was threatened with total disruption.

GABRIEL RIESSER

Gabriel Riesser (1806–63) was born in Hamburg, the son of a modest communal employee. He studied law at Kiel and Heidelberg universities but, like Gans and many others before him, was prevented from adopting an academic career because he was a Jew. In 1830 he was refused admission to the bar in Hamburg on the same grounds. At the same time the subject of Jewish emancipation was once again topical and had been debated in the Landtag of Württemberg as recently as 1828, when the word 'emancipation' became the slogan of its champions.[81] Riesser decided to join the battle and in December 1830 wrote a famous pamphlet, *Ueber die Stellung der Bekenner des Mosaischen Glaubens in Deutschland*, which he addressed to 'Germans of all faiths'.[82] His analysis of the problem was revolutionary in its originality and militancy. He stipulated nine points of approach to his argument. First, he rejected a widely-held view that the weak should not demand, but should rather plead their case with humility and constraint. Humility, he argued, was a virtue only in the strong. He for one was not prepared, by appealing to those who withheld emancipation, to pay 'a cowardly tribute of servility'. Second, the time when men were martyred for their beliefs was past. Freedom of conscience posed problems of law, of honour and of freedom, not of faith. Third, Riesser made no claim or pretence that he was representing either the Jewish people or the Jewish religion and assumed sole responsibility for any views expressed. Fourth, he freely admitted his personal involvement and motivation in challenging the state. He was a man denied the fulfilment of his interests and ambitions on purely religious grounds. Fifth, he had neither the intention nor the ability and knowledge necessary to present a reasoned account of 'Mosaic theology'. Sixth, while it was true that among Jews there were varying opinions on the theology and practice of Judaism, he felt that, as a man and a Jew, 'he owed no account regarding his views on religion to any earthly power'. In his seventh point, Riesser rejected absolutely any notion that demands for civil rights could be met by displacing 'an aristocracy of faith with an aristocracy of enlighten-

47

ment'.[83] The state had every right to confine civil rights to those who were willing to carry out their civil duties, and Riesser emphasised that all Jews in Germany were not only willing, but were actually fulfilling their civil duties. Eighth, he insisted that the state had no right to use its powers to intervene in matters of conscience and the religious convictions of its subjects. Finally, the state could not and must not impose standards of behaviour and performance on adherents of minority religions when it could not, and did not, do the same for those who subscribed to the religion of the majority.

As far as Riesser was concerned, he was not dealing with the conflict of one religion with another, or the truth or superiority of the one against that of the other—his concern was solely and exclusively one of law and right. For Christianity to insist that Jews convert to gain civil benefits was not only coercive and immoral, it denigrated Christianity itself and made a mockery of its teaching. He confessed himself quite indifferent to Jewish religious practice, which he had long since abandoned, yet he denied the state and its Christian theologians, who were in any event appallingly ill informed on Judaism, the right to criticise Jews for adhering to Judaism and the right to demand of Jews that they relinquish their ancestral faith to be accepted by the state. He, Riesser, would refuse 'to pay the admission-tax of lies' which was demanded of him. Nor would he accept that, by concerning himself with the question of Jewish emancipation, that made him particularistic. In demanding civil rights for Jews, he was 'pursuing the same aims as those who wanted to further the progress of mankind'.[84]

Although Riesser's pamphlet made little impact on the non-Jewish world, apart from sparking off a vigorous and ultimately significant polemic between him and the Heidelberg theologian H. E. G. Paulus, its effect on the Jewish community was explosive and lasting. Riesser's pamphlet was published in January 1831; a second edition was issued in February of that year. He was challenged by Paulus, who had already established a reputation as an opponent of Jewish emancipation (see *Die jüdische National-absonderung nach Ursprung, Folgen und Besserungsmitteln*, Heidelberg, 1831). Riesser's reply was marked by its unusual sharpness of tone and aggressive response. The original lack of interest outside the Jewish community in Riesser's work is illustrated by an article published in 1842 by H. B. Oppenheimer,[85] who wrote: 'Riesser's brilliant articles are unknown even to those who make the laws, yet petty pamphlets of pietistic country parsons who derive their hatred of Jews from such as Eisenmenger provide the ammunition for anti-Jewish arguments and are treated in the *Literatur-Zeitungen* with great respect—as if they had rescued the immortality of the soul from the Promethean fire of the Young Hegelians.' It might be argued that with the advent of Riesser's intervention, the Jews of Prussia (and indeed of Germany) achieved a *de facto* emancipation and that henceforth their evolution was a dual one. In relation to their political situation, their fight was a deliberate campaign to gain *de jure* recognition for what they felt they had already achieved. Internally they were now sufficiently confident to embark on a series of searching self-examinations which were to change the structure and content of Judaism, but which left the struggle for emancipation untouched. For Riesser had changed the nature of the debate and the subject of the controversy. The Jews, Riesser maintained, were Germans. Since even the law recognised that their status was different from that of foreign nationals, it was implicitly accepting this fact. Again, if the Jews of the middle ages were defined and treated as a 'trading caste', the state could not operate on the assumption that medieval estates had been abolished and still maintain a medieval classification for the Jew. As far as the predominance of Jews in trade was concerned, Riesser charged that the state could not discriminate against Jews because they were traders and at the same time block their access to other professions and occupations. Similarly, where in the past Jews had been at pains to defend and explain their religion, Riesser saw no justification for this—'the final agonising efforts of mankind's two vampires—the spirit of caste and religious hatred'[86] were too repellent and repulsive to warrant serious regard.

Riesser thus transformed the debate on the Jewish question by persuading the Jews that it was not the state that had a right to demand that they align their great tradition with that of the state, but on the contrary it was their right to demand civil equality provided only that they fulfilled their civil obligations. In Marx's terms, Riesser called for a transfer of religion from the public to the private domain. His militancy found a strong echo among the leaders of Jewish thought and led to vigorous attacks on opponents of Jewish emancipation in the Jewish press.[87] Thus, while *Sulamith* saw itself as 'a mediator and peacemaker between this nation and its opponents',[88] the *Allgemeine Zeitung des Judentums*, in a review of its first year of publication, poured scorn on 'the selfishness and prejudice' which had taken hold of public opinion in Germany when it came to decide on Jewish emancipation. 'All the old accusations are dragged up and perpetuated in endless harangues.'[89] For Riesser, besides giving a lead to the Jews in challenging the attitudes of the state, was equally fearless in attacking the hitherto sacrosanct Christian churches for their hostility and arrogance:[90]

> When you call your religion, whose hatred has throttled generations, and drowned centuries in blood, a religion of love ... do you not blush ... to level charges against the sister religion that has been your victim and to say that only *we Jews* must purify our religious tenets, so as to make ourselves fit for full civic equality, while the tenets of Christianity are above requiring any such purification?

It was not only the fact that Riesser dared to turn the tables on his opponents that so impressed his fellow-Jews. In spite of it, or more probably because of it, his gaining the respect and admiration of his German fellow-citizens persuaded the Jews that his militancy was right. Riesser, the Jew who began his fight because he was denied the right to practise law, ended his career as a German judge, and one of a delegation of citizens who was to offer Friedrich Wilhelm IV the imperial crown of a united Germany.

CHAPTER III

The Prussian State and the Jews

In England the industrial revolution provided the impetus for a professional civil service, but in Prussia it was the civil service that initiated an industrial revolution. Friedrich Wilhelm I (1714-40) of Prussia selected his administrators from the bourgeoisie and treated his Jews harshly because he had a genuine religious aversion to them, which caused him to be indifferent to their needs as human beings but did not prevent him from encouraging and supporting those among them whose wealth or manufacturing skills made them an asset to the state. This meant that, while as a despotic ruler he perpetuated the medieval concept of the Jew as the property of an overlord, he also recognised that the future of the Jews lay in their systematic absorption into the emerging middle classes in Prussia. His policy therefore was to foster Jewish participation in unrestricted competitive economic activities without, however, affording them the general freedom to which the middle classes normally aspire.

His successor, Friedrich II (the Great) (1740-86), although he intended to pursue the same policy towards Prussia's Jews, was a very different character, and the consequences of his rule produced somewhat unexpected results. As a 'philosopher of the enlightenment' he scoffed at religion but did not display any more sympathy towards his Jews because of that. On the contrary, his antipathy was even more pronounced than that of his predecessor. It was also more irrational and unpredictable. Unlike his predecessor, he chose his civil servants in the main from the ranks of the nobility and greatly extended their numbers and functions, while characteristically remaining cynical and sceptical towards them and their activities, no matter how devotedly they fostered the interests of the state.[1] The effect of Friedrich's irrational hostility to Jews and his determination to accelerate the progress of Prussia gave rise to an intense ambivalence which was continuously reflected between and within his administrators. While he despised Jews and longed to 'diminish' their numbers in Prussia, he also recognised the important part they could play in furthering commercial and industrial developments. His appetite for war exhausted the wealth of his state and strongly reinforced the need for promoting industrial progress, in which the Jews were an essential catalyst. The difficulties he faced were compounded by the unusual nature of his state, which[2]

> was not built around the political ideal of liberty like the Western nations, nor around the cultural traditions of the German folk, nor around the natural factor of the German race; it was as remote from liberalism as from any German nationalism. It was a conscious and political creation . . . but it did not spring from the will of the people, or from a desire for greater justice and more human happiness . . . it was the result of a will imposed upon the people from above. Hierarchy, authority, obedience and devotion were the foundations of the army and of Prussianism. King, aristocracy and people, each one within his rank, served the one idea. The growth of Prussia was dominated by only one goal—power, by only one norm—Prussia. Everything else counted only in so far as it served that goal and norm.

The king and his administrators liked to think that their decisions and actions were wholly determined by the nationally perceived interests of Prussia. As Selma Stern has described it:[3]

> What was of interest to [Friedrich II] was simply and solely the question whether Jews were useful or harmful, essential or superfluous, to the Prussian state. Whether he was likely to succeed in exploiting their business acumen, their entrepreneurship, their innovatory skills for his as yet undeveloped, poorly financed and poorly industrialised national economy. Whether he could deprive

a living historical organism of its own laws, customs and attitudes and consolidate these into a rational purpose which would foster the needs and demands of the state, so that they might contribute in transforming the militarily powerful but territorially incomplete, nay impossible state into the best organised, the best disciplined, the most admired and the most feared trade-finance and industrial power in Northern Europe.

It would probably be right to argue that the infamous *General-reglement und Generalprivilegium* of 17 April 1750 (which Mirabeau once described as 'a law worthy of a cannibal'[4]) was intended to stimulate Jewish participation in industrial expansion, but it also provided an opportunity for Friedrich to give concrete expression to his intense hostility, since it included rules restricting Jewish marriages, excluding Jews from most forms of skilled labour, from innkeeping and specified other trades, and similar petty restrictions. It also institutionalised a variety of 'protected', 'specially protected' and 'naturalised' Jews and by its direct intervention in personal status law initiated a process of selection which was almost Darwinian in character, in that it eliminated many of Prussia's unsuccessful Jews by expulsion, while at the same time facilitating the rise of a ruthless commercial class whose loyalty was secured by making their public and private well-being dependent on the whims and goodwill of an autocratic ruler. Much as a Carlyle might rant against Ephraim and Itzig because they 'wallowed in the dirty wealth gained from the ruin of their neighbours',[5] Itzig was rewarded by Friedrich by being appointed permanent Chief-elder of Prussian Jewry, because his work was important for Prussia. Lest this should be interpreted as a mark of respect, however, when Itzig applied for permission for his daughter to marry, Friedrich granted it only on condition that the couple left Prusia after the nuptials. And when Prussian Jewry's pride, Moses Mendelssohn, was nominated for membership of the Prussian Academy of Sciences, this was vetoed by him,[6] on the ground that a Jewish philosopher contributed nothing to the economic progress of Prussia. Friedrich gave formal expression to this dichotomy of approach to the Jews in the administrative framework he created. He established a number of specialist

53

departments, including a department which was to deal with 'trade, industry and urban settlement', in addition to his central administrative department[7] and, characteristically, ruled that commercial and industrial questions relating to Jews were to be dealt with by the new department, while all questions relating to the personal status of Jews were to be decided upon by the central department.[8] Since the king also reserved the right to overrule any of his administrators, no matter how well founded their recommendations might be, on the grounds that 'a ruler need no more take the advice of his ministers than a Newton would have to consult Leibniz and Descartes to discover the law of gravitation',[9] Friedrich's absolute power over the Jews of Prussia was firmly entrenched, and the duality of his approach was bound to find an echo among his advisers. Some of these were inclined to apply his rationalism to their analyses of issues concerning the Jews, some would apply the humanistic principles of their time, some would follow their king in his ferocious antipathy towards Jews, while yet others would endeavour to emulate their ruler by applying a combination of such diverse trends in their desire to serve the interests of the state. Thus, Manitius, Friedrich's minister of finance, recommended in 1745 that the restrictions and special taxes imposed on Jews should be abolished as unethical and unnecessary. Unethical because the hostility to Jews was no more than a heritage of the Catholic Church, 'the source of all persecution', and unnecessary because Jews should devote themselves to business and for that they only needed to be honest—'in that respect we could only wish that Christians were as scrupulous as Jews'.[10] In 1772 the central department argued that it would be improper to withhold 'natural rights of humanity' from people enjoying the status of 'subjects' (*Untertan*), especially since they served the interests of the general and national good.[11] More emphatic was an earlier report which argued that 'it would be ridiculous to accuse [Jews] of being in many respects useless people, when they are prevented at the same time from becoming useful'.[12]

Then there were civil administrators who could see only grave danger for Prussia if it permitted Jews to develop their commercial activities while 'the flower of Prussia's youth' was conscripted to fight for the country. Others felt that they could best serve the royal will by making sure that restrictions on Jews were rigorously enforced, lest 'Jews should fare better than Christians'.[13] The third group, those who tried to resolve the institutionalised ambivalence towards Jews by combining rationality and brutality in their recommendations, also revealed, albeit unintentionally, the untenable foundations of many of the assumptions made about Jews and their social and economic roles in Prussian society. Inspector Domhardt of the central department was instructed to prepare a report on the feasibility and desirability of expelling Jews from West Prussia in 1780. His report (which we shall quote verbatim) is remarkable because it clearly demonstates not only the ambiguous position so characteristic of his time, but also the extent to which Jews were fulfilling social functions, which implied a much more constructive integration into the structure of the Prussian economy than the traditional folk-image of the Jew as exclusively occupied in commerce and money lending would suggest. Referring to himself in the third person throughout, Domhardt wrote:[14]

He went to West Prussia and discussed the Jewish question and emigration with the chamber (*Kammer*). The number of Jews to be expelled—4,430 souls—constitutes almost half of all Jews established in West Prussia. The Deputies have already expressed proper concern about the negative and harmful effects for the country. It is known that the Jew does not carry out all and every duty of a citizen and that he contributes nothing to the protection of the country; it can also not be denied that an unusual number of them, who maintain themselves by usury and sharp practice, must be a burden for the rest of the state. Hence it is necessary that the excessive number be curtailed. For all that, he cannot agree to an abrupt expulsion of a considerable number of these people. The king has made his reign memorable by tolerance for all and every religion and faith. An abrupt expulsion would not only go against general principles of humanity, but especially against such lofty attitudes [of the king].
  Added to that is the fact that the province can benefit only from a gradual expulsion of Jews. It is unlikely that the benefit which the Jews derived from the exercise of various trades (*Gewerbe*) will pass immediately to Christian inhabitants. These are not yet in a position

55

to take over occupations (*Nahrungsstellen*) vacated by an emigration. Aliens cannot be brought in without great expense or very quickly. The consequences would be a complete disruption of trade, a shutting down of all factories and a considerable shortfall in taxes and profits which a reduction in consumption by more than 4,000 souls would involve.

A gradual reduction would be better. It could be achieved thus:

1. Not a single Jewish family to be granted domicile in the plains, nor a single trade carried out by a citizen (*Landmann*) to be permitted to them. Therefore Jews who have acquired land on the estates of the nobility on which they have settled and where they deal in cattle or fodder or distil brandy should be instructed to sell their lands, move to the city or leave the country.
2. Apart from those resident here, foreign, Polish or mendicant Jews are not to drift into the country (*einschleichen*).
3. It is impossible to forbid Jews to practise professions or trades (*Handwerke*). Deutsche-Krane and Flatow [areas of East Prussia] would lose most of their professionals. As soon as Christian guildcraftsmen settle in these places, Jewish quacks should be debarred.
4. Only impediments to marriage can reduce this extraordinary number without invoking serious consequences. If Jews who are not suited to be ordinary or extraordinary protected Jews were to be granted a marriage certificate only if they could prove that a foreign Christian, carrying on the same profession had already been settled for at least three years, then marriage would become more difficult. There is no danger that numbers will increase outside marriage, since the Talmud strictly forbids such licence and holds the sanction of excommunication for offenders.

On balance, rational considerations and humanitarian principles came to dominate the attitudes of the Prussian civil service; shortly after Domhardt's report another Counsellor of State, Christian Wilhelm von Dohm (1751–1820), a liberally inclined administrator and a friend of Moses Mendelssohn, issued his famous *Ueber die bürgerliche Verbesserung der Juden* which laid the foundations for the formal emancipation of the Jews.[15] He argued that the condition of the Jews was the result of their treatment at the hands of Christians: 66 per cent of Jews were petty traders and pedlars; 10 per cent were servants; 8 per cent were manual workers and fully 84 per cent would have to be reckoned as belonging to the poorest sections of the community. To improve their condition would be of benefit not only to them, but to all of society and to the state. Dohm rejected any suggestion that the Jewish religion made the Jew inferior: 'From what we know of the Jewish religion, it contains no harmful principles; only the mob, which feels free to cheat a Jew, accuses him of having a law which permits him to cheat a Gentile and only persecuting priests have fairy tales of [Jewish] prejudices, which merely prove their own.'[16] He insisted that 'the Jew is a human being more than he is a Jew', and if he is more corrupt (*verdorben*) than other people, then this is 'an inevitable and natural consequence' of the oppression to which he has been subjected.[17] To improve the position of the Jews, Dohm recommended that they should be given access to all trades, crafts and guilds, that the state should provide the best possible education for them and that they should share the privilege of military service but retain their communal autonomy and freedom of religion. Given the reforms he advocated, he thought that the Jews might be able to free themselves from the effects of their oppression but that they should be debarred from public office so as not to offend Christians.[18]

In 1791, as a result of the French revolution, the Jews of France became the first full and equal citizens of any state in Europe. One of the results of this event was a commission set up by Friedrich Wilhelm II to review his predecessor's legislation on Jews. After two years' deliberation, the commission concluded that emancipation could be granted to Jews only when they had attained a culture like that of the Christians—this, they thought, would take sixty or seventy years, a span of three generations. A more significant consequence was the emergence of nationalism, the movement which challenged the identities of groups and communities. To Fichte, the prophet of German nationalism, that meant the explicit and dogmatic exclusion of Jews. In 1793 he proclaimed:[19]

> There is spread throughout nearly every country of Europe a powerful, inimical state which was continually against all others and often succeeds in bitterly oppressing their peoples—this state is Jewry . . . The only way I can see of giving [the Jews] civil rights is

to cut off their heads in a single night and equip them with new ones devoid of every Jewish idea . . . to protect ourselves against them, again I see no means except to conquer their promised land and pack them all off to it.

From Napoleon to Fichte the idea of the Jews as a separate nation, as 'a state within a state',[20] became the dominant concern. The Sanhedrin summoned by Napoleon (1807) rejected the concept, but did not convince Europe. The Jews failed to come to terms with the conflict they had themselves generated by opposing the German image of Jews as a people with their own notion of themselves as a creed.[21] The Napoleonic Wars and the crushing defeats suffered by Prussia exacerbated the problem, because it intensified romantic nationalism and thereby sharpened the contrast between the 'alien race' of the Jews and the 'true German', for 'Christian Teutomania' was the emotional response to military humiliation. At the same time, however, Prussia after the Peace of Tilsit embarked on extensive social and administrative reforms under the Stein–Hardenberg administrations. The municipal law of 1808 gave some Jews citizenship rights in cities, serfdom and the monopolies of the guilds were abolished, and the liberalism of Hardenberg and Humboldt[22] combined to create the Edict of Emancipation which was signed by the king on 11 March 1812. Under this edict, all Jews resident in Prussia were granted citizenship. Jews were to have the same civil duties and rights as Christians, including the right, explicitly stated, to hold teaching and academic posts. They were to adopt German names and to use the German language in all their legal transactions. Jewish communal autonomy was thus largely abolished, and its final forms, together with questions relating to their admission to the civil service and their educational institutions, were to be dealt with in later legislation.[23]

The Jews expressed their gratitude and delight by devoted service in the Wars of Liberation and passionate expressions of loyalty to Prussia: 'Now . . . we have obtained freedom as Prussian citizens; now we have only one fatherland—Prussia— and we have to pray for it. We have only one mother-tongue— German', wrote David Friedländer,[24] but the German historian

Heinrich von Treitschke (1834–96) saw the effects of the edict of 1812 differently: 'The hatred against the Jews was so strong and general that public opinion adopted a hostile attitude to them almost unanimously even in a case where they were obviously treated unjustly'.[25] The reaction was not slow in coming and was given implicit support both by the refusal of the participants in the Congress of Vienna of 1815 to adhere to the spirit of the peace settlement, which guaranteed civil rights to Jews by exploiting a textual ambiguity in the treaty,[26] and by Prussia's refusal to extend the benefit of pensions to Jewish wounded veterans and widows of the War of Liberation.[27] Rights granted under the edict were curtailed or withdrawn, and the open riots against the Jews in 1819 (the Hep Hep riots)[28] persuaded the Prussian administration to reverse the trend of legitimating the social aspirations of its Jewish population and to reconsider its attitude to the Jewish question. Thus, in 1820, Jews were deprived of the right to become military surgeons, in 1822 they were debarred from all other military offices, their right to hold teaching and academic posts was abolished and restrictions were imposed on the type of landed property Jews might own, with an absolute ban on the acquisition of mines and quarries. A decree of 1823 specified that elected representatives had to be Christian and in 1825 further restrictions on land ownership were imposed. In 1827 Jews were excluded from the office of executioner, in 1831 from the higher local government offices of mayor and lord mayor while Jewish landowners were excluded from hereditary rights in landed property (*Patrimonalgerichtsbarkeit*). In 1833 they were excluded from the office of village head (*Schulzeämter*), in 1835 from military conscription and in 1841 from the magistracy. Those Jews who had acquired estates were debarred from wearing uniforms appropriate to their station.[29]

By 1840 the struggle for emancipation had been resolved for the Jews who had followed the guidelines set out by Dohm sixty years earlier, but for the rulers and people of Prussia, the problem had been reformulated anew into 'the Jewish question', for, in addition to the trends and developments we have described, fate in the shape of a new king and an unexpected event took a hand in giving the struggle for emancipation new directions. The constant and voluminous reiteration of arguments for and against the Jews, presented as they were in every conceivable form from crudely religious to political, economic and philosophical, in the result only obscured rather than clarified the real issues. That this was true was noted by many of the participants in the debate, notably Bauer and Marx, but so strong were the influences of traditional images and hostile prejudices that even the most radical writers could not escape their influence and unwittingly perhaps, but also unmistakably, perpetuated ideas generated in earlier and less sophisticated centuries.

THE JEWISH QUESTION AND CLASS CONFLICT

By the time the Jewish question became the catch-phrase of Germany in 1842, the concept itself was almost a century old. It arose originally in England in 1753 in connection with the 'Jew-bill' of that year which raised questions about Jewish land owner-ship and the naturalisation of Jews.[30] In the English context, these two questions were seen as problematic because they had religious and economic implications. Thus granting Jews civil rights meant accepting them into a Christian society as well as undermining their own view of themselves as temporary residents awaiting sal-vation through their Messiah. On the economic level it was recog-nised that the Jew might present a threat at all class levels: the landed gentry feared that they would acquire all land, merchants feared their competition, small shop-keepers feared that Jews might displace them and labourers feared that Jews would work for less money and thus lower wage-rates. In England, therefore, the real nature of the Jewish question was recognised correctly very much earlier and thus perhaps did not degenerate into the virulent movement it ultimately became in Germany. There was a national and a social class issue. At the national level the problem of converting a Christian into a pluralistic society was recognised and, at the social class level, each social group appeared to acknowledge the possibility of conflicts of interests in relation to a socially stratified but classless group whose members might be expected to move into the national framework at any class level. It would follow from such a situation that the Jews would meet the greatest hostility at the most deeply entrenched class levels and the least at those levels which were already in transition and which represented more fluid group interests. We have already noted that the Jews of Prussia met more vigorous hostility at the highest and lowest, i.e. the most strongly entrenched, social class levels. If we bear in mind the extent to which the German evolution of the Christian state hardened opposition to any form of religious pluralism and look again at the pattern of legislation which whittled away the emancipated status the Jews were accorded in 1812, we will see that the situation in Prussia was very similar to that of England a century earlier, in that the Jewish question was simultaneously a national and a class conflict, which was more complex in Prussia because the two conflict levels existed in much stronger form and because in the Prussian situation authority linked with ascribed status was held to have much greater significance than in England.[31]

Although the class structure of Prussia is often described in a simple three-tier grouping of nobility, citizenry and peasantry,[32] the same criticism that R. S. Neale has directed against such a simplistic classification in England[33] could also be directed at such a view of the Prussian class structure. If we are arguing that the pattern of restrictions reimposed on the Jews of Prussia between 1812 and 1841 was as much class- as nation-based, this would be difficult to demonstrate if one employs a crude three-level description of Prussian society, but will appear more convincing if we apply for example the more sensitive and discriminating structure suggested by Marx for French society.[34] Marx suggested five groups: the big landowners, the financial and industrial aristocracy, the higher echelons of the army, universities, churches, law and press, the petty bourgeoisie and the proletariat. Except for the last group which in Prussian contemporary terms were represented predominantly by the peasantry, this classification reflected the social-structural hierarchy of Prussia more realistically and could therefore be used to illustrate our tentative analysis. We would stipulate that Prussian legislation had two objectives. First, to protect the value-system of the German-Christian state from influences emanating from non-Christians and, more especially, to prevent Jews from achieving authority derived from ascribed status positions. Second, to protect class interests which might feel threatened by Jewish competition and again to ensure that social classes would not be subjected to Jewish authority based on ascribed status. Thus the German-Christian state is clearly the object of protection in the decrees of 1823 and 1831 which laid down that elected representatives and higher local government dignitaries must be Christians and would also protect representatives of the financial and industrial aristocracy from being swamped by Jewish interests speaking on their behalf. The decrees of 1822, 1825, 1831 and 1841, which restricted Jewish land ownership, excluded them from hereditary privileges, prevented them from owning mines and quarries and debarred them from wearing the uniforms appropriate to their stations, protected the interests not only of the big landowners and eliminated Jewish competition for property of high industrial potential, but also of peasants and proletarians from the threat of coming under Jewish industrial control, since Jews were effectively prevented from owning the great mining operations which lay at the root of industrial expansion.[35] There was also the additional advantage that by prohibiting Jewish ownership of mines and quarries, the likelihood of employment of Jews in heavy industries would also be prevented.

The senior positions in the universities were protected from Jewish competition and authority by the decree of 1822, as were schoolteachers and students. While the higher echelons of the army were protected by the decrees of 1820 which prevented the admission to the army of Jewish surgeons, another of that same year closed other specialist army offices to Jews, and all ranks were protected by the decree of 1835 which forbade Jews to carry out military duties for a Christian. The petty bourgeoisie was protected by the decree of 1841 which prevented Jews from being appointed magistrates and thus assuming positions of authority over them as well as over other sections of the lower classes, while it would probably have been the peasantry that would have seen the 1833 decree which prevented Jews from becoming heads of villages as being in their interest. Finally for all Prussians the idea, however improbable in practice, of a Jewish executioner must have been a painful one and the decree of 1827 allayed their fears on this score.

If the restrictive legislation highlights the elements of class conflict that formed an important, though at that time mainly ignored, part of the tensions between Christians and Jews, it would also appear reasonable to suggest that the Jews responded by seeking out those sections in the social structure in which they found least resistance or, better, the greatest degree of acceptance, namely in the middle classes, the bourgeoisie—the fast rising, expanding, ambitious and least tradition-bound sections of the community. It would be interesting to examine[36] whether the Jewish predilection for the bourgeoisie was a result of the difficulties they experienced in breaking into tradition-based levels of society, or if their consistent movement towards bourgeois capitalism was rooted in the historical consequences of landlessness which Ber Borochov has suggested.[37] According to Borochov, Jews, by being deprived of ownership of and contact with the soil, lost contact with primary forms of production and concentrated all their skills and energies on those elements of production which utilised human rather than natural forces. They manifested a preponderance of 'mental' over 'physical' labour and a tendency to choose spontaneous self-employment rather than wage labour. Whatever the real situation may be, R. A. Kann is likely to be correct when he argues that 'wherever Jewish-Gentile friction does exist, disparity, difference in social stratification, always is the premise of Jewish identification on which all other issues are based. Without the experience of such disparity the Gentile world would not even become conscious of the existence of a problem of majority-minority relations.'[38] It is equally true, however, that 'in order that resentment and aggression released by economic hardship turn to a specific target, the target must be present in the minds of the embittered',[39] even, we might add, where the consciousness of economic hardship is less apparent than the objects of the resentment it concentrates upon.

As we shall see, Marx put forward a hypothesis that 'the Jew' was a socio-economic category as well as a religious identity, a view which has had wide-ranging ramifications ever since, particularly in Marxist and neo-Marxist theories. Here we have indicated at least two alternative hypotheses to explain the phenomenon of 'the Jew' and, implicitly, of anti-semitism, which, because they are more closely related to empirical evidence, deserve to be taken seriously. Toury wrote about English Jews, Kann about German and French Jews, Borochov about Polish and Russian Jews, and I have suggested a class-conflict model for Prussian Jews. This, to say the least, would suggest that there is an approach here which offers a fruitful field for further research.

CHAPTER IV

Unexpected Developments

1840 was a momentous year both for Prussia and for the Jews, a year of excitement, of anxiety, of promise and of euphoria. It was the year in which the seeds of the 1848 revolution, the rebirth of Israel and the birth of the socialist movement began to germinate. It was the year in which Friedrich Wilhelm IV became king of Prussia and the Jews of Damascus faced a blood-libel.

FRIEDRICH WILHELM IV

Even if the people of Prussia had heeded the warnings implicit in the actions of their crown prince—his condemnation of the rationalist theologians Gesenius and Wegscheider, his attack on the distinguished theologian Baur on the fictitious grounds that he sided with 'the views of a Dr Strauss', or his refusal to support the appointment of the Hegelian theologian Vatke—even so, they were bound to heave a sigh of relief when, after forty-three years, the garrulous, surly Friedrich Wilhelm III died in June 1840 and Friedrich Wilhelm IV ascended the throne.[1] A man of considerable intellectual gifts, charming, volatile and sensitive to public acclaim, he was nevertheless a romantic mystic, an absolute ruler cast in the mould of feudal kings, a conservative pietist wholly divorced from the realities of his time and his people.[2] The new king hated the dry, pragmatic unemotional civil service he had inherited from his father, and longed for a full restoration of the traditional estates in Prussia, for the revitalisation of the nobility and for a greatly strengthened Church to give meaning and substance to his cherished faith in Prussia as a great 'Christian–Germanic' state, a Prussia modelled on the Christian Ständestaat as advocated by Karl Ludwig von Haller.[3] As yet the king was unaware of, or indifferent to, an industrial revolution that was gaining momentum, of a rapidly increasing urban proletariat that was likely to be hostile to his paternalism and his pietism, and above all to a powerful, liberalistic bourgeoisie that was forcefully pushing for constitutional recognition.[4]

So desperate was the hunger for change that the people of Prussia were willing to take Friedrich Wilhelm IV's first liberal actions as proof of a new era that would meet their needs. Censorship of the press was relaxed, and a general amnesty offered to political prisoners. Ernst Moritz Arndt, the German nationalist, was restored to his Chair at the University of Bonn after an exclusion of twenty years, and other nationalists in disgrace, such as 'Turnvater' Jahn, were restored to favour.[5] In particular the freely expressed dislike of Prussian bureaucracy was misread as a sign of freedom. In Prussia there was euphoria and rejoicing. At the University of Bonn a festive dinner was held to celebrate the return of Arndt. Jubilant *Privatdozenten* toasted the hero. Even the disgraced and churlish Bruno Bauer was temporarily swept away by the current of joy: 'My name was called; I had to rise; the enthusiasm with which I joined the celebration was boundless. I embraced Arndt; hurray, I am to be allowed to be part of the faculty! I was supremely happy.'[6]

Yet even whilst the people rejoiced, the king was beginning to show his true colours to the more perceptive of his subjects. An early audience granted to the poet Herwegh was a disaster.[7] The arch-conservative, Julius Stahl, was summoned to Berlin. When the liberal and tolerant Minister of Education, Altenstein, died he was replaced by the boorish Eichhorn.[8] Within a year of his accession, in February 1841, Friedrich Wilhelm IV received a copy of a pamphlet, 'Four Questions Answered by an East Prussian', which was addressed to the members of the East

Prussian provincial Parliament (Landtag) on the eve of their meeting and called for a constitution as a matter of right. Although this created a great stir, it was confiscated by the police of Leipzig. Its author, a Jewish physician from Königsberg, Johann Jacoby (1805–77), sent a copy to the king. If any of the king's subjects still had hope, his response on receiving the pamphlet finally put an end to it. Jacoby was arrested, charged with lèse-majesté and subversive criticism and sentenced to two and a half years' imprisonment. This sentence was revoked on appeal and Jacoby became something of a national hero.[9] The bitterness of the Prussian people was greatly increased because the earlier relaxation of censorship had released a flood of provocative and challenging material which greatly intensified the political atmosphere, and which made the re-imposition of censorship especially hard to bear.[10] Discontent, aggravated by the start of an economic recession, was paving the way for the rise of the radicals and the revolution of 1848.

Along with their fellow-citizens, the Jews of Prussia were also filled with hope and expectation when the new king ascended the throne. They were greatly encouraged by his determination to settle the quarrel with the Catholic church over mixed marriages, and promptly despatched a deputation to greet him and to appeal for emancipation. The king received them graciously and responded as follows:[11]

> His Majesty has not yet been able to extend those rights to all your co-religionists in all provinces which have been granted to those in the old provinces; it would not have been possible, without dereliction of duty, since, especially those of your co-religionists living in the Posen province stand—if I may so express it—too low still; meanwhile, I learn with pleasure from local reports that more and more of them have advanced sufficiently to be granted those civil rights which are already extant in other provinces. This work of ennoblement will be continued as far as it lies in the power of the king to influence it.

The Jews received this message 'with boundless joy'.[12] They followed it up with many petitions in which their grievances were set out in detail, foremost amongst which was the shameful

Napoleonic decree of 1808 which should have been rescinded in 1818.[13] Again like their fellow-countrymen, the Jews did not have long to wait for the king to reveal his plans. In 1841 a draft law was circulated which stunned Prussian Jewry because it advocated nothing less than a return to the middle ages.[14] It was this draft law which initiated the debate which Hermes, Bruno Bauer and Marx subsequently joined. As far as the Jews were concerned, it was not their demand for emancipation which was at issue here, but resistance to an attempt to return them to a status of a bygone age because the draft law called for the creation of separate entities which the state would control:[15]

> The Government recognises a miraculous essence in the extraordinary historical development of the Jews, the causes for which have not been established [by research]. Legislation must allow this special essence to unfold from within without drawing it into the life of the Christian state; all a Christian state can do is to secure such provisions and facilities and their continuance, which will enable them [the Jews] to find an adequate field of action (*Wirkungskreis*), albeit one which would not impinge on the Christian state. To this end it is planned to recommend the introduction of Jewish corporations on the model of Posen as the most appropriate method, at the same time excluding Jews from military service and, self-evidently, from offices and positions of honour for ever, and generally to keep Jews and Judaism totally outside the state.

The draft law raised a storm of protest from all sections of the Jewish community. Ludwig Philippson (1811–89), scholar, rabbi and author, founder and long-time editor of the *Allgemeine Zeitung des Judentums*, was also a leading figure in the German liberal movement and in municipal politics. Eighty-four Jewish communities appealed to him to fight the draft law.[16] All the initial attacks were concentrated on the military service clause. The government tried to counter this by suggesting that Jews might be permitted to volunteer, but this was rejected. The objection, the Jews said, was to the deprivation of a 'duty' to defend the fatherland. Even they themselves were surprised by the volume and vigour of their opposition, and were equally taken aback at the strong support they received from non-Jewish quarters. Newspapers in Cologne, Trier, Dusseldorf, Hamburg, Königsberg and Leipzig drew attention to the wider implications of a return to 'corporationism' and called for equal rights for Jews.[17] The Rhein Landtag voted strongly in favour of Jewish rights.[18] The government tried to calm the situation by inviting both provincial authorities and Jews to submit their views. It hinted to the provinces that they might like to demand greater restrictions on Jewish mobility and occupations. At the same time it tried to reassure the Jews that the real object and intention of the proposed corporations were to remove Jewish disabilities, to give them greater independence and autonomy and to allow them to work with Christians for their mutual advantage. It was pointed out, however, that the king took the view that it was essential to protect the nature of the Christian state and to ensure that Jews would never exercise any kind of authority over Christians or enjoy rights which might diminish those of Christians.[19]

Hostility to the plan was clearly more vigorous than the government had anticipated. Although the plan was quietly shelved, arguments continued with unabated acerbity, which owed much to yet another event of 1840 which profoundly influenced both Prussians and Jews and initially, at any rate, may well have encouraged Friedrich Wilhelm IV to proceed with his 'corporation plan'.

THE DAMASCUS AFFAIR

For a decade the Middle East had been restive and the European powers were manoeuvring for positions of influence, notably in Turkey and Egypt.[20] Sultan Mohammed, the strong ruler of Turkey, had died and been succeeded by his seventeen-year-old son, Abdul Meguid, in 1839. While the new sultan celebrated his accession by issuing a manifesto proclaiming the inviolability of the person and properties of all non-believers (i.e. non-Muslims), his viceroy in Egypt, Mehmet Ali, rebelled against Ottoman rule, declared himself independent and occupied all Palestine and Syria. In this conflict, France—which under its then Foreign Minister,

Thiers, was pursuing a strongly aggressive, expansionist policy[21] —decided to back Mehmet Ali; the sultan, on the other hand, was supported by a coalition of England, Austria, Prussia and Russia. The new approach to religious freedom proclaimed by the sultan had given rise to a certain amount of tension between the different communities which the powers were trying to exploit. Mehmet Ali tried to seek support from the hostility of Muslims to infidels, while France was relying on Catholic hostility to Jews, especially in Syria, to gain influence. Since there was no substantial Protestant population in the Middle East, Palmerston thought that English influence might best be secured by supporting the Jews of Syria and even by propagating the idea of a strong Jewish resettlement in Palestine.[22]

In 1840 Damascus had a fairly small Jewish population, most of whom were poor, illiterate petty traders and artisans, but included a small percentage of wealthy merchants. On 5 February of that year a Capuchin (Franciscan) friar, Father Thomaso (Thomas), and his servant disappeared in Damascus. There was some evidence that the friar had been involved in a quarrel with a Turkish mule-driver, but since his disappearance remained a mystery the monks turned to Count Ratti-Menton, the French consul, for help.[23] Ratti-Menton, with the connivance of the governor of Damascus, Sherif Pasha, and a number of dubious characters, implicated the Jewish community and suggested that Father Thomas had been slain by the Jews and that his blood had been sent to Constantinople for use at Passover by the Chief Rabbi. A number of leading Jewish citizens were arrested and tortured to extract confessions. When this did not succeed, sixty Jewish children, aged from three to ten, were locked up without food or water in the hope that their cries would induce their mothers to confess. This also failed. More Jews were arrested and tortured. Some died, some converted to Islam to escape, most of them were crippled for life. Among the new suspects was a young man, Isaac Levi Piccioto, an Austrian subject, who appealed to his consul, M. Merlato, for protection, and thus the Damascus affair became an international incident. Merlato protested about the tortures and sent detailed accounts of the events in Damascus to

Metternich. Ratti-Menton in turn defended his actions in despatches to Thiers, who held daily press conferences in Paris. Throughout Europe the blood-libel became a major discussion point in the press. Most of the French and a number of German newspapers welcomed this opportunity to attack the Jews and their religion.[24] At the same time, the Jews of Damascus sent appeals for help to their co-religionists in Europe.[25] Throughout Europe the Jewish communities were deeply disturbed. They were concerned about the suffering in Damascus and they were concerned about the readiness with which some European newspapers and people accepted the crude falsehood of the blood-libel. In Paris Adolphe Crémieux (1796–1880), champion of the underprivileged and the most famous Jewish lawyer in France, decided to defend the Jews of Damascus, although he had to face hostility and obstruction from the French government. In Germany Gabriel Riesser protested, and the Jews were horrified, but curiously there was no call for action. In England the great champion of oppressed Jewry, Moses Montefiore (1784–1885), summoned a meeting which Crémieux attended and to which he brought the sad tidings: 'La France est contre nous.'[26]

Austria's Metternich turned directly to Mehmet Ali in Egypt and demanded justice. He, eager to placate the European powers, appointed the Austrian, English, Prussian and Russian consuls in Cairo as a tribunal to investigate the situation. Thiers, on the pretext that the exclusion of the French consul from the tribunal implied a serious slight to the honour of France, pressed Mehmet Ali to cancel the tribunal. Montefiore summoned another meeting in London at which it was decided that he and Crémieux should go to Cairo and Damascus to plead for the Jews. Money for this journey was contributed by Jewish communities all over the world. The actions of the French consul were challenged in the Chamber of Deputies in Paris by Benoît Fould, a Jew (1792–1858), without success. A very different response came from the House of Commons in London where Sir Robert Peel initiated a debate on 22 June. Palmerston promised full support from the British government. During the debate the fiery Irishman, Daniel

71

O'Connell, took a swipe at the Front Brench which directed attention at the real issue: 'Observations upon this subject would have been stronger if a member of this House belonging to the creed of the accused had been able to make them. The government ought to introduce a bill for the complete emancipation of the Jews.'[27] There were public meetings of protest, notably in London and in Philadelphia. Montefiore and Crémieux sailed for Alexandria with the full support of Britain and the blessing of Queen Victoria.[28]

By now Russia and the United States[29] had joined the protests and when Montefiore arrived in Cairo (August 1840), Mehmet Ali tried to resolve the problem by issuing a pardon for the imprisoned Jews in Damascus. Montefiore refused to accept this, and demanded and received the release of all prisoners and the rejection of the blood-libel. With strong European support, the sultan reasserted his authority over Syria and Palestine and Montefiore went to Constantinople where he received a Firman from the sultan in which Jews were promised freedom of religion, and the blood-libel was declared to be false. Before returning to Europe, Crémieux encouraged oriental Jewry to provide education for their children, and by October had established two schools for boys and one for girls. He returned to Europe in November–December 1840 and received an ecstatic welcome from all the Jewish communities he passed on his way home. Montefiore returned somewhat later, hailed, acclaimed and idolised by Jews throughout the world as deliverer and protector.[30] He was honoured by Queen Victoria in a citation which briefly outlined the events at Damascus.[31]

The Damascus affair had a profound effect on Jews everywhere. Those in the more advanced countries were shattered by the ease with which a medieval superstition could gain credence even in cultured Europe. They were disturbed by the deep hostility, especially in Catholic and conservative circles, which had been displayed. They were dismayed that France, the first country to grant Jews full emancipation, could be so hostile, and equally shocked to discover that in oriental countries there were large Jewish communities living, by any standards, in abysmal poverty and ignorance. At the same time they were proud and elated because here, for the first time in perhaps 2,000 years, Jews acting on the world stage in the interests of oppressed Jews had achieved a remarkable diplomatic victory. The event created a sense of unity among Jews which they had not known for centuries. 'Generally, this event had a revitalising, invigorating effect on the Jews themselves. A new era had arisen for Judaism, a note had been struck which found an echo in all, and a rapprochement had taken place between followers of our faith in the farthest lands.'[32] Even some alienated and baptised Jews expressed a sense of identification with the victims of Damascus. J. A. W. Neander (1789–1850), a descendant of Moses Mendelssohn and favourite theologian of the Prussian government, protested strongly about the blood accusation.[33] Heine warned that the fanaticism behind the blood-libel was an infectious evil which would spread in diverse forms until in the end it would rage against all Jews.[34] He also described Crémieux as 'the advocate of the Jews who, in pleading their case, speaks for all humanity'.[35] He bitterly attacked those baptised Jews who out of cowardice or in order to hide their origins attacked Jews or failed to defend them.[36] Moses Hess described his feelings some twenty years after the event:[37]

> Twenty years ago, when an absurd and false accusation against the Jews was imported into Europe from Damascus, it evoked in the hearts of the Jews a bitter feeling of agony. Then it dawned on me for the first time, in the midst of my socialist activities, that I belong to my unfortunate, slandered, despised and dispersed people. And already then, though I was greatly estranged from Judaism, I wanted to express my Jewish patriotic sentiment in a cry of anguish, but it was unfortunately stifled in my heart by a greater pain which the suffering of the European proletariat evoked in me.

Ferdinand Lassalle, though only fifteen, had no doubts where his loyalties belonged.[38] He confided to his diary early in 1840:

> I believe I am one of the best Jews there are, without observing the traditional law. Like that Jew in [Bulwer-Lytton's] *Leila*, I would stake my life to pull the Jews out of their present oppressed state. I would not even be afraid of the guillotine, could I make them a respected people again. Oh, when I lose myself to my childish

73

dreams, it has always been my favourite idea to stand at the head of the Jews, with arms in my hand, to make them independent . . .

From Marx we have only a 'Freudian slip' to suggest that he was aware of the events in Damascus. When he entered the debate on the Jewish question, like Hermes and Bauer before him, he made use of a debate in the French Chamber of Deputies in December 1840 in which Benoît Fould spoke on the Sabbath. In 'On the Jewish Question', Marx refers to this debate without mentioning names, whereas in the *Holy Family: or Critique of Critical Critique*, he wrote: 'Monsieur Crémieux declared on behalf of the French Jews'.[39] But Crémieux was not elected until 1842—he was in any event at that time ending his triumphal tour of Europe after his success in Egypt. Hermes and Bauer both stated Fould's name correctly.[40]

If the events in Damascus had created a warm band of fellow-ship between Jews, it also showed up in stark relief the positions of the different communities. In England, Jews were not yet fully emancipated, but they were respected and accepted by both government and people. In France, the Jews were emancipated but ignored. In Germany, and especially in Prussia, although the Prussian government co-operated through its consul in Cairo in helping the Jews, the Jews were not emancipated, not respected, not accepted. They were fearful of the impact of the affair on their own position in Prussia. They prided themselves on being the intellectual leaders of world Jewry—Leopold Zunz had written the most scholarly refutation of the blood-libel and Riesser had published his 'Jüdische Briefe' to protest against the libel—but when it came to taking action, Riesser, 'who might easily have joined Montefiore and Crémieux', did nothing.[41] A later Jewish historian defended Riesser, who could 'go to the capital of Egypt only as a civil pariah of Hamburg. Would that have impressed Mehmet Ali? Unfortunately there was no major power then called Germany and still less a civil equality for Jews in most German states'.[42] But this is not likely to have been the real reason. For one thing, such an argument could equally well have applied, at least in part, to Montefiore; for another, Crémieux's position was even more difficult because his own government was actively working against him in Egypt. The real reasons for Prussian Jewry's inaction lie deeper and can be summarised briefly under two headings. First, the Damascus affair was seen as a challenge to Prussian Jewry's image of itself as a group of Prussian *nationals* of the Jewish faith. This is well illustrated by a letter from Abraham Geiger of 1840: 'It is more important to me that the Jews of Prussia should be able to become pharmacists and lawyers than the rescue of all the Jews in Asia and Africa, in whose fate I am interested as a human being.'[43] Amongst the elite group of the Jews, and notably amongst many of the intellectuals, there was an underlying fear that identifying with Jews in Asia would detract from their status in Prussia.[44] The second reason, closely linked to the first, was the unallayed hostility from many German intellectuals and politicians who exploited every opportunity to denigrate and malign the Jews or Judaism or both. Although there was a growing acceptance of the broad masses of Jews by the broad masses of Germans, the constant harassment to which Jews were subjected in books and newspapers undermined the confidence of many who might otherwise have been quite happy to assert their Jewishness.

CHAPTER V

The Political Image of Jews

Damascus had created a sense of solidarity, of mutual responsibility among the Jews of the world,[1] but the Jews of Germany were fearful of the consequences of identifying too closely with such a movement lest it diminish their status as nationals of the German fatherland. These fears were not exaggerated. The events of Damascus and the draft bill on Jewish corporations had once again made the Jewish question a major topic of the early 1840s. Only this time the familiar conservative-liberal debate received a new impetus from political radicals eager to make their voices heard and delighted to find in the Jewish question a topic in which restraint and circumspection, even accurate information, were superfluous because Prussian censorship was quite content to allow its constraining influence to be set aside when Jews were the subject of debate.[2]

In the course of time the Jewish question had assumed a uniform, three-dimensional character for all who were concerned with it, politicians, civil servants, radicals and Jews. For all of them the real issues were the meaning of Jewish history, the meaning of Jewish law and the relationship of the Jew to the state. In the intellectual climate of the period, the Hegelian tradition was supreme and it was precisely this tradition which appeared to make the three-dimensional Jewish problem insurmountable. It was not so much Hegel's position, which was not opposed to Jewish emancipation, but the Hegelian ethos which gave rise to the kinds of answers these three categories were eliciting from conservative and radical thinkers. There was in the Germany of the 1840s a deep empathy with Hegelian notions of state, law and history.[3]

> All the worth which a human being possesses—all spiritual reality he possesses only through the state . . . the state is the Divine Idea as it exists on earth . . . law is the objectivity of spirit; volition in its true form. Only that will which obeys law is free: for it obeys itself . . . when the subjective will of man submits to laws—the contradiction between Liberty and Necessity vanishes.

If Jewish law was what its defenders claimed it to be, then it could only be seen as the basis of a Jewish state—the Jews would indeed be 'a state within a state' and their claim for emancipation would be as unreasonable as that of the Quakers.[4] If Jews did not see their law in this light, if they were willing to forgo their law for state law then there was no objective basis for remaining Jewish and baptism would resolve the emancipation issue. Logically the Jew without law relinquishes his statehood and therewith his claim for a place in history—he must, therefore, choose between the German state and Christianity or Jewish law which can offer him a tolerated status in Germany until his law succeeds in restoring him to independent statehood.

In one way or another this was the core of the argument. There were separate emphases and orientations. In the case of Marx there was also some originality in the transformation of the religious into an economic issue but the fundamental argument did not change. The German climate of opinion stood in stark contrast to that prevailing in England, where the Jewish question assumed a much less traumatic character. This is well illustrated by Macaulay's essay on the civil disabilities of the Jews, in which he puts forward the English ideal of a state:[5]

> Government exists for the purpose of keeping the peace, for the purpose of compelling us to settle our disputes by arbitration instead of settling them by blows, for the purpose of compelling us to supply our wants by industry instead of supplying them by rapine. This is the only operation for which the machinery of government is peculiarly adapted, the only operation which wise governments ever propose to themselves as their chief object.

77

Such simple pragmatism could not evoke the fervour of a Prussian *Erziehungsstaat* with its conforming and rebellious subjects, whose views we must now consider.

HEINRICH HEINE

Heine (1797–1856) published his 'Damascus Letters' and *Ludwig Börne: eine Denkschrift* in 1840 and both are important not only for the views they expressed on current topics, but also for the comments he made on Jews and Judaism, some of which find a remarkable echo in Marx.[6] This is not to say however that Marx took his views from Heine, or even that they were basically agreed in their views. Heine's paradoxical nature[7] is well illustrated in the 'Damascus Letters'. For all his pungent comments, there is a sense of balance, a capacity to take a wider view, a generosity of perception which is lacking in Marx. Heine refused to see the Damascus drama as a narrowly Jewish tragedy. On the contrary, he saw it as the thin end of an obnoxious wedge which would in the long run become a weapon against all humanity. In the same way he did not regard Crémieux's mission as an exercise in destroying the unpleasant torturer Ratti-Menton, or as an exercise in restoring the Jews of Damascus to favour. 'We are not really concerned here with the great virtue of a Ratti-Menton or the un-savouriness of the Jews of Damascus—there is probably little to choose between them. The former is likely to be as unworthy of our hatred as the latter are of our love.'[8] Heine saw Crémieux's achievement in the destruction of a vile, medieval superstition and in the diminution of torture as part of the judicial process in the Orient. He had many harsh things to say about Jews, but restricted himself to those of France, whom he takes to task for not being more active on behalf of the Jews of Damascus: 'French Jews are too emancipated; they have been submerged or, better, dissolved in French nationality'.[9] Like Marx, Heine was con-temptuous about the way Jewish religious practice was carried out, though he was still concerned only with French Jews and, unlike Marx, did not necessarily reject religious practice as such:

'Many [French Jews] still carry out Jewish ceremonials as an external cult, mechanically, without knowing why, merely from habit; there is no trace of an inner faith, because in the synagogue, as in the Christian church, the acid wit of Voltaire has been too destructive. *For French Jews, as for all other Frenchmen, gold is the god of the day and industry is the dominant religion.*'[10]

Rothschild and Fould are sarcastically referred to as 'the rabbis of finance', although Heine acknowledged Rothschild's genuine efforts on behalf of Jews in distress and later confessed that he had misjudged Fould. 'How ready I am', he admitted, 'to be put to shame when those to whom I have done an injustice disprove my accusations by their actions.'[11] Heine regarded the response of both practising and baptised Jews as wholly inadequate. The Jewish community of Paris had been only 'lukewarm' in its response, and offered no money to help those in Damascus: '*The financial resources of the Jews are indeed great but experience shows that their avarice is greater still.*'[12] Converted Jews were strongly criticised: 'Among baptised Jews there are many who from cowardly hypocrisy spread more vicious slanders about Israel than its natural enemies. In the same way, certain writers express themselves viciously, or not at all about Jews in order to hide their origins. This is a well known, sad, ridiculous fact.'[13]

If Heine despised the way French Jews were practising their religion, he could, nevertheless, defend the religion *per se* against the blood-libel:[14]

To listen to M. Thiers one could easily come to believe that Capuchin flesh was the favourite dish of the Jews, but no—great historian and petty theologian—neither in the Orient nor in the Occident does the Old Testament permit its believers such dirty food.[15] The Jews' revulsion to any form of blood consumption is quite peculiar to them. It is expressed in the earliest dogmas of their religion, in all their sanitary laws, in their purification ceremonies, in their basic views on clean and unclean, in their profound cosmogenic revelation on the material purity of the animal world, which is at the same time a physical ethic which Paul, who rejected it as a fable, failed to understand. No, these descendants of Israel, of the pure, elect nation of priests, eat neither pork nor old Capuchins, they do not drink blood any more than they drink their own urine . . .

Heine also appealed for a sense of perspective in looking at values in different cultures. 'Servitude', he explained, 'lies in the nature of man. Let us not judge whether the German who serves a person is as worthy of respect as the Roman who serves a country. The loyalty of the one is as good as the patriotism of the other and both are deviations as sincere as the dedication to a supernatural idea, as for example, the worship of God by the ancient Hebrews.'[16]

In a final comment Heine returned again to the theme of the displacement of the worship of God by the worship of money. He castigated the cringing, awe-stricken, servile, spineless creatures adoring Rothschild, 'For money is the god of our time and Rothschild is his prophet'.[17] The Rothschilds appear also in Börne and were defended against Germany's 'preachers of freedom' who were foolish and unjust in attacking them. For the Rothschilds are the real revolutionaries. Thus Baron James Rothschild, 'the Nero of finance',[18] is, like his precedessor, the Roman Nero, a mighty destroyer of privileged patricians and the founder of a new democracy. 'I see in Rothschild one of the greatest revolutionaries who create modern democracy. Richelieu, Robespierre and Rothschild are for me three terroristic names and they mean the gradual destruction of the old aristocracy. Richelieu, Robespierre and Rothschild are the three most fearful levellers of Europe.'[19] Heine praised the Rothschilds for not seeking baptism. 'Baptism is the order of the day for rich Jews.' Did these rich Jews think that baptism would change them: 'Did they think that you can change lice into fleas by pouring water over them?'[20]

Like Marx, Heine saw the United States of America as the epitome of greed and remarked on the persistence of religion there: 'the Americans make a great deal of fuss about Christianity and are the keenest church-goers', but 'worldly need is their real religion and money is their god, their only, almighty god'.[21] Heine's views on Jewish law and Jewish history were Hegelian in origin and not unlike those of the German radicals, but differed in that they were tempered by a positive understanding which is wholly lacking in men such as Strauss, Bauer and Marx.[22]

As the prophet of the Orient [Mohammed] called them 'the people of the book', so the prophet of the Occident [Hegel] . . . called them 'the people of the spirit'. Already in their earliest beginnings, as we can see in the Pentateuch, the Jews show a preference for the abstract. Their whole religion is nothing but a dialectic act by which matter is separated from spirit and the absolute is recognised solely as spirit. What a terribly isolated position they had to occupy among the nations of antiquity, who, dedicated to the joyful service of nature, saw spirit in pictorial and symbolic representations of matter. In what dreadful opposition they must have stood to colourful Egypt, the Temples of Joy of Astarte in Phoenicia, lovely, fragrant Babylon, and finally to Greece, the flourishing home of art.

It is a curious drama how the people of the spirit gradually freed themselves entirely from matter. Moses gave the spirit a kind of material bulwark against the real pressure from neighbouring peoples. Around the field in which he had sown spirit, he planted the rugged ceremonial law and egoistic nationalism as a protective hedge. But when the sacred spirit-plant had struck roots that were so deep and shot upwards to such a height that it could no longer be wrenched out, then Jesus came and tore down the ceremonial law that had no further meaning; he even pronounced a verdict of death on Jewish nationality . . . he called the peoples of the world to share the Kingdom of God which hitherto had belonged only to a single chosen people; he gave the whole of mankind Jewish civil rights . . .

But the Jews themselves remained aloof from all this, their own history took a different course: 'Nations rose and disappeared, states blossomed and withered, revolutions stormed across the world, but they, the Jews, were bent over their books and noticed nothing of the wild chase of time that tore over their heads.'[23] This led Heine to his ambivalent image of the Jews of his own day, whom he saw as a stark contrast. He related how Hegel had once drawn his attention to the fact that, in nature, that organ which serves man's highest function also serves the lowest, and that was how Heine saw the Jews:[24]

The Jews are made of that substance from which gods are moulded; if they are kicked today, they will be worshipped tomorrow. While some of them wallow in the shabbiest filth of peddling, others ascend the highest pinnacles of humanity, and Golgotha is not the only mountain where a Jewish god has bled for the salvation of the world. The Jews are the people of the spirit and whenever they return to their principle they are great and magnificent and put their foul tormentors to shame . . . what curious creatures of the grossest paradox. Amongst them are found all kinds of caricatures of vulgarity, yet there are also those amongst them who are ideals of purest humanity. Just as they once led the world towards new directions for progress, so the world can perhaps expect further inspiration from them . . .

For, to Heine, it seemed likely that the Messiah, so fervently hoped for by religious Jews, might be the same redeemer who would liberate Germany.[25]

CARL H. HERMES

Hermes (1800–56) is important in our context mainly because he provoked Bruno Bauer and Karl Marx to write on the Jewish question and because he provided the frame of reference within which they conducted their debate. Hermes was a conservative, an apostle of the Christian-Germanic state. Compared with Bauer and Marx he may well have been a mediocrity, but his style was persuasive, his argument effective and as an editor of the *Kölnische Zeitung* he made sufficient impact to persuade Marx not 'to allow him to continue his blabbering'.[26] Hermes was clearly perturbed by the strong reaction which the Prussian bill on the civil and political position of the Jews had called forth from Jews and liberals. Hermes published his first article on 6 July 1842 on the front page of the *Kölnische Zeitung* (no. 187) under the heading 'Köln, 5.Juli'. The second article was a reply to Ludwig Philippson who, as editor of the *AZJ*, had published an 'Open Letter to Dr. Hermes' as a leading article on 18 July. This second article was published (again starting on the front page) on 30 July (no. 211). Philippson responded with a further leading article on 8 August. Hermes replied to this in the Beilage, no. 235 of 23 August, under the heading 'Letztes Wort an Herrn Philippson zu Magdeburg'. This was the end of the affair for Hermes, although Philippson published a further rejoinder on 1 November 1842 When Marx asked Dagobert Oppenheim to send him Hermes' article,[27] he probably did not realise that two of the three articles were direct replies to Philippson. Marx had told Oppenheim that he wanted to give the Jewish question 'a new perspective' but did not do so until the following year. H. Hirsch[28] thinks that Marx had too many other things to deal with and also wanted to study the problem first. It seems to me, however, that it is more likely that Marx postponed his plan to write on the Jews when he found that two of the three articles were mainly a polemical dispute between Hermes and Philippson.

To Hermes the proposed bill was eminently reasonable, since the variety of laws concerning Jews in different Prussian provinces made it very desirable that a uniform system be established. The liberals had insisted that it was 'medieval barbarism' to differentiate between citizens on the basis of their religion and wanted complete equality for Jews. Hermes thought that that might be a very nice ideal, but it would require a rational state (Vernunftstaat) which did not yet exist anywhere in the world. He professed great humility: 'We are frail, passionate, prejudiced men and cannot be changed by legislation'. Like the Jews, he too believed that men needed religion 'to raise us to a higher, better, purer and more moral way of life', and Christianity would do just that. That is why Prussia had based its civil and political system on it. But it follows that 'as long as our religion is the basis of our system, we cannot grant Jews equal rights without creating an impossible internal contradiction'. Whatever legislation is proposed, therefore, can be concerned only with more or less restrictions for Jews, never with the abolition of all restrictions.

Some people, argued Hermes, point to countries where Jews have been granted civil equality: Holland and France, for example. But the situation there was very different and, besides, he did not think that emancipation was working. Prussian Jews in any case were too divided among themselves. Those who were religious did not really want emancipation and those who were not, but still regarded themselves as Jews, could hardly expect the state to create special provisions for them. 'If they are dissatisfied because they are treated as Jews when in their hearts they have long since ceased to be Jews, then they have only themselves to blame.' Those educated Jews who were impatiently demanding emancipation were in error if they believed that the restrictions imposed on them as Jews were a sign of contempt or hatred—Jews who deserve respect will receive it. However, and Hermes carefully deferred the weight of his argument to his final sentence:

> If Jews as such are not despised, it does not follow that they should be granted full civil rights which so far have been reserved for Christian citizens and from which they are excluded partly because of their faith which they will not relinquish, and partly because of the moral degeneration (*sittliche Verwahrlosung*) which, though due to centuries of unjust persecution, is nevertheless a problem which cannot be resolved very quickly and which affects the large majority of their tribe (*Stamm*).

In his reply Philippson concentrated on showing Hermes to be wrong in his facts. A vigorous debate ensued between the two over the criminality of the Jews[29] and by the time Hermes wrote his final reply his cool, calm, superior style had collapsed and he indulged in very crude, very violent anti-Jewish polemic. Since the days of Tacitus, he exclaimed, Jews had been the *odium humani generis*, and 'Jews will not cease to offend us until they cease to be Jews'. The Talmud, according to Hermes, represents 'debased' Judaism, a level of debasement no other nation on earth has equalled. Jewish children were trained to usury as early as possible. He could enumerate other vices but did not want to go into too much detail because some of his friends were Jews. He was only really interested in protecting his people and his country.

Leaving aside the polemical nature of Hermes's articles, he did highlight a number of key issues which remained dominant in subsequent discussion. The first was the nature of the state in relation to its citizens, the second was the nature of Jewish law and its role in determining Jewish–Gentile relationships, the third concerned the dynamics of Jewish history and, arising from that, the conditions for social change. As a traditionalist, Hermes saw the 'Jewish question' as a simple issue. The constant factor was the Christian-Germanic state. The abnormality of the political situation lay in the Jews, who created and perpetuated a problem by remaining Jews. While it would be unthinkable and unreasonable to expect the state to adjust itself to a Jewish minority, it was obvious that the Jews ought to adjust themselves to the state if they wanted full equality, or to be content with a tolerated status if they wished to remain Jews. Hermes saw no contradiction in his assumptions that the majority of Jews were so 'degenerate' that they could not be elevated to full citizenship with Christians, while the simple act of baptism would not only provide citizenship, but would also remove the 'degeneration' at a stroke.

THE SEVENTH RHINE-PROVINCE LANDTAG

The Prussian proposals to avoid the question of Jewish emancipation by introducing the corporation bill, the impact of the Damascus affair and the growing volume of books and pamphlets focused public attention once more on the Jewish question and led to a prolonged debate on the subject in the chamber of deputies of the Rhine Province.

On 13 July 1843 the Landtag met to discuss two resolutions. The first called for the abolition of the decree of 1808, which was in any event enforced only on the left bank of the Rhine. The second demanded the complete emancipation of West Prussia's 27,000 Jews, who represented a mere 1 per cent of the total population of the province. In support of these motions the chamber had submissions from the citizens of Cologne, Aachen, Trier, Düsseldorf, Bonn, Saarbrücken and other areas, petitioning on behalf of the Jews. The subject had last been discussed in 1827 when the delegates refused to make a recommendation either for or against.[30] The motions were introduced by a clergyman acting as *Referent*.[31] The case put forward by the *Referent* was typical of the widespread liberal position in Prussia at that time. He began by explaining that Jews had lived on the Rhine since Roman times, i.e. even before its conquest by German tribes, and that they could not, therefore, be regarded as aliens although they had been continuously ill treated and persecuted. He explained the anomaly of the 1808 decree and showed how, in practice, it was a boon to every dishonest Christian moneylender and borrower, it was an insult to every respectable Jew and said that such a law had never been found necessary on the right bank of the Rhine.[32] Many of the restrictions imposed on Jews had no legal basis at all. He rejected all suggestions that the Talmud led Jews to anti-social behaviour and, towards the end of his argument, dealt with two further important issues. The first was the oft-quoted objection that the poor moral condition of the Jews meant that, at best, they were not ready for civil emancipation:[33]

> This is an argument put forward at all times and by all nations who are trying to prevent the emancipation of an oppressed class of people. I have heard it put forward in all earnestness against the Catholics in Ireland; who does not remember the same objection to the emancipation of the Greeks in Turkey? Who does not hear it daily as an argument against granting independence to coloured peoples in European colonies?

The second point concerned the effect of emancipation on Jews in other European countries. Moses Montefiore is quoted as an example (his name came up frequently in the course of the debate), as well as Jews in France, Holland and Belgium who had achieved positions of honour and importance and occupied them with credit. The *Referent* rejected the notion that Jewish emancipation was incompatible with a Christian state. Christianity's highest principle was love of one's fellow-men regardless of their faith, and this love could ensure the ultimate victory of Christianity throughout the world.

The debate which followed faithfully reflected many of the current views.[34] Some defended Judaism as a religion, and the Talmud. 'What', demanded a townsman, 'was the basis of the Jewish state in ancient times? Obedience.' Just as it is in Prussia. The Talmud was much maligned and misunderstood and in any event was largely ignored by most Jews. A nobleman agreed. The charges brought against the Talmud were all derived from a book by Eisenmenger, but it must be remembered that this was written as an act of revenge by a man who felt slighted by Jews. Many speakers described the faults and behaviour that were held against Jews as consequences of the way they had been treated in Christian countries and felt sure that, given emancipation, the Jews would adopt higher standards. One speaker expressed the conviction that political emancipation would, by its great moral impact, lead to the human emancipation of the Jews. Some arguments tended to be more factual: during the War of Liberation, thousands of Jews flocked to the colours to defend the fatherland and 6,000 of them died for their country; if Jews could be noblemen, like Baron Rothschild, surely they could also be citizens; emancipation was likely to be the best means of ensuring the eventual conversion of all Jews to Christianity; the Jews of Trier were model citizens who would grace any community and all Europe was looking to the Landtag; to grant Jews civil rights was a matter of honour—could we do less than defend it? A nobleman explained that the Jewish proclivity for money was no more than a characteristic of the oppressed. 'When a nation is oppressed, its main efforts will be directed towards the acquisition of money which offers the only means of softening hearts and of gaining influence in an indirect way.'[35] The Landtags-Marschall added somewhat caustically that if the existing restrictions had not prevented Jews from indulging in undesirable business activities, emancipation would do no worse and that, in any event, the correct answer to usury was state-run savings banks. A town delegate fiercely attacked the proposed corporation-plan[36] for Jews and called on the assembly to resist it with all the influence at their disposal. The problem of the Jew in the Christian state was not taken very seriously. What, after all, demanded a townsman, is a Christian state? 'The Christian state is an invention of modern philosophy . . . wherever thoughts are lacking, words are put in their place.'[37] The so-called Christian state, he charged, can claim to have inspired only religious hatred, prejudice, superstition, envy and avarice. The sooner such a state decides to make amends, the sooner it will become truly Christian. A state, argued another, can demand only the duties of citizenship, it cannot and must not interfere with an individual's freedom of conscience. Similarly, argued another, the law may judge men only by their actions, not by their religion. There were some, yet another townsman pointed out, who saw the Jews not primarily as a religious group but as a nation. But what are 'the signs of nationality'? Language? Jews speak the language of their country of residence. Service?

Jews serve the state wherever they are permitted to do so.
Fulfilling civic duties? Jews do so as well as any other citizen.

Finally, there was the problem of Jewish isolationism. Most
speakers were sure that Gentile hostility was more to blame for
this than the Jews themselves, and one nobleman confessed that he
preferred to love Jews from a distance.[38]

Those who were opposed to the emancipation of the Jews
produced many arguments current in conservative circles and a
few others peculiar to the speakers concerned. Very few, even of
those who opposed emancipation, argued for the retention of the
decree of 1808, but there were some lurid views on Jews. A
nobleman denied that the Jews were a religion (*Glaubensgemein-
schaft*). What, he demanded, did the simple Hebrew of the Old
Testament have in common with the Jew of the Talmud and the
enlightened Jew of the nineteenth century? Only one thing—
descent. Hence the Jews must be an alien nation and would
remain so as long as they insisted on remaining Jews. A second
nobleman saw in the Jews 'the core of mankind', combining in
their nature all that was best and worst in human beings. That is
why they would always be the chosen people and why they would
always be hated. A third nobleman held a similar view. The Jews
were gifted, crafty, intelligent, able; in fact they had all the virtues
and vices of mankind—to emancipate them would be dangerous,
to say the least. A townsman was fearful of what emancipation
might lead to. The law of Moses was not only religious law, it was
also civil law. If, after emancipation, a Jew were to be appointed
judge, what would happen if he came across another Jew who
had broken the laws of the Sabbath? Would he not have to
sentence him to be stoned to death? With all the restrictions
imposed on them, argued another, the Jews already possessed 'the
power of money'.[39] They owned a quarter of the liquid assets of
the state—what would happen if all restrictions were lifted? Jews,
said a townsman, by adhering to Jewish law, had ceased to
develop.[40] They could not be emancipated until they joined
Christians in their historical progress. Only those who openly
severed all connections with Judaism and Jews could be emancipated, said one nobleman, but another disagreed. A Christian

state was essential, because a humanist state could lead only to materialism and brute force, and Jews who were alienated from their religion would greatly increase this danger. The burden of emancipation was seen as a task of the Jews rather than the state by several speakers, but for others this was going too far. The Catholic Church had not recommended emancipation, said one, therefore it could not be right; another argued even more forcefully that the suffering of the Jews was ordained by God for all times, and to emancipate them would interfere with the will of God; it was not the task of the Landtag 'to eliminate this symbol in world history'.

When it came to the vote, the first motion recommending the abolition of the decree of 1808 caused no difficulties: sixty-eight delegates voted in favour and only five against. The second motion created some problems. The *Referent* had proposed to submit to the king that 'all existing restrictions which prevent complete equality between Jews and his Christian subjects be removed'. The wording of this motion seemed to many delegates to be going too far. There were demands for the insertion of such qualifying phrases as 'gradual' removal, 'preparing for', etc. After further prolonged debate, the following motion was agreed: That the king be requested 'to prepare for the removal of all existing restrictions which prevent equality between the Jew and his Christian subjects in civil and political matters'. The motion was put to the vote: fifty-four delegates voted in favour and nineteen against.

The vote in the Landtag shocked many Prussians. One of the first to react to it was Philipp Ludwig Wolfart who wrote in October 1843 a short but powerful pamphlet in which he took to task the delegates who had voted for civil rights for Jews.[41] His arguments, although similar to those of Hermes, were more cogent and persuasive and not only influenced the conservative elements in Prussia, but also had a stimulating effect on more radical thinkers. Wolfart began by seeking to define the Prussian state. Prussia, he argued, was a Christian-evangelical monarchy. Its Christian character derived not so much from the Christian character of the state as from the Christianity of its monarch, who was not primarily a head of state but the divinely appointed leader of a Christian community (*Gemeinschaft*). Hence the Jews were disqualified from equal citizenship not because they were Jews but because they were not Christians; i.e. they chose and continue to choose the right to opt out of the *Gemeinschaft* which alone gives meaning to the state.

Second, Wolfart maintained that a proper appreciation of the law demanded that, while the Jews had a claim to equality *before* the law, they could not and must not be granted equality of rights *through* the law, since this would make a mockery of the Christian foundations of the law. Third, there was an inherent incongruity in a Christian state which admitted its non-Christian subjects to full civil rights which would *ipso facto* include administrative, judicial and control positions. The idea, however, of a Jew participating in the government of a state based on an absolute belief in and allegiance to Christ, when he himself rejected and denied the supremacy of Christ in the state, could only be a form of betrayal and must 'inevitably' lead to state-sponsored treason.

Nevertheless, although hostile voices continued to be heard and traditional prejudices and fears remained, the general trend in Prussia was positively and unmistakably moving towards an acceptance, however reluctant, of the Jews as equal citizens in the state and loyal subjects of the king. This was the trend, until the radical critics of state and society issued a renewed challenge to the Jews.

PART TWO

The Radical Critique
of Judaism

Introduction

The welter of views and opinions on Jews and Judaism in the political arena was closely intertwined with the intellectual debates of that period. The conceptual difficulties which had to be overcome in the early nineteenth century were threefold. The first was the problem of reducing Judaism to a single category or manifestation; that is to say, finding a formula which would simultaneously explain *biblical Judaism* and its relationship to Christianity without according it a significance which might be seen as extending beyond the advent of Christianity and, at the same time, demonstrating that Judaism, as the antecedent of Christianity, must perforce be regarded as a lesser phenomenon. In other words it was necessary to establish that *talmudic* (i.e. post-biblical) *Judaism*, partly because it emerged sequentially from biblical Judaism, and partly because it might be seen as a challenge to the Christian dogma of the transference of divine election from the earlier to the later religion, was a 'petrified' remnant of a decayed religion or, at least, to show that there was no real, organic link between the two religions. It would also be necessary to account for and accommodate *contemporary Jews* in an 'enlightened' manner, without relinquishing the condemnatory judgments on their origins and beliefs.

Second, philosophical and theological thought had to search for a coherent explanation of the discrepancy between the universalism and rationalism of the Enlightenment, which seemed to exemplify the contrast between true Christianity and the much despised Jewish particularism and casuistry, with the emergence of romanticism in which the German-Christian state shared much greater affinity with Jewish-particularistic aspirations than with a genuine Christian universalism. Third, the advent of French materialism, coupled with the shift in social values associated with the emergence of industrial capitalism, again seemed to transform predominant societal concerns from the superior, spiritual other-worldliness of Christianity to the crude, materialistic and 'egoistic' this-worldliness of Judaism as depicted in the European intellectual tradition.

It will be sufficient to look only briefly at some of the leading philosophers and theologians, not least because their work has been extensively discussed in existing literature, both generally and specifically in relation to Jews.[1] Voltaire anticipated the German radicals when he argued casually that Judaism and Christianity were so much alike that 'Christians are Jews without circum-cision',[2] but German thinkers treated the subject more seriously. Kant may well have served as a model for Marx when he argued that the philosopher cannot use the Bible as textbook but only to illustrate patterns of thought. Since true religion is the realisation of ethics, which in turn is a product of thought, rational truth need not concern itself with views about the past, either to assert or to refute them. The more so in the case of Judaism, which for Kant was less a religion than a community of related individuals, a kinship group, united by a religiously constructed constitution of Moses. In this respect Kant argued very closely along the lines of Spinoza and the Deists.

Like many others he was particularly interested in the complete absence of any reference to immortality in the Pentateuch and regarded this as proof of his contention that the Mosaic code only contained enforceable laws precisely because it was a political instrument. Hence, if Christianity, with an infinitely greater potential for ethical evolution, did contain the concept of im-mortality, then the connection between the two religions was purely chronological and had no real significance. If biblical Judaism thus presented no problem, neither did talmudic Judaism.

Kant rejected the idea of Jewish survival as part of a divine plan, because such an assumption would lead to one of two hypothetical propositions. Either that God would restore his scattered people to their land, or that God was punishing his people, which suggested a political rather than an ethical Messianism. The reason for the survival of the Jews was for Kant a logical consequence of the constitutional character of their religious code, which withstood the destruction of their state. Since Kant saw no real significance in either the history or the religion of the Jews, his solution for contemporary Jewry was simple. All they had to do was to relinquish Mosaic law, establish a Jewish church in accord with evangelism and thus continue as 'a well behaved, fully emancipated' nation. This 'euthanasia of Judaism' seemed to Kant to be the only possible solution.[3]

Hegel was primarily interested in biblical Judaism, or better, the influence of the Old Testament. The essence of Jewish being was the separation of the group from alien influences, an aspiration made more difficult in a country like Palestine, traversed as it was by all the world's trade routes.[4]

Jewish worship served an exclusive goal of obedience to God, and since this meant the equation of virtue and worship with observance of meaningless rules, observance *per se* became the supreme principle against which Jesus, as a true revolutionary, asserted the principle of freedom, the dominance of the free, moral will over the demands of a rigid legalism. It ought to be noted here that neither Hegel nor any other writer we have to consider in this context considered the existence of 'public' and 'private' law in the Pentateuch. There are some laws of conduct which are enforced by the community (e.g. public observance of the Sabbath, adultery, murder, theft), and others the observance of which cannot be regulated by public sanctions (e.g. the private observance of the Sabbath, dietary laws, laws of sexual conduct). The implication of such dual legal demands on the individual could be interpreted as providing a 'public' law to protect the community and 'private' laws which impose a requirement of free choice, i.e. the exercise of a free, moral will.[5]

In the Pentateuch, according to Hegel, the existence of God is the focus of state law, not as a theorem but apodictically, as a command which makes it truth. 'What greater truth is there for slaves', he commented, 'than that they have a master.'⁶ For truth to have meaning in philosophical thought, there must be a condition of freedom between subject and object, a condition which the Jewish conception of God failed to meet. This conception was equally at fault in its exclusivity. When the heathen worshipped his god, he accepted implicitly that other worshippers would have their gods. The Jews on the other hand regarded it as axiomatic that only they had God. Like many other critics of Judaism, Hegel stressed biblical Judaism's lack of sympathy with, and devaluation of, nature. Because all life and history was governed by God's will, nature was incidental to the affairs of men, a force as lifeless in the events of men as men were themselves. For Hegel too was struck by the absence of any reference to immortality in the Pentateuch, which meant that there was no idea of a continuation of the personality of the individual. The Jews' drive for survival was based on the material assumptions of their existence.

Hegel did not devote much thought to talmudic Judaism, which was to him essentially the same as biblical Judaism. But he did comment on the position of the Jews of his own day. The hostility they had faced through the centuries was put down to their self-exclusion from nature and other men. Jews would be ill treated as long as they refused to recognise the world in its beauty and to make their peace with it. Although in his later work Hegel went even further by making a total separation between Judaism, which he placed historically on the fringes of the oriental world, and Christianity, which he described as a product of a declining antiquity (i.e. Greece and Rome), he nevertheless argued for the emancipation of the Jews and against those whose 'bellowing' (*Geschrei*) tried to oppose it. A state, argued Hegel, can demand that all its citizens should belong to a religious community because such membership would have an educative (socialising) influence. But an advanced state should not concern itself with the particular denomination of a religious community. While he agreed with opponents of Jewish emancipation that Jews tended to regard themselves as more than a religious denomination, this was no justification for denying them formal rights, because they were human beings and it was on this fact that their claim for civil rights was based.[7]

German theologians were naturally more concerned with the relationship between Judaism and Christianity. Wilhelm Vatke (1806–82), a Hegelian, historical theologian, saw spirit and nature opposed to each other in ancient Judaism. Christianity completed the religious evolution of man's self-consciousness by demonstrating that the experience of the senses can be understood as a product of spirit. He thus restored the sequential occurrence of Judaism and Christianity which Hegel had rejected, and solved the problem of talmudic Judaism by describing it as a mixture of disintegrating sectarianism of biblical Judaism mixed with alien ideas from Alexandria. Friedrich Schleiermacher (1768–1834), who was friendly with many Jews of his day and a devoted visitor of Berlin salons, was nevertheless extremely hostile to Judaism. It was his ambition to show the absolute truth of Christianity by analysing other religions. In the case of Judaism it would be necessary to eliminate all concepts, laws and ideas which were political, social and practical in order to isolate Judaism in its true essence, the real *Judaismus*, which he then described as the idea of retribution. Man is free to act and thereby invokes a divine response of reward, correction or punishment. Judaism ceased to be a living religion with the end of its Biblical period. What remained was an empty shell, a mechanical movement without life or spirit. Hence there was no real relationship between Judaism and Christianity. If the Old Testament were included in the Christian canon, this was due to the synagogal origins of Christian worship and the support in prophetic writings for Christian claims of authenticity. Both Schleiermacher and Neander laid great stress on the role of Philo Judaeus of Alexandria in the formation of early Christianity.[8]

August Gförer (1803–61) also assigned great importance to Philo and to Alexandrian Judaism in the development of Christianity, though he was quite original in stressing the significance of the rabbinic tradition of the Talmud for an understanding of the New Testament period, more particularly because he took the view that the isolation of the Jews in hostile environments until the eighteenth and nineteenth centuries kept this rabbinic tradition free of any Christian influence. Gförer also drew attention to the complete lack of historiographical trends in talmudic writing, i.e. chronological sequences were largely disregarded and this enabled modern scholars to study and evaluate norms and values that have persisted over time. Unlike most theologians, Gförer had studied the Talmud with the help of some rabbis and was familiar with the work and aspirations of contemporary Jewish scholars such as Abraham Geiger and Leopold Zunz, the earliest representatives of 'the science of Judaism'. In line with later scholars, he saw the Pharisaic movement as a precursor of talmudic Judaism which strove to preserve both Jewish law and the Jewish people. He pointed out that the rabbis of the Talmud who were all artisans or professionals offered leadership without exploiting the people, and contrasted this with the role of Catholic priests who, if they had acted similarly, would have made the reformation of the late middle ages unnecessary. Gförer was strongly opposed to the treatment of contemporary Jews as 'white negroes',[9] but thought that the cause for this was Jewish exclusivity (*Sonderexistenz*). He advocated full assimilation, complete civil rights and access to state service for Jews, but this final privilege to be given only after they had converted to Christianity.

If we now turn to the radical writers (and we shall concern ourselves only with their somewhat neglected views on Jews), particularly Strauss, Feuerbach and Bauer, we shall meet in one form or another many of the ideas which we have briefly outlined here. The basic issues do not change for the radicals, though they do show a greater propensity to search for the 'core' of Judaism, the 'essence' of the Jew, or the 'real' Jew hidden behind metaphysical or theological mystifications. We have seen how Mendelssohn tried to adapt his religion to conform with the norms of rational belief. The Jews at that time tried to absolve themselves from the burden of accusations levelled against them by claiming for themselves and their religion the same ethical standards as those of their critics. Gabriel Riesser rejected the very concept of a critique by arguing that Jews were seeking equality

as citizens, that their beliefs and religious convictions were irrelevant and in any event a purely private matter. Both Hess and
Marx changed this flow of polemic, for both sought to define a
social role for Jews and Judaism which, whatever the ultimate
outcome of the theological debate, would leave a radical demand
requiring a radical response. But their radicalism was rooted in
and drew much of its justification from earlier philosophers,
especially those whose radicalism was derived much more from
their attitudes to their political situation than from their views on
Judaism. Nevertheless the Jews were also made to feel the weight
of the growing political discontent, not least because to criticise
them incurred no sanctions from the state, and this enabled their
critics to give voice to many of the frustrations imposed on them
by an absolutist regime.

CHAPTER VI

The Radical Image
of Jews

DAVID FRIEDRICH STRAUSS

Strauss (1808–74) was the pioneer of a new radical trend in German theology. His most important work, *Das Leben Jesu*, 'provided the first impulse' for a systematic attack on religion and, indirectly, on politics.[1] Here he argued that the Gospels in the New Testament should not be regarded as history, but as myths. There is a substantial introductory section in the book, which described the background to the Gospels, and in this context, Strauss discussed the history and religion of the Jews until the advent of Jesus. Like Hegel and most Hegelians, he relied heavily on Philo Judaeus of Alexandria (20 BC–55 CE)[2] and Josephus (c. 37–100 CE) for his source material, but rejected the Talmud because it was completed too late to be reliable.[3] This rather suggests that Strauss was unfamiliar even with the contents of the Talmud: had he had the most elementary knowledge of its structure, he would almost certainly have made use of the Mishnah, which had been codified in Palestine by the end of the second century CE.

According to Strauss, Judaism emerged as a monotheistic religion from polytheistic animal and idol worship, which it rejected, but whose sacrificial cult it retained. The worship of an invisible God, coupled with bloody sacrifices, set up a 'contradiction' which constantly pulled the people back towards idol-worship.[4] The prophets tried to resolve this conflict by calling increasingly for spiritual worship of God, who was defined as a spiritual moral being.[5] But they never entirely rejected ritual worship, because it became increasingly the only means to maintain Jewish identity and independence in the face of the constant threat presented by the rise of imperial powers.[6] Under this threat the temptation to revert to idol-worship, which was closely identified with alien rulers, disappeared, and a growing concern with the observance of ritual and ceremonial took its place.

Alexander the Great brought Greek thought and custom to Judaism, but the religious and national peculiarities of the Jews were strong enough to expel these alien influences through the Maccabean revolt, after which the people 'clung even more rigidly and harshly to their self-righteous ceremonial worship'.[7]

Strauss saw the Maccabean victory as a regression from the prophetic period. Because it led to a trend towards the multiplication and 'sophistic extension of externalised worship', it moved much further from the God it sought than the prophets, who had understood his presence in man and recognised true worship in righteousness and love of man. The prophetic missions had added a further dimension to the religious conceptions of the Jews. They created an image of former glory, an idealised version of the Davidian era, which Israel could enjoy again if they 'returned' to true piety. That is how the concept of David restored, i.e. the Messiah concept, arose.

The Messiah idea persisted as a mixture of moral-religious and national-political striving. As a result of political misfortunes it was increasingly associated with the nation-idea of an oppressed and unhappy people. In the final stages of the Jewish state it had disastrous consequences in that it led to 'senseless and destructive revolts' against the might of Rome.[8]

Following the successful Maccabean revolt, three main sects, which Strauss then described, emerged among the Jews. The largest, the Pharisees, was very similar to the romantic movement in Germany, 'which was the unhappy result of the healthy rebellion against French rule'.[9] In both cases, the people rejected the imposition of alien rule, customs and religion in order to restore their own independence. In such a situation it was easy also to reject the good features of an alien system, to intensify national isolation and to emphasise that which separates one nation from another. Once their historic mission was completed, the people adopt an 'externalised spirit' (*Ausserlichkeitsgeist*) in which form obliterates content. 'Such a movement develops a rigid pride which will not relinquish one iota of its nationalistic striving, which will make no allowance for changed conditions, and which will therefore rebel and mutiny against any ruler whom time and conditions may impose upon them.'[10] The Pharisees could only have succeeded, Strauss claimed, if they had been able to infuse a new spirit into the people, to offer them an inner religious and moral revival. This, they did not even try to do. Instead they drove the people towards an illusion that *externalia* were all, that a meticulous observance of ceremonial law would persuade God to grant them total salvation and mastery over all other nations through the Messiah.[11]

The Sadducees stood in opposition to 'this sect of rigid, narrow Judaisers (*Judenthümler*)'. They accepted only biblical law as authoritative, which gave them 'a certain protestant aura'. They rejected the Pharisaic reward-concept (*Lohnsucht*), wanted good for its own sake and came close to Epicurean materialism in their denial of resurrection and angels. This may have been Greek influence, although there are signs of such an attitude already in Solomon.[12] The 'cold, refined, moral severity' of the Sadducees made no headway among the people and was represented by an upper, priestly stratum. It could no more offer a national rebirth than 'the sanctimonious, reward-seeking piety' of the Pharisees.[13]

All the deeper religious and moral drives of the Jews appear to Strauss to have merged in the Essenes, whose asceticism and self-denial very closely resembled that of the early Christians. Their object was to free the soul from the body.[14]

In summing up his account of Jewish history, Strauss underlined his basic assumption that Christianity would never have become the dominant religion of the West if, even in its origins and first beginnings, Western and Greco-Roman cultural influences had not been present as well as oriental and Jewish influences. Christianity was the product of a fusion between Judaism, which also embodied other oriental religions, in search of God, and Hellenism, which also embodied Roman politics, in search of man.[15] The Pharisees, the true ancestors of modern Judaism, were seen as 'wholly negative'. They established an externalised ritual and ceremonial worship which led to religious petrification of the people. Their Messiah idea assumed 'a sterile, political, Jewish-particularistic form which ruined the true piety of the people. They entirely misconceived the idea of God, of worship and of a Messiah who could help them and mankind'.[16] The Sadducees saw where the Pharisees went wrong but had nothing positive to offer in its place. The Essenes had the right idea in concentrating on the purification of the inner man, but were too extreme. However, their concept of the impurity of all non-members of their sect, which included fellow-Jews, 'was such a blow to Jewish national pride that it helped to prepare for the eventual rejection of Jewish particularism'.[17]

It only remained for Strauss to show what alternatives Christianity adopted in place of Jewish preoccupations with law and national particularism. The Greeks offered an alternative to law: 'Just because the divine did not appear for the Greek in the form of a dominating law, he had to be a law unto himself. Because, unlike the Jew, he did not see his life ordered step by step through religious dictates, he had to seek a moral norm within himself.' To overcome nationalism, Christianity had to go further because particularism, the concentration on one's own people, was characteristic not only of the Jews but also of Greeks and Romans: 'The Greek was as exclusive towards Barbarians as the Jew towards heathens.' Even Plato and Aristotle were not free of 'national prejudice'. It was the Stoics who were the first to argue that, since all men are reasonable, they must also be equal and belong together.[18]

Strauss may have been a radical to orthodox theologians, but he did not reject either Christianity or religion as such. On the contrary, he argued fervently that by placing Jesus squarely in a human context, the power of his mission would only be enhanced.[19] Needless to say, he was violently attacked by conservative theologians, some of whom even went so far as to suggest that his *Das Leben Jesu* had been 'financed by Jews', that it represented 'the vengeance of Judaism on Christianity', and similar charges.[20] Although he regarded himself as a 'critic', he did not go far enough for the radicals who followed him, particularly Ludwig Feuerbach and Bruno Bauer. But the level of his scholarship was never disputed, and his interpretations of Jewish history and Jewish law were taken over by other radicals, either completely or in part. The image of Jews as a static remnant of a once world-historical mission became a commonplace in the radical tradition, even though Strauss's image could easily be shown to be devoid of any real knowledge of Jewish history and Jewish law. It was however an image in the tradition of Hegel, and as such exercised a profound influence on later writers.

Strauss's attitude to the Jews of his own day and the question of their emancipation was characterised by the same sympathetic antagonism that pervaded his historical account. He set out his position in two long articles in 1848 which followed riots against the Jews, especially by the peasants of Odenwald and other areas.[21] He explained the contrast between the open hostility of peasants and the favourable attitude of 'humane theorists' towards Jews by claiming that only the peasant knew 'the real, actual Jew' who would deprive them of their last cow if they could not meet their debts, while the humane theoretician knew only 'the cultural Israelite' of the city. The problem was, however, not only an economic one, determined by Jewish dishonesty in business. There was also the persistent particularism of the Jews who deliberately separated themselves from their German fellow-citizens by their ritual and ceremonial laws. While Jewish dishonesty was largely due to the persecutions they had suffered, their particularism was an expression of their spiritual isolation (*Sondergeist*), which would have to be overcome. As a true Hegelian, Strauss rejected the idea of converting Jews to Christianity and, even more strongly, any suggestion that the state should abolish such religious rites as circumcision, dietary laws and the Jewish Sabbath. Instead he wanted Jews to intermarry with Germans so that they merged completely with the German host nation. Only then could equal rights be accorded to them, albeit gradually. Full emancipation was to be a privilege reserved for those who, having shed their Jewish identity, were so immersed in modern culture that Germans could regard them as 'belonging to us'. Strauss thus completed a full circle. Christianity had emerged as a reaction to Jewish particularism which, having remained unchanged for nearly two thousand years, must now, in turn, be rejected by the Jews themselves if they wished to be regarded as equals of German Christians.[22]

LUDWIG FEUERBACH

Unlike Strauss, Feuerbach (1804–72) chose a 'historico-philosophical analysis'[23] rather than a historical mode of presentation. The sources for his analysis of Judaism were the Old Testament, Philo Judaeus, Spinoza and, certainly for his second edition, J. A. Eisenmenger.[24] Although he insisted that his analysis of Judaism was valid 'to this day', he, like Marx, appears to have treated his personal experiences with Jews as totally irrelevant. Like Bauer and Marx, Feuerbach was supremely arrogant and confident of his 'genius'.[25] He considered his *Essence of Christianity* to be 'a world-historical event', yet like Bauer, but unlike Marx, he sank into almost total oblivion after his meteoric rise to fame in the 1840s.[26]

Feuerbach's enigmatic character is much more difficult to evaluate than those of his contemporaries. He was much less hostile and negative in his approach, without however being less critical or radical. He held aloof from the great radical figures of his period and did not indulge in the scathing sarcasm or contempt of a Bauer or a Marx. His search for balanced argument is evident, though occasionally obscured by his predilection for dogmatic aphorisms, yet he could also display a naivety which suggested a certain gullibility. He was enchanted by Christian Wilhelm Weitling (1808–71) and his comrades and cheerfully adopted their communism, even though he predicted that their inevitable victory would not lead to a 'classless' society, but would invert

the ruling strata in society.[27] He was friendly with Georg
Friedrich Daumer (1800–75) and in contact with Friedrich
Wilhelm Ghillany (1807–76), both of whom were neurotically
obsessed with their researches into 'human sacrifices as practised
by Jews, ancient and modern',[28] and referred to their researches
in his book,[29] but does not appear to question the approaches of
these researchers in the light of his own knowledge of and
friendships with Jews, or the overwhelming evidence against
them which would have been readily available to him, since he
wrote at about the time of the Damascus blood-libel when the
question of the use of Christian blood by Jews was widely discussed and almost universally rejected as a medieval fable.
Feuerbach's ambivalence is evidenced by his own experiences with
Jews. During his later school years when he was planning to study
theology, he took private lessons in Hebrew from the local Rabbi
Wassermann and in return taught the rabbi's son Latin. This
caused a furore in Ansbach because the lad was the first Jew there
to learn Latin and the boy was frequently beaten up on his way
to Feuerbach by local youths. Towards the end of his stay in
Erlangen, presumably while he was studying anatomy and
physiology in 1837, Feuerbach formed a friendship with Jakob
Herz (1816–71), a famous physician whose career clearly reflected
the position of Jews in Germany. Herz qualified MD in 1839 and
taught at the university without the status of *Privatdozent* from
which he was debarred as a Jew. He served in the Austro-
Prussian War with distinction, was awarded the 'freedom' of
Erlangen in 1866 but did not achieve the title of professor until
1869. He distinguished himself again in the Franco-Prussian War
of 1870–1, and a monument in his memory was set up in Erlangen
in 1875.[30]

Feuerbach's analysis of Judaism was predicated on three fundamental characteristics which, he claimed, distinguished the Jews
(who were also referred to as Israelites and Hebrews). First, that
'Israel is the most complete presentation of positivism in religion';[31]
second, that 'creation is the fundamental doctrine of the Jewish
religion',[32] and third, that 'utilism is the essential theory of
Judaism'.[33] Feuerbach built his case for Jewish egoism on a

comparison of heathen (Greco-Roman) and Jewish attitudes to nature and life. He then contrasted Judaism and Christianity and finally offered his views on the meaning of Jewish law.

The heathen is strongly idealised. He identified God with nature and accepted nature as it is. His relation to the world was 'aesthetic or theoretic';[34] he studied fine arts and philosophy and heard 'heavenly music in the harmonious course of the stars'.[35] He developed science and art because these arise 'only' out of polytheism. Study of nature is the worship of nature and therefore idolatry. The fundamental humanity of the heathen is demonstrated in that he subordinates the individual to the whole of mankind—'men pass away but mankind remains'.[36]

The contrast with the Jew is total. The Jew 'makes nature merely the servant of his will—and hence in thought degrades it to a mere machine, a product of the will.'[37] He approaches the world from a practical standpoint and makes nature 'the abject vassal of his selfish interest, of his practical egoism'.[38] Jewish contact with nature is through the stomach; they have only 'an alimentary view of theology': eating is 'the most solemn act of initiation'[39] in the Jewish religion. The god of the Jews is egoism: 'Egoism strengthens cohesion, concentrates man on himself, gives him a consistent principle of life; but it makes him theoretically narrow, because indifferent to all which does not relate to the well-being of self'.[40] The concept of creation was the result of Jewish egoism: the egoist cannot tolerate postponed gratification, 'the chasm between the wish and its realisation'. The Jew therefore made the world ' a product of a dictatorial word, of a categorical imperative, of a magic fiat'.[41] And so 'the creation out of nothing had its origins in the unfathomable depth of Hebrew egoism'.[42] Creation, in turn, provides the justification for egoism. In this way egoism became the god of the Jews, the reflection or projection of their ego: 'God is the ego of Israel which regards itself as the end and aim, the lord of nature'.[43]

The difference between Judaism and Christianity lay mainly in the fact that the Jew's religious consciousness 'was circumscribed by the limits of a particular, national interest';[44] while the Christian had freed himself from this limitation. Hence 'Judaism is worldly

Christianity; Christianity spiritual Judaism—the Christian religion is the Jewish religion purified from national egoism'.[45] Whereas the Israelite made his national needs the law of the world, the Christian made human feelings absolute. This is illustrated by the function of biblical miracles. Old Testament miracles have only the welfare of the nation as their object, whilst New Testament miracles are concerned with the welfare of men, albeit Christian men. Similarly, the desire for earthly happiness of the Israelitish religion becomes the longing for heavenly bliss in Christianity, because Christianity has spiritualised the egoism of Judaism into subjectivity, which is, however, expressed as 'pure egoism'.[46]

Feuerbach then considered the meaning of Jewish law by contrasting, in much the same manner, law and love. The Jews are a national, and therefore a political, community. Their political system is expressed in the form of religion, and the highest conception, the god of such a system, is law, 'the consciousness of law as an absolute, divine power'.[47] Where apolitical, unworldly feelings are supreme, as in Christianity, the highest power, the god, is love.[48] But Jewish law has force only if it is associated with a divine will which perceives the evil-doer and punishes.[49] The Jew does not see his laws as having subjective value because they are 'adventitious and arbitrary'; they are only fortuitously based on reason or ethics; their true force lies in their being God's commandments.[50] Since he has no real relationship with the moral imperatives of his law, 'he must separate from himself that which gives him moral laws and place it in opposition to himself'.[51] The inevitable result of this is that 'the law has authority, has validity, only in relation to him who violates it'.[52]

There are many difficulties in the Feuerbachian conception, some of which he dealt with in a casual, offhand manner. Thus the fact that the book of Jonah appears to extend the Jewish idea of God's love beyond national boundaries 'does not belong to the essential character of the Israelitish religion'.[53] Philo Judaeus' argument that love is the highest virtue only showed that 'even the Jews, by imbibing the principle of humanity contained in Greek culture had by this time mollified their malignant religious separatism'.[54]

Strauss's thesis that Jewish national particularism made it essential for Christianity to break away from it and to adopt a universalistic world view from Greco-Roman heathenism was thus repeated by Feuerbach, but he also needed a conceptual basis which would allow him to account for this in an analytic-anthropological framework. Like Marx, he found it difficult to free himself from his philosophical background and was led into somewhat confusing, even contradictory, positions by the un-qualified transfer of philosophical concepts into anthropological explanations.[55] This applies particularly to the key concepts he employed in relation to the Jews, egoism and creation, which were also destined to play a major part in the subsequent analyses of Judaism by Bauer and Marx.

Feuerbach's 'egoism' was partly derived from Kantian ethical theory. Jewish egoism was seen not as the subjective idealism of the theoretical egoist, but as the practical expression of a moral egoism which simultaneously explained the contradictions of Judaism's universal God whose primary concern is the well-being of his 'chosen people' (i.e. the national particularism of the Jews, as Strauss called it, and the narrowness of Jewish society, as Bauer and Marx were to call it) and the more traditional concept of moral egoism as the self-centred 'atomistic' view of the individual Jew conceiving himself as an end in himself. Thus this single concept with its dual meaning was almost enough to explain the difference between Judaism and heathenism in antiquity and the conceptual superiority of the Christian universal spirit, even if this was projected on to heaven. At this point Feuerbach must have recognised that his philosophical analysis was leading him straight back into the Hegelian system and he therefore applied the concept of egoism to the practical expression of Christianity as well, that is to say, for all its universalistic aspirations, by its emphasis on the individual's relationship to God instead of to his fellow-men, by defining human relationships only in terms of their value as an act of service to God, or, as Feuerbach put it, because the individual 'does good not for the sake of goodness itself, not for the sake of man, but for the sake of God',[56] Christ-ianity too was a religion of egoism. Jewish egoism thus becomes, in anthropological terms, ethnocentrism[57] as opposed to Christian egoism.

The model that emerges from this is therefore not unlike the Hegelian model 'anthropologised'. For Hegel, the developmental sequence of religion was:

(a) Religion of the Hebrews—man has neither freedom nor consciousness
(b) The advent of Jesus—i.e. man with consciousness
(c) Religion of the early Christians—with community consciousness.

For Feuerbach, this becomes:

(a) Jewish ethnocentrism enslaved by law
(b) Christian individualism—constrained by other-worldly love
(c) Community—the unity of I and Thou—freedom and infinity.

What still remained to be explained was the Jewish concept of law, the Jewish desire to subject man to the objective rule of divine law rather than to the capricious rule of human lawmakers. Feuerbach extracted a key characteristic of practical egoisms, i.e. active satisfaction of the two-dimensionally described personal and national needs of the Jews. That leads us, as Rotenstreich[58] has shown, to the concept of action. Action is 'practical' because it is utilitarian, but lest the realities of human inadequacy became intolerable, i.e. unable to gratify needs immediately, the Jews, according to Feuerbach, conceived of the idea of creation—'the fundamental doctrine of Jewish religion'. Creation was the dynamic principle, which not only led to magical solutions to the problem of unsatisfied needs at the individual level, but also provided the rationale for a divine, immutable law which revolved around the personal and national needs of the Jews. Whereas the Christian dissipated himself in a search for other-worldly love, the Jew sought roots and refuge in a divine law which encompassed his worldly existence. Thus, all that Marx had to do was to strip the Feuerbachian thesis of its religious context to produce his 'real' image of the 'worldly' Jew, and Bruno Bauer was the man who inspired him to do so—but it was Moses

Hess who first recognised the need to extend the Feuerbachian analysis beyond its preoccupation with religion.

MOSES HESS

Hess (1812–75) has often been described as an important influence on the young Marx. More particularly, his essay 'Ueber das Geldwesen' ('On the Essence of Money')[59] has been referred to as a major influence on Marx's essays 'On the Jewish Question'.[60] Edmund Silberner, Hess's biographer, has no doubts about this. He maintains that Marx was 'inspired' by Hess and quotes Cornu, who described Hess as 'une influence profonde' on young Marx.[61] McLellan goes even further. He claims that the similarities between the essays of Hess and Marx 'are remarkable and can only be accounted for on the supposition that Marx copied heavily from Hess's essay',[62] and that many of the themes of Marx's essays 'are taken directly' from Hess.[63] Tucker is also of the opinion that 'the reasoning [in 'On the Jewish Question'] turns wholly on Hess's thesis'.[64]

A close examination of the available evidence, however, suggests that these confident assertions need not necessarily be correct. Material covering the life and work of Marx in 1843–4 is at best confusing, and often contradictory. In this chapter I shall look particularly at four problems, the solutions to which might lead us to a more accurate assessment of the situation.[65] The first of these will be concerned with the justification of an assumption that Marx had in fact seen Hess's essay *before* he wrote 'On the Jewish Question'. The second will deal with the problem of why Marx did not publish Hess's essay. The third problem concerns supposed similarities in the two essays. The fourth issue is a suggestion that Hess's influence on young Marx can more readily be seen in the 'Economic and Philosophical Manuscripts' (Paris, 1844) which would mean that, while Hess's influence was important in leading Marx towards revolutionary communism, it was insignificant in providing a model for Marx's analysis of Judaism.

1 Marx first decided to write on the Jewish question in

August 1842, following the publication in the *Kölnische Zeitung* of a series of articles by C. H. Hermes (1800–56).[66] He thought that he could give this problem 'a new perspective',[67] but did not go ahead with his plan. Bruno Bauer had meanwhile published his own responses to Hermes.[68] Marx read Bauer's essays, decided that they were 'too abstract',[69] and wrote a critical analysis of them which he published in the *DFJB* in 1844. There is some confusion, however, about the period when Marx actually wrote the two reviews of Bauer which constitute his contribution to the Jewish question. In the letter of March 1843 he was already negotiating with Ruge about the founding of the *DFJB* and informed him that he planned to marry and live for a while in Kreuznach, where he intended to write, because 'before we start work, we should have some items ready',[70] the more so because as late as October 1843, Marx was planning to bring out the first issue of *DFJB* in November of that year.[71] In the event, Marx went to Kreuznach in May 1843, married on 19 June and remained there until October–November 1843. In spite of the painstaking researches into his life, there appears to be considerable uncertainty about this particular period. The longer Marx did in fact remain in Kreuznach, the more likely it is that he wrote his contributions for the *DFJB* before he went to Paris, i.e. before he saw Hess's manuscript. Franz Mehring thought that the essays on the Jewish question were written in Kreuznach 'at least in their fundamentals', and that Marx stayed there until November 1843.[72] Werner Blumenberg[73] and Joel Carmichael[74] also give November as the date of departure. Marx's wife, Jenny, gave the date as 'the beginning of October',[75] McLellan and Cornu as 11 October,[76] the Moscow Institute for Marxism-Leninism[77] and Banning claim it was at the end of October.[78] From Marx himself we have only the last letter he wrote from Kreuznach to Ludwig Feuerbach, saying that he was about to go to Paris 'in a few days' time'. But, incredibly, no less than four dates have been published for this letter. *MEW* published the letter in full under the date of 3 October 1843.[79] McLellan, in spite of his assertion that Marx arrived in Paris on 11 October, published a shortened English version of the letter dated 20 October,[80] while Bolin published a shortened version dated 30 October.[81] Mehring gave the date (but not the text) of the letter as 23 October. This much is certain, that whenever in October Marx wrote that letter, he was sure that a first issue would be ready within a month, which suggests that his own contributions were ready. Such a conclusion is supported by Marx's letter to Froebel dated 21 November 1843 in which he stated that he was only waiting for Ruge to arrive to start printing.[82]

We also know from Marx that the first task he undertook in Kreuznach was to write his 'Critique of Hegel's Philosophy of Right'.[83] This increases the likelihood that he wrote the essays on the Jewish question in Kreuznach, since the first essay is very much a follow-up of his work on Hegel and follows the line of thought developed in that manuscript and in the Introduction to the 'Critique', also written at that time.[84] At the risk of being guilty of 'psychologising', it also seems possible that Marx grasped the opportunity of analysing the Jewish question at that time to work through the bitterness of his recent experiences with his own family. This would make the violent polemic of his second essay more understandable.[85] On balance, then, it seems reasonable to assume that the essays 'On the Jewish Question' were written in the summer of 1843 in Kreuznach or, at the latest, in the autumn of 1843, after Marx and his wife had moved to Paris.

Now Silberner suggests that Hess's essay was written 'at latest' early in 1844[86] and that would also appear to be the view of McLellan. It is at best very unlikely, therefore, that Marx had seen Hess's manuscript *before* he had written his essays 'On the Jewish Question'.[87] Of course Hess was in Paris when Marx arrived and we may safely assume that an exchange of ideas took place, but even that is speculation.

2 McLellan has suggested that Marx 'copied heavily from Hess's essay, presuming it would not be published'.[88] Why should Marx presume that? In fact, why was Hess's essay not published by Marx? It is generally assumed that the failure of the *DFJB* after the first issue accounted for this. Yet we know that when Hess submitted his MS. he was paid for it by the publishers,[89] which must mean one of two things: that the MS. was submitted

early enough to be included in the first issue or that the publishers did not realise, until the first issue was published in February 1844, that the journal would fail.[90] If we look again at available evidence we ought to draw a conclusion that Hess's essay could have been published in the first issue of *DFJB* but was suppressed by Marx because it ran counter to the policy he had laid down for the review. Thus, for example, Hess's essay embodied an un-equivocal call for the adoption of communism as the only solution to the problems facing industrial (i.e. capitalist) societies. 'We would only destroy each other', Hess maintained, 'if we do not adopt communism.'[91] Such an uncompromising position went too far for Marx. In the third letter to Ruge (dated September 1843) published in the *DFJB*, in which Marx elaborated on his plans for the new publication, he wrote: 'I am opposed to setting up a standard of dogmatism. On the contrary, we must help the dogmatists to clarify their own assumptions. Thus, communism particularly is a dogmatic abstraction, and by com-munism I do not mean some imagined or possible but real, existing communism.'[92]

The gap between Marx and Hess during the latter half of 1843 was already too wide for Marx to publish Hess's essay. From the way Marx reported this to Julius Froebel in his letter of 21 November of that year, we may assume that it led to vigorous arguments between them.[93] Nevertheless Hess's essay, as we shall see, exerted a profound influence, as Cornu put it, on the in-tellectual development of the young Marx.

3   Let us now briefly outline the main arguments in 'Ueber das Geldwesen'. Hess's essay has a wide sweep and a grand design.[94] It reviews man in nature, man in history, man in the future. The description of man in nature is almost Darwinian, whilst the description of man in history has a Comteian grandeur. And the key to it all is that 'all life is an exchange of productive activity'. At that level man shares a common bond with plants and animals, but only at the physical level. Because he is man, social exchange and communal life are as essential to him as air for his physical existence. Social exchange, i.e. social relations, is proportional to man's productivity. The greater the social

relations, the greater the productivity. 'Social relations do not arise from man's essence (*Wesen*), they are his real essence.' Free activity is 'a species act which realises productivity. This is a final truth. It took man a long time to recognise it through a history filled with conflict'. This is quite normal. Like all real things, shared exchange activity has an origin, or developmental history. Man's social development is not yet complete, 'but the end is in sight. We see in the distance the promised land of organised mankind'. Hess rejects those who proclaim an apocalyptic doom and those who are prepared to accept the *status quo*. 'If prehistoric animals had had consciousness, they would have argued and reasoned just like our present-day philosophers, theologians and clerics'. Hess is insistent that man's real history will only begin when he has completed his social evolution.

He now puts forward his theory which is to account both biologically and historically for the evolutionary process. Man began to function as an isolated individual who could satisfy his needs only through raw animalistic struggle. Hence man's first exchange of production was robbery with violence (*Raubmord*); his first activity was slave labour. That is to say, because man did not produce enough for all, the stronger robbed the weaker or, in the language of the day, the contradiction between men's social nature and their isolation made them mutually destructive. Having once established patterns of robbery and slavery, man institutionalised them by raising them into laws and principles. What began spontaneously and unconsciously was elevated into 'right'. 'History so far is nothing but the regulation of, and justification for, robbery and slavery'.

The implication of this process was that man came to regard his isolated state as normal and right, and 'egoism' became his dominant characteristic. His social nature was placed outside himself, his 'species being' was vested in God and the individual strives to live for ever by assuming an immortal soul. Hence, 'Christianity is the theory, the logic of egoism'. But life is not only theoretical. It also has a practical side where species life is external to the individual and this is represented by money. 'Money is for practical life what God is for theoretical life in the topsy-turvy world'. Hess has now reached the core of his essay. Money 'is the alienated wealth of man, his commercialised life activity. Money is the quantitative expression of human worth, the hallmark of our slavery, the brand of our servitude. Money is the coagulated blood and sweat of those who market their inalienable property, their real wealth, their life activity, in exchange for something called capital in order to feed cannibalistically off their own fat.'

If Hess condemns, he does not do so, in marked contrast to Marx, as an 'objective' observer. Where Marx analyses, Hess preaches:

> This applies to all of us. No matter how clearly we see this, as long as we do not actively work against it, we must continue to purchase our existence by losing our freedom. Make no mistake, not only we proletarians but also we capitalists are the victims who suck our own blood, consume our own flesh. We, all of us, cannot work for each other, we can only devour each other if we do not want to starve. The money we consume, for which we work, is our own flesh and blood, which, in its alienation must be acquired, looted and consumed by us. We are all, to be honest, cannibals, predatory animals, blood-suckers. We will remain such for as long as each acquires for himself instead of all working for each other.

Hess then attacks political economy, which measures man's worth and productive capacity by his money. 'Human beings are not goods.' Hence economics, which measures man by his money, and theology, which measures man by his faith, are equally undesirable because neither is really interested in man. The attack on economists allows Hess to explain a further developmental stage of man. Capital has two facets: accumulated labour and production. Only that which can be bought or sold has value; that of course includes man. Economists established that free men are worth more than slaves because 'hunger is a greater incentive than the whip and greed for money is more important than the approval of a master'. What the economists forget, according to Hess, was that the value of 'freedom' must depreciate, the more general it becomes. The more 'free' men demand slave labour the more mercenary they become. Competition ruins the price of 'free' men. The change from 'slave' to 'free' labour is therefore seen as degrading. Ancient slavery was not only the most natural form of robbery, but also the most human, because 'it is human and natural that one submits only unwillingly to being sold, while it is unnatural and inhuman to sell oneself'. The modern labourer is thus a direct descendant of the medieval serf who sprang from Christian slaves descended from heathen slaves. The perpetuation of this human slavery was made possible by Christianity, which assured man that his alienation was right, normal and proper. The Christian separates the inner from the outer man, rejects the outer man and describes the suffering of the inner man as good because it leads to heaven. As a result, slavery was accepted and justified— one did not sell men but only bodies. With the principle of trade in bodies established, the way was open for universal, mutual and voluntary marketing of the self (*Selbstverschacherung*).

Thus the essence of the modern pedlar-world (*Krämerwelt*) is money, the modern pedlar-state, 'the so-called free state is the promised kingdom of God just as, inversely, God is idealised capital, heaven the theoretical pedlar world'. Christianity had no difficulty in adjusting either to slavery or to serfdom. With the advent of enlightenment, it tried to realise its ideas on freedom and equality but inevitably had to find a social counterpart to its separation of body and spirit. This was achieved by 'sanctioning private egoism', by declaring the single individual to be the true man, by proclaiming the rights of man, but men independent of each other, 'windowless monads', who could no longer be bought and sold; they were free, equal—and isolated. What separated them from each other and from the state was property, money, which had become all-powerful. 'In the modern state, money, not man, is the law-giver.' Property sanctifies egoism which in turn destroys the real life of the individual. So the freedom man received was the freedom of the predatory animal. The equality he received was the equality of death. Hess then compares ancient slavery, the slavery of the American Negro and Europe, where men 'are slaves of each other'. On balance the latter is the worst because in the modern pedlar-world, 'visible slavery becomes invisible'. Equally the medieval world with its guilds and corporations was preferable to the modern world. The former at least had some sense, however restricted, of association, of community; the latter has only money, and money is alien. Man can never own it, hence he can never serve others with it.

The perfection of man's egoism, a conscious egoism, means that he is now at the peak of the social animal world. 'We are no longer herbivores, like our gentle ancestors; we are carnivores who consume each other.' As the predator relishes the blood of his prey, so man enjoys his money in a brutal, bestial, cannibalistic manner. 'Money is social blood, but alienated, spilt blood.' It was the Jews' 'world historic' mission to turn mankind into predators, and they have completed their mission. The mystery of the blood of Christ, like the mystery of Jewish blood-worship, is now revealed as the mystery of the predator. In the modern Jewish-Christian pedlar-world, the symbolic and mystical has become actual.

For all his contempt for money, Hess maintains that in its own way it has played a useful part. 'It acted as a mediator between alienated men, as religion is the mediator of love for alienated men.' But it has outlived its usefulness, for the time has come to unite men in real relationships.

In his final 'message', Hess again becomes a preacher. The organic community for which we are striving could not come about until our development was complete. We have fought over the material means which, in our isolation, we needed for survival. We needed them because we were not yet united, although we need unity, which is our life. Hence we sought our life outside ourselves. Now that our full strength is developed, we will destroy ourselves if we do not adopt communism. Our conflicts will not develop further because our development is complete. Our enormously increased productive capacity will condemn most of those who live by the work of their hands to abject misery, because their labour has lost its value, while a few who accumulate capital will wallow in surplus and will degenerate through excesses unless they listen to the voice of love and reason—or yield to force. 'The evolution of society is completed; the final hour of the social animal world has struck.'

4   As we have seen, Silberner,[95] McLellan[96] and Tucker[97] have no doubts that Hess's essay 'Ueber das Geldwesen' was a major influence on Marx when he wrote 'On the Jewish Question'. Silberner and McLellan agree that the most important 'clues' for such a statement are the similarities of view on the rights of man, the nature of medieval guilds and corporations, and the nature of money. Silberner also points to a similarity of vocabulary. How reliable are the comparisons?

In discussing the rights of man, Hess is scathingly contemptuous and sees the results as wholly negative. Under pressure from the impact of the enlightenment, 'modern legislators and practical Christians' could not be content with heavenly comforts; they had to offer man some of these spiritual delights here on earth. They did this simply by declaring the alienated, isolated, abstract 'personality' of the medieval citizen to be 'sacred'. All that happened, therefore, was that the 'practical alienation of life, like the theoretical (religious) alienation, was raised into a principle so that heavenly egoism was also realised on earth'. This is what happened. The abstract, naked person was declared to be the true man, his isolation and independence from others was proclaimed freedom. With the abolition of slavery, not robbery—but only arbitrary robbery—was abolished.[98]

Hess's argument is a consistent extension of Feuerbach's critique of religion into socio-economic fields.[99] His approach is moralistic, his premises are philosophical. All his fervour must lead to an ultimate rejection of everything that does not lead him directly to communism. Hess does not assign any functional significance to human rights nor does he build their emergence into his evolutionary framework. They are seen quite simply as evil in intent and evil in effect.

For Marx the question is a very different one. His starting-point is Bauer's claim that the Jew cannot be granted the rights of man because his Jewishness 'is his true and supreme nature before which human nature has to efface itself'.[100] Marx deals with this objection in a coldly analytic manner. 'Let us consider for a moment the so-called rights of man.' To do this he turns to France and North America, i.e., 'those who have discovered them'. Marx points out that the rights of man are in part political rights. 'Their content is participation in the community life, in the political life of the community, the life of the state.'[101] Marx thus takes a view which is contrary to Hess's, since the latter insisted that the rights of man *only* increase his already existing isolation. Marx then systematically examines liberty, property and security,[102] the main constituents of man's rights which justify his important earlier conclusions that political emancipation is the best form of 'real' emancipation in 'the prevailing social order'[103] and that, through the establishment of the rights of man, the state becomes free (emancipates itself); though man remains unfree, he is not yet a 'species being'.[104] These conclusions also lead Marx to his analysis of the great (French and American) revolutions and why they did not free man. The 'political revolution dissolves civil society into its elements without revolutionising these elements themselves'.[105]

On balance, then, while it is true that Hess and Marx agree that the rights of man are not enough, in the case of Hess this is argued as a polemic, while Marx reaches his conclusion by systematic logical analysis which also underlines the importance, historically, of the emergence of the human rights concept. Marx explained the emergence of the rights of man as a product of political revolution, while Hess described them as an imposed fraud.

Marx and Hess were not alone in stressing the positive aspects of medieval estates and corporations: Bauer made the same point in 'Die Judenfrage'.[106] There is also a marked difference between Hess and Marx. Hess's point of reference is a moral imperative, and he therefore underlines the fact that the serf ('who has nothing and is nothing') is specifically excluded from any advantages in the system. Marx's touchstone is the relationship of the individual to the state. Any advantages or disadvantages accruing to the individual are presented as logical manifestations of that relationship. According to Hess, there were in the middle ages persons who had some social position, who had a social character, who were somebody. 'The estates and corporations, although only egoistical associations, had a certain social character, they had a communal spirit, albeit a limited one; the individual could be absorbed in his social sphere and he could, in an incomplete manner, merge with the community.'[107] Hess then described the effects of the feudal system. Marx, however, was more concerned with the *causes*. In the feudal state the individual as such had no relation with the state. The state recognised only estates and corporations and its relationships were concerned only with these. Each individual was, therefore, only a social role *within* the estates and corporations, but by sharing the same social role in relation to the state, individuals enjoyed a communal existence.

The two main points of similarity between Marx and Hess, then, do not appear to justify a conclusion that 'Marx *copied* Hess's ideas at this stage'.[108] If anything, it is possible to argue a much stronger case to show that the 'Economic and Philosophical Manuscripts' of 1844 show signs of Hess's influence. There can be no question that, by the time these were written, Marx had seen the essay 'Ueber das Geldwesen'. From Marx's handling of Bauer's 'Die Judenfrage', we know that he sometimes picked up ideas with which he did not necessarily agree, or even recollect as belonging to a particular author, but which he subsequently developed in his own particular way.[109] There appear to be many ideas in the 1844 'Manuscripts' which are strangely reminiscent of Hess's essay. To demonstrate this I shall tabulate some of the arguments developed by Marx and set Hess's ideas in juxtaposition.[110]

1844 'Manuscripts'	*'Ueber das Geldwesen'*
'The demand for men regulates the production of men . . . the existence of the worker is reduced to the same conditions as the existence of any other commodity', p. 69	'The more "free" men demand slave labour, the more mercenary they become. Competition ruins the price of "free" men', p. 168
'Land ownership has its source in robbery', p. 103	Robbery as the source of all property is the persistent theme throughout Hess's essay
'The misery of the worker increases with the power and volume of his production', p. 120	'The hundredfold increased productive power will reduce the majority of those who live by the work of their hands to abject misery', p. 186

'The worker is related to the product of his labour as to an alien object . . . It is just the same as in religion. The more of himself man attributes to God, the less he has left in himself', p. 122

'Religion is the spontaneous activity of human fantasy, of the human brain and heart', p. 125

'The external character of work for the worker is shown by the fact that it is not his own work but work for someone else; that in the work he does not belong to himself but to another person', ibid., and

'Alienation is apparent . . . in the fact that my means of life belong to someone else', p. 177

Note the comparison of man with animals, pp. 126–7

'Productive life is species life', but now 'life itself appears only as a means of life', p. 127

'Political economy expresses in its own fashion the moral laws', p. 174

'The economist establishes the unity of labour and capital . . . capital is accumulated labour', pp. 174–5

How love, sexual relations, honesty and learning are dependent on money, p. 191.

'What God is for theoretical life, money is for practical life . . . the alienated wealth of man, his commercialised life activity', p. 166

'Man's noblest and least alienated organs, e.g. brain and heart', p. 159

'Every free activity—and there is only free activity, because whatever a being creates that is not free activity is not his own but someone else's action', p. 160

Another persistent theme in Hess; see esp. pp. 165 and 181–2

'in the natural world order, "the species is life itself, the individual only a means of life. The opposite world order is supreme in the condition of egoism" ', p. 165

'National economy is the science of the earthly, as theology is the science of heavenly acquisition', p. 167

'Capital, by national economic definition, is accumulated stored labour', p. 168

'Love, sexual relations and exchange of thought are dependent on money', p. 173.

We see, therefore, that a case could be argued for assuming that many of Hess's ideas stimulated Marx's thinking and that this is more apparent here than in 'On the Jewish Question', especially because both Hess and Marx argue here for the inevitability of communism, which Marx does not do in his earlier essays.

The closest parallel between the two writers is in the evaluation of money, which is embodied in a single section in Marx's second essay on the Jewish question, but more diffuse in Hess's article.

Marx, on 'Die Fähigkeit'	*'Ueber das Geldwesen'*
'The god of practical need, self-interest is money. Money abases all the gods of mankind and changes them into commodities. Money is the universal and self-sufficient value of all things. It has deprived the world of man and of nature of their proper place', pp. 36–7	'What God is for theoretical life money is for practical life—it is the alienated wealth of man, his pedlarised life activity. Money is the quantitative expression of human worth—money is the coagulated blood sweat of the exploited', p. 166
'Money is the alienated essence of man's work and existence—this essence dominates him and he worships it. Politics is in principle superior to the power of money but in practice it has become its bondsman', ibid.	'Money, the essence of the modern pedlar-world, is the essence of Christianity realised', p. 170
	'In the modern state, not man but money is the law-maker', p. 174
	'Money is social blood, but alienated, spilt blood', p. 82

Silberner indeed thinks that the comments on money by the two men 'differ only in the mode of expression',[111] but even this may be assuming too much, if only because the moral revolt against 'money' was such a strongly felt and widespread attitude in the radical circles of that time.[112] In this context we might also look at the quotation on which Tucker based his claim that Marx's 'reasoning turns wholly on Hess's thesis';[113] 'The Christian was from the beginning the theorising Jew; the Jew therefore the practical Christian . . . Judaism is the lowly application of Christianity'.[114] Hess made no comments along these lines, but Feuerbach and Bauer expressed themselves in very similar terms. Thus Feuerbach: 'Judaism is worldly Christianity; Christianity spiritual Judaism—the Christian religion is the Jewish religion purified';[115] and Bauer: 'Christianity is completed Judaism—Judaism is unachieved Christianity'.[116]

McLelland has suggested that Marx's negative views on Judaism are derived from Hess,[117] while George Lichtheim thought that Hess had drawn 'an even more repellent picture' of Judaism than

Marx.[118] Although Hess was destined to become the pioneer of modern Zionism, what were his views on the nature and function of Judaism *at this particular period*?[119] In 1842 F. W. Ghillany published a book in which he claimed that the ancient Hebrews offered human sacrifices to Moloch.[120] The book evoked a considerable reaction, and appears to have made an impression on Moses Hess, who, in his 'Philosophie der Tat',[121] presents a historical picture in which Moloch is the archetypal god who demands human sacrifice. This god then becomes 'the Jewish Moloch—YHWH' who at first demands the sacrifice of every first-born. In the *juste milieu* era of Judaism, the sacrifice is replaced by money; i.e. the first-born is 'redeemed' and animals take the place of humans in the sacrificial cult. The Christian god is a copy of the Jewish one because he allows his first-born son to be crucified.[122] The underlying historical trend developed here is continued in 'Ueber des Geldwesen'. The main thrust of the attack on religion is directed throughout against 'the Christian pedlar-world', and the Jews receive only one serious mention, which is closely linked with the earlier one. We have seen how Hess's essay is built on the image of man evolving through the sequences of animal life, and how money was equated with blood, 'the alienated, spilt blood' of man. This leads Hess to the Jews: 'The Jews, in the natural history of the social animal world had the world-historic mission to bring out the predator in mankind. They have finally completed their task'.[123] The 'proof' for this assertion is built on the 'blood mystique' of Judaism and Christianity. The reverence for blood in ancient Judaism[124] is 'revealed as the mystique of the predator'. But this mystique was only 'prototypical'. In medieval Christianity it was 'theoretically, idealistically, logically realised' in that 'the alienated, spilt blood' of man was symbolically consumed (communion), so that in 'the modern Jewish-Christian pedlar world, the symbolism becomes actuality'.

Hess's gruesome imagery is not very profound and lacks the incisiveness of Marx. It hardly seems fair to summarise Hess's comments by saying that 'Judaism represents in their grossest form the evils of bourgeois society',[125] or indeed to claim that

Marx's image of the Jew or of Judaism owes very much, if anything, to that of Hess. Probably the only conclusion that can be drawn with any degree of certainty is that 'so far as the transformation of humanism into socialism is concerned, Hess was Marx's precursor and, so to speak, his "John the Baptist".'[126]

CHAPTER VII

The Radical Challenge
to Jews

BRUNO BAUER: THE MAN

We have seen how the draft bill of Friedrich Wilhelm IV to organise the Jews of Prussia into 'corporations' and the repercussions of the Damascus affair led to a renewed and vigorous debate on the Jewish question, to which C. H. Hermes contributed in the *Kölnische Zeitung*. The subject was thus highly 'topical', and Hermes's dispute with the editor of the *Allgemeine Zeitung des Judentums*[1] attracted the attention of Bruno Bauer (1809–82), ex-theologian, former *Privatdozent* in the University of Bonn and, since April 1842, an independent writer, resident in Berlin and keen to contribute to the questions of the day.[2] Jewish protests about being singled out for special restrictions also irritated Bauer who saw himself as being equally, if not more, oppressed than the Jews.[3]

Before we consider the substance of Bauer's contribution, it will be necessary to take a brief look at the personality and immediate background of the man, since both have important implications for his approach to the Jewish question and for his relationship with Karl Marx, for it was over the Jewish question in the first instance that the break occurred between two hitherto close friends. Bauer was educated in the University of Berlin where he began to teach theology after graduation in 1834. Throughout his years in Berlin he moved increasingly towards a radical criticism which led him to attack E. W. Hengstenberg, the head of the theological faculty in Berlin.[4] Altenstein, the Prussian Minister of Culture, who was kindly disposed towards Bauer, sent him to Bonn where he was accepted by the faculty with considerable reservations.[5] Bauer was asked outright if he intended to continue to attack his colleagues as he had done in the past. He assured the Dean that he only wanted to sort things out for himself. Altenstein, who was possibly motivated more by his dislike of Hengstenberg than by any really positive feelings for Bauer, expected Bauer to make his own way in Bonn. Bauer was a brilliant, dedicated scholar whose searing arrogance isolated him from colleagues and students. He despised the entire faculty at Bonn,[6] maintained polite but superficial contacts with fellow-academics and preferred to throw himself into his work. He was not amenable to direction by superiors or advice from well-wishers and frankly admitted his own unsuitability to work in the context of an organisation.[7] Less than six months after Bauer's arrival in Bonn, Altenstein died and the New Minister, Eichhorn, had no particular sympathy for Bauer. Yet throughout his stay in Bonn, Bauer was in continuous contact with the Ministry in Berlin, always demanding, never showing appreciation when he received help,[8] and not deigning to accept advice which might have resolved his difficulties.[9] It was a characteristic of Bauer that he did not express his views in open discussion but, while listening to others, would plan devastating attacks in his forthcoming publications which would silence all opposition.[10]

Bauer's isolation and furious energy resulted in a prolific output in Bonn. In 1840 he published his *Kritik der evangelischen Geschichte des Johannes* and in 1841–2 his *Kritik der evangelischen Geschichte der Synoptiker*, his most important contributions to theology. He also developed his 'pure criticism' which assumed ever greater significance in his own eyes until he came to see 'die Sache' ('the affair', as he called it) as the ultimate weapon with which he would change the world. Bauer was an elitist, an intellectual rapist,[11] who eventually elevated his loneliness, his ability and his academic superiority into philosophical virtues which would 'destroy' his opponents, terrorise 'pure theory' and eliminate the need 'to put his hand to anything' because 'the true and pure critic' had, in Marx's words, 'transformed himself into a "transcendental power"'.[12] Bauer's *Kritik der Synoptiker* led to a demand by the theological faculties of all German universities for his dismissal.[13] This demand, coupled with his incidental involvement in the demonstrations in Berlin in sympathy with Professor Karl Theodor Welcker, dismissed from his chair in Freiburg in 1841,[14] resulted in the withdrawal of his *licentia docendi*. Bauer, whose position had been described as a national tragedy by Arnold Ruge,[15] completely ignored the genuine efforts of his faculty to help him, even after his dismissal.[16] Other radical academics like Strauss, Feuerbach, Ruge, Max Stirner and Marx recognised that their political views made teaching positions at universities at that time untenable. Bauer alone seemed to think that his total rejection of all theology and theologians was no obstacle to his continued presence in a theological faculty and he remained in Bonn for two and a half years to prove it. He was the last radical academic to leave the stage, and his dismissal was seen as an apocalyptic event by the 'metaphysical revolutionaries'.[17] Interestingly enough, it also earned him the respect of leading Jewish figures who attacked 'Die Judenfrage' but also argued that a man who sacrificed his career for his convictions deserved to be taken seriously.[18]

'DIE JUDENFRAGE'

There are two facets to Bauer's 'Die Judenfrage' which are of interest in our context. The first is his basic premise and the second is his critique of Judaism. In his basic premise Bauer rejected those who advocated the emancipation of Jews and those who opposed it. He argued against those who advocated emancipation because they were not critical of themselves, were not conscious of their own lack of freedom, and assumed their own freedom. Nor were they critical of those for whom they advocated emancipation; the 'non-self-critical' failed in not being critical of the Jews, 'a consequence of a consequence' (to use Hermann Jellinek's phrase).[19] Those who opposed Jewish emancipation were also one-sided critics because they carried out a theological critique of Judaism without being critical of themselves. Bauer, who had already criticised himself and Christianity, would now resolve the question by criticising Judaism and the Christian state and thereby show that the Jewish question was a human question and the human question a Jewish question. He would show that since Christians were not free, Christianity could not emancipate —how then could it emancipate the Jews? Only when Christianity and Judaism criticised themselves and recognised that they were not free—when both discarded their prejudices—only then could emancipation come about—that is, the emancipation of all mankind.

In the result, Bauer's long essay on the Jewish question is little more than an anti-Jewish polemic. Unlike Feuerbach, Bauer had no substantive theory on which he could build an argument, nor was he a 'critic' by his own definition, i.e. he did not explain things out of themselves, but contented himself with 'negations'.[20] His method was simple. He took a series of arguments from the debate on Jewish emancipation. If they were for the Jews he refuted them; if they were against, he rejected them and added his own ideas on Jews, which as often as not turned out to be little more than rephrased prejudices which frequently led him into insurmountable contradictions. This method gives the essay a spurious semblance of balance, which does not, however, survive any kind of systematic analysis.

Advocates of the Jews, Bauer proclaimed, often argued that Jews had been ill treated in the Christian world and that any faults they possessed were consequences of this.[21] His reply to this was that if Jews were under pressure, they must have provoked this by their determination to retain their identity. Had it not been for this determination, there would not and could not have been external pressure.[22] Later in the essay, he took up this subject again, as a complaint of the Jews. In reply to a Jewish author, Bauer explained that all men, not only Jews, suffer in their own way. The Jews are deluding themselves if they think that they would be free if restrictions on them were lifted. A civil servant is also restricted as long as his whole being is filled with the completion of forms. The privileged classes were not free, even though they could express their views in provincial parliaments, because their views carried no weight. Not only Jews—all had to carry exceptional burdens.[23] Some people maintained, Bauer continued, that Jews were hated because they were misunderstood, but this was not so. True understanding *ought* to lead to hatred; it is those who argue otherwise who misunderstand.[24] There are those who said that they preferred Jews to keep their religion. Did they mean the religion of Moses, or that of the Talmud? The law of Moses was relevant only in Palestine. If Jews abided by that then they ought to be taken back to that country and given the same corrupt environment. But Jews had since evolved talmudic Judaism which was even less real than Mosaic Judaism. Adherence to either was, therefore, meaningless.[25] Others said they preferred Jews who were 'enlightened', but this was wrong because the more enlightened a Jew, i.e. the less specifically Jewish he was, the more his claims were seen to be a pure demand for privilege. On the other hand, a provincial delegate had asserted that the 'empty shallow deism' of the educated Jew was even less desirable than the 'religious uncouth' Jew. This was also wrong, argued Bauer, for shallow deism was in fact the dominant religious system in the state.[26]

Jewish demands for emancipation and Christian support of such demands showed that barriers were coming down. But the orthodox Jew could not reasonably demand emancipation;[27] emancipation did not make sense because Jews always lived in a world in which only they were real while other nations were unreal; they were dedicated to the future because it could establish their unique reality, and to the world beyond because it was part of their reality.[28] Jewish emancipation would merely be a question of extending an existing system of privilege. It was not therefore a Jewish question. Those who were not themselves emancipated could not emancipate. This was an emancipation question for all, for none were free. Jews must give up Judaism, Christians Christianity; the real solution was the rejection of subordination and faith and the adoption of freedom and humanity.[29]

Bauer reviewed some of the arguments put forward against the Jews in the Bavarian Landtag in 1831. It was said that religious hatred was still a barrier to Jewish emancipation. How is it, asked Bauer, that this hatred was silent when Jews died in battle as common soldiers and cropped up only when they wanted commissioned rank?[30] Another delegate had suggested that the people of Bavaria were not ready to agree to Jewish emancipation. Did this mean, asked Bauer, that claims for justice and humanity should be subordinated to the arbitrary wishes of the people?[31] Yet another delegate insisted that before emancipation could be granted to Jews, 'the yoke of foreign legislation, the whole Pharisaic-talmudic rabbinic system, must be removed unconditionally'. Should this apply only to Jews, asked Bauer? What about the yoke of alien Holy Scriptures with its baptism and communion—should these not also be abolished?[32]

Like Hermes, Bauer took up the debate in the French Chamber of Deputies in 1840 regarding the introduction of Sunday as a general rest-day. Although the Jews in France were emancipated, Bauer protested, which would presumably include the right to observe their Sabbath, they were also compelled to observe Christian holy days. While in the Christian state there was an inherent right to disadvantage the Jew, in a 'free' state he was subjected to 'the tyranny of the majority'.[33] Bauer also complained that in 1791 not a single Jew intervened in the French revolution— they merely exploited it.[34] Jews and Christians might think that Jews could be good citizens until their Messiah came, but they would never be fully involved as long as they looked towards a better society only with the coming of the Messiah.[35] He also discussed the way in which the Great Sanhedrin set up by Napoleon dealt with this question in 1807. The Sanhedrin had stated that Jewish religion and French citizenship were in no way incompatible. This, Bauer said, was a contradiction. How could the Sanhedrin accept a French ruler when Jewish law recognised only God as ruler; how could it accept social obligations to the state when Jews recognised only obligations to God?[36] In fact the entire proceedings of the Sanhedrin, their exclusive concern with Jews, Bauer found 'tiring and eventually disgusting'.[37]

These examples illustrate how he dealt with aspects of the

continuing debate on Jewish emancipation. His essay also contained his own substantive contribution in which Hegelian dialectic and orthodox theology were used indiscriminately to carry the burden of 'proof'. The weight of Bauer's thesis was directed at two key issues: Jewish history and Jewish law. The nature of the relationship of the Jew to the Christian state was largely derived from the nature of the Jew himself, as constituted in law and history.

Bauer on Jewish history

Bauer's model of Jewish history is complex. Although all his arguments led to the same conclusion, they were nevertheless contradictory. As a nation Jews were represented alternately as static and dynamic: they had a determination to survive which was based on their unhistorical character and which demonstrated their incapacity for historical evolution—it was symptomatic of their static oriental heritage.[38] Since they were a nation standing outside the movement of history, Jews had lost interest in the progress of man and concentrated entirely on personal advantage because they had lost any feeling of honour. Nor could this lack of morality be explained by the pressures to which they had been subjected because they had evolved no moral principle from their suffering either for themselves or for mankind.[39] In fact the suffering of the Jews was really the logical result of their own inability to recognise (or accept) the natural development of their own consciousness. Jews were martyrs not to a higher ideal but to a past which they refused to recognise as such. Hence in the course of time they had become 'a chimerical nation' in a Christian world fighting for truth, for men and for freedom.[40] The Jew's obstinacy in not accepting the true consequences of historical development was due to his 'egoism'—his belief in himself forbade the Jew to have a history—he resists history (*geschichtswidrig*) until 'the Jew makes his very existence an injustice'.[41] To remain a Jew, even though an illusion, meant a war against history, a total war. Those who suggested an equality of value in Jewish and

Christian morals were denying Christianity as the natural progression from, and elimination of, Judaism.[42] Judaism had been truth once, but it had long since been superseded—instead of fighting for new truths, Jews continued to uphold a discredited one.[43]

Bauer appeared to follow the Hegelian view of Judaism as unachieved Christianity and Christianity as completed Judaism.[44] This explained why Christianity, the daughter of Judaism, hated the mother. Bauer described it as the behaviour of 'the consequence towards its assumption',[45] an inevitable process because that which follows could not exist if that which preceded it remained. This was wholly in accord with the Hegelian theological view that the Jewish mission ceased with the advent of Jesus. Yet he also claimed that Jewish history ended with the completion of the Talmud,[46] i.e. five centuries after Jesus, and that it was then that the Jews became 'a collection of atoms' without a national consciousness or a historical function, incapable of contributing either leaders or thinkers. Accordingly Moses Mendelssohn's contribution was 'a fruitless, unsuccessful game'.[47] Moses Maimonides' (1135–1204)[48]

> unclear, confused, slavish sophistry can only be an object of curiosity, whilst Christian scholastics—and how many of them are stars of the first order—will for ever belong to world history. What clarity in their questions and deductions compared with the mumble of Jewish dialectics! What magnificent structures worked out down to the smallest detail their works are in themselves, and how much more so in comparison with the confused dustheap in which Maimonides manipulates the meaningless dictates of [Jewish] tradition.

However, at the end of the essay, Bauer offered yet another view of Jewish history.[49]

> Judaism has followed Christianity in its conquests through the world, as a constant reminder of its origins and true nature. It is the incorporated doubt about the heavenly origin of Christianity, the religious foe of the religion that proclaims itself as the completed, only true one, which could not overcome even the small group from which it sprang. Judaism is the touchstone by which Christianity offers the clearest evidence that its essence is that of privilege.

Bauer thus offered four models of Jewish history. The first described Jews as a petrified people which had opted out of the history of man and devoted its dynamic life to an exclusive, egoistic relationship with its law. This model is, therefore, very close to the Strauss–Feuerbach conception. The second model described the Jews in terms of a Hegelian thesis which defied both its antithesis (Christianity) and synthesis (atheistic free man). The third model, a naturalistic one, saw Jews as a dynamic national unit until the beginning of the middle ages, after which it disintegrated into unrelated atomistic individuals who would eventually be absorbed by world historic peoples, while the fourth was an inverted Hegelian model in which Jews operated antithetically in relation to Christianity.

Bauer on Jewish law

In the orthodox Christian tradition, Jewish law had two characteristics: it was preparatory and impossible to keep. It was preparatory in the Paulinian sense that it brought man to consciousness of sin; it was impossible to keep so that, through a constant awareness of sin, the right gulf between finite man and absolute God would be created. The advent of Jesus freed man from sin and *ipso facto* from the law. Bauer's view of Jewish law differed from the orthodox Christian view only in that he sharpened the Paulinian conception[50] and extended the Christian view to give it a philosophical dimension. In line with his overall approach, Bauer regarded Jewish law as wholly negative. We have already seen that he divided it into Mosaic law, which he described as meaningless because it had no relevance outside a Jewish state, and talmudic law which he saw as a continuation of Mosaic law, 'but a chimerical, illusory, mindless continuation . . . the Talmud does not break the form of the old, to give its spiritual content some air, but is only a collection of fragments and bits into which the old had crumbled'.[51] Hence, if Mosaic law was not real, talmudic law was even less real. Since the laws of a people reflected their true being, their own laws made the Jews

133

a fettered people. Their law was arbitrary, had to be served without questioning, and hemmed the people in by petty regulations.[52] Since Jewish law lacked reality it was never implemented, and it was impossible for Jews to come to terms with it; yet it nevertheless met the needs of the Jews who wanted to be a people unlike all other people, and who therefore evolved a law unlike all other laws. Thus the Jews became a unique people with a unique law, albeit an unreal law for an unreal world (*Wunderwelt*).[53] As a result of this the Jew feared nature,[54] lacked inner moral strength,[55] was unable to form a true relationship with his environment[56] and separated himself from other nations by his dietary laws.[57] If then Jewish law kept the Jews separate, i.e. made them special, how could a general (state) law make them equal?[58]

Not the least important consequence of the law was that not a single Jew took part in the creation of European culture because their national spirit was opposed to arts and sciences,[59] because their spirit lacked liberalism, a dimension for making contact with other peoples or the will to master the meaning of nature.[60] They were forbidden to indulge in arts and sciences, for these raise man beyond his immediate needs.[61] Bauer concluded therefore that a follower of Jewish law could neither live in a real world nor take an interest in its affairs.[62] He saw the Jew as an unhistorical phenomenon that had opted for an illusory relationship with an illusory law in order to avoid real relationships with the world of man. Until therefore the Jews made a transition from the servitude of Judaism to the freedom of Christianity and beyond that to the ultimate freedom of critical, scientific man, they were neither capable of receiving, nor entitled to demand, emancipation, least of all in a Christian state which had itself not made the transition from religious privilege to secular freedom. Critique had solved the problem, had shown Judaism to be 'a medieval luxury, a mere appendage to the history of Christianity' which had forfeited its right to exist.[63]

'DIE FÄHIGKEIT'

Although he did not say so, Bauer's second article[64] clearly incorporated some responses to criticisms which his 'Die Juden-frage' had attracted. It introduced very little material that had not already been dealt with in the earlier book, apart from two new factors. The first was a continuous emphasis on the superiority of Christianity over Judaism, a subject made clear in the book, but extended here into a basic principle.[65] The second concerned what Bauer might have regarded as an omission. In 'Die Judenfrage' Bauer had dealt with traditional, reform and en-lightened Judaism as adaptations to the Christian state and rejected all three as inadequate. Since the rise of Gabriel Riesser, however, there had arisen yet another version of the claim for emancipation, a claim based not on the suitability of a follower of Judaism to be emancipated, but on the demand of a right to emancipation *in spite of* adherence to any particular religion. This claim was now also rejected. Bauer's insistence that a Jew who gave up his Judaism gave nothing and lost nothing would appear to be a response to criticism, as was his rejection of a suggestion that Jews had initiated the process of emancipation.

Bauer began by repeating that the problem of emancipation was a general one. The Jew was circumcised and the Christian baptised to estrange them from their human essence. But if he had said that Jew and Christian must work together for freedom, he was not saying that together they constituted a stronger force, or that Jewish demands for emancipation had stimulated those of Christians, or yet that Christians did, or should, need the help of Jews. He was merely asserting that emancipation must be pre-ceded by a recognition that the essence of man was neither circumcision nor baptism. What needed to be determined, Bauer continued, was whether Jews had contributed to the present historical situation.

If Jews claimed that the moral basis of their law enabled them to participate in social affairs and to be good citizens then such a claim had no more significance for the critic than a desire of a Negro to become white. If it is argued that Jews want to be emancipated not because of their moral law but in spite of their Jewishness—that they will be citizens first and then Jews—their limited Jewish essence will always predominate over human and political obligations. Citizenship would be in appearance only; it would be contrary to their true essence. Jews, as long as they want to remain Jews, do nothing towards becoming free men.

Bauer then looked at the way Jews had responded to the efforts of criticism which Christians directed at religion to liberate man from his most dangerous self-deception. He thought that they were interested only in attacks on Christianity, in critics who assaulted their erstwhile tormentors. They were so shortsighted that they did not see that, if Christianity—the perfection of Judaism—fell, their religion must also fall. They were so apathetic that they did not oppose criticism. Hence the Christian foe of criticism is the more human; those who fought criticism did so because they saw its challenge as a matter of concern for mankind. Meanwhile the Jews felt secure in their egoism. If they did nothing against Christianity it was because they lacked the creative strength which such a battle required. The struggle against Christianity was possible only for a Christian, because only he had grasped the meaning of consciousness. The Jew, however, was far too involved in the petty details of his law to even think about the problem of man's essence. He could not share in the fight against Christianity because he did not even know what the fight was about. Every religion is a form of hypocrisy because it makes man worship that which he is himself, but a spark of the real man remained. It made the Christian fight for freedom, while the Jews in their narrowness remained without consequence for history and mankind, a capricious sect living on the sidelines of history.

Bauer then contrasted Jewish and Christian 'jesuitism'.[66] Whereas Jewish jesuitism was only 'animal cunning',[67] Christian jesuitism was the hellish labour of spirit fighting for freedom. When the Jewish casuist, the rabbi, debated whether an egg laid on the Sabbath may be eaten, this was pure farce, the contemptible consequence of religious pettiness. Christians were superior because their lack of freedom was all-pervasive and must lead inevitably to full freedom. Jews stood much lower and were, therefore, less able to be free. Christianity was conceived when, in a weak moment, 'the manly spirit of Greek philosophy and classic culture embraced lustful Judaism'.[68] After giving birth to the results of that union, Judaism turned its back on it, while Christianity remembered and loved 'the magnificent form of godless, worldly philosophy'.[69] If Christianity was more adept in its inhumanity to man this was due to its ability to grasp the real essence of man. Judaism, which remained tied to religious obligations, family, tribe and nation, i.e. to specific human interests, never recognised the universal essence of man. Enlightenment, therefore, had its real roots in Christianity. Because Christianity had such a comprehensive conception of man, it could resist all attacks on its inhumanity. Christian teaching of freedom and equality was so profound that it was difficult to challenge, although its concept of love, because it sprang from religion, could bring about for unbelievers exclusion by hatred, persecution, sword, and pyre.

There were enlightened Jews before there were enlightened Christians because it was easy for them—all they had to do was to give up their law—but 'the Jew gives nothing to mankind when he turns away from his narrow law; the Christian who gives up his Christian essence gives mankind everything'.[70] It was untrue to suggest that Jews influenced the enlightenment of the eighteenth century; their achievements were far below those of Christian critics and represented no more than a reflection of what these had stimulated. Jews could claim emancipation only because the time was ripe for all to claim it. To suggest that they had initiated demands for general emancipation by their claims was a ridiculous exaggeration. Jews were not leaders, but merely followers of progress. But Bauer also insisted that equality and freedom could not be granted or given, they had to be fought for. He offered an extended discussion on the inevitability of a process which led from Christianity to criticism and liberated self-consciousness, a process which also showed that 'Christianity stood high above Judaism, the Christian high above the Jew, and his capacity to be free was very much greater than that of the

Jew'.[71] If Jews wanted to be free, it did not follow, however, that they had to become Christians. This would merely mean exchanging one privilege for another. Some Jews deluded themselves that they could gain advantage through baptism, but baptism did not make a Jew free and even if all Jews were baptised, they would add nothing to Christianity. It was, in any event, too late for that. To be free, the Jews must accept a Christianity in dissolution, i.e. criticism, free humanity. They must relinquish the chimerical privilege of their nationality, their fantastic, groundless law, they must deny their Jewish essence and break with the ultimate religion, to the perfection of which they had contributed nothing. The Christian needed to take but one step to overcome his religion. It was harder for the Jew to achieve freedom.

THE IMPACT OF BAUER

In spite of his prolific output and inordinate claims, Bauer remained without any real influence on the theology and philosophy of his time;[72] in particular the radical writers, including Strauss, Feuerbach, Ruge and eventually, and most dramatically, Karl Marx, turned away from him. Bauer was described as the last theologian who, 'precisely because he was not free of the faith he attacked, pursued theology with theological fanaticism'.[73] Ruge's view that Bauer negated rather than criticised and that he had misunderstood the social and political character of human existence was underlined by Marx's critique of his essays on the Jewish question. Bauer's concepts of 'self-consciousness' and 'mass' were finally rejected in the *Holy Family* as 'a finite, anthropological subjectivity with claims to absolute significance'.[74] Accordingly there was little response to Bauer's essays from non-Jewish quarters.[75] The situation was very different for the Jews who considered Bauer's essays to be a new threat in their struggle for emancipation. As they saw it, Bauer's premise was not the traditional animosity towards Jews; he disclaimed prejudice and did not appear to be motivated by personal advantage.[76] Second,

Bauer, both by reputation as a theologian and by the apparent range of his sources, spoke with an authority on Judaism which impressed all but the most learned. Third, Bauer's position as a leading radical, coupled with the public sympathy he had gained over his dismissal from the University of Bonn, suggested that his views might be unduly influential. Fourth, Bauer had raised the same critical questions as Spinoza on the meaning of Jewish law. Like Spinoza, he denied its relevance and like Spinoza he suggested that it could have meaning only in a national context. Hence his attack was seen as a threat by those committed to Jewish law and by those fighting for the recognition of Jews as German nationals. Finally and most significantly, to attack the Jews, Bauer had made effective use of many of the arguments which were currently being used within the Jewish community about the need for reform. As Nathan Rotenstreich has pointed out, it was mainly 'the chief spokesman of the reform movement [who] rushed into print to refute Bauer's views'.[77]

Bauer's reception in the Jewish press was at once respectful and hostile. Thus the editor[78] of the *Israelit des neunzehnten Jahrhunderts* reproduced in his paper parts of Bauer's original essay from the *Deutsche Jahrbücher*, after introducing the author as a member of 'the eccentric left of the Hegelian School'[79] who were characterised by 'a fanaticism of dialectics'. The author 'storms against every thing that does not fit into the scheme of his fanatic dialectic. Past and present are equally damned. All history is blasphemy, Christianity, Judaism, in fact all religions are a denial of morals, a mockery of humanity, the work of deceptive sophistry and hypocrisy because they contradict their philosophical principles'.[80]

After presenting long excerpts from Bauer, Hess published his own critique in two issues[81] which we can summarise briefly as follows:

1 Since Bauer wants Christianity no more than he does Judaism, he does not regard his arguments to be about a *Jewish* question. Why then should a Jewish weekly consider it? Because the reality is such that Christians can laugh at Bauer, whereas Jews are saddened because lack of civil rights is their reality.

Bauer, at the same time scolding and comforting, says that Jews cannot be oppressed because in their own view they are nothing, and a nothing cannot be oppressed. Yet we are oppressed as human beings and always have been.

Bauer claims that Judaism is an illusion, an error. He also claims that Christianity is a progressive development of Judaism. How can the development of an error be progress? Christianity believed that it had brought salvation to mankind, but it obviously had not, so how can Jewish resistance to it have hindered progress?

2 Hess was offended by Bauer's description of the Jews as 'orientals', and argued that since Judaism, Islam and Christianity all originated in the East they must all be 'oriental'.

3 Hess then attacked Bauer's concept of Jewish law. He quoted Hegel's *Encyclopädie der philosophischen Wissenschaften* where the master had stated that 'religion is the means by which truth comes to general consciousness'. Only that which is in man can reach consciousness, hence the Mosaic revelation served only to bring to consciousness what already lay in the minds of the Israelites. It was intended to unfold the Israelites' moral life according to the demands of time and place. Wherever man's development is furthered by law, there will also be provisions for an evolution of the law, so that moral progress will be continuous.

4 Pure Mosaism, as taught by Moses and the prophets, had no other purpose than to make the Israelite into a man, hence some biblical laws were abrogated when they were shown to be outdated, without, however, attacking the underlying spirit. Although Bauer is right in his comments on the Talmud, Jews see it as a true, if anachronistic, element in the evolution of their law, because it was itself, in its time, an instrument for the reform of biblical law.

5 Bauer shows 'an unequalled lack of knowledge', 'a total ignorance'[82] of present-day Judaism. He does not know that talmudic views 'have long since been eliminated from the consciousness of all Jews,[83] that Jews regard the land which offers them protection as the fatherland, and that Jews are actively interested in all questions of national welfare and national

freedom. He knows nothing of the great patriotism of the emancipated Jews of Holland, France and Belgium. Since he knows nothing of all this, 'we have to suffer the barb of his dialectic, which, based on assumptions, condemns us as narrow-minded, separatist Jews'.[84]

Hess ended his polemic by asserting his belief in evolution, the gradual achievement of perfection, while 'those who take up positions inappropriate to their time, who want to free themselves by crude opposition—and such there have been amongst the dreamy youth of all time—would be mocked and rejected by their contemporaries'.[85]

Six months later[86] Hess published a long interview of one of his correspondents with Bauer, part of which deserves to be quoted at length because it conveys a good idea of the man and his views.[87]

A few days ago I was with Bruno Bauer to discuss your article on his 'Die Judenfrage' with him. It is curious that scholars, no matter how advanced they are in their scientific and academic disciplines, no matter how much they can detach themselves from their subjective needs and attitudes, when it comes to their personal habits almost always suffer from subjective peculiarities which defy all common sense. Thus I found Bauer in his room, which serves a threefold purpose as visiting-living room and study,[88] wrapped in such a cloud of smoke that no matter which way I looked I saw nothing but smoke; a locomotive could have been driven by it. The critic remained hidden for a long time, and his presence could be ascertained only from his invitation, 'Do come in.' At last a window was opened and the smoke drifted away and the man was revealed who with his pen destroyed a structure that took 1,800 years to build. He is a haggard, studious man of middle stature with high forehead, sharp eyes and fair hair. Generally his appearance is not very inviting, but it improves somewhat in conversation: his expressions are precise and his demeanour is very confident and self assured. He is not particularly industrious but manages cleverly to live on his writing. Since we were already acquainted, I was well received. Regarding your article which I had sent him in advance, he acknowledged the popularisation of a complex presentation of the Jewish question, which is more than he could say for other reviews of his critique of emancipation, but stressed immediately that you had no more countered his arguments than any other anti-critic. He particularly objected to your accusation that he was prejudiced against the Jews.

He had defended the Jews in his pamphlet on the Bavarian Parliament because truth forced him to do so; but in his essay he had to explain facts, and the explanation of facts led him to concepts from which were derived arguments and results which he recorded in 'Die Judenfrage'. He was, he maintained, a critic and had nothing to do with prejudice; in any event arguments were not prejudices. Besides, he continued, he had, both here and elsewhere, been just as critical about the Christian religion and offended the antiquated leaven of Christian theological feeling. I have come, he said, to explain facts by their nature and history, but not to flatter a prejudice which I have never entertained. If we look at the history of religions and their principles we find that every religion is a caste system which excludes all opposing castes from its privileges, whose rights it denies and must deny. As long as man is religious he is only a partial man, not a real man. Religion is constantly challenging true humanity, which, as long as man thinks, stands armed against religion which rails against humanity as long as man only feels, i.e. as long as he does not illuminate and clarify his feelings with thoughts, and eventually elevates them to pure thought. The time will and must come where this oppression will disappear in one state, when true humanity will ascend the throne. This state will in both friendly and hostile ways demonstrate to other states how man can be a real, whole man all over the world. Just as now there are states which are democratic, others which are republican and yet others which are only absolutist, so there will be a purely humanitarian state whose example all other states will sooner or later follow.

The interviewer then reported at length (nine out of twelve columns) what *he* said to Bauer, inviting the editor (and his readers) to 'imagine' Bauer's replies. The interview lasted 'several hours', during which two further points made by Bauer were recorded. The interviewer had challenged Bauer's view of Jewish separatism by insisting that it applied only in relation to Gentiles, whose 'religious conception of God differs qualitatively from that of Israel'. Since Christians and Jews shared the same basic concepts, Bauer's analysis of Jews in Christian states was wrong. Bauer replied that history suggested otherwise—Judaism and Christianity had fought each other as long as they existed together, which suggested that they did differ in their basic views on the absolute. The interviewer rejected this reply, arguing that there had also been continuous conflict *within* Christianity between different denominations, and that if Bauer wanted to use history, he would also have to explain why Jews had been involved in the civil and political life of so many Christian states and not in non-Christian states.

As a final attempt to convince Bauer, the interviewer argued: if he were to accept Bauer's thesis that Christians, as a different caste from the Jews, *had* to withhold emancipation from them, what would happen if the situation were reversed? Would the Jews be right in withholding emancipation from Christians? Bauer replied that the situation did not permit a simple reversal. Christians remained superior to Jews because they had made the all-important declaration that God is man. The interviewer interjected that this idea was already implicit in the Old Testament statement that God breathed his spirit into man and that Christians, in any case, did not say that God is man but that Jesus (i.e. one man) is God: 'He looked at me as though he were surprised by this argument; tried to evade the question and made other interesting observations on the Jewish question which I might report on some future occasion'.[89]

Mendel Hess returned to the challenge of Bauer's 'Die Judenfrage' when Gotthold Salomon published his polemic against Bauer[90] in a long review spread over four issues. This contains an introduction on the relationship of Judaism to philosophy which deals especially with the Hegelian left, and is therefore of considerable interest.[91]

When Kant's system dominated philosophy, Hess argued, and its rationalism was uppermost in Christian theology, the Jewish question was debated accordingly. Christianity was seen as a religion of reason (*Vernunftreligion*), as the purest manifestation of moral consciousness, and its mission as the removal of all separatist and nationalist elements in Mosaism. Dogmas in the New Testament were explained away or described as accommodations to the religious views of the time, which more enlightened periods could reject. In this context the capacity of the Jews to be granted civil and political rights were made dependent on whether Jews could rid themselves of any nationalist element which isolated them from fellow-citizens and debarred them from citizenship of a state based on a universal humanitarianism. Jews responded to this position by arguing that Judaism and Christianity were built on the same foundations, that neither the Old Testament nor the Talmud were contrary to pure morality and that Jews were not isolating themselves by their ritual law, but used it as an instrument for increasing their religious awareness and as a symbol of the historical processes through which God manifested himself to man.

A fundamental change was brought about by Hegel with his idealism and pantheism. While Hegel tried to adjust his philosophy to Christian dogma, either from conviction or in deference to the church, his disciples saw the contradiction and rejected a peaceful covenant between religion and philosophy, since the two were diametrically opposed. For Hegel's disciples, truth was philosophy, reason, self-consciousness. Religion was error, fantasy, a product of the emotions and of anthropomorphic imagination. Leftist Hegelians went even further. They saw in Christianity the alienation of man from himself, the denial of everything physical and sensual, a contradiction of humanity, political freedom and independence of spirit.

Hegel constructed reality from spirit and had to do the same with history. If life is the evolution of divine self-consciousness, both in history and in historical religions, then the religion of the greatest self-consciousness (i.e. the latest) is the closest approximation to true religion. Thus Hegel saw Christianity as the mission of Judaism to the heathen. It was therefore an offspring of Judaism, albeit a superior one. This was how Bauer analysed the relationship. Bauer's position is therefore on the left of Hegelian philosophy.

There were five ways of dealing with the critique of the Hegelian left:

1 Disproving Hegel's basic concept. This would be difficult because Hegel's system was not based on mathematical certainties but on probabilities. Thus, for example, Schelling's attacks on Hegel had no effect on Hegelians.

2 Attacking left-wing Hegelians by showing that the Hegelian right made possible a synthesis of religion and philosophy. If this were to be done, Bauer could be refuted by demonstrating that Jewish-Christian views on the God–world relationship are the same.

3 Arguments which begin with a Christian premise could be invalidated by showing that there is no uniform Christian concept; hence a Christian position could be held as the opposite of a Jewish one.

4 If Christian moral teaching is made the focus, then it could be shown that historical events which went side by side with these refute their moral influence.

5 If Bauer is refuted on details it can then be argued that, if his evidence is wrong, his conclusions cannot be right and his basic assumptions must be rejected.

The editor of the *Allgemeine Zeitung des Judentums*, the most important and most popular Jewish newspaper in Germany, was deeply shaken when Bauer's article first appeared.[92] Because he was ill at the time, Ludwig Philippson promised to publish a separate pamphlet 'to disentangle Bauer's web and attempt a complete refutation'. In the meantime he complained that Bauer's method of criticism treated all things as if they were dead or inanimate, that he forgot that he was dealing with a world of people, their feelings and their thoughts. He warned Bauer that his critical acumen was itself becoming a passion and that he was wholly negative in his views. The promised pamphlet never appeared. Philippson explained in the following year that 'the eternal polemics wearied him'. Instead he contented himself with long reviews of the replies by Gustav Philippson, Abraham Geiger and Samuel Hirsch.[93]

Der Orient and its important Literaturblatt[94] remained cool in the Bauer dispute. The editor regaled readers with little pieces of gossip about it and carried a few reviews of some of the replies published. The most important reviews were those by Hermann Jellinek, himself a radical, who accepted Bauer's basic premise but wholly rejected his argument.[95] Jellinek's views are of interest because they show some similarities to those of Karl Marx. This is most apparent from his review of Gustav Philippson's polemic against Bauer[96] in which the young reviewer explained how Philippson ought to have criticised Bauer. Jellinek began with the change in speculative philosophy from the 'ought' of Kant and Fichte as the equivalent of 'is' to a point where only that which is real is seen as rational. Judaism was unlucky when the Hegelian system assigned it a place between two worlds, i.e. the point where the orient with its dull, natural religions left the world stage and the spirit of the occident began to dawn. Yet in his philosophy of history Hegel contradicted himself by assigning a different place to Judaism. Hence those who fought for Jewish emancipation were wrong to appeal to Jewish history instead of attacking the principle of the Christian state. An opponent of Bauer should examine the church–state relationship which Hegel had suggested, to disprove the assumption that the state must be Christian, because it is precisely from Hegel's system that a conclusion can be worked out that it is not the task of the state to ensure that man is enrolled as 'a citizen of heaven' (*Himmelsbürger*), but merely to ensure that an individual is capable of being a member of the state (i.e. a citizen).[97]

Bauer had argued that Jews had confined themselves to trade and had not contributed to any other social activity. This, said Jellinek, should also have been dealt with by reference to Hegel. Hegel had always insisted that the state was an organism consisting of individuals. Since every individual, i.e. every citizen, has needs, this system of needs, like the family, is a basis of the state and in the system of needs lay the division of labour of civil society. Needs place people into positions, and these positions (*Stände*) are divided into 'substantial, reflective and general'. If a person adopts his trade as his (reflective) position, then he works in a social context and his work, therefore, has a moral basis; i.e. in trading, the Jews are working for society. Bauer's attack on the Talmud, Jellinek continued, should have been answered by showing it to have been a stage in the developmental process of Jewish consciousness. Jellinek ended his review by stating that Bauer, 'the youngest of the young Hegelians', had misunderstood Judaism, had no real knowledge of the literature of Judaism and was entirely destructive.

The debate on Bruno Bauer's 'Die Judenfrage' continued to occupy the German-Jewish press for years. While the Hegelian element gradually disappeared, its theological and historical features continued to concern many writers, especially when the rabbinical conferences in Brunswick in 1844 and 1845 tried to resolve many of the issues which the Reform movement had made the substance of its critique of traditional Judaism.[98] If the Jews over-reacted to Bauer's critique, the volume and intensity of the debate certainly misled Bruno and Edgar Bauer into overestimating its importance. Bauer had no influence at all on the legislative processes in Germany[99] and his essay would most probably have sunk into oblivion had not Karl Marx used it as a springboard for his analyses of the relationship between state and religion and the nature of Judaism.

Bauer returned to the Jewish question twenty years later, as a leading conservative historian. In this book he described Jews as 'white Negroes' whose racial characteristics made conversion to Christianity or spiritual baptism impossible.[100] He died a forgotten man, whose life work was wasted and in the main rejected, even by so generous a person as Friedrich Engels.[101] Although Bauer denied an anti-Jewish bias all his life,[102] Ludwig Philippson was probably right when he described him as 'the real father of anti-semitism',[103] because Bauer was one of the first intellectuals to put forward the thesis that the Jews were *racially* incompatible with the German people.

CHAPTER VIII

The Marxian Response

THE CRITIQUE OF RELIGION

Marx's famous statement that 'the criticism of religion is the premise of all criticism' is unambiguous as an assertion about the fundamental importance of a critique of the *role* of religion, but it leaves us with considerable difficulties concerning the Marxian concept of the *nature* of religion. He appeared to have accepted the sharp distinction which Kant, Fichte and Spinoza drew between morality and religion and argued that, while the former was based on the autonomy of the human spirit, the latter was based on its heteronomy. While morality was rational, religion represented 'the sanctity and inviolability of subjective belief'.[1] The extensive literature on Marx and religion does not really go far enough in elucidating Marxian views on religion.[2] For we need not only a much more sensitive appraisal of the distinction between morality and religion, but also a systematic analysis of the analytic distinction which Marx may or may not have made between religion as a category and Christianity as the typification of such a category. There also remains the problem of determining the extent to which Marx's use of the concept of religion owes its origins to the relatively undifferentiated ideas of the enlightenment period on the one hand and to the Hegelian philosophical tradition on the other.[3]

A comprehensive critical appraisal of the Marxian view of

religion has not yet been attempted. Such an appraisal would have to go much further than anything that, to my knowledge, has yet been written. Not surprisingly, Marxist scholars have tended to explicate a militant atheism from Marx's writings,[4] while Christian scholars have tended to soften the Marxian critique by acknowledging the justice of Marx's rejection of Christianity as the willing and active collaborator in the oppression and exploitation of the lower social classes,[5] or by trying to deduce some evidence of a positive regard for Christianity in Marx's comments on the revolutionary role of Luther,[6] or other positive observations.[7]

A number of issues would need to be studied systematically before a really authoritative summary of Marx's critique of religion could be attempted. That such an attempt is important can best be argued by suggesting that Marx represents an important stage of transition from the philosophy to the sociology of religion. The difficulties that have to be overcome can be summarised under a number of headings.

1 For all his rejection of religion, Marx constantly refers to it, in whole essays, in paragraphs, in sentences and in casual phrases. To draw together every reference to religion would in itself be a herculean task, but it is essential precisely because it might help us to extract a more accurate definition of what Marx meant by religion.

2 Marx did not define 'religion', nor did he differentiate between form, content and organisation, as is done in contemporary sociology. Whether 'religion' as used by Marx can be used as an analytic category ought to be questioned, like the use of concepts such as 'crime' or 'disease', or as Sartre questioned the use of the term 'philosophy' in other contexts. In each instance the trend has been to concentrate on particular crimes or diseases or philosophies in order to achieve meaningful results.[8]

3 There is a difference between Marx and Engels, and Marx's views on religion after his association with Engels ought to be analysed separately, if only because, unlike Marx, Engels was interested in form and content problems.

4 While it is perfectly legitimate to evaluate the Marxian

critique of religion in the context of the Hegelian heritage, this cannot be regarded as a definitive analysis because Marx was influenced not only by contemporary philosophers and theologians but also, and particularly, by his and their experiences of and in a *German-Christian state*. Or, to put this another way, Marx's relationship to Hegel, Strauss, Feuerbach and Bruno Bauer was one reality, the other was that he was reared to a 'Protestant ethic' in a Christian state without the benefit of Max Weber.

In the context of this study, however, we must confine ourselves to one further aspect of the Marxian critique of religion. Marx produced one single comparative analysis in the field of religion, his essays 'On the Jewish Question', in which he contrasts some aspects of Christianity and Judaism. Most scholars so far have treated the critique of Christianity as a critique of religion and the critique of Judaism as a critique of 'capitalism' or 'commercialism', but Judaism is a religion, and I would venture to suggest that the Marxian critique of religion would be more meaningful sociologically if we take account of the comparative elements of the two religions which are contained in these essays.

Marx was not an atheist. To deny the existence of God was not only 'a negative recognition of God'; he regarded atheism as positively damaging, because this negation was the atheist's means of asserting the existence of man, while Marx was concerned only with man—man as the source, creator and recipient of all that pertained to man.[9] Questions concerning the relationships of man to transcendental beings were contemptuously assigned to theologians and were of no interest to Marx. His real interest lay in the social functions of religion, that is to say the way religion affects men's relationships to each other and the values they assign to such religiously determined relationships. Man, in this context, is 'unemancipated', he either 'has not found himself or has lost himself again'.[10] Marx thought that for man in that condition, religion had two distinct social functions. First, it made the world in which he lived meaningful, it offered an antidote to his natural fears and it offered him compensation, albeit an illusory compensation, for 'man's inhumanity to man'. For religion was 'consolation and justification' for and of man's condition. Yet here we have a typical instance of Marx himself using 'religion' when he means 'Christianity', even though his analysis of the Jewish religion, written almost at the same time, suggests quite different functions for 'religion'. Second, because religion gave a rational appearance to man's distorted relationships, Marx described it as a major instrument of social control.

For Marx, the apparent contradiction of a German *Jew* demanding emancipation in a German-*Christian* state was too good an example of religion being employed as an instrument of social control to be allowed to pass.[11] A state may have the right to impose control, but when it uses religion to do so, it forgoes its own authority and subjects itself to an altogether different one. A state, as a state, must not deny any citizen the right to political emancipation, because the citizen in turn acknowledges the right of the state, but not of religion, to exercise control. This issue is the essence of Marx's first essay on the Jewish question. If, however, the result of Marx's analysis demonstrates that religion, as a 'public' component in the state, has a social control function— as evidenced in the German-Christian state where Christianity has been incorporated into the formal social system—can a social control function also be demonstrated for Judaism, a 'pariah' religion, a religion that is explicitly rejected in the formal power structure?

Before attempting to answer this question, we must first briefly glance at both the sources of Marx's concept of Judaism and his favourite mode of analysis at that time. In discussing the position of the Jew in the German-Christian state, Marx needed no definition of a Jew other than the category so described within that state.[12] For an analysis of Judaism, however, this was not enough. Marx needed a meaningful concept, but deliberately excluded both personal knowledge of the Bible and personal experience of Jews. Thus one need only consider Marx's extensive knowledge of the Bible,[13] which stands in striking contrast to the complete lack of any reference to biblical law. Equally, it is worth noting that the Jews Marx knew or knew of, quite apart from his rabbinic ancestors and relatives, were quite unlike the 'Jew' of Marx's essays, e.g. Spinoza, Moses Mendelssohn, Börne,

Heine, Eduard Gans, Dagobert Oppenheim, Moses Hess. Nor did
Marx make the slightest attempt at finding an empirical basis for
his 'real Jew'. Instead, he took the descriptions of his intellectual
predecessors from Kant to Bauer as absolutely authentic images of
Jews and Judaism, leaving us with the inescapable conclusion that
Karl Marx—the man who had just completed a brilliant critique
of Hegel, who had shown convincingly that Hegel had erred
because he had deduced real life from abstract ideas, because he
had failed to look for an empirical reality exactly as it was—that
same Marx was guilty of precisely the same methodological error
when it came to analysing Judaism. So that his accusation regarding Hegel's 'mystifications' must in our context also be applied
to Marx.

We have already considered in some detail the concepts of
Judaism on which Marx relied. Let us now try to recapitulate by
showing the line of thought that began with Kant and ended with
Marx, for the continuity is quite startling.[14]

The problem facing Kant in the period of enlightenment and
the search for a rational religion was that, while the basic dogmas
of Christianity, resurrection and life after death were not really
susceptible to 'rational' explanation, no such difficulty was
presented by the laws of the Old Testament. It was necessary
therefore to denigrate Judaism lest the primitive version of true
religion should prove to be more rational than the ultimate (i.e.
perfect) form. Kant did this by describing Jews as slaves of the
law and, what is perhaps even more significant, as 'a people
composed solely of merchants'.[15] Hegel in his early work
'analysed' the story of Abraham in order to deduce from it some
characteristics of the Jews. He pointed out that the Old Testament
shows no interest in the problem of life after death. 'The Jews'
drive for survival was directed toward material conditions of
being.'[16] Feuerbach further elaborated this interest in material
conditions by equating it with a lack of interest in 'higher' values,
described by him as Jewish egoism. Both Feuerbach and Bauer,
as we have seen, also abstracted the significance of Jewish law from
Jewish being by suggesting that the law was only something the
Jews refused to observe. Marx now completed the picture by

making Jewish egoism the essence of Judaism, the source of human greed.[17] We might say that there is here a notion of the continuity of Jewish self-imposed slavery first to the law (Kant), then to God (Hegel), to egoism (Feuerbach) and to money (Marx).

The method by which Marx achieved the final reduction of the Jew, to expose his 'real social significance', is the same he had employed so effectively in his *Critique of Hegel's Philosophy of Right*, the so-called 'transformative method of criticism',[18] the method which had enabled Marx to turn Hegelianism, which was standing on its head, back on its feet. This was accomplished by reversing subject and predicate, so that if, according to Hegel, reality is the appearance of the idea, then to Marx the idea is the appearance of reality. If for Hermes, religion makes man, then for Marx, man makes religion. If for Bruno Bauer, the secret of the Jew is in his religion, then for Marx, the secret of the religion is in the Jew. Finally, then, if for Kant (and indeed for most of Christian Western Europe) the Jew is a trader, then for Marx, *the trader is a Jew*.

Marx relied on phenomenological verification for his thesis. If the trader was a Jew in the consciousness of Western European society, then that was the reality—that was what the 'real' Jew was—with this reservation, however. Even if the image of the Jew could be shown to be objectively valid, such an image was still predicated on an idealised self-concept of Christian society. To that extent, therefore, Marx accused his critical predecessors of describing the 'real' Jew in a distorted—or better, idealistically conceived—society. Once this Christian society is itself subjected to the same vigorous critique, the Jew will appear no better, except in that he is a natural and proper constituent part of Christian society itself, rather than an 'eyesore' within it. At this level, Marx argued, an attempt to deny the Jew political emancipation would be entirely contradictory, an assertion of an idealised community rejecting one of its elements on objective grounds. Only so contradictory a structure as a 'Christian state', which by definition is an incomplete and therefore 'underdeveloped' state, could be guilty of such a flagrant act of self-deception.

Let us now return to the problem of demonstrating a social

control function for Judaism, a tolerated religion in Germany, without a role in the formal hierarchy of power. In the Marxian description of feudal society, we see that members of the various guilds, corporations and estates stand in a relationship to their interest-groups which go beyond the actual needs and interests of any one individual. Land for both peasant and landowner, authority for both aristocrat and civil servant, have meaning and value which transcend personal considerations. It is different for the trader. He owes loyalty neither to his calling nor to his colleagues. He can satisfy his needs by merely ensuring that he serves the needs of others. This sort of schema fitted in perfectly with Marx's conception of the Jew in feudal society. Inevitably, when the old order gives way to a period of transition, when feudalism disintegrates through revolution or through its own 'contradictions', the trader finds himself in a most fortunate position. For, no matter what changes are likely to occur, what will remain constant in a fluid situation are the immediate needs of the community; the trader, the key-link in the need-satisfaction chain, finds himself able to manipulate and exploit unstable conditions. To be able to manipulate means exercising power, and even if this power is neither recognised nor legitimated, it is real and will grow in proportion as the structure of the old order declines. This power represents informal social control. Marx was not interested whether this situation applied to all, some or no Jews; since he had 'transformed' Judaism into the trading process itself, he had shown that, while Christianity as embodied in the German-Christian state was an instrument of formal social control, Judaism, as embodied in the trader, exercised informal social control.

The conflicts which initiate the transition from feudal to industrial society are social conflicts and the religious categories that appear to be in opposition here are meaningless 'super-structures' which obscure the real issue. Sooner or later the state will have to relinquish its 'public' association with religion and institutionalise the growing social control forces in the trading processes. That is political emancipation in which religion is 'privatised' and the real dynamic forces in society create a new social structure which will still be far from perfect, but which must certainly include the Jew on equal terms.

What Marx had established, then, was not a critique of religion, but a critique of the *relations of religion* in social processes. Since he ignored the components of religion, he viewed it as a *social institution* in the state to which men relate as they were assumed to do with other social institutions. Hence the real substance of his critique would seem to be the existence of religion as a social institution, whereas he regarded it as more properly a private element in the life of the individual.

Accordingly, his solution to the problem of religion is presented here in two phases. Political emancipation is achieved when the state ceases to utilise religion in formal social control processes and replaces it by adopting informal processes of trade and industry (i.e. a feudal changes to a capitalist economy). Human emancipation is achieved when these control forces in turn give way to the only legitimate forces of control—man's inherent, but so far alienated, communal character, when the power implicit in social control no longer 'separates man from community, from himself and from other men'.

If Christian-feudal society projects man's human essence onto heaven and 'Judaised' civil society turns man's human essence inwards into an isolated and isolating egoism, then, to the extent that that is true, Marx succeeded in his critique of both systems and the means of control they employ to maintain themselves. The question that remains unanswered is why man should tolerate and even be content to live under such alienating conditions. Marx answers this question in his *Contribution to the Critique of Hegel's Philosophy of Right*, where the relations of religion to the individual are discussed.[19] For here, religion is an expression of as well as a protest against suffering, it is an opium for the people, trapped as they are in a 'vale of tears'. Although a detailed discussion of this aspect of the Marxian critique falls outside the scope of our discussion, enough has been indicated to enable us to summarise and briefly criticise Marx's analysis. The case against religion, for Marx, is threefold: that it distracts man from his real essence in this world (either upwards or inwards);

that while thus distracted he allows himself to be shamefully exploited and controlled, and that the consequent distracted, exploited and controlled man is thus deprived of his 'human essence', i.e. he has no autonomy and neither at the social nor the individual levels does he assume responsibility for his own destiny. In criticising this analysis, the following points ought to be made. First, that Marx provides no empirical evidence to support his arguments;[20] second, that, to the extent that what he claimed is true it is certainly not new, in fact it constitutes in its essentials (though not in its semantics) the prophetic critiques of *society* rather than of religion.[21] This is probably inherent in the essence of the Marxian critique which, as I have argued, is concerned with the relations of religion and not with religion. Not only does such an approach leave religion uncriticised, but beyond that, since all relations are social relations and faulty relations diagnose faulty social situations, it would certainly be possible to make a case *for* both Judaism and Christianity from the Marxian analysis, if for example we stipulated that, since both religions are predicated (though in rather different ways) on fundamental demands for community, and since the ideal-type Christian and Jewish communities are very close to Marx's own 'messianic' vision of human emancipation, the failures of both religions in their social relations are failures which leave the religious ideal untarnished and uncriticised. The relations of religion are in the last resort relations between men and cannot be equated with the 'essence' of religion. Third, and in much the same way, the fact that an object can be abused is not a criticism of the object but of the user or, better, abuser. There is ample evidence of man's ability to abuse his physical, emotional, social and religious environments. The real target of Marx's critique therefore is man himself, not the institutions he has created and all too often abused.

THE 'DEUTSCH-FRANZÖSISCHE JAHRBÜCHER'

In the foregoing section, indeed throughout this study, we are endeavouring to understand Marx's critique of Jews and Judaism in the intellectual and historical contexts in which it was written. Before going on to consider the actual essays, however, it might be worth while to look at them also in the somewhat narrower context of the *Deutsch-Französische Jahrbücher* in which they were published.[22]

The first and only issue of the *DFJB* runs to 237 pages. Although edited jointly by Arnold Ruge and Karl Marx, it carried no evidence of Marx's editorship.[23] The Introduction by Ruge (pp. 3–16) is pedestrian and 'mild' compared with most of the other contributions and is followed by an exchange of letters between contributors and Ruge (three letters from Marx to Ruge,[24] three from Ruge to Marx, an exchange of letters between Ruge and Bernays[25] and a singularly non-committal letter from Feuerbach to Ruge[26]). Although the Prussian and Austrian governments strongly resented the publication of the *DFJB* and exerted great pressure on France to expel its contributors, it is unlikely that the famous contributions of Marx and Engels were the cause of Prussian anger. Prussian charges of lèse-majesté and Metternich's fears that the book might get into Austria were related much more to other items[27] which we might look at briefly.

There was first the witty but insolent poem by Heine, 'Songs of Praise to King Ludwig', in which both the king and the Catholic church are subjected to bitter scorn (pp. 41–4). This is followed by a detailed documentation of the political scandal concerning the charges of high treason and lèse-majesté levelled against Dr Johann Jacoby when he sent his 'Four Questions' to Friedrich Wilhelm IV. The account is presented at length by Jacoby himself (pp. 45–70).[28] This is followed by Marx's 'Zur Kritik der Hegel'schen Rechts-Philosophie' (pp. 71–85) and Engels's 'Umrisse zu einer Kritik der national Oekonomie' ('Outline of a Critique of Political Economy') (pp. 86–114). Next came Moses Hess's 'Briefe aus Paris'[29] (pp. 115–25), in which Hess's ideas are much closer to those expressed by Engels than either of them stand to Marx.[30]

The next item is a report on and excerpts from the ministerial

conference in Vienna of 12 June 1834: a particularly strong attack
on Metternich which also attacked the complete impotence of the
various German Landtage. This was presented by Bernays
(pp. 126–48) and is followed by a highly emotional and somewhat
nationalistic poem, 'Treason', by Georg Herwegh, in which he
charged that in Germany, loyalty had become treason and treason,
loyalty (pp. 149–51). Engels's second contribution, a long-
winded but vigorous review of Carlyle's Past and Present, was
intended as a first instalment of a series on 'Die Lage Englands'[31]
(pp. 152–81), and this leads to Marx's reviews of Bauer's 'Die
Judenfrage' and 'Die Fähigkeit' (pp. 182–214).[32] The final contribution, again by Bernays, is a review of the German newspaper
world, 'Deutsche Zeitungsschau' (pp. 215–37).

It is difficult to believe that the volume which eventually found
its way to printer and public (however limited) corresponded in
many ways to the ideas Marx had wanted to implement.[33] It
must have been a severe disappointment to him that there was not
a single French contributor, that his co-editor turned out to be
very much less than either a radical or a philosopher, and that the
man he most wanted to involve, Ludwig Feuerbach, kept a cool
and disinterested distance from the entire project, even though
his impact on the more important articles is scarcely less than that
of Hegel. Marx would not have noticed the rather heavy
Schwermut (nostalgia) for Germany and all things German
which must have been an additional alienating factor for French
readers, since he himself was not entirely free of this sort of
exile's lament, but it cannot have escaped him that the contributions of Jacoby and Bernays, important as they might be today
to the historical researcher, were already dated and of relatively
little interest to a European public he was trying to attract.

We will of course never know whether Marx might have been
at all embarrassed by the fact that this particular publication,
which was destined to carry his fateful attack on Jews and Judaism,
was written predominantly by Jews or men of Jewish origin, all
of whom, since they had repudiated religion and were not
therefore 'Sabbath Jews', must necessarily have been 'everyday
Jews' or, in Marx's term, 'a contemporary anti-social element'

in society. Leaving aside the two poems, which must be evaluated at a different level, and discounting the topical items of Jacoby and Bernays, it would be right to describe the essays of Marx and Engels as the most substantial and the most important items in the issue. The difference between the two men is both instructive and illuminating. Marx towers not only above Engels but above all other contributors. The depth of his argument, the brilliance in style, his sharp wit and overall intellectual detachment characterise his writing. Even when he indulges in polemic, his words are chosen with care and his commitment is only occasionally allowed to break through his logic. He is above all sharp and concise, in marked contrast to the plodding style of Engels, but this is as much a product of his arrogance as of his skill. Engels builds his arguments with care and patience, using and acknowledging every reference, every item, every detail, even if his sole purpose was to demolish it. No less than twelve important English contributors to the science of political economy are discussed, and in each case arguments are pitted against observed and recorded realities in the English factory system and class structure. The same applies to his review of Carlyle. Engels is both laudatory and critical, but always in relation to what he knows and has experienced in the English social situation. When he attacks Carlyle's views on religion, though no less radical than Marx, he pays tribute to Feuerbach and Bruno Bauer as his mentors, perhaps being even a little chauvinistic about the importance of 'German philosophy' and too contemptuous of 'English empiricism', but building his case exclusively on what he has learnt and seen in books and in life. Not so Karl Marx. Important as Feuerbach is to Marx's own critiques, he does not refer to him by name and for all the painful situations to which the unemancipated Jew in Germany was subjected (some of which, as we shall see, even find a place in the *DFJB*), the Marxian critique or, better, destruction of Judaism, never moves outside the abstract conceptualisations of his philosophical predecessors. In these two long essays, Engels savagely criticises the plight of the English working class and the indolence of the ruling classes. He then ends his second essay thus: 'The condition of England is of immeasurable importance for history and for all other countries; for socially England is far ahead of all other countries' (p. 181). Marx, on the other hand, analyses the Jewish question briefly though no less critically, and concludes: 'The social emancipation of the Jew is the emancipation of society from Judaism' (p. 214).

In chapter VI we discussed Marx's refusal to publish Hess's essay 'Ueber das Geldwesen' and the probable reasons for it. It ought therefore to be noted that, if a case can be made for showing the influence of Hess's essay on Marx's later 'Economic and Philosophical Manuscripts', one should also draw attention to the apparent affinity in thought and language between Hess's essay and Engels's contributions to the *DFJB*. Thus, like Hess, Engels wrote of competition turning men into predatory animals who devour each other (p. 92), of the alienation of man through *Selbstverschacherung* (p. 99) and, above all, of the effects of the right to property, 'because private property isolates everyone in his raw individuality' (p. 101). It would be fair to say that, similar as Hess's and Engels's ideas are in many respects, Engels presents them more academically, more coherently and more effectively than Hess, and this might well have determined Marx's editorial decision to accept one and reject the other.

Finally we might look particularly at the place of the Jew in the *DFJB*, for not only were most of its contributors Jewish, but Jews are referred to on several pages apart from Marx's essays on the subject. One point of interest in this area again refers to the difference between Marx and Engels.

Like Marx, Engels is concerned with trade, commerce and peddling. His 'Umrisse' set the tone in his first sentences: 'Political economy arose as a natural consequence of the expansion of trade, and with it, simple, unscientific peddling was displaced by a sophisticated system of authorised fraud, a complete science of acquisition' (p. 86).[34] Merchants, speculators and owners of landed property are subjected to bitter attacks, as well as the economists who rationalise and justify their activities. In his second article, Engels strongly supports Carlyle's attack on 'the gospel of Mammon', the religion that has replaced Christianity, in which the idea of a society is characterised by separation, isolation and competition of and between fellow human beings (p. 160). In other words, everything that Marx was to attack and criticise in civil society is anticipated here, except for one single feature. In neither article does Engels mention Jews or Judaism. Where Engels attacks facts and practices which he abhors, Marx concentrates his entire critique on a metaphysical abstraction called 'the Jew', whom he has equated with every facet of an emerging capitalist system.

Apart from the sophisticated philosophical material in the *DFJB* there are two 'stories' to illustrate the indignity and pettiness arising from the social and legal disenfranchisement of the Jews. Since neither of these are likely to find their way into the general literature on Marx and Marxism, we might mention them here, more particularly because one emanates from Arnold Ruge, the man who was to describe Marx as 'an insolent Jew',[35] while the other stands in marked contrast to the Marxian analysis of the Jewish question. In his letter to Bernays (June 1843, pp. 31–4), Ruge relates the following to illustrate how even in Saxony there is some progress. 'The Jews are bad Christians and therefore do not share the liberties of the Saxon people; they have no civil rights and there are many things they may not do that those who are baptised can do.'[36] In Dresden there was a park called Brühl's Garden which was surrounded by high walls and had only one entrance, at which a sentry controlled admission. The park was open to the public except on those occasions when members of the royal court used it. But Jews and dogs were never admitted. One day a general's wife arrived with a dog in her arms, but the sentry would not let her enter. Furiously, she complained to her husband, who issued an order lifting the restrictions on dogs. Thereupon the Jews complained and asked for equal rights with dogs. The general was greatly embarrassed. To rescind his instruction admitting dogs would incur the wrath of his wife and her friends, while the Jews would create a great rumpus if the equality with dogs which they had enjoyed throughout the middle ages were to be denied them in the nineteenth century. The general on his own responsibility decided to allow admission to Jews as well as dogs. This caused considerable indignation in the populace, but the old general stood his ground.

The second story, by Bernays, is contained in his 'Deutsche Zeitungsschau', a vigorous, though appallingly written, polemic in which he attacks in turn the Bavarian, Prussian and Baden peoples for their impotent and inconsequential Landtage. He mocks them not only because these representative bodies have no legislative powers, but also because even some of their 'liberal' representatives appear at times more reactionary than the conservative government ministers. Thus in the Baden Landtag debate on Jewish emancipation, the minister of justice, Christof Franz *Trefurt*, argued in favour, while the liberal opposition and its most noted figure, Johann Adam von Itzstein, argued against.[37] Bernays is particularly contemptuous of the people of the grand duchy of Baden, who had just celebrated the twenty-fifth anniversary of the constitution granted to them by Grand Duke Karl Ludwig Friedrich on 22 August 1818, which severely restricted the rights of Jews in Baden.[38] To celebrate the anniversary, the citizens organise and perform a drama which is performed with 'mediocrity, without art and without enthusiasm'. The nobility opposed to the dominant, reactionary head of the Baden government, Freiherr Friedrich Karl *Blittersdorf*, therefore decide to produce their own play 'The Expulsion of the Jew—Baron von Haber', which was more likely to produce political unrest than the dreary performance of the citizens. The 'play' described by Bernays turned out to be an actual *cause célèbre* which took place in Baden at about that time and which is recounted fairly accurately, though with some unsubstantiated embellishments. It begins with a tender scene between the Grand-Duchess Sophie, her lover Baron *Moritz von Haber* and their bastard child, 'whose black curls convinced the Jewish man that his dark, oriental blood was not averse from mixing with the paler, Germanic sap'. The officers of the palace guard resent having to present arms to the Jew, insult him, and provoke a duel between Lieutenant *Göler* and a Russian who defends the Jew in which both are killed. This leads to great fury among the officer corps and the citizenry. They assemble that night, storm and wreck the baron's house (and, while they are about it, a few other Jewish houses as well) and the baron has to flee for his life. No action is taken against the rioters, and Grand-Duke *Leopold* goes for a drive with his wife to show the populace that all is well (pp. 217–21). In fact this is more or less what happened. In 1842 or 1843 Baron Moritz von Haber, a member of one of Germany's leading banking families, had an amorous affair which led to a duel between Baron Julius von Göhler and a Russian cavalry officer, Werefkin, in which both were killed. Some months later Haber himself fought a duel over this affair with a Spanish nobleman, Uria de *Sarachaga*. There was a riot in Karlsruhe in which Haber's house was invaded and wrecked and he fled to Paris, where he remained.[39]

If we now summarise this brief review of the main contributions to the *DFJB*, we see that they undermine the main Marxian thesis on Jewish emancipation. Marx had argued that Jews had a right to emancipation in spite of their 'anti-social' role in society, because the whole of society was adopting their 'anti-social', i.e. commercial, practices. Ruge's story illustrates how Jews are subjected to indignities and restrictions which have nothing to do with the social functions of Jews and which go well beyond the restrictions which, Bauer had claimed, applied to all. Engels's essays demonstrate at length the development of both commercial and industrial capitalism without a single reference to Jews as instigators of those processes and finally Bernays's story is the antithesis of the Marxian argument. For here at the centre of the story is a Jew who is the embodiment of everything Marx attacks. A financier, a man who in a deeply anti-semitic environment has achieved power and status through his money, yet it is his Jewishness which evokes the hostility of both nobility and citizenry—the conflict is racial not social, and for all his money and the power that goes with it the Jewish capitalist is forced to leave the country.

ON 'DIE JUDENFRAGE'

It is quite easy to see why many scholars have expressed the view that Marx was not really interested in Judaism, in the first essay at any rate.[40] For there is considerable emphasis throughout on the intention to look at the place of religion in the state, to extend the discussion beyond Judaism to Christianity, indeed to all religion. The criticism of religion is the starting-point of all criticism,[41] though here, as elsewhere, it is sharply reduced to a mere category among categories. In this sense, however, the Jewish question 'is resolved into the general question of the age'.[42]

Bauer asked whether Jews had a right to demand political emancipation. Marx inverts the question—'has political emancipation the right to ask the Jew to abolish Judaism—or man to abolish religion?'[43]

Marx quotes Gustave de Beaumont, Tocqueville and Thomas Hamilton to show that in the United States religion persists as an essential element, even though wholly divorced from the state.[44] The problem thus becomes a general problem of the relationship of complete political emancipation to religion.[45] The need to go beyond Judaism is made explicit: 'We express in human terms the contradiction between the state and a particular religion, *for example Judaism*, by showing the contradiction between the state and particular secular elements, between the state and religion in general' (my italics).[46]

The need to generalise is continued: 'The political emancipation of the Jew or the Christian—of the religious man in general—is the emancipation of the state from Judaism, Christianity and religion in general'.[47]

If the malaise is general, then so is the cure, in which 'man emancipates himself politically from religion by passing it from public to private law'. He creates a process which aims at 'the separation of man into Jew and citizen, Protestant and citizen, religious man and citizen—this *is* the process of political emancipation'.[48]

The importance of the first essay lies in the ideas which are explored here on a number of fundamental issues. Using religion as his key variable, Marx constructs a theoretical model of the state in 'logical' evolution and demonstrates how this is borne out historically by reference to different periods and different countries. He argues a case for the incomplete nature of the French revolution and the American War of Independence, and concludes that these revolutions must go further to achieve an ultimate position of perfection on a continuum that moves from feudal society via political emancipation to human emancipation. It is clear, therefore, that the essay contains in rudimentary, but unmistakable, form some of the most fundamental concepts in the Marxian system, namely:

1 the criticism of civil, i.e. bourgeois, society;
2 a materialist approach to history;
3 the analysis of 'the rights of man' as inadequate;
4 the call for a revolution more profound than the earlier ones;
5 the vision of a 'perfect' society.

It is the misfortune of the Jews that these substantive ideas should have been developed under a heading 'On the Jewish Question', which has thereby given credence and circulation to his second essay, which is incomparably weaker and less convincing.

Let us now look briefly at the main arguments which are important in our context because they make clear why Marx, who, as we shall see, held such a wholly negative view of Jews and Judaism, nevertheless argued strongly for the Jews' right to political emancipation. It will become apparent, however, that it is not quite correct to argue as Avineri and McLellan have done that Marx championed political emancipation for Jews. It would be more correct to say that the Marxian concept of political emancipation made it impossible to exclude any category in civil society from it.[49]

In his discussion of the relationship between the state and religion, Marx wholly rejects the claim of Hermes and Bauer that there can be a 'Christian' state. Such a 'so-called Christian state' is not a political state, it is 'no state at all',[50] as is shown by its characteristics, which Marx describes as follows:

(a) it is the Christian negation of the state;

(b) it is an uncompleted state using Christianity to complete and sanctify its imperfection;

(c) it needs the Christian religion to complete itself;

(d) it has a political attitude towards religion and a religious attitude towards politics;[51]

(e) it is in its own consciousness an 'ought' whose realisation is impossible;

(f) it is a state where alienation, not man, prevails; where only the king matters, but he differs from other men and relates himself to God. His relationship to the people is based on faith.[52]

A more advanced form of state is the 'constitutional state' (as in France) where the state as such has 'emancipated itself from religion' but which continues to be dominated to some extent by 'the religion of the majority'. Since in such a state the relationship of the Jew to the state 'retains a semblance of religious opposition', political emancipation is incomplete.[53] There is no 'logical' justification for this argument. As Marx himself states, the key to civil society (i.e. political emancipation) is the regulation of relations through law,[54] a condition which was certainly fulfilled in France. What Marx was trying to resolve here is a problem raised by both Hermes and Bauer about the introduction of Sunday as a rest-day in France. When, during the debate on this, a deputy raised the question why a Christian rest-day should be introduced in a state which gave equal recognition in law to Judaism, the answer was that Sunday corresponded to the wishes (i.e. the religion) of the majority. Marx may have wanted to show that the debate 'proved' that religious differences were still in the awareness of the people, and that this would be valid, but not when the next 'higher' stage of state is the American state, where such religious discrepancies could equally well have occurred.[55]

Only in some of the United States does the state have no 'theological attitude to religion'. Here, therefore, there is complete political emancipation, and criticism becomes criticism of the political state. The need for such criticism is demonstrated by the persistence of religion within it, which, since it is a 'defect', shows that there must be something wrong in the state.[56] To demonstrate this thesis Marx moves from a consideration of the relationship between religion and the state to the problem of the relationship between the individual and the state. The secular state has liberated *itself* from religion, but it has not liberated man.[57] Man continues in his alienation because, although the secular state has abolished the distinctions between categories, 'distinctions of birth, social rank, education and occupation' between citizens, 'it does not thereby abolish the effect of these distinctions as they act on the citizenry'.[58] Marx appears to be too concerned with the Hegelian source of this observation to consider its full implications. The whole tenor of his discussion would suggest that, at this point, he might have drawn attention to the limitations inherent in state action, and to the need for man himself to overcome the effects of distinctions once they have been formally abolished by the state, as he did in fact by calling on the Jews to emancipate themselves.

The secular state in its emerging form Marx called 'civil society', and the outstanding characteristic of that society is that every man functions as a private individual: his motives are egoism, selfishness and personal need. Against this Marx posits the perfect state, the state where man is 'a communal being', his real essence.[59]

In the imperfect state, therefore, there is a constant tension between the political state and civil society. This is not a conflict between, but a conflict within, the citizen and the Jew, the citizen and the shopkeeper, the citizen and the landowner. It is a conflict between 'the living individual and the citizen'. In general terms, then (i.e. the secular version of the Jewish question), there is a conflict between 'the general interest and private interest . . . between the political state and civil society'.[60]

Nevertheless, since man in civil society acts at least partly as a 'species-being', political emancipation in the present world order is real (and essential) progress.[61]

Both Hermes and Bauer argued that, while it may be possible to grant Jews some civil rights, they cannot claim full equality or the rights of man because 'human nature has to efface itself' before the Jew's 'true and supreme nature'.[62] Marx therefore asks: 'What then are the rights of man?' Using the Declaration of the Rights of Man, Marx argues that the rights of man are the rights of egoistic man, of man in civil society. This conclusion effectively removes the Hermes/Bauer objection to granting Jews the rights of man.[63] More importantly, it leads Marx to the conceptualisation of historical models of three societies (past, present, future) which are so important to his intellectual development.

What needs to be explained, said Marx, is how 'political liberators' could attempt to create a political community 'by proclaiming the rights of egoistic man'. By doing that, the revolutionaries 'invert means and ends . . . they suffer an optical illusion of consciousness'.[64] The answer Marx offers is that the revolution must not be seen in terms of political state versus civil society, but in terms of feudal society versus civil society.

'In feudalism, elements of civil life such as property, family and occupation are raised into political categories, viz. lordship, caste and guilds. The individual's relation to the state, therefore, is expressed in terms of the relation of his status group to the state, which itself now represents the rulers and their servants, unconnected with the people.'[65]

The revolution shattered the estates, the corporations and guilds, it dissolved society into its 'basic elements', man, but selfish man, egoistic and unrestrained.

'In the new political state consisting of individuals, relations are regulated by law—where relations between feudal estates were regulated by privileges.' 'Man, as a member of civil society . . . is an individual separated from the community, withdrawn into himself, wholly preoccupied with his private interest and acting in accordance with his private caprice.' In this condition, 'the only bond between men is natural necessity, need and private interest, the preservation of their property and their egoistic persons.'[66]

Thus, although this process of political emancipation 'is a reduction of man', it also elevates him, in his role as citizen, 'to a moral person'. This process must now be completed to achieve the final goal, human emancipation, 'when the real individual man has absorbed into himself the abstract citizen; when as an individual man, in his everyday life, in his work and in his relationships, he has become a species-being; and when he has recognised and organised his own powers as social powers, so that he no longer separates his social power from himself as political power'.[67]

Marx's 'messianic vision' of a perfect society (which he abandoned soon afterwards) owes its 'ideology' to Feuerbach's anthropology. It is a conception which reads almost like an inverted version of the Freudian system. For Feuerbach the heathen represented natural man, that is, man in harmony with the objective reality of the material world which satisfies his needs. The Jew, by subjecting the material world to his egoism, deprives it of its objective essence and thereby alienates man from his world and from himself. The Christian, in an attempt to redress this imbalance, projects his true essence onto heaven, onto a divine figure, which means anthropologically that man knows his true essence but cannot live it. The essence of man here is an innate 'goodness', by which Feuerbach meant the ability of man to live in harmony with his needs and the objects which satisfy his needs, i.e. the opposite of the Freudian essence, which is a primeval, selfish, pleasure-seeking force, which seeks to subjugate rather than to harmonise.

Marx expressed this analysis in sociohistorical terms and, at this juncture, thought that, if the 'false consciousness' which has led man into 'Jewish' egoism could be overcome, then man would achieve the harmonious state of the heathen and, beyond that, the more sophisticated projection of his real essence as expressed spiritually in Christianity. In the result, however, Marx became increasingly interested in one facet of this problem, namely overcoming man's inclination to reduce his fellow-men into objects of his need-satisfaction, a conception which Marx sought to derive in the first instance from the utilitarian approach of Judaism as stipulated by Feuerbach.

ON 'DIE FÄHIGKEIT'

If Marx went to great lengths in his first essay to stress the generality of his approach by extending every argument from Jews to Christians to religious man, his approach in the second essay is very different, for here he is predominantly concerned with the 'real' Jew, though he also has something to say about money.

Marx's starting-point is the inability of Bauer to free himself from his 'theological' outlook. Bauer saw 'the ideal, abstract essence of the Jew, his religion, as his whole nature'. Marx wants 'to try to break with the theological formulation'. To do this, he considers Judaism not only as a religion, but more particularly as a social and historical phenomenon.[68]

Judaism has a 'special position' in the modern world, and the question of Jewish emancipation is, therefore: 'What special *social* element has to be overcome to dissolve (i.e. emancipate) Judaism?' The answer to such a question must lie not in the religion of the Jew but in his social role in society. For his social role will also explain his religion: 'Let us not seek the secret of the Jew in his religion but let us seek the secret of the religion in the real Jew', the famous prescription which was subsequently extended to all religions ('Man makes religion—religion does not make man'). 'What is the secular basis of Judaism? Practical need, self-interest. What is the worldly cult of the Jew? Bargaining. What is his worldly god? Money. Very well! Emancipation from bargaining and money, and thus from practical real Judaism would be the self-emancipation of our era.'

The social role of the Jew is the epitomisation of the selfish, money-seeking man. Beyond that he has no existence. As soon as 'the basis of bargaining is abolished', the Jew would cease to exist; 'his religious consciousness would dissolve like a dull mist'. Once the Jew recognises the futility of his social role, he would be working for general human emancipation. He would not, as Bauer claimed, still have to work through a superior stage of Christianity to eliminate 'human self-alienation'.

But why would the mere rejection of Judaism on the part of

the Jew help general human emancipation? Because the Jew's social role has been extended into the Christian world. The Jew has 'made money a world power' and thereby made 'the practical Jewish spirit . . . the practical spirit of Christian nations'. 'The god of the Jews has been secularised and has become the god of the world.'

'The bill of exchange is the Jew's actual god.'
'His god is only an illusory bill of exchange.'
'The chimerical nationality of the Jew is the nationality of the merchant, generally of the "Geldmensch".'

We have seen in the first essay how Christian (i.e. Western) nations evolved from feudal to civil society. Civil society is characterised by having as its main constituent selfish, egoistic man. It follows therefore that Judaism, which is predicated as selfish self-interest, 'reaches its height with the perfection of civil society'—'which (in turn) achieves perfection only in the Christian world', i.e. by being adopted as a formal social system.

Christianity, of course, arose out of Judaism, but 'it overcame real Judaism only in appearance'; in fact it 'dissolved itself again into it'. It thus enabled Judaism 'to attain world dominion and convert externalised man and nature into alienable and saleable objects'.[69]

This then is the case for 'discerning in Judaism a universal anti-social element of the present time' which leads to a logical 'cure'.

'When society succeeds in transcending the empirical essence of Judaism—bargaining and all its conditions—the Jew becomes impossible because his consciousness no longer has an object; the subjective basis of Judaism—practical need—is humanised and the conflict between the individual sensuous existence of man and his species existence is transcended', because 'the social emancipation of the Jew is the emancipation of society from Judaism.'

The anti-social nature and universality of Judaism are based on a systematic association of Judaism with money and anti-social aspects of society:

'Practical need, egoism, is the principle of civil society.'
What actually was the foundation of the Jewish religion?—practical need, egoism.

'The god of practical need and self-interest is money.'
'Money is the jealous god of Israel before whom no other god may exist.'

Having thus established the direct association between Jews and money, the argument can be generalised:

'Money degrades all the gods of mankind and converts them into commodities.'

Money is the general self-sufficient value of everything.

It has robbed the whole world of man and nature of its proper worth.

Money is the alienated essence of man's labour and life—'this essence dominates him as he worships it'.

Again:

'Under the rule of private property and money, nature is despised and practically degraded.'

In the Jewish religion, nature exists only in the imagination:

'Selling is the practice of externalisation. Man, captivated by religion, knows his nature only as objectified and thereby converts his nature into an alien, illusory being, so under the dominion of egoistic need he can only act practically, only practically produce objects by subordinating both his products and his activity to the domination of an alien being, bestowing upon them the significance of an alien identity—of money.'

Judaism has attained 'universal dominion' and has converted 'externalised man and nature into alienable and saleable objects'. In one sense, therefore, it is possible to argue that Marx equated Judaism with what he later came to call 'capitalism', because he deliberately associated Jews and Judaism with money and commercialism. Since he regarded these as essentially anti-social, he also described Jews and Judaism as anti-social. He even appears to suggest that money and trade were *created* by Jews though this is done by extending the Feuerbach–Bauer conceptions, rather than by historical analysis.

If Marx had confined his analysis of Judaism to the social issue, those who have maintained that he was really talking *only* about commercialism, that Judaism 'has very little religious and still less racial content for Marx', and that he was only indulging in 'an extended pun at Bauer's expense',[70] might have been right. But Marx does not content himself with an analysis of 'the social significance' of Judaism (and admits as much later on, as we shall see). He confirms and supports Feuerbach and Bauer's criticisms of the Jewish religion and Jewish history and adds some comments of his own, which are even more contemptuous and certainly less well informed than those of his predecessors.

In the Marxian conception, the Jewish religion is wholly negative. Christianity has at least some redeeming features: it proclaims that 'every man is a sovereign, supreme being'; it 'was too noble, too spiritual to eliminate the crudeness of practical need', but the Jew 'contributes nothing to mankind if he renounces all his Judaism'.

Marx gives one example of Jewish practice: 'The Jews' monotheism . . . makes even the toilet an object of divine law.' This solitary example of Jewish religious practice is a good illustration of the point I made earlier that Marx went beyond his predecessors to make Judaism appear contemptible. In *Essence of Christianity*, Feuerbach had stated: 'The Christian religion distinguishes inward moral purity from external physical purity; the Israelites identified the two.'[71] Marx was saying the same, but in a very different way.

He repeats the by now familiar attack on Jewish thought: 'In the Jewish religion [there is] contempt for theory, for art, for history, for man as an end in himself'; and he identifies entirely with Bauer in his attack on Jewish law:

The Jews' unfounded, superficial law is only the religious caricature of unfounded, superficial morality and law in general, the caricature of merely formal rites encircling the world of self-interest. Here . . . the highest relation of man is the legal relation, the relation to laws which apply to him not because they are laws of his own will and nature, but because they dominate him and because defection from them will be avenged. Jewish jesuitism [i.e. the Talmud] is the relationship of the world of self-interest to the laws governing it, and the cunning circumvention of these laws is that world's main art.

Indeed the movement of that world within its laws is necessarily a continuous abrogation of that law.

Judaism does not reach only its peak in civil society—it reaches its full completion because it 'could not develop further as a religion, could not develop further theoretically'. Nevertheless, it is a historical phenomenon. 'Judaism has been preserved, not in spite of history but by history.' As a contemporary anti-social element it is the product of 'historical development', to which it has actively contributed, but only in its 'harmful aspects'. Historically, therefore, Judaism is not only 'a religious critique of Christianity' but also the perpetuation of 'the practical Jewish spirit'—'The Jew who exists as a special member of civil society is only the special manifestation of civil society's Judaism.' Equally, the Jew's will to survive, his 'tenacity', is not due to his religion, but to his selfishness and practical need.

The Jew is thus firmly placed into a sequence of historical development, to which, however, in its positive aspects, he contributes nothing. On the contrary, he sits on the sidelines of history, ever ready to take advantage of the achievements of others. Even for his own progress he is dependent on the goodwill of non-Jews. 'Judaism could create no new world: it could only draw the new creations and conditions of the world into the compass of its own activity because practical need, whose rationale is self-interest, remains passive, never wilfully extending itself, but only finding itself extended with the continuous development of social conditions.'

So it is and so it has always been. The Jew has never changed, nor has his role in history ever changed. 'Thus not only in the Pentateuch or Talmud but also in present society we find the nature of the contemporary Jew, not as an abstract nature but a supremely empirical nature.'

MARX'S REVISED CRITIQUE OF JUDAISM

It is curious that in spite of the extensive literature which has analysed, discussed and interpreted the essays 'On the Jewish Question', virtually no attempt has been made to explain why Marx practically re-wrote them both in *Die heilige Familie* (*Holy*

Family)—why he should have considered it necessary to do so and how far this second version agrees with, or differs from, the first essays. While it is true that Avineri and McLellan[72] have noted the less hostile attitude to Jews in this later version, they have offered no explanation for it. Most of the scholars who have written on Marx's 'Jewish question' have ignored the second version altogether.

There are, however, substantial differences between the two versions. We can explain these partly by a careful comparison of the texts and partly by noting the reasons which Marx himself has suggested in the text of the second version, or later on. There is widespread agreement that the first essays were of critical importance in Marx's intellectual development and it has already been indicated that they represent a rudimentary formulation of what was later to be known as 'historical materialism'.[73] In addition, Marx wanted to demonstrate the social and political aspects of the Jewish question. He also clearly wanted to create a distance between his own Jewish origins and his intellectual stance. In the earlier essays, however, he does not entirely succeed. His discussion is still largely determined by religious and philosophical arguments which blur the socio-political concepts. They are also peppered with anti-Jewish expressions which, though intended for a reified concept of 'Judaism', nevertheless suggest something less than a 'scientific' analysis. Again, since Marx intended to suggest a historical pattern of development, he would have to avoid moral judgments, if these patterns are to be represented as a logical sequence. The task was to present Judaism as a social and historical phenomenon in such a way that the question of Jewish emancipation could be shown to be a political issue free of religious overtones. To do this it would be necessary to show the Jews as a sociohistorical factor in the political evolution of states. 'On the Jewish Question' succeeded only partly in doing this. First, they began by presenting Judaism and Christianity, indeed all religion, as a single category. This tended to obscure the Jews' historical role. Second, they made value-judgments about Jewish social characteristics. This tended to distort the presentation of their function. Third, the problem of their emancipation was, in part at least, discussed in a philosophical context. This tended to weaken the argument. Fourth, essential dialectical processes of history had clearly to be shown to have a balance. This was only partially achieved in the earlier essays.[74]

Accordingly, Marx set out to correct the inadequacies of the earlier essays in the *Holy Family*, as follows:

1 The order of discussion is reversed. It begins with 'the social significance' of Judaism and is followed by a discussion of the political characteristics of the state in evolution. No attempt is made to generalise from the Jewish to other religions.

2 The theoretical point about internal conflicts between individual and citizen is elaborated by reference to a Jewish writer, and the vigorous polemic of the first essays is transferred from the Jews to Bauer.

3 The concepts of 'species-life' and 'species-being' are abandoned. So is the 'vision' of a future society.

4 The historical necessity of social and political development is emphasised by a sharper contrast of the positive and negative aspects of civil society and implicitly by a more positive view of the role of the Jew in civil society as an agent of change. Without actually referring to Jews, Marx also makes this clear in the 'Economic and Philosophical Manuscripts' of 1844 when he refused to shed 'sentimental tears' over the transformation of land into a commodity, a process often initiated by Jews in Prussia.

Marx presents his second version in the form of three sub-sections of 'the campaigns of absolute criticism'. The first two 'campaigns' deal with Jewish criticisms of Bauer and the third is the revised version of the first essays. Marx mocks Bauer by showing how such *triste* opponents as 'a few liberal and rationalist Jews' are more than Bauer can handle.[75] It is tempting to speculate, however, that the few arguments against Bauer, which Marx reproduces from the vigorous debate Bauer had inspired, all have some bearing on weaknesses in Marx's own analysis, which he subsequently corrects. In the first campaign he quotes a Jewish critic who had argued that Bauer 'imagines a peculiar kind of state . . . a philosophical ideal of a state'.[76] Marx agreed—but he also left his own 'philosophical ideal' of human emancipation out of his second version.

Another Jewish critic challenged Bauer's contradictory concept of Jewish history. While on the one hand Jews are described as a static element in history, they are also said to have contributed to their own persecution by the role they played in history. Marx agrees with the Jewish critic. Although he had suggested much the same contradiction in his first essay, he puts forward a less ambiguous view in the second.[77]

In the second campaign Marx deals with three substantive objections against Bauer put forward by Gabriel Riesser. In the first, Riesser argued that Bauer's ideal state must exclude both Jews and Christians. Marx strongly agrees. He points to the danger of creating a situation where 'persons representing adverse elements' are eliminated in 'terroristic' fashion. 'Herr Bauer must have both Jews and Christians hanged in his critical state.' Marx must have been aware that his own prescription for 'abolishing Judaism' could also be interpreted in this way and, in my view, tried to reject such a conclusion here.[78] Riesser also accused Bauer of failing to distinguish 'what belongs to the domain of law and what is beyond it'. Again Marx agrees with Riesser, and, as we shall see, also deletes from his own comments on Jewish law 'what is beyond it'.[79]

It does appear reasonable to suggest that Marx reviewed his own contribution 'On the Jewish Question' in the light of the voluminous criticism of Bauer's essay, since his own essays remained virtually unknown at the time.[80] This is further supported by the third campaign, which opens with a particularly vicious attack on Bauer's 'self-apology'. Bauer was given to public self-analysis (criticism is everything) and public self-defence. He is thus the very opposite of Marx, who systematically dissociates himself from his subject. Bauer had earned the respect of Riesser and other Jewish critics because he had lost his position in the University of Bonn by standing up for his convictions. Marx only makes fun of him.[81] It is also worth noting that Bauer had accepted some of Marx's main criticisms, but excused himself on the grounds that his errors had been penned two years previously. Marx belittled Bauer for that explanation and then went on to present his own revised version of what he himself had written two years earlier.[82]

Before turning to the text of the revised version of 'On the Jewish Question', it might be appropriate to look briefly at Marx's call for the 'abolition' of Judaism, a concept which has disturbed many Jewish writers and which may also have been seen as a justification for some of the vicious attacks on Jews, Judaism and even Zionism. The Moscow translation of the *Holy Family* uses the term 'abolish' for Marx's '*auflösen*', i.e. to dissolve.[83] This faulty translation may certainly have given rise to some of the anxiety felt in English-speaking countries.[84] The real problem, however, is a conceptual one. Marx did not mean to provide 'a warrant for genocide'. He was trying to reduce Judaism, which he equated with the 'money system', into an abstract 'principle' in civil society that would have no function and therefore no place in a communist society. The abstract nature of his argument can best be illustrated by Marx's concept of 'labour'. Like religion, including Judaism, 'labour is free in all civilised countries'. This freedom is 'free competition of the workers among themselves'. But in the society of the future, 'it is not a matter of freeing labour but of abolishing it'.[85] Whether Marx is right about this is a different matter; what concerns us here is that Marx was determined to elevate Judaism into an abstract element like labour and that he no more intended personal harm to individual Jews by calling for the dissolution of Judaism than he would have wanted workers to be attacked when he called for the abolition of labour.[86]

Let us now turn to the text itself. Marx begins by explaining one small problem. Bauer's second article, 'Die Fähigkeit', had neither the force nor the substance of 'Die Judenfrage', and Marx's reasons for according it a separate review seem obscure. One reason undoubtedly was simply to enable him to separate the political from the social and religious aspects of the question. He now explains his second reason, namely that in this article Bauer treated the Jewish question as 'purely religious'. But 'religious questions of the day have at the present a social significance'. It is this 'social significance' which matters, and Marx now admits that the *DFJB* 'committed the injustice of not stopping at the word "social" '. There is no further elaboration of this cryptic admission, but the context makes it clear that Marx is referring to his own contemptuous assault on Jewish law.[87] In the first version Marx felt that he could make his point without denying Bauer's basic views on Judaism, which he fully accepted. All that was necessary was to go further than Bauer, to extend a valid analysis beyond the limits which Bauer had set for it. Bauer had expressed extreme contempt for Jewish law. Jews might claim that it was 'moral, ethical law', but since they honoured it more in the breach than in the observance, it was really no more than 'a fantastic, groundless law'.[88] Marx agreed with this and added his own scathing comments on this 'caricature of purely formal rights'.[89] But this criticism, like Bauer's, is a religious criticism. The Jew's relation to his law is irrelevant at a general socio-political level. Marx had declared that in the 'new' political state, consisting of individuals, *relations are regulated by law*.[90] At the level at which Marx wanted to conduct his analysis, therefore, what mattered was that Jews had a law which governed their relations, not how far they went beyond or accepted these laws. The existence of the law meant a stage in political development— to make fun of the law meant obscuring the political and historical processes which Marx wanted to illustrate in his essay. This is not to say that Marx changed his views on the quality of Jewish law. He admits that 'the Jewish question is also a religious question' and on a later occasion repeats, albeit in more moderate tones, his critique of Jews in their relation to Jewish law.[91]

The 'Sabbath Jew', who is now described as *scheinheilig* (i.e. only appearing to be holy), is merged with the 'everyday Jew' because he is only a 'fantastic reflection' of the latter.[92] A new emphasis is laid not only on the historical nature of Judaism but on the developmental aspect of this phenomenon. Whereas before, 'Judaism was preserved by history',[93] it now appears that 'Judaism has maintained and developed itself through, in and with history'.[94] Whereas before, 'the worldly god of the *Jew* was money',[95] *Judaism* now developed not as 'religious theory' but as

179

'commercial and industrial practice', as the 'money-system'.[96] In this wholly abstract context (in which the term 'Jew' is avoided and 'Judaism' is stressed more strongly), it is easy to show how the human emancipation of Judaism is not a task of the Jews but of a civil society which is 'Jewish to the core' because it is dedicated to the 'money system'.[97]

Marx's analysis of Judaism, for all its emphatic pungency, remains 'doctrinal'. He still produces no evidence of any kind to support his sweeping assertions.

After a concise delineation of the 'social' aspect of the Jewish question, Marx turns to a revision of his longer analysis of the political problem. He repeats his earlier deduction—Jews are politically emancipated in some states—neither Jews nor Christians are humanly emancipated. Therefore, as there is a difference between political and human emancipation, those states in which Jews do not have full political emancipation 'must be considered as underdeveloped'.[98] This is followed by a repetition of the difference between 'the German Christian state' and 'the absolute Christian state' which not only 'can emancipate Jews; it has done so and by its nature must do so', because 'it is not contrary to political emancipation to divide man into non-religious citizen and religious private individual'.[99] Marx then again discusses 'the rights of man' and again stresses the Jews' historical role in civil society. 'The Jew has all the more right to the recognition of his free humanity [i.e. rights of man], as free civil society is thoroughly commercial and Jewish and the Jew *is a necessary link in it*' (my italics).[100]

Marx then deals at length with the Sabbath debate in the French Chamber of Deputies which was alluded to only briefly in the first essay and which had been discussed (and, according to Marx, misunderstood) by both Hermes and Bauer.[101] Briefly, the suggestion in the Chamber was to institute a day of rest for working children—Sunday was suggested and an objection was raised that Sunday was a Christian day, whereas French law insisted on total equality of Judaism and Christianity. It was argued, however, that Sunday was still the appropriate day for the majority of the population. Marx argued that this sort of issue illustrated no more than the imperfection of the constitutional state, which he contrasted with 'the democratic representative state'.[102]

This leads Marx to what appears to be his main purpose in restating the political argument, namely to show both the historical necessity for and the inherent imperfections of the transition from feudal to civil society, but this time leaving the need to transcend the limitations of civil society implicit in its defects rather than by proposing a messianic solution. Bauer, Marx claims, is wrong in supposing that 'the abolition of privileges will also abolish the object of privilege'.[103]

> Industrial activity is not abolished by the abolition of the privileges of the trades, guilds and corporations but, on the contrary, real industry begins only after the abolition of these privileges . . . ownership of the land is not abolished when privileges of land ownership are abolished but, on the contrary, begins its universal movement with the abolition of privileges and the free division and free alienation of land; . . . trade is not abolished by the abolition of trade privileges but finds its true materialisation in free trade.

In the same way, 'religion develops its *practical* universality only where there is no universal religion (as in North American states)'.[104] This last sentence is the weakest link in the Marxian analysis, to which we shall return, but first it should be shown how Marx leads from these developmental aspects to their drawbacks.

'Free industry and free trade abolish privileged exclusivity', but they also 'isolate man from the social whole', for now he is 'no longer bound to other men by even the semblance of common ties'.[105] Instead there is 'a universal struggle of man against man, individual against individual'. This is 'the war of civil society as a whole', where individuals strive against each other, exploiting 'the uncurbed movement of elementary forces of life freed from the fetters of privilege'. 'The individual considers as his *own* freedom, the movement, no longer curbed or fettered by a common tie or man the movement of his alienated life elements, like property, industry, religion, etc; in reality this is the perfection of his slavery and his inhumanity. Right has here taken the place of privilege.'[106] The final conclusion of this indictment is that 'anarchy is the law of civil society emancipated from disjointed privilege—and this anarchy is the basis of the modern public system'.[107]

This, then, is the revised version of the earlier argument, a version which could be only 'indicated' in 'On the Jewish Question', but which is made more explicit here as 'the materialistic outlook on the world'. Because the earlier versions did this in 'philosophical phraseology, the traditionally occurring philosophical expressions such as "human essence", "genus" (species) etc. gave the German theoreticians the desired excuse for misunderstanding the real trend of thought'.[108]

Perhaps it was not just, or not only, the 'philosophical phraseology' which led to misunderstandings. For example, one assumption in the Marxian analysis leads to confusion because no rationale is provided to substantiate it, namely the classification of religion with industry, land ownership and trade. Marx showed that these three categories exist with *different* religions in both feudal *and* civil society. It is also quite possible for a civil society on the Marxian model to exist without any religion, but not without the other categories being represented in one form or another. If it is argued that alienation in such a society leads to a religious expression of the human spirit,[109] in other words, that alienation can be expressed *only* through religion, then the classification would appear to be justified. But where would this leave the analysis of Judaism?

If Judaism is the alienated form of practical need, and Christianity is the alienated form of human spirit, then different religions have different functions, and religion *per se* cannot be described as a unitary category. If the alienated essence of Judaism becomes part and parcel of Christianity as these two interact, then Judaism has a functional role; it may indeed be 'a necessary link'. But if Judaism develops its practical universality only where there is no universal religion, i.e. where it would not interact with Christianity, as in the United States of America, then Judaism has no historical role and Bauer's argument that Judaism has remained a static element in history has not been refuted.

A more general criticism of the Marxian analysis of the Jewish question emerges from his failure to look at the historical and empirical realities of Judaism. At the historical level we must note that, whatever Marx may have regarded as the causes for Jewish survival and however genuinely he was convinced of the purely economic significance of Jews, Judaism was a system of beliefs and, even as a 'superstructure', its early concerns with and legislation on some of the most critical social issues which were to concern Marx all his life (e.g. land ownership, the rights of workers, condemnation of exploitation, etc.), ought to have been accorded, if not approval, at least some recognition. At the empirical level, it is noteworthy that he appears to have failed to recognise or acknowledge the significance of the class factor in the struggle for Jewish emancipation which was noted earlier, and which is worth resummarising.

Until the end of the eighteenth century, Prussian Jews did constitute a society within a society: they existed as a legally defined, autonomous unit. This meant that as a society they evolved a pattern of stratification which, though not equivalent to that of Prussian society, was nevertheless sufficiently well defined to make it inevitable that the movement towards integration into the larger society was represented by different thrusts towards social class levels and attempts to overcome varying resistances. These resistances appear to have been greatest at the 'top' of the social hierarchy—i.e. the aristocracy and senior civil service establishment (the ruling elite), and at the 'bottom'—i.e. the industrial proletariat; both of which represented well-entrenched sociocultural elements whose social and economic positions were conditioned by their feudal roots as estates and guilds. The least resistance was offered by those sections of the middle classes (the bourgeoisie) who were beginning to emerge as new groups through the industrialisation process and who therefore had no prejudices rooted in tradition, those whose feudal trading associations with Jews had made Jews acceptable to them, and some sections of the professional intelligentsia whose roles had not been sufficiently well established to offer an organised resistance to Jewish emancipation.

Marx had the necessary personal experience of Jewish communal structures to have been aware, at the very least, of the fact that such stratifications existed and to call for an explanation. His insistence on treating 'the Jews' as a uniform entity, therefore, seriously weakens the credibility of his analysis.

PART THREE

On the Jewish Question and on the Questions of Jews

CHAPTER IX

The Quest for a Jewish-Socialist Synthesis

EARLIEST RESPONSES TO MARX

There can be little doubt that the volume of literature inspired by Marx's review-essays on the Jewish question is out of all proportion to their substantive content. There are many reasons for this. To begin with, several interest groups have continuously interpreted and reinterpreted the essays in the light of changing conditions and situations. Jews, Marxists and Marxian scholars alike have had to adjust their positions in relation to the rise of political anti-semitism, the emergence of political Zionism, the extermination of millions of Jews by Hitler and the less open anti-semitism of Stalin, the re-establishment of the State of Israel and the constantly changing sectarianism of left-wing political movements. Coupled with all this are the fluctuating attempts now to isolate the Jewish question as a particular problem, now to generalise it into a universal social issue, as indeed Marx tried to do. As we shall see, neither Marxists nor Jews have been successful in ridding themselves of an inevitable ambivalence in their approaches. Before we turn to a review of the literature which has emerged mainly in the present century, we might briefly look at the available material on the responses to Marx's essays in his own lifetime. It has already been noted that since most of the copies of the *Deutsch-Französische Jahrbücher* were confiscated at the Prussian border, very few people in Prussia knew about or commented on them.[1] One German-Jewish newspaper published a review,[2] while another carried news of Marx's contribution to the Bruno Bauer controversy in its gossip columns.[3]

The solitary review, which is in the form of a report from a correspondent, is interesting because it welcomed Marx's first essay, which is brilliantly summarised, but totally ignored the second. 'Your readers will certainly be interested,' it began, 'in a critique of Bauer's "Jewish Question" which comes from a literary group whose politico-philosophical approach concedes nothing to Bauer in extremism of critique or in dialectic brilliance —the group of Ruge and Marx's *Deutsch-Französische Jahrbücher*, the journal of our philosophers who have emigrated to the fatherland of the revolution.' In his summary, the reviewer then contrasted Bauer's demands, that Jews must give up Judaism and that man generally must give up his religion to be able to claim political emancipation, with Marx's argument that, on the contrary, political emancipation only orders the relationship between the state and its individuals *cum* citizens who are in conflict not only over religion but also over all other individual-istic categories such as birth, class and occupation; in short the categories of civil society. Political emancipation is less than human emancipation, but in the present world order it properly provides for the individual to enjoy his civil rights which include unrestricted religious freedom. The reviewer ended on a note of praise and reassurance: 'By rejecting religion for the citizen, Marx saves it for the man. The practical consequence, then, is the feasibility of political emancipation in spite of religion; religion meanwhile need not worry unduly about its fate in the so-called human emancipation, because "the existing world order" still has a long way to go'.

Heine, as a contributor to the *DFJB*, had certainly seen Marx's essays, and when the *Holy Family* was published, Marx personally asked the publisher to send him a copy.[4] Although, as we have seen, Heine would certainly have agreed that Marx's analysis applied to *some* Jews, he criticised its superficiality and rejected the Marxian conclusion. Some nine months after receiving the *Holy Family*, he wrote a long letter to Ferdinand Lassalle which strongly suggests that he might have been responding to Marx. Its immediate subject was the election of Achille Fould and other Jews to the French Chamber of Deputies. Heine expressed great satisfaction that in France Jews appeared to have achieved real civil equality, because Fould's election proved that, like the Christians in France, Jews could now achieve high office even though they could 'neither think nor feel'; they only had to have money. Heine promised to take the successes of rich Jews into account 'in my historical researches into the national wealth of Jews from Abraham to the present day'. He continued:[5]

> To avoid misunderstanding, let me say at once that the results of my researches into the national wealth of the Jews are most laudable for them and do them great honour. Israel owes its wealth exclusively to that belief in God to which they have adhered for thousands of years. The Jews worshipped a higher being, who rules invisibly from heaven, while the heathen, incapable of raising themselves towards the purely spiritual, made all sorts of gods of gold and silver which they worshipped on earth. If these blind heathen had turned all this gold and silver which they wasted on idol-worship into money and invested it at interest, then they would have become as rich as the Jews, who knew how to utilise their gold and silver to greater advantage—perhaps in Assyrian-Babylonian state loans, in Nebuchadnezzar's gilt-edged, in Egyptian canal shares, 5 per cent stakes in Sidon or in other stocks of antiquity which the Lord blessed, as He blessed present-day stocks and shares.

Two years before his death, Heine wrote his *Confessions* in 1854 in which he settled his account with many of the dominant themes that had preoccupied him and his intellectual contemporaries for a lifetime. Without relinquishing his status as 'a revolutionary and fighter for democratic principles',[6] he rejected atheism, expressed some reservations about communism (as represented by Weitling),[7] and underlined the positive characteristics of both Protestantism and Catholicism. He disparaged the philosophy of Hegel by arguing that the snake in the biblical story of the Garden of Eden, 'the little *Privatdozentin*, taught the entire Hegelian philosophy six thousand years before Hegel's birth. That blue-stocking without legs cleverly demonstrated the relationship between being and knowing, how man becomes God through consciousness, or, what amounts to the same thing, how God achieves consciousness of himself through man'.[8]

Heine then attacked the radical conception of Jews and Judaism, and lest there should be any confusion about the nature of his target, inserted a long quotation from his preface to the second edition of *On the History of Religion and Philosophy in Germany* in which the 'godless, self-gods', Ruge, Feuerbach, Daumer, Bruno Bauer and 'his obdurate friend' Marx, are mentioned by name[9] as the authors of misconceived analyses of Judaism. Heine deplored the ignorance and superficiality of those who wrote about the Jews: 'Neither the deeds nor the real essence of the Jews are known to the world. Some think they know the Jews because they have seen their beards, which is all they have ever revealed of themselves, yet now, as in the middle ages, they remain a wandering mystery.'[10]

To understand the Jews, he insisted, it was necessary to understand the Bible, and particularly the grand figure of Moses, who was 'already a socialist, though, as a practical man, he tried to change existing practices especially in regard to property. Instead of trying to effect the impossible by foolishly decreeing the abolition of property, he strove only for its moralisation, by bringing the rights of property into harmony with the laws of morality and reason'.[11] In fact, Heine went on,[12]

> Moses did not want to abolish property; on the contrary, he wanted to ensure that it was possessed by all, so that no one would sink, through poverty, to the status and mentality of the slave. Freedom was always the real goal of the great emancipator, freedom breathed and burned in all his laws concerning pauperism. He hated slavery absolutely and totally, but even he could not eliminate this inhuman practice, it was rooted too firmly in the life of antiquity, and he had to content himself with laws restricting its usage.

He recalled the law which ordained that a freed slave who refused to accept his freedom should have his ears pierced and remain a slave for ever.[13] 'O Moses, our teacher, Moshe Rabenu,[14] exalted champion of freedom, give me hammer and nails that I may nail our complacent long-eared slaves, in their black-red-gold uniforms, to the Brandenburg Gate.'[15]

If Marx claimed that the Jews had been preserved not in spite of, but through, history, Heine rejected that idea and described Jewish survival as a supreme achievement of a stubborn people, made possible by their 'portable fatherland',[16] the Bible:[17]

> I see now that the Greeks were only beautiful youths, but the Jews were always men, mighty unyielding men, not only then but right through to the present day, in spite of eighteen hundred years of persecution and misery. I have learned to respect them . . . these martyrs who have given the world a God and morality and who fought and suffered on all the battlefields of thought.

Similarly, if many Western European nations had been 'Judaised', had adopted 'a pork-eating Judaism',[18] this was not, as Marx maintained, because they had adopted the egoism and commercialism of Jews. In a passage which poetically anticipated the later work of Max Weber and Wernet Sombart, Heine offered a different view:[19]

> Perhaps it is not only because of their capacity to acquire culture, in the nations I have mentioned, that Jewish customs and ways of thought have been accepted so readily. The reason for this pheno-menon may perhaps also lie in the character of the Jewish people, which has always shown a great affinity with the character of the Germanic and to some extent the Celtic races. Judea has always seemed to me to be a fragment of Occident lost in the Orient. In fact, with its spiritual faith, its severe, chaste, even ascetic customs—in short, with its abstract inner-worldliness—this land and its people always presented the most marked contrast to neighbouring countries and peoples who, with their sensuous, varied and fervent modes of worship, devoted their lives to a Bacchantic feast of the senses.

Although, like Marx, Heine saw Luther as a revolutionary figure, he differed from him in that he ascribed Luther's greatness to his achievement in making the Bible accessible to all men, so that it could create 'a great democracy in which every human being is not only king, but also bishop of his castle', so that an empire could be founded, 'an empire of the spirit, of religious feelings of neighbourly love, an empire of purity and true morality, which would not be transmitted through meaningless dogma but through parable and example, as depicted in the beautiful, sacred educational text for young and old—the Bible'.[20]

In the most telling passage of his *Confessions*, Heine wrote with some force against the hostile and arrogant conceptions of Jewish history of both Bruno Bauer and Karl Marx. He dismissed Bauer's argument that Jews were themselves responsible for their persecution and, like Max Weber, totally rejected the Marxian thesis that the Jew is a trader because he is a Jew. With consummate skill Heine wove his arguments into the Marxian conception of class conflict, and, by linking the persecution of Jews with the 'interests' of both the ruling and the working classes, destroyed Marx's contention[21] that the Jews were the eager creators and representatives of a capitalist bourgeoisie.[22]

> The evil man of Cologne[23] believed that the spiritual salvation of the world was endangered, and that any means, falsehood as well as murder, were justified, especially against the Jews. The poor, downtrodden people, the heirs of unending poverty, hated the Jews because of the wealth they had amassed, and what today is called the hatred of the proletariat against the rich was then called hate against the Jews. In fact, the latter were excluded from all ownership of land and from all manual trades, being relegated to trading and finance, activities which the church spurned as too low for true believers. In this way the Jews were legally condemned to be rich, hated and murdered.

While thus rejecting Bauer and Marx's versions of Jewish history, Heine did not, however, reject the Marxian view that religious conflict is often only 'a fantastic reflection' of underlying social tensions—'a protest against real suffering'. He supported this by a clever comparison of two facets of social unrest:[24]

> Such murders [of Jews], it is true, were in those days committed under cover of religious zeal. It was said that those who killed our Lord must die. How strange. The very people who had given the world a God, whose whole life was permeated by the worship of God, were stigmatised as deicides! The bloody parody of such madness was seen at the outbreak of the revolution in St Domingo [Haiti], where a Negro mob, led by a black fanatic who carried a huge crucifix, devastated the plantations with murder and fire amid bloodthirsty cries of 'The whites have killed Christ—let us kill all whites!'

MOSES HESS

The three questions into which the 'Jewish question' had been divided, namely the meaning of Jewish history, the meaning of Jewish law and the relationship between the Jew and the state, had been 'resolved' by Marx into one: the relationship between Jew and state, and even that was generalised into a general socio-political question. The other two were dealt with by denying their reality. Many Jews were attracted by Marxist teaching, but the more they knew about Jews and Judaism, the less able most of them felt to accept the Marxian analysis. The task they set themselves, therefore, was to create a synthesis between the uncompromising Marxian position and a Jewish reality. Various attempts were made by Jewish Marxists and socialists. The first, perhaps the most important of these, was by Moses Hess,[25] not only because he challenged Marx's and indeed his own earlier analysis of Judaism but especially because he re-established that the 'Jewish question' had a fourth dimension, that of Jewish nationality. Following the challenge to the Sanhedrin issued in 1806 by Napoleon, and the persistent hostility of the romantic-national movement in Germany, Western European Jewry had at first demurred, then denied absolutely that they were anything other than a 'confession'. Moses Hess challenged this view, restored the concept of a Jewish nation and thus gave the 'Jewish question' in Germany and indeed in history a further dimension.

Moses Hess was, and remained all his life, a dedicated socialist. If he lacked the capacity for systematic thought of a Karl Marx, he was a more sensitive and perceptive visionary who had the courage and the determination to attempt a total synthesis of 'economic socialism' with national religious Judaism.

Just as Marx did not mention Moses Hess by name when he attacked him viciously in the *Communist Manifesto*,[26] so Hess did not mention Marx when he eventually took issue with the whole radical literature on the Jewish question in *Rome and Jerusalem*.[27] It would be beyond the bounds of this study to deal in detail with Hess's vigorous and imaginative response to the extensive critiques of Judaism, some of which have been reported here.

193

There clearly is a need for such a systematic analysis, the more so since virtually no attempt has yet been made to do this.[28] The stony silence with which Hess's socialist contemporaries met his analysis[29] has largely been maintained, except for a few disparaging studies 'by faithful Marxists, to the greater glory of their own creed but at the expense of the facts of history'.[30] Perhaps one ought to blame 'the narrowness of socialist thinking' for this treatment. There is at least one factor in Hess's essay which raises its importance beyond its immediate Jewish focus. This is his central thesis, which questions the overriding role of class struggle and which, historically, at any rate, appears to be well founded. 'Behind the problems of nationality and freedom,' Hess argued, 'there is a still deeper problem . . . the race question, which is as old as history itself and which must be solved before attempting the solution of political and social problems.'[31] This proposition was then made explicit: 'The entire past history of humanity originally moved only in the context of race and class struggle. The race struggle is primary, the class struggle secondary . . . Along with the cessation of race conflict, class conflict will also come to an end. Equality for all classes in society will necessarily follow the emancipation of the races.'[32] This essay contains a number of uncanny predictions, notably on the Jews both of Germany and of Eastern Europe.[33] He thought that 'a final race war would seem to be necessary before the Germans absorbed social and humane ideas',[34] and that 'if Germany were to conquer France and Italy . . . it would result in placing the entire German people under police law and in depriving the Jews of their civil rights'.[35]

Hess was determined to resolve the contradictions of the radical tradition in one fell swoop. He asserted a Jewish nationalism without relinquishing his universalism, he upheld religion without forgoing socialism, he proclaimed his faith in revolutionary change without accepting materialism. He also rejected the narrow view of Jews and Judaism which had become an integral feature of the radical tradition.

Any suggestion that a commitment to Judaism implied being 'particularistic' was spurned. Marx had maintained that 'when the Jew recognises his practical nature as invalid and endeavours to abolish it . . . [he] works for general human emancipation'.[36] 'When I work for the regeneration of my people,' Hess replied, 'I do not thereby relinquish my humanistic aspirations.'[37] He went even further: 'I cannot accept these humanitarian efforts which obliterate all differences in the organism of mankind in the name of such misunderstood ideas as "freedom" and "progress".'[38] Nor did Hess regard religion as incompatible with socialism, though he did think that religion in a socialist era would be radically different from the religions of his own time, because it would not be the product of the oppression of individuals.[39] In any event, he regarded Mosaism as being based on 'socialistic principles'.[40] Not surprisingly, therefore, he wholly rejected Marx's image of Judaism. If for Marx, 'it is from its own entrails that civil society ceaselessly engenders the Jew',[41] then for Hess, Judaism's only dogma—unity—is 'a living, creative perception which constantly produces itself out of its own spirit'.[42] If for Marx the basis of the Jewish religion is 'practical need, egoism',[43] for Hess, 'nothing is more foreign to the spirit of Judaism than egoistic salvation of the isolated individual',[44] and, what is more, 'no nation refutes egoism more strongly than the Jewish'.[45] For Marx, 'the practical Jewish spirit—Judaism or commerce—has perpetuated itself in Christian society'[46] or, as he put it later, 'Jewry has maintained itself . . . only in commercial and industrial practice.'[47] For Hess, it was 'a false reason' (*Scheingrund*), offered by 'Jewish rationalists', that 'Jews must act as industrial and commercial promoters [to] be the leaven of such activities among the civilised nations in whose midst they live.'[48] On the contrary, because unity is the theme of Judaism, it has always rejected any one-sided view of life, 'it is neither one-sidedly materialistic, nor one-sidedly spiritualistic; body and spirit merge into one another'.[49]

Hess also used the opportunity to express dissatisfaction with the materialist conception: 'I do not assert with the materialists that the organic and spiritual world is subjected, like the inorganic world, to the same laws as an external mechanism.'[50] He reproached his socialist colleagues: 'The masses are never moved to progress by mere abstract conceptions; the springs of action lie far deeper than even the socialist revolutionaries think.'[51] He developed his plan for Jewish people without for a moment relinquishing his universalistic and socialist outlook:[52]

> With the Jews, more than with other nations, which, though oppressed, yet live on their own soil, all political and social progress must necessarily be preceded by national independence. A common, native soil is a primary condition, if there is to be introduced among Jews better and more progressive relations between capital and labour. The social man, just as the social plant and animal needs for his growth and development a wide free soil; without it, he sinks to the status of a parasite, which feeds at the expense of others.

Hess gently chided the socialists for using his Jewishness as a weapon against him, 'not only . . . opponents, but even my own comrades (*Gesinnungsgenossen*) . . . have always used anti-Jewish weapons in every personal quarrel, which is always effective in Germany'.[53] It also seems likely that Hess replied to comments in the *Communist Manifesto* by copying Marxian rhetoric. Where Marx made fun of 'the role of speculative cobwebs embroidered with flowers of rhetoric steeped in the dew of sickly sentiment',[54] Hess mocked 'the theoretical, anti-national humanitarianism [which is an] idealistic dream [without] a semblance of reality. We become so saturated with spiritual love and humanistic chloroform that we become entirely unconscious of the pain and misery that the antagonism . . . between the various members of the great human family causes in real life'.[55]

Hess was thus the first Jewish socialist to attempt a synthesis between socialism and Judaism, and in many ways the most original and the most important. His essay, like Marx's, sank into oblivion soon after it was published, and, again like Marx's, did not re-emerge until early in this century when the socialist revolutionary of the nineteenth century became the prophet of political Zionism. Inevitably, in purely Marxist terms, Hess's thesis was totally unacceptable, mainly because it denied the predominance of economic factors as determinants of history, but also because it accorded religion an independent function. Nevertheless Hess had pinpointed the critically important factor of nationalism, which was destined to complicate socialist thinking for many years and to dominate Jewish socialist and anti-socialist thought.[56] Hess might be said to have 'discovered' Jewish nationality independently and then tried to adapt it to his socialist-philosophical background.

BER BOROCHOV

Although Borochov (1881–1917) was deeply committed to finding a solution to the Jewish problem which, for him, in contrast to Marx and Hess, meant the much larger and, at that time, much more serious problem of Eastern European Jewry, and although he, like Moses Hess, evolved a national solution, he remained faithful to his materialist outlook, and argued his case within the strict confines of Marxist theory as expounded by 'Russian Marxism'.[57] It is not certain, and on balance even unlikely, that Borochov was familiar with Marx's essays 'On the Jewish Question', but he was a brilliant Marxist theoretician and produced the most cogently argued case for Jewish national restoration—which, indirectly, also served as the most convincing Marxist analysis of the problem of nationalism.

Borochov's starting-point was Marx's statement that the relations of production constitute the economic structure of society. But specific societies have their separate relations of production and corresponding superstructures; in other words, in addition to the *relations* of production, there are differing *conditions* of production which Marx himself had classified as natural environment, race, external and historical influences, etc. 'In this conception of the "conditions of production",' said Borochov, 'we have a sound basis for the development of a purely materialistic theory of the national question.'[58] He postulated two sorts of human groupings. Groups divided by conditions of production are societies, and groups divided according to their role within the system of production of any given society, i.e. their relations to the means of production, are classes. From this basis Borochov developed a model of 'national struggle' which stood in the same relationship to conditions of production as the class struggle stood in relation to the means of production. He then pointed out that Marx used the concept of class in two ways.[59] On the one hand it meant every social group which differed from others in the same society in its relation to the means of production. On the other hand it meant a group that, in relation to its place in the system of production, had already achieved a degree of self-consciousness and had formulated its own interests and demands. Similarly, a group which developed under the same conditions of production, Borochov called a people, which, if it was also united through 'a consciousness of kinship', became a nation.[60] Again, just as under conditions of harmony in relations of production we have class solidarity, so, when there is harmony in conditions of production, we have national kinship or nationalism. But there is an element of antagonism between class consciousness and national consciousness. Stable conditions of production weaken national consciousness and increase class antagonism, while unstable conditions of production (national danger) have the reverse effect. Ruling classes in all nations take advantage of the antagonism between class and national consciousness by presenting stable conditions as unstable in order to exploit national consciousness and reduce class antagonism. Hence they do not think nationally but nationalistically,[61] the former being progressive, while the latter is reactionary.

Borochov argues that the most important factor in the conditions of production is territory.[62] Each class has its own particular interest in the national territory (e.g. a source of income for landowners, a base for capturing world markets for the grand bourgeoisie, a consumers' market for the middle class and a place in which to work for the proletariat). In the Borochovian dialectic, therefore, nationalism is wholly compatible with a materialistic interpretation of history and with the inevitability of class struggle. From this model, Borochov derived his answer to the Jewish question. Instead of concentrating on the traditional concern with Jewish commercial activities, he emphasised constant Jewish migration as a 'stychic' (i.e. elemental) process of a Jewish proletariat seeking a solution to the constant problem of its unstable existence in the Diaspora.[63] Not anti-semitism, but the Diaspora itself, was a social aberration, partly because the alienating forces in society exacerbated the tension between Jew and non-Jew and partly because the Jews' position outside basic industries made their proletarisation a slow, haphazard process. 'We must understand once and for all,' he insisted, 'that he who has no national dignity can have no class dignity.'[64] Zionism was, therefore, the only solution which would preserve Jewish cultural values which, like the Sabbath, were 'not only a religious tradition, but a deeply rooted socio-economic institution',[65] and which would also create the framework for allowing a Jewish proletariat to involve itself in a natural class struggle.

Even had Borochov not seen Marx's contribution to the Jewish question, he was fully alive to the consequences of the failure to formulate a coherent approach to problems arising from national differences. Borochov's analysis, designed to meet the need for such an approach, was carefully balanced in that it offered the logic of Marxist materialism, the emotional appeal of Zionism, an answer to Marxist assimilationism and a justification for the choice of Palestine, coupled with a socialist role for a Jewish proletariat in the Diaspora.[66] In short, although less imaginative and all embracing than Hess, he nevertheless offered a complete synthesis of a socialist orientation with a national-culturally defined Judaism.

CHAPTER X

Varieties of Marxist Solutions
to the Jewish Problem

Jewish Marxists or Marxists concerned with the Jewish problem tend either to develop solutions in which Marxist theory is adapted to a Jewish reality or opt for reality-based solutions which are then formulated to bring them into harmony with Marxist theory. There are, of course, some who insist on following an orthodox Marxist line and therefore argue for abstract solutions which are rigidly derived from the logic of Marxist theory. However, historical materialism applied in such dogmatic fashion fares no better than traditional religion faced with the challenge of secularism. Thus we shall see how a Western European Marxist argued for assimilation which Western Europe rejected, Eastern European Marxists argued for Jewish 'cultural autonomy' which Eastern Europe rejected, and international Marxism arguing for an international solution which is likely to disintegrate in its own contradictions. Since we are primarily interested in the influence of Marx's analysis on subsequent developments, we must also note that there appears to be a pattern from which a rule emerges that, the more realistic a solution appears to be, the greater its theoretical distance is from the Marxian position.

ASSIMILATIONISM

Otto Bauer (1881–1938), the Austrian social democrat and one-time foreign minister, devoted a special chapter to the question of Jewish national autonomy in his book on the national question.[1] Although his definition of a nation as 'a totality of men united through a community of fate into a community of character' admirably fitted the position of the Jews, and although he recognised their role in history, he nevertheless rejected the idea of Jewish autonomy as being contrary to the interests of the proletariat. Like Engels, Bauer described the role of Jews as mediators of trade and commerce in the pre-capitalistic era, and like Marx, he thought that, with the advent of capitalism, Christians had been 'Judaised'.[2] Jews had therefore fulfilled their historic role and should assimilate themselves culturally and economically with their host societies. In Western Europe this was already happening, while in Eastern Euope Jews were an oppressed and exploited group which, because it was not stratified by class, could not play a part in the processes of history. Only class struggle could endow a group with a historical task, but since capitalism inexorably meant the end of Judaism,[3] the Jews were 'doomed' to disappear; they would disappear (*aufgehen*) among the nations of the East as they had already disappeared in the West.[4] Bauer skirted casually over the problem of the resistance of Eastern European workers to the acceptance of Jewish workers in industry, a problem carefully analysed by Borochov.[5]

Bauer's advice to Jewish workers (strongly reminiscent of the early religious reformers of Judaism) was that they should make every effort to adapt themselves to their cultural environment in speech, dress, manner and custom if they wanted to be accepted and employed.[6] His refusal to extend his concept of 'cultural national autonomy' to the Jews did not serve to make him any more acceptable to traditional Marxists. He was branded as a 'reactionary' by Lenin,[7] and lived just long enough to see the Nazi attacks on even the most assimilated of Jews. In May 1938 the London *News Chronicle* published an appeal by Bauer to the world to rescue the 300,000 Jews of Austria who were threatened by the German invasion. He died as a refugee in Paris on the day the appeal was published.

CULTURAL AUTONOMISM: THE BUND

Otto Bauer's concept of autonomy for national groups was destined to play a part in Jewish history, though not in the way he had intended. We have frequently had occasion in the course of this study to draw attention to the fact that Marx's analysis of the Jewish question was marked by its lack of reality and complete unawareness of the real situation of Jewish people either in his own time or in earlier periods of history. There is a certain irony in the historical observation that, if Marx had never existed, socialism would have emerged during the nineteenth century anyway, and Jews would have been its pioneers even without Marx, Hess and Lassalle.

Throughout the middle ages and well into modern times, the basic Jewish social organisation (inside and outside the ghetto) was the *Kehilla*. Within the *Kehilla*, especially in Eastern Europe, there were associations of employers and employees concerned with mutual aid schemes and sick and unemployment funds,[8] but during the 1840s, just about the time when Marx was writing his essays, these joint associations tended to drift apart, Jewish workers began to develop a consciousness of their social situation and to use strikes as a means to force improvements in their working conditions, and formed themselves into *Chevrei Baalei Melachah* or working men's associations.[9] Since Jewish trade unionism antedates the normal facility of state-centred authority, the 'oath' became an important form of social bond. Members would swear by some Jewish religious object. In addition they would organise places of worship by trade groups. This natural assimilation of religious tradition into the early foundations of workers' movements was to have important repercussions later in the century, when Jewish workers met Marxist theorists to whom 'the criticism of religion is the premise of all criticism'.[10] To Jewish workers, resentful of the poor working conditions of most of their members at a time when industry was developing at a rapid rate, when more and more Jews began to labour in factories and workshops for fixed wages, the problem was not really a new one, it was constantly becoming bigger quantitatively, but qualitatively it was the traditional conflict between rich and poor Jews, a conflict already well expressed in the Hasidic movement of the eighteenth century. Hence the profound religious and spiritual element in the Jewish 'class struggle'. Towards the end of the nineteenth century, additional forces began to make themselves felt. Haskalah, the movement for enlightenment, which was spreading secularisation and a taste for European culture as well as socialism spread by a Jewish intelligentsia, gradually merged into a socialist movement which sought to emancipate the Jewish masses, bring them into free and brotherly association with the proletariat of Eastern Europe and work with them for the liberation of mankind in general and Jewish workers in particular. Out of these elements the Bund was created in 1897.[11] Originally, the Jewish socialist intellectuals had hoped to spread a knowledge of Russian with their attempts to provide secular education.[12] They failed to spread education among Russian workers because, as one of them put it, 'They could not make me a drunkard and I could not make them class conscious',[13] while Jewish workers saw little use or need for Russian. Yiddish thus became an important factor in the new Bund, tied as it was to Jewish consciousness and a form of Jewish nationalism. Equally, although Marxist theory prescribed the complete subjection of nationalist aspirations to the class principle, the Bundists recognised the particular position of Jews by advocating a Jewish national autonomy within a framework of Russian and Polish nationalism, but acknowledging the Marxist teachings by repudiating the idea of international *Jewish* solidarity and the ideology of a contemporary Jewish movement, Zionism.

In summary we might say that the Bund emerged when an active but unassimilated Jewish proletariat merged with a Marxist oriented and Jewish-cultural oriented intelligentsia to form an autonomous organisation, because they recognised that the Russian workers' movement would neither 'Russify' the Jews nor stem the anti-semitic excesses of the Russian workers. As such, they affiliated to the Russian Social Democratic Labour Party in 1898 where they became an influential force, particularly during the revolution of 1905. From 1901 onwards the political

ideas of the Jewish historian Dubnow, the Jewish socialist
Zhitlovsky and the ideas of the Austro-Hungarian Marxists on
national autonomy were adopted by the Bund as the appropriate
Marxist theory for their demands to be treated as a 'nationality'
in Russia, especially since they had disowned the idea of a world-
wide Jewish entity and claimed only to represent the Jewish
population of Russia. The bitter attacks to which the Bund was
subjected, and the violent internal dissension which their position
made inevitable, at first led the Bundists to move towards a
'neutralist' position on vital political issues and to shift the weight
of their activities to the cultural and educational fields. When the
Russian revolutionary movement split into Bolsheviks and
Mensheviks, the Bundists sided with the Mensheviks.[14] During
the First World War, largely perhaps due to the extensive
emigration of Bundists to North and South America, the
Bundists became less Russia- or Eastern Europe-centred and
increasingly acknowledged the existence of and a sense of
fraternity with Jews in other parts of the world. With the advent
of Hitler, the Bund was eventually destroyed by Stalin in Russia
and Hitler in Poland, though remnants of it are still active,
notably in America and Israel.

In terms of Marxist theory, the Bund was too full of internal
contradictions, too much of an amalgam of ideologies, to survive,
and Plekhanov was probably correct when he described them as
'Zionists afraid of sea-sickness',[15] but Plekhanov's Jewish wife
Rosalia Bograd, a socialist revolutionary, did better in explaining
the confused ideology of the Bund when she wrote: 'Deep down
in the soul of each one of us, revolutionaries of Jewish birth, there
was a sense of hurt pride and infinite pity for our own, and many
of us were strongly tempted to devote ourselves to serving our
injured, humiliated and persecuted people.'[16]

From a Jewish point of view, the story of the Bund is not
unlike that of the bitter conflicts among the Jews of Western
Europe over the issues of assimilation versus national (i.e. Zionist)
revival. The Western Jews who sought salvation in a total
integration within bourgeois-capitalist systems were no less
universalistic than their socialist-revolutionary counterparts in

the East, who, like Rosa Luxemburg, Victor Adler, Otto Bauer and Leon Trotsky, looked to an international proletariat for the coming millennium. Some tried to create a genuine synthesis out of incompatible foundations, while others paralysed themselves by advocating one course of action knowing it to be inadequate as a solution. An interesting example of this is Julius Martov (Iulii Osipovich Tsederbaum 1873–1923),[17] the most important Marxist theoretician to have been associated with the founding of the Bund, at least in its earliest stages (1897) and also its most hard-hitting and vigorous opponent in the Russian revolutionary movement. Martov, the companion of Lenin, founder of Menshevism and ideologue *par excellence* of the Russian revolution, was too much of an internationalist to understand the needs of the Jewish workers and too Jewish to anticipate the anti-semitic excesses of the Russian proletariat. He could no more reconcile the national-cultural aspirations of the Bundists with proletarian universalism than in his later career be able to reconcile the 'terrorism' of revolutionary change with his thoroughly bourgeois humanism. Opposed as he was to the Bund, he was yet typical of its stubborn, messianic persistence. He lacked the brutal pragmatism of a Lenin and the caustic detachment of a Plekhanov —his role in the Russian revolution—like that of the Bund—was important but ineffectual, dedicated but misconceived. In a sad little pictorial record of the Bund which is filled with photographs of long forgotten men and women who were murdered either by the Nazis or by the Soviet NKVD, there is an entry which in its own way typifies the incongruity of the Bundist conceptions, albeit unwittingly. After detailing the part played by members of the Bund in bringing socialism to Russia and in fighting Hitler Germany during the Second World War, it records: '1945–46— Bundist organisations and their auxiliaries are re-established in Poland. In 1948 Polish Bund is forced by Communists to liquidate. Overwhelming majority of Bundists leave the country.'[18] It would appear that Jewish socialist workers' movements survive only in capitalist societies.

LENINIST–STALINIST TERRITORIALISM (OTTO HELLER)

If Hess and Borochov built their Jewish-socialist synthesis around what they considered to be the errors and omissions of Karl Marx, Otto Heller and Abram Léon made Marx's 'ingenious approach'[19] and his 'brilliant thought'[20] the starting-points for their respective treatments of the Jewish question. Both were totally committed to Marxism, both were violently opposed to anti-semitism, Zionism and Jewish nationalism, both presented a historical-materialist interpretation of Jewish history—but Heller was a Leninist–Stalinist and Léon was a Trotskyist—and the sectarian gulf between them was as wide as the gulf between either of them and the most 'reactionary, bourgeois historian'. Hence Léon, although familiar with Heller's book, ignored its materialist thesis, just as Heller ignored the Trotskyist approach to the Jewish problem.[21] Of the two, Heller is the more polemical, Léon the more widely read, but both felt able to compress three thousand years of Jewish history into a single book and both took considerable liberties with the facts of history and the work of historians to make the Jews fit into their theories. Yet the fate of both men is the tragic and final refutation of their arguments, for Léon died in a German extermination camp, and Heller, perhaps more significantly, with 'many other Jewish communists lost their lives in Nazi extermination camps or in one of the Soviet prisons from which there was no return'.[22] Though 'emancipated from Judaism', they nevertheless died as Jews.

Although Heller was convinced that Marx had found the key to a correct solution of the Jewish problem, he conceded that his approach had been 'too narrow, too one-sided',[23] by which he meant that, while Marx had found the true solution to the social aspect of the Jewish question by reducing it to its real economic foundations, his opponents ought not to call him an anti-semite because he had failed to consider the question of 'Jewish nationality' and had thereby left the impression that the abolition of the Jewish social role in society must mean the abolition of the people as such.[24]

Once, a long time ago, Heller argued, the Jews were a nation. Today they are a caste. Both as a nation and a caste they have been mainly concerned with trade. This is not to be explained by reference to restrictive legislation during the middle ages, because the very fact that the original nomadic nation chose Palestine—a centre bisected by the ancient world's trade and caravan routes—as its territorial base showed that even then the Jews were a *Handelsvolk*, a trading people.[25] The rules of historical materialism demand, Heller insisted, that no assumptions may be based on 'mystical' factors such as innate human or racial characteristics. There must be no talk of 'essence', which Marx had already refuted in Bauer, and there must be no talk of race, as Sombart had it. Jewish disinclination for agriculture and industry, according to Heller, must be shown to be 'a co-incidence of natural and social factors, especially in their economic geographic and historical development'.[26] The Jews were a trading people because as nomads they had no experience of agriculture, because Palestine was a barren country and because it also had important trade routes. Here we have an interesting and typical example of the problem of making the facts fit the theory. The nomadic character of the early Hebrews and the existence of trade routes in Palestine are deduced from biblical references, although Palestine in the Bible is 'a land flowing with milk and honey'. For Heller it was too barren to sustain a wide agriculture, and for Léon the flow of milk and honey was a poetic expression for its profitability as a commercial centre.[27]

Long before the destruction of the second temple the Jews established trading centres in many parts of the Mediterranean basin, so that when their national independence was destroyed by the Romans, the Jews were recognised universally as traders and could survive the loss of political independence by becoming a caste defined by its religion. 'The misfortune of their national destruction was their salvation.'[28] Heller described three periods in Jewish history. In the first, from the end of antiquity to 1300 CE, Jews continued their role as traders, founded cities, financed kings and dukes and held a general monopoly of money, but did not indulge in usury. The second period from 1300 to 1650 is the most tragic because Jews now came into conflict with the emerging forces of capitalism in Europe. They were driven from traffic in commodities and were forced into the money trade. They were thus brought into direct conflict with the trade in goods, many were exterminated, and the Jews as a whole were stigmatised as pariahs and subjected to ill-treatment. The third period represented the advent of capitalism. The Jews as a caste lost their social role because the money monopoly they had held was taken over by the ruling classes who eliminated the caste through emancipation and assimilation.[29] The staggering superficiality and indeed inaccuracy of this panorama of nearly two thousand years of history needs no comment, but it did persuade many readers that this kind of materialist interpretation had a ring of truth. In this way, then, 'modern capitalism sealed the fate of Jewry'.[30] But only of Western Jewry, those living in areas where capitalism was most advanced and who were now faced with the unmistakable death signs of the caste, i.e. falling birthrates, mixed marriages, emigration and conversion to Christianity.

The situation was different for the Jews of Eastern Europe, where, because it lagged behind the West by one and a half centuries, the Jewish caste was maintained in full strength. Although many emigrated, Jewish migration must not be regarded as a characteristically Jewish proclivity, as Sombart suggested (and as Borochov did, though Heller does not mention him);[31] emigration to more advanced, i.e. capitalistic, economies would lead only to total assimilation. How then are the Jews of Eastern Europe to be saved? Zionism, any revival of Jewish nationalism, is 'a Utopia doomed to bankruptcy', a reversion of history,[32] and capitalism offers only oblivion. The only answer is the proletarian revolution, the establishment of an autonomous Jewish region in Biro-Bidjan in the Soviet Union,[33] where a Jewish proletariat could maintain its autonomous 'nationality'.

Heller also devoted some space to analyses of the Jewish religion and of anti-semitism. His comments on Judaism as a religion are modelled on Marx and vie with the master in expressing contempt. He went further than Marx by relating the developments of the religion to socioeconomic determinants. His description of Jewish law is reminiscent of Marx: 'The Jewish religion . . . is a constitution, a law, a calculating law, an account-book for the credit and debit of the soul, a balance-sheet, a dossier in which the exchange-rate of salvation is recorded.'[34] Fortunately, 'the destruction of the Jewish religion through the proletarian revolution enables those of Jewish nationality still living in the East to survive'.[35]

Anti-semitism is a feature of capitalist society. Since Engels, Bebel and Lenin explicitly rejected it, it has no place in socialism. Nevertheless it remains a weapon of reactionary ideologies, particularly in its racial form. This includes not only those who serve the swastika but also those who follow the star of David.[36] Heller is thus one of the pioneers of the charge that Jewish nationalism is 'racialist', although he argued quite emphatically that Jews are 'the product of racial mixtures'.[37]

TROTSKYIST INTERNATIONALISM (ABRAM LÉON)

Although highly critical of Karl Kautsky, Heller clearly followed him in many of his main arguments[38] just as he was influenced by Werner Sombart, although he too was frequently criticised.[39] These two men were also key figures in Abram Léon's version of Jewish history. He is more critical of Sombart than Heller, yet his main complaint against Sombart might well be applied to his own and to Heller's excursions into Jewish history: 'The theory of Sombart is completely false. Sombart claims that he is portraying the economic role of the Jews, but he does so in a completely impressionistic way, rearranging history to suit his theory.'[40] In marked contrast to Sombart, Heller and Léon make the suffering and persecution of the Jews throughout history their dominant themes, not however from any excess of sympathy, since all persecution is described as a direct result of Jewish economic function, but in order to reinforce the 'message' of their theses that, unless and until Jews join the proletarian revolution, they always have been and always will be subjected to persecution and misery. Neither appears to have considered a fairly obvious difficulty in this thesis, namely that if the peasants, petty bourgeoisie and middle classes always and instantly rebel violently against economic oppression—even if that oppression, in Hannah Arendt's terms,[41] is 'functional'—why should this only or at least predominantly be when the oppressors are identified as Jews? In other words, if the victimisation of Jews is exclusively and directly economic, why and how do other ruling minorities such as an aristocracy maintain their power and position?

Léon, after explaining the need 'to reject the fundamental error of all idealist schools' of Jewish history, showed how Karl Marx 'puts the Jewish question back on its feet', not by looking for the secret of the Jew in his religion, but by looking for the secret of the religion in the real Jew,[42] and 'real' means 'the Jew in his social and economic role'. Like Heller, Léon stressed that Jews emigrated from Palestine long before the destruction of their national state and since, in ancient times, merchants were always foreigners, it was natural that Jews in dispersion should adopt that role.[43] He quotes Kautsky in support of this claim, but neither he nor Kautsky has adequately explained why neither in ancient nor in modern times some emigrant peoples become traders while others do not. In our own day, for instance, we have had Asians in East Africa and Chinese in Indonesia and Singapore predominantly as traders, even though the Asians originally came as labourers (i.e. proletarians) whereas the Irish in America or the Turks in Western Europe have, Léon claimed, not become traders. Historically, the Jews must be seen as 'a social group with a specific economic function. They are a class, or more precisely a people-class'.[44] For Léon, race, class and people meant much the same thing and there is 'a continuous interdependence between racial or national and class characteristics'.[45] The Jews were not, however, capitalists. For capitalism is the bearer of a new mode of production, whereas merchants (i.e. Jews) intervene only in the spheres of production. There is also a direct relationship between being a merchant and being a Jew, for as soon as the Jews adopt 'normal' economic roles, they cease to be Jews. This Léon called 'the law of assimilation—wherever the Jews cease to constitute a class, they lose, more or less rapidly, their ethical, religious and linguistic characteristics; they become assimilated'.[46]

Like Heller, Léon describes 'periods' of Jewish history: pre-capitalism, medieval capitalism, manufacturing and industrial capitalism and the decline of capitalism. These periods are not directly derived from Jewish history but from general European history. Their particular relevance for the Jews is then explained. Again, as in Heller, the final stages of capitalism are described as the most disastrous for the Jews, who 'are being crushed between the jaws of two systems, feudalism and capitalism, each feeding the rottenness of the other'.[47]

Léon is less interested in the content of the Jewish religion than Heller, but more concerned with the relationship between Judaism and Christianity. Early Christianity was 'a reaction of the labouring masses of the Jewish people against the domination of the wealthy commercial classes'.[48] But from about the third century it became the ideology of the landowning ruling classes and 'a religion of consolation for the popular masses'. For Kautsky this was a process similar to the emergence of 'social democratic revisionism' from orthodox Marxism. Léon preferred an analogy with the socialist content of fascism, 'which also attempts to make use of "socialism" in order to strengthen the rule of finance capital'.[49] Since Christianity had initially been a proletarian revolution, it followed for Léon that all poor (i.e. non-commercial) Jews became Christians, while those who were merchants remained Jews; hence the triumph of Christianity completed 'the selective process which transformed the Jews into a commercial class'.[50] Léon agreed with Heller that the Jews had been preserved 'not despite their dispersion but because of it',[51] but sharply opposed his view of the role of the Jews as usurers. To claim that this occurred only after their elimination from trade was 'a vulgar error', because 'usurious capital is the brother of commercial capital'.[52]

If it is 'infantile' to see Jewish economic activity as a result of any 'predisposition', it is 'puerile' to ascribe it to persecution and legal restrictions. Léon denied that medieval guilds excluded

Jews except on rare occasions when they did so only because, as traders, they were reputed to be 'dishonest'.[53] The expulsion of Jews from European countries during the middle ages was a true reflection of the economic processes there which had caught up economically with the Jewish position and therefore had no further need of them.[54]

Léon then turned his attention to the problems of the Jewry of Eastern Europe, where the majority of Jews were not merchants but artisans, i.e. a proletariat, but a proletariat concerned exclusively with the production of commodities for consumption. Since he had rejected the exclusion from ancient guilds as a possible cause, he used the structure of the Jewish community as an explanation: as the peasant was drawn into heavy industry (e.g. mining, steel), with the advent of industrial technology (thus the peasant serving the landowner became the labourer serving the mineowner), the Jewish artisan, serving the trader and merchant within the community, remained to produce consumer goods for the same 'employer' but now at factory and sweatshop level.[55] Even Léon felt the superficiality of this analysis and added a rider that such an explanation was 'necessarily schematic' and that those who criticised such an approach 'have not completely understood this dialectical interdependence'.[56]

Dialectical interdependence was also called upon to explain a smaller 'contradiction', namely that, while capitalism created the conditions for the elimination of Jews by economic and cultural assimilation, it also produced a revival of Jewish nationalism by creating conditions for mass migration and concentration of Jews in urban centres.[57] Léon described the emergence of German racism[58] and the rise of Zionism[59] as direct consequences of a decaying capitalism—both therefore doomed to be transient phenomena. 'Only a world-wide socialist planned economy would be capable' of transplanting millions of Jews to a new territorial centre, and that would presuppose an international proletarian revolution.[60] Since the Zionist movement had been prepared to go ahead without waiting for the proletarian revolution, it had proved itself to be 'an ideological excrescence'.[6]

In a final chapter, having rejected all of Jewish history as mere economic manifestation, Jewish religion as merely the false consciousness of economic functionaries, Jewish nationalism as a mere aberration of a Jewish people-class which 'history' had 'doomed to disappearance', he nevertheless needed a 'solution for the Jewish question. He argued confidently that 'the very fact that a solution had not been found in two thousand years best demonstrates that it was not necessary'.[62] If a solution was now required, it was because capitalism was collapsing and with it 'the social basis of Judaism'. This was also reflected in the high percentage of Jews in the proletarian movement, where 'the intellectual faculties of the Jews' have become 'an important support for the proletarian movement'.[63] And when the great revolution came, there would be an important part for the Jewish masses. After all, 'socialism is not at all interested that all Jews should take up manual occupations. On the contrary, the intellectual faculties of the Jews should be put to widest use'.[64]

As a Trotskyist, Léon had no faith in the Soviet Union. Writing only a decade after Heller, he knew that Biro-Bidjan was a forgotten dream, that time and reality had overtaken the confident polemic of an earlier Marxist.[65] Like Heller, he sought a meaningful existence for the Jewish people, but demanded 'unconditional surrender' before this could be granted. Materialists they may have been, but in their absolute belief in Marx, Heller and Léon resembled their ancestors, who also clung to their faith, even in death. Perhaps the greatest irony lies in their conception of Judaism. Although they both sought to vindicate Marx's youthful essays by applying the 'science' of historical materialism, they ended up by defending Bruno Bauer's Christian-theological conception of a static Judaism. It differed only in that in the theological tradition Judaism was permanently encapsulated in its law, while in the materialist tradition it was equally firmly enclosed in the trading process.

CHAPTER XI

Marx and the Sociologists

Sociologists have, generally speaking, ignored or avoided the Marxian analysis of the Jewish question, partly perhaps because the rise of political anti-semitism since the days of Marx and its consequences have made this a 'delicate' subject, but more probably because 'it would require more than a lifetime to acquire a true mastery of the literature concerning the religion of Israel and Jewry, especially since this literature is of exceptionally high quality.'[1] There were two noticeable exceptions—Max Weber and Werner Sombart. Both dealt at length with the Marxian hypothesis, though neither did so specifically in answer to Marx. Both had an infinitely greater knowledge than Marx of Jews and the literature on Jews, though neither intended to 'defend' the Jews against the Marxian polemic. Although Weber explicitly refuted Marx while Sombart tended to support him, it was Sombart who was subjected to more frequent attacks by Marxists.[2]

MAX WEBER

Weber (1864–1920) did not respond directly to Marx's analysis of the Jewish question, except in the sense that much of his work can be seen as a response to 'the ghost of Marx'.[3] Since the *Wirtschaftsethik* of the world religions was a dominant theme in

Weber's work, he was bound to be interested in the Marxian hypothesis of Judaism as the 'embodiment' of bourgeois commercialism, indeed in the entire Marxian critique of religion. Weber frequently disclaimed any originality in his presentations, arguing that his main aim was to organise his data 'in a manner to emphasize some things differently',[4] yet his precision of analysis and insistence on defining his critical variables stand in marked contrast to the wild polemics of the young Marx. If we noted earlier that the Marxian critique of religion throws doubt on the very use of religion as an analytic concept, Weber divides the concept into a number of discrete variables, each one of which is then investigated independently and comparatively.

Although Bruno Bauer and Marx prided themselves on the way in which they transformed the problems of their day into the 'right' questions, they were both too deeply enmeshed in the Hegelian dialectic to give adequate consideration to either subject or predicate in their assumptions. If the problem was Jewish emancipation, then the answer lay for Bauer in the nature of the Jew and for Marx in the nature of emancipation. It was, as we have seen, in this way that Bauer was caught in an insoluble tautology and Marx was left with a critique of religion that did not really extend beyond the external relationships of one particular religion. Marx had stipulated two functions for religion in feudal Europe. It made the life of the exploited groups bearable by giving meaning to their existence, and it provided the legitimation for ruling groups to maintain the disparate distribution of wealth. Religion, or better Christianity, thus proved to be a valuable instrument for exercising social control and for justifying the emerging capitalist order. Max Weber, who started from a historical-comparative perspective, argued that while religion was universal both in time and in space, capitalism was not. Within Christianity the economic order differed according to whether he considered Catholic or Protestant states. Even where Protestants were minority groups they tended to move towards a capitalist economy—as did the Huguenots in France under Louis XIV, the nonconformists and Quakers in England and, 'last but not least, the Jew for 2,000 years'.[5] Hence Weber argued that particular religions might propagate specific ethical principles which fostered or prevented the rise of a capitalist system.

Marx did not analyse Judaism as a religion. Since he had no time for religion anyway and since Bauer had, in his view, fully demolished Judaism as an ideology, he concentrated his attack, as he did in the case of Christianity, on the 'social significance' of Judaism, which he described in Feuerbachian terms as selfish need and egoism. Since bourgeois-capitalism was also predicated on selfish need and egoism, Marx attempted to equate the two phenomena—Christian Europe was being 'Judaised', its feudal order was giving way to a bourgeois-capitalist order which was 'Jewish to the core'. To Weber this was an untenable proposition. 'The universal reign of absolute unscrupulousness in the pursuit of selfish interests by the making of money has been a specific characteristic of precisely those countries whose bourgeois-capitalistic development . . . has remained backward.'[6] Thus the Marxian notion that any religious ideology is little more than a *post facto* superstructure of a given economic system, in which the relations of production are the only meaningful determinants of a dominant ethic, cannot explain the variations in either economic development or ethical values as they manifest themselves in different societies.

It would be beyond our frame of reference to discuss the Weberian thesis and the vigorous controversy it has inspired.[7] We must restrict ourselves to some of Weber's views on Jews and Judaism and their relationship to the Marxian thesis. Since Weber's starting-point was the origin of modern capitalism, he, like Marx, naturally looked to the middle ages. Although critical of the methodology of the then famous economic historian Wilhelm Roscher (1817–94), Weber was undoubtedly influenced by Roscher's analysis of the economic role of Jews in the middle ages[8] in which he argued that both the predominance of and hostility to Jews during that period could be explained as follows. During the earlier middle ages the economically underdeveloped European societies actively encouraged the immigration of Jews, who were commercially experienced and had well-established trading contacts, in order to provide basic goods and raw materials. Under Jewish tutelage a Christian commercial middle (i.e. merchant) class arose which, having acquired trading skills from Jews, increasingly saw them as competitors and exploited religious differences to promote hostility. This eventually led to the expulsions of Jews, particularly from areas of their greatest concentration, the larger urban commercial centres.[9] Roscher credited the Jews with the introduction of a number of commercial instruments, a credit which was to play an important part in Sombart's view of the Jewish role in creating modern capitalism. Max Weber accepted and indeed restated this view but insisted on restricting it to trade and commercial activities. He introduced a sharp differentiation between Jewish-pariah and modern Protestant capitalism. Though they were both rational, in that neither was handicapped by notions of magic and supernatural forces and both were based on 'self-righteous and sober legality',[10] Jewish capitalism was politically orientated (financing wars, tax-farming), adventurous or speculative, while Protestant capitalism was rationally organised and based on the use of free labour and industrial entrepreneurship. Weber therefore assigned less importance to competitive clashes between Christian middle-class and Jewish capitalism and sought to explain the hostility between the groups by the voluntary pariah status which characterised the position particularly of the medieval Jew and which he attributed to their Israelite origins in antiquity.[11]

There is every likelihood that Weber did not originally intend to study Judaism to the extent that he did and intended to do before his untimely death. Following the success of his earliest and most famous excursion into the sociology of religion, *The Protestant Ethic and the Spirit of Capitalism* (1930), he planned to study the economic ethic of the world religions—by which he meant Confucianism, Hinduism, Buddhism, Christianity and Islam. Judaism was added, partly to test the theses of Marx and Roscher and partly 'because it contains historical preconditions decisive for understanding Christianity and Islamism, and because of its historic and autonomous significance for the development of the modern economic ethic of the Occident'.[12] It could be argued that Weber might not have continued his interest in Judaism had not Sombart developed the Puritan ethic thesis in relation to Jews, who, as a separate problem, had been 'entirely omitted' from the earliest essay.[13] As a result of the Sombartian essay and perhaps also from a natural interest which grew with his increasing knowledge of Judaism, Weber published a number of essays bearing on Judaism and, towards the end of his life, completed his *Ancient Judaism*, which he even then regarded as only a first section of a more comprehensive treatment of the Jewish religion and its evolution.

Weber's characterisation of and attitude to Jews are, to say the least, problematic in a way that he himself, preoccupied as he was with the problem of 'value-free' sociology, did not seem to appreciate. For all his undoubted genius and originality, his pervasive liberalism and dogmatic insistence on the integrity and autonomy of human beings, he made a number of contradictory statements and false assumptions about Jews, which, at times, appear to owe more to the complex ambivalence to Jews among the liberal German middle classes than to any objectively derived assessment. Let us take, for example, the problem of whom Weber regarded as a Jew. This was simple enough in relation to his discussion of the Jews of antiquity, but far from clear in relation to those of his own day. In his *Sociology of Religion* he distinguished between a 'Jewish freethinker', 'pious orthodox Jews', 'reformed [sic!] Jews', 'baptized Jews' and 'assimilated Jews'.[14] These categories would suggest that there is no escape for any individual from his Jewishness, even if he has explicitly rejected it by converting to another faith.[15] Still more perplexing and, to my mind, significant, is the sharp distinction Weber draws between reformed Jews who, unlike orthodox Jews, 'were actually welcomed by Puritan nations, especially the Americans', and the situation of Jews in Germany, who 'remain—even after long generations—"assimilated Jews"'. Quite apart from the fact that it was not Puritanism *per se* that made Jews welcome in America, it is surprising that he did not recognise in this very phenomenon he discusses here the implicit weakness of his own 'pariah' concept.[16]

Weber's friends and admirers saw no difficulty in describing him as a German who thought like a European, and a European who was fiercely loyal and devoted to Germany.[17] If he himself could live with a dual identity, why did he insist on describing Jews as a self-chosen pariah people? The important issue is not, as Gerth and Martindale have suggested, that the concept might be thought, although it was not intended, to suggest a contempt-uous attitude toward Jewry—the objection, as Baron has explained, is a conceptual one, it is a rejection of an underlying sociological premise that even if there had not been, or where there is no hostility toward Jews as a religious group, they would still insist on an in-group/out-group barrier to maintain their identity.[18] Just what, in concrete terms, the Jews would have to do to escape, in Weber's conception, from a situation which would leave them permanently 'assimilated', and would obviate the need to counsel an aspiring Jewish academic with Dante's words 'lasciate ogni speranza',[19] remains shrouded in a mystical allusion to Isa. (21:11–12) at the conclusion of the famous lecture, 'Science as a Vocation', where the Jews are described as the people that has 'enquired and tarried for more than two millenia, and we are shaken when we realise its fate.'[20]

The most frequently reiterated characteristic of Jews is their 'dual morality', the moral dichotomy between standards applying to relations with brothers and with aliens.[21] This concept is so fundamental to the Weberian construction and has attracted so much attention also in Marxist circles that we might look at it here in some detail. The basis of Weber's assertion is biblical law, particularly Deut. 23:20, which stipulated that, while the Hebrew may lend on interest to an alien, he may not do so to a 'brother'. Although Weber has received some support for his dual morality thesis from Jewish scholars because he extended its existence to other national and religious groups,[22] there are some general observations which ought to be made and some specific difficulties which arise from a careful analysis of the Weberian argument. To begin with, like Marx and so many other observers, he appears to assume that any generalisation made about Western European Jews from the eleventh century to modern times will also hold good for all Jews at all times, even though this is patently untrue.[23] Second, Weber gives insufficient attention to the separate but equally important consequences of the Deuteronomic law on usury for Christian Europe.[24] Third, he appears to underestimate the importance of the perpetuation of in-group/out-group dichotomies, not only in Catholic Europe but also in Puritan America, as a general sociological variable.[25]

Let us now look at Weber's argument in detail. 'The separation of economic in-group and out-group ethic has remained permanently significant for the religious evaluation of economic activity.'[26] What Weber is suggesting here is that, because the Jews once had a clear dictate linking certain economic behaviour to a specific economic ethic, the same link would always manifest itself no matter what social and historical factors might intervene. The argument further assumes that not only did the Jews of biblical and post-biblical times interpret the law in the same way, but that they all shared this interpretation with Weber. Both assumptions are questionable, for apart from any lack of unanimity about the intention of the usury law, it also underwent constant change according to the position of the Jews. Thus there were those who considered that the purpose of the law was to prevent Israelites from coming into contact with idolaters, while others thought that it was meant to prevent the Israelite from indirectly fostering idolatry by supporting the idolaters' economy.[27] Some rabbinic authorities regarded the law as mandatory, while others (a majority) considered it to be permissive legislation. There were those who, referring to Exod. 22:24, argued that taking interest from a poor Jew or Gentile was forbidden, whereas lending on interest to a rich man was permitted.[28] In fact both of Weber's assumptions, and much of his argument derived from them, can be called into question by a more methodical and comprehensive review of the relationship between socio-historical change and rabbinic exegesis. Note, for example, the following sequence of comments. First, two early talmudic teachers: Rabbi Joseph, commenting on the text of Exod. (22:24): 'If thou lend money to any of my people that is poor by thee', as follows: 'My people that is poor by thee—

means that if the choice is between Jew and idolator, lend to the
Jew; if between rich and poor, lend to the poor; poor relative
or poor townsman, lend to the poor relative; poor townsman
and a poor man from another town, lend to the poor townsman.'[29]
Another Tana explained the statement in Psalm 15:5, that only
he who 'putteth not out his money on interest' shall sojourn in
God's tabernacle, to apply only 'to him who refrains from taking
interest from Jew and Gentile alike'.[30] In subsequent centuries,
important changes took place in Europe which were destined to
be of considerable consequence to the social position of Jews.
Stein has summarised these as the Christianisation of Europe with
its concomitant anti-Jewish legislation; the development of the
feudal system which, because it demanded a Christian oath before
the acquisition of land, alienated the Jew from the soil; the
resultant rise in Jewish migrations; their economic insecurity and
need for religious ritual facilities—all these combined to transform the Jews' economic activity and with it their interpretations
of traditional economic ethics.[31] Rashi (1040–1105), the most
famous and authoritative rabbinic commentator in early medieval
Europe, had witnessed the first Crusade (1096) and recognised the
need to reinterpret the in-group/out-group ideal of Deuteronomy.
'We cannot,' he wrote, 'maintain ourselves unless we do business
with them, because we live amonst Gentiles and our maintenance
comes from or through them, and also out of fear.'[32] His grandson
Rabenu Tam (1100–71), who had himself suffered severely during
the second Crusade (1145–7), went further:[33]

> Today people usually lend money at interest to Gentiles and we
> decide leniently . . . because we have to pay taxes to the king and
> princes and everything is 'Kedei hayeinu' [for the sake of our
> survival]; we live among the nations and it is impossible for us to
> earn a living unless we deal with them. It is therefore no more
> forbidden to lend at interest because one might learn from their
> deeds, than it is to engage in any other business.

Maimonides (1135–1204) and Nachmanides (1194–1270), the
renowned Spanish rabbis, not being subjected to the same
hostility as their north-western European counterparts, took a
more detached and somewhat less conciliatory view. Maimonides'

primary concern was the problem of contamination. He regarded lending money on interest to Gentiles as a positive commandment in Deuteronomy, but pointed out that this might only be done 'to the extent that this may be necessary for the Israelite in order to earn a livelihood'. A scholar, on the other hand, who was not likely to learn from the heathen, might lend at interest 'for the mere sake of making a profit'.[34] Nachmanides, however, contented himself with the moral counsel that it was best to refrain from lending money at interest to Gentiles.

From the thirteenth century onwards there was a trend to regard the major monotheistic religions not, as even Maimonides did, as idol-worship (the extreme evil in Jewish law) but as worship of the true God, albeit in unacceptable form. Meiri (Don Vidal Solomon, 1249–1306) is described by Stein as the first rabbi to express this view, although others credit Rashi with its introduction.[35] Meiri therefore argued that 'no one cares about refraining from business dealings with, and loans to, Gentiles . . . these laws refer only to real idolators and their images, but all transactions with Christians are perfectly legal'. A more outspoken expression of the changing Jewish attitude came from David Kimchi (Redak, 1160–1235):[36]

> the Torah forbade the charging of interest to the Israelite but permitted him to do so to the alien . . . The Hebrew must not overreach or rob the alien or steal from him, but interest which he takes by full agreement [of the non-Jew] is permitted . . . The Jew is under no obligation to lend to Gentiles without interest, because generally they hate the Jews. But if the Gentile is kind to the Jew, the Jew must certainly be kind and good to him.

By the fifteenth century, Rabbi Joseph Kolon observed casually that moneylending was the main occupation of the Jews of Italy, and Rabbi Kapsali at about the same time noted that the Jews of Venice were 'owners of loan-banks and God has blessed them with wealth, because they devote their time to the study of the law'.[37]

With the advent of the sixteenth century and the emergence of modern capitalism, it is possible for a famous Jewish exegete to offer an economic theory which, while remaining strictly within the limits imposed by Jewish law, yet proposes a rational defence of the biblical commandment. Don Abarbanel (1437–1508) argued thus:[38]

> There is nothing unworthy about interest *per se*, because it is proper that people should make profit out of their money . . . if someone wants money from someone else, why should the borrower not give the lender a certain amount of interest? . . . This is neither despicable nor contemptible. It is an ordinary business transaction and correct. Nobody is under obligation to give his money away to somebody else, unless it be for the sake of charity. Equally, one cannot be compelled to lend one's money free of interest, unless for the sake of charity.

And that is how Abarbanel saw the injunction of giving interest-free loans to fellow-Jews. It was an extension of charity which, certainly in the middle ages, would not have been seen as extending beyond one's immediate parish or brotherhood. An equally 'rational' defence of the Jewish position came from a contemporary of Abarbanel, Abraham ben Mordecai Farissol (1451–1525), who wrote:[39]

> The urban communities who pay interest [to Jews] derive great benefit from the Jewish taxes for the betterment of their cities. If people in need of money do not find Jews or other money-lenders they will lose more than by paying interest, because they will either buy what they need from someone else on credit and at a high price, or they will bring along garments or precious possessions in exchange . . . This is well known to the merchants of the Gentiles who have an understanding of the times. They sell their ware on credit at certain seasons [when prices are high] and do twice as much damage as the fixed rate of interest known to be charged by the Jews. This rate is law, quite apart from its being based on mutual agreement.

Josel of Rosheim (1478–1554) drew up a financial code of practice for Jews which limited rates of interest, curbed aggressive methods of debt collection and forbade 'obnoxious' loans. He persuaded the leaders of Jewish communities to adopt this code.[40]

A seventeenth-century Jewish writer, Leon da Modena, argued along lines which we will discuss later in defence of Jewish business ethics:[41]

> The Torah did not forbid interest at all, only usury [Neshech], i.e. something that bites, something improper and against ethical

223

conduct. The whole question is to be judged [even amongst Jews] according to the viewpoint of the leaders of a given place, according to business usage and according to time . . . It is proper to organise a community in such a way as is customary amongst some of the other nations.

Even this brief survey of rabbinic views set out in historical sequence shows the pattern of adaptive interpretation which Jewish law underwent in order to enable its followers to co-ordinate the demands of Jewish law and the pressures of the external environment into a coherent and ethically meaningful life-style. It is surprising that so acute an observer as Max Weber should have missed the pronounced evolutionary trend in Jewish commercial ethics, that he should have discussed those comments and concerns of rabbis that he came across as 'mere difficulties for Jewish ethical theorists', and that he should have regarded any disapproval of usury expressed in 'late Judaic ethic' as being inconsequential 'in the face of the robust words of the Torah'.[42] In this context it would be relevant to note that it is really quite remarkable that not even present-day writers, Jewish or other, have seriously considered the possibility of taking the biblical usury law at face value. If an independent political state adopts legislation which is intended to further the interests of its citizens, but which has no parallel provisions in neighbouring states, then it is both logical and even essential to create a dual system. If a ban on usury is ethically desirable and introduced unilaterally, then the legislating state can survive economically only if it introduces dual legislation which would prevent outsiders from taking advantage of a law, the provisions of which are not reciprocally binding. A modern example would be the need in Britain to deny the foreigner the advantages of a free national health service if his own country has no such facility. Just as the existence of dual legislation is *not* an expression of 'superiority' but a means of protecting a social innovation from exploitation, so the absence of dual legislation would mean that, whatever the unilateral provision, it would have been unworkable.

Another point that might be made here is to emphasise the simple fact that the usury law is one of 613 biblical commandments. It is only among non-Jewish analysts that it finds such disproportionate significance. In Jewish literature it does not feature as a dominant issue to anything like the same extent. Historically it has been important as a focus of conflict between Christianity and pre-capitalism, rather than as a precept of Jewish religious practice.

The statement by Modena which we quoted earlier clearly indicates that among Jews, as among Christians, a more universalistic ethos, coincidental with the rise of the Calvinist approach, was emerging, which not only invalidates the Weberian thesis of a voluntary pariah capitalism, but also calls into question an important distinction he made between Puritan honesty and Jewish legality. For not only were the Jews themselves committed to an 'honesty is the best policy' ethos, except in situations where they used legal but harsh commercial practice as a form of retaliation for indignities to which they were subjected, but the outside world too was beginning to see their value as 'honest brokers', as is suggested by the comments of Abarbanel and the activities of Josel of Rosheim on the one hand, and an interesting comment by Manitius, Friedrich II the Great's minister of finance, on the other. In the memorandum of 1745, Manitius recommended the removal of restrictions and special taxes on Jews. 'Business,' he wrote, 'knows no difference between religions. All it demands is honest dealings. And in that respect we could only wish that Christians were as scrupulous as Jews.'[43]

The main weakness of Weber's ideal-typical 'dual morality' model is, first, that it ignores the continuous development of economic values in the Jewish tradition, as I have just tried to indicate in a very brief review of the continuous changes in rabbinic attitudes. Second, that it treats an essentially *rational* piece of legislation as an *ideologically* significant construct for which a permanent validity is assumed. It would be only fair to note, however, that, like Weber, many Jewish commentators have also attempted to establish biblically derived economic legislation within ideological frameworks. Nevertheless, since Weber developed an ideal-type rationality as a factor in the economic development of Protestantism, his insistence on an

225

ideological interpretation of the usury laws in Judaism is somewhat perplexing.

Another Weberian thesis stipulates that, because Jewish
capitalism was political, speculative or adventurous, it did not
develop rationally organised industries based on free labour. As
a historical observation this is essentially true, but the explanation
is likely to be more complex. Parkes, for example, has put forward
an interesting counter-explanation to Weber's. He assigns responsibility for the pariah status of Jews to 'Christendom', and
explains the lack of Jewish participation in industrial capitalism
by describing their position at the end of the middle ages as 'so
completely ruined that their share in the beginnings of the new
commercial and industrial order was negligible'.[44] Similarly we
could note that Weber's view, that the infusion of a religious
ethic into economic relations made 'the brutal accumulation of
money'[45] objectionable to Puritans, was the exact opposite of a
charge made against Puritans by Marx.[46]

There are some points on which Weber is factually wrong.
Thus, it is incorrect to say that 'no religious premium' existed for
exercising economic restraint.[47] The principle of 'Chilul hashem'
(desecration of the Holy Name), which has existed since ancient
times, is precisely the 'premium' which could and generally did
determine the ethics of economic relations with Gentiles. Subject,
of course, to the possibility of application. That is to say, religious
leaders in Judaism always frowned upon and indeed curbed
economic behaviour, if it brought Jews, and through them their
God, into disrepute. But in situations where the Jew *per se* was
despised and persecuted, such a principle would be difficult to
apply since whatever the Jew did would reinforce his evil
reputation. If for example there appeared to be no ethical restraint
on Jewish economic activity, this would be due not to the
absence of a restraining code but to its inefficacy as a mediator
between in-group and out-group.[48] Weber is also wrong in
claiming that 'the highest form of Jewish piety is found in the
religious mood (*Stimmung*) and not in active behaviour'.[49] The
highest form of Jewish piety is carrying out religious precepts
(*Mitzvot*), most of which involve action of one kind or another.

Our primary objective in taking issue with some of Weber's historical and analytic arguments has been to demonstrate that, unlike most of his predecessors in Germany, notably those in whom we are interested, such as Hegel, Bruno Bauer and Karl Marx, he was not concerned with 'abolishing' Judaism or nullifying it, or demonstrating the need for eliminating it. Neither were his analytic categories such that they would allow him to reduce Jews and Judaism into irreversibly fixed elements which made all further argument superfluous, as Sombart attempted to do. In this respect he stands in the tradition of Ludwig Feuerbach, whose *Essence of Christianity* 'was not a critical destruction of Christian theology and Christianity, but an attempt to retain what is essential in Christianity in the form of a religious "anthropology" '.[50] In this sense Weber also differed from Marx in that he did not attempt to eliminate Judaism but tried to isolate its ideal-typical characteristics, recognising both the need for a continuous refinement of his variables through empirical research and the impropriety that empirical research should 'wish or even be able to deny anybody the opportunity to evaluate, as "revelations", facts which science seeks to explain empirically as far as the resources permit.'[51]

WERNER SOMBART

Sombart's (1863–1941) *The Jews and Modern Capitalism* (1911)[52] owes its origins directly to Weber's *Puritan Ethic*.[53]

> That the religion of a people, or of a group within a people, can have far-reaching influences on its economic life will not be disputed. Only recently Max Weber demonstrated the connection between Puritanism and capitalism. In fact, Max Weber's researches are responsible for this book. For anyone who followed them could not but ask himself whether all that Weber ascribes to Puritanism might not with equal justice be referred to Judaism, and probably in a greater degree; nay, it might well be suggested that that which is called Puritanism is in reality Judaism.

Unlike Weber, however, Sombart is not primarily analytical nor is he particularly interested in a comparative approach. Instead he builds his argument mainly on historical and descriptive data. Again, unlike Weber, he begins with a hypothesis and selects his data to substantiate it, a process which leads him inevitably into a set of immutable determinants, though he himself was convinced of 'the unimpeachable objectivity of my Jew-book (*Judenbuch*)'.[54] Sombart makes direct references to Marx and also plays with ideas put forward by Heine and Bruno Bauer. He described his approach as 'statistical and genetic', though both terms are really meaningless in his text.[55]

Like Weber, Sombart has the greatest difficulty in deciding who is a Jew, or what he means by it. At first we are told that his references to Jews include 'renegade Jews', that is to say those who have themselves, or whose parents have, converted, because 'historically they remain Jews'.[56] Later on in the book he writes that he is not interested in Reform Judaism and its 'ethics of Judaism', because only those concerned with detailed rabbinic law are involved in his thesis.[57] Still further on, various categories of Jews are contrasted, including the categories suggested by Marx: 'Western Jews are different from Eastern Jews, the Sephardim from the Ashkenazim, the Orthodox from the Liberals, the everyday Jew from the Sabbath Jew (to use a phrase of Marx). This . . . there is no need to deny. But it does not by any means preclude the possibility of common Jewish characteristics.'[58]

Sombart's essay could be seen as an attempt to restate the Marxian thesis in sociological terms. What Sombart seeks to provide are the historical and anthropological proofs to substantiate the Marxian claim that Judaism was 'the spirit of capitalism'. Methodologically he followed Weber—in fact, copied him—but he lacked the capacity to formulate theoretical principles and the distance from his subject to explain those aspects of Jewish history which went against his basic suppositions.[59] In the first part of his book, he set out to show the dominant influence of Jews in the development of modern capitalism in Europe: 'Israel passes over Europe like the sun: at its coming, new life bursts forth; at its going all falls into decay.'[60] In Sombart's view, the importance of the Jews for the economic development of Europe was twofold: 'they influenced the outward form of capitalism [and] gave expression to its inward spirit'.[61] Like Marx, he regarded the colonisation of America as a direct transfer of 'the Jewish spirit' to the new world, Jews 'swarmed' there as soon as settlement began[62] and filled it 'to the brim with the Jewish spirit',[63] so that Americanism is nothing other than 'the Jewish spirit distilled'.[64] Like Roscher, Sombart claimed that Jews contributed, indeed invented, important instruments of finance, e.g. securities, which made it possible to progress from personal to impersonal moneylending.[65] Sombart strongly disagreed with Weber about the economic role of the Jew. 'Not his "usury" differentiated [the Jew] from the Christian, not that he sought gain, not that he amassed wealth; only that he did all this openly, not thinking it wrong, that he scrupulously and mercilessly looked after his business interests.'[66] The difference between Sombart and Weber then was that Weber regarded the Jewish pariah status as a product of the Jews' own in-group/out-group ethic, whereas Sombart inclined to the view that pariah status was imposed on the Jew by a tradition-bound Christian society. The Jew therefore felt free to reject accepted Christian ethical standards which regulated commercial life and to adopt instead the dominance of market factors to order his business. He thus became the innovator *par excellence* in a conformist environment. The contrast was not between Christian honesty and Jewish legality, but between Christian traditional ethic and 'capitalistic spirit'.[67] The Jews thus disregarded barriers between industries, states and prevailing codes of etiquette, introduced modern advertising, founded the cheap press and created demands for goods.[68] They introduced new business methods such as marketing cheap goods, accepting the idea of small profits with large turnovers, gimmick selling and credit buying. They introduced waste-product trades, the 'general store' and payment by instalments.[69] In short, the Jew was 'modern' and created modern commercial practices. Sombart dismissed the question of Jews' disabilities and their persecution because 'they were of no moment whatever for the economic growth of Jewry'.[70] Nor did he recognise that the problems created by legal restrictions on

Jews did not affect so much their economic growth (which was in any event always distorted by the emergence of a small number of exceptionally wealthy families) as their economic structure which, by concentrating them in commerce and finance, misled him (and many others) into regarding this enforced occupational structure as a racial characteristic. Like Bauer and Marx, Sombart argued that the legally disadvantaged Jew compensated for his inferior position by acquiring wealth: the Jews 'became lords of money and through it lords of the world'.[71]

In considering the chief characteristic of Jews, this time clearly following Heine, Sombart stressed their rationalism or intellectualism, which was opposed to mysticism and the natural world, 'to that creative power which draws its artistic inspiration from the passion world of the senses . . . when the faithful of other religions hold converse with God in blissful convulsions . . . in the shool [synagogue] . . . the Torah is publicly read'.[72] But Sombart disagreed with Marx on the question of the relationship between religion and the nature of man. Marx had stated emphatically in relation to religion in general that 'man makes religion; religion does not make man',[73] and for Jews specifically that the secret of the Jew was not in his religion, but the secret of his religion was in the real Jew.[74] Sombart however took the view that 'external legalism does not remain external; it exercises a constant influence on the inner life, which obtains its peculiar character from the observance of the law.'[75] He argued that 'self-control' was an essential ingredient of Jewish law, and therefore life, that this was demonstrated in their sexual mores, where 'the rationalisation of conduct is its best expression'.[76] There follows an extremely tendentious discussion of Deut. 23:20 in which Sombart shows himself to be better acquainted than Max Weber with post-biblical Jewish literature, but also more selective in choosing his data to suit his argument. Certainly, like Weber, he failed to perceive how closely Jewish thought evolved alongside Christian thought in interpreting the functions of the law. This led Sombart to the crux of his argument, that in both Judaism and Puritanism are to be found those characteristics which are essential for the emergence of modern capitalism, in fact, 'Puritanism *is* Judaism'.[77] Nevertheless, Jews have certain peculiarities which Sombart posits like Weberian analytic categories, and of which all those who wrote about Jews, including Marx, were conscious.[78] These peculiarities were extreme intellectuality (they behold the world not with their soul but with their intellect), rationalism (they are interested always in the result of a thing, not the thing itself), mobility and energy (both mental and physical) and adaptability.[79]

Since, according to Sombart, Jewish characteristics 'have been constant through the ages in a most extraordinary fashion',[80] and because Jews are 'more' than a religion, a nation and a people, he opted for the concept of race and speculated what the significance of a race with such special characteristics and such a special history might be. Notwithstanding his earlier assertion that the Jew's peculiar character was the result of the influence of the law, he now argued against himself and with Marx, that 'the fundamental characteristics of the Jewish religious system . . . must have been in existence . . . even before the religion was developed.'[81] Thus not the Diaspora, not the middle ages, but Jewish traits created their characteristics. Sombart thought that 'Jewish characteristics are rooted in the blood of the race and are not in any wise due to educative processes.'[82] In an interesting parallel to Bauer, he claimed as an established fact that the 'capitalistic civilisation of our age is the fruit of the union between the Jews [with their] extraordinary capacity for commerce and the Northern peoples, above all the Germans [with their] remarkable ability for technical innovations.'[83] In a final contradiction, Sombart explained how 'throughout the centuries . . . Israel has remained a desert and a nomadic people', while at the same time 'they became towndwellers . . . and towndwellers they have remained.'[84]

If Weber wrote in the tradition of Ludwig Feuerbach, Sombart is very much a latter-day Bruno Bauer. Like Bauer, Sombart began as a radical (Marxist) and ended at the other extreme of the political spectrum (Bauer became a conservative, Sombart a fascist). Like Bauer, Sombart strenuously denied being antisemitic, but steadily moved his position until he was in agreement with the racial anti-semitism of the National Socialists. He may not have moved quite as much on this as would appear at first sight. Although in his *Jews and Modern Capitalism* he expressed the hope that no one would think so badly of him as to regard him as anti-semitic (p. 279) and referred contemptuously to anti-semitic pamphleteers as 'prejudiced scribblers' (p. 303), his own position was highly ambivalent even then. In his article in *Judentaufen* published a year after *J&MC*, he expressed the view that the unification of the human species through intermarriage would be terrible (*schauerlich*) (p. 14), that even if Jews changed their names, their 'physiognomy' would betray their origin (p. 18), and that there were some Jews he liked, but 'objective Jewish cultural life' he did not find very sympathetic (p. 20). Also in 1912 Sombart published *Die Zukunft der Juden* (Leipzig), in which he expressed support for Zionism because since no one can 'leave his race', the exodus of Jews to Israel would 'free the German national soul (*Volksseele*) from the grip of the Jewish spirit' (p. 85). By the time he published *Deutscher Sozialismus* (Berlin, 1934), he is openly anti-semitic. For Sombart to move his position does not appear to have been unusual. Hoselitz noted that 'it is interesting to note that [Sombart] discovers the Jewish influence in the development of capitalism at a time when he is, on the whole, critical of capitalist economy, whereas, after World War I, when he has become a violent opponent of Marxian socialism he finds that "proletarian socialism" is strongly influenced by Jewish thoughts.'[85] Sombart's tendency to shift his position is also described by F. Friedlander.[86] For all that, it probably was not any preoccupation with Jews that led Sombart to write about them. As was the case with Bauer, there appears to have been an ulterior motive, which in Sombart's case may well have been the need to compete against Max Weber, for in his later book, *The Quintessence of Capitalism*, he also argued against the 'prevailing' view that Puritanism, and in particular Calvinism, fostered the spirit of capitalism. He put forward the view that the essential ingredients for capitalism were already inherent in the teachings of the Catholic church and that, if anything, 'Protestantism has been all along the line a foe to capitalism' and 'it would be but a narrow conception of the capitalist spirit . . . to see its various manifestations springing from Puritanism.'[87]

We cannot here delve further into this issue. As far as Sombart's analysis of Judaism is concerned, we have seen that in its essential conception it supports the Marxian thesis, albeit in less objectionable terms. Its main weaknesses are that Sombart virtually ignored the persecution of Jews in Western and Central Europe, particularly since he confines his attention to these very Jews. If one were to take his insistence on the existence of Jewish characteristics seriously, then it would be difficult to see why the Jews did not make better use of their 'intellectuality and rationality' to discover (as Sombart and Marx did) the relationship between their economic activities and their persecution, and to opt for a less hazardous economic role. Like Marx, Sombart ignored the position of the great majority of Jews throughout history, not least perhaps because the Jews of Eastern Europe, North Africa and Arabia provided little evidence of that 'genius' which changed the economic destiny of the Occident. We have already noted that it was not until Sombart had moved towards a position of positive hostility to socialism that he attempted to explain why so many of the initiators of capitalism should have been drawn so strongly to the creed dedicated to its destruction.

Sombart's ability to transform traditional religious and political polemic into respectable pseudo-social scientific theses is also displayed by Ferdinand Tönnies in a remarkable passage on Jews in a famous paper, 'The Individual and the World', in which we once again meet 'the Jews' as typified by the numerically insignificant Western European Jews, in which Marxian principles are reasserted and even anti-semitism is made to sound quite normal.

Jews, wrote Tönnies, were 'predestined' for the role of intermediaries. Their financial transactions during the middle ages caused them to be 'hated, feared and persecuted' until the advent of Protestantism brought emancipation, which, while giving Jews legal equality, did not counteract 'sentiment and opinion' about them. In a single sentence Tönnies managed to summarise both Marx and Sombart: 'The conception of what Jews are came to blend so completely with trade, that is, with capitalism, that many traits which we regard as Jewish are in fact characteristic of trade in general—notably of dealings in money and capital—although Jewish peculiarities will often enhance them.' Tönnies predicted that Jews would increasingly concentrate in the great cities where, like other small groups (e.g. the Swiss and the Quakers), they would form communities—'a sort of conspiracy' —to behave recklessly against all but their fellows.[88]

MAX HORKHEIMER

Although Horkheimer (1895–1973) was a social philosopher rather than a sociologist, his close connection with Marxian approaches to history, his dominant influence on the Frankfurt School, both before and after the Hitler era, and his keen interest in religion generally and Judaism in particular make his contributions highly relevant to our deliberations.

Like most of the members of the Frankfurt School, Horkheimer was a middle-class Jew whose early associations with Judaism were tenuous and whose early intellectual activities were dominated by revolutionary Marxism.[89] There are a number of factors, however, which make his contribution to the Jewish question, indeed to 'critical theory' generally, unusual and interesting. The first of these is the constant and admitted influence of personal experiences on his social theory. If any attempts to relate events in Marx's life to his theoretical views are daring speculation, in Horkheimer's case such influences are all too apparent and he himself readily admits them.[90] Second, because Horkheimer's starting-point in the analysis of the Jewish question was Marxist, but underwent considerable change, and third, because he was a very rare neo-Marxist thinker who succeeded in making an original contribution to the sociological analysis of religion without relinquishing his historical-materialist approach or allowing his analysis to degenerate into a blind, hostile or contemptuous rejection of everything even remotely associated with it.

In order to convey some idea of the way in which Horkheimer's thought developed, largely as a result of the events in his own lifetime, let us look first at his concept of the role of religion in society, his analyses of Christianity and Judaism as historical phenomena, the effect of German anti-semitism and, finally, his reassertion of a positive Judaism.

Horkheimer began as a Marxist.[91]

> It is true—I was a Marxist, a revolutionary. I began to study Marx after the first world war, because the danger of nationalism was obvious. I believed that national socialism could only be overcome through revolution, a Marxist revolution. Being a revolutionary, a Marxist was a response to totalitarian domination from the right, but I doubted even then, that the solidarity of the proletariat, demanded by Marx, would, in the end, create the right society. Marx's starting-point was the oppression of the proletariat, a condition of which the proletariat had to be made aware. They would then discover that they had a common interest—the radical elimination of oppression. But in this respect Marx was wrong. The social position of the proletariat improved without revolution . . .

If he was a Marxist, it was never as a blind follower of a creed, but rather as an intellectual attracted to a particular approach to history. If he was a revolutionary, it was never in the accepted sense of that term. Critical theorists have often been attacked for their lack of involvement in political action, none more so than Horkheimer.[92] It would seem however that his notion of being a revolutionary was itself a romantic, intellectualised concept which saw its praxis embodied in its critical contemplations.[93] We will not be surprised, therefore, to find a considerable unorthodoxy in his views whenever he felt sufficiently unconstrained to allow his thoughts to develop. That his Jewish origins were an embarrassment and a handicap is clearly reflected in his early writing on the Jews,[94] but this was not the case with his 'Marxist' analysis of religion.

For Marx, the critique of religion was the important thing, whereas for Horkheimer, to whom religion was a historical more than an actual problem and who had to a considerable extent also been influenced by the work of Max Weber, the need was more to understand than to undermine, to explain rather than to destroy. Hence religion must not only be seen as a concomitant of domination, as 'a sigh of the oppressed', because even beyond oppression there were problems to which men sought solutions, problems which did not have their roots in, and could not be alleviated by, material conditions. There was, first and foremost, death, which, 'in so far as it is not alleviated by religious or meta-physical comfort, is absolute destruction.'[95] That is why 'death as an unavoidable end has always been the basis of religious and metaphysical illusion.'[96] Some aspects of religion certainly owe their origin to material conditions and wants but there are also other human aspirations which give rise to images of the divine and men's relationships to those images. Once these have been created and become established, they acquire their own dynamic and begin to influence men just as men, in the first instance, influenced religious conceptions. 'While it is true that religion receives its entire content through psychic integration (*psychische Verarbeitung*) of worldly events, it acquires in that process its own *Gestalt*, which in turn acts on the spiritual nature (*Veranlagung*) and destiny of men and, as a whole, gives a reality to social evolution.'[97] Since almost all aspects of religion are discussed by Horkheimer (as they are by Marx) in a Judeo-Christian context, it is interesting to note that in this instance he chooses examples from Chinese and Indian cultures to illustrate his point. Thus, ancestor-worship among the Chinese is explained in that it had its origins in conditions of production which made the young dependent on the experience and techniques of the old.[98]

> [These] conditions of production are in the first instance experienced in religious forms and then gain their own history and significance. The ancestor-cult, which influences each individual through educa-tion, custom and religion as a living social force, constantly receives new impulses, not only through the experience of the child and young man with his parents and grandparents, but also through many spiritual elements which are activated in each person by events and which utilise cultural forms. Thus, the idea that ancestors retain their power in the world beyond, especially their power to bestow blessing, extends the possibilities of influencing an unpredictable fate.

The ability of religious traditions to integrate themselves into the lifestyles of groups and individuals has important consequences for social change. Just as it is 'wrong to regard religious ideas as anything other than the mediated reflection of worldly events dictated to man through his labour, so it would be wrong not to recognise that these ideas exercise a definite social effect on each individual.'[99] It would be foolish, for example, to assume that 'theoretical enlightenment' could eliminate the evils of the Indian caste-system. In that system, the idea of earning a better place in another existence has become so important that any attempt to change it would be regarded as a step to deprive the destitute and despised of a well-deserved and just reward. That is one of the reasons why 'even the lower orders would react to any forcible attempt at change with fury and fanaticism at the slightest provocation'.[100]

The implication of such a view of religion must lead to criticism of the Marxian position on religion. 'The maintenance of anachronistic social norms is due, not necessarily to sheer force or the deception of the masses about their material interests—these are themselves determined by the nature of man—but this perpetuation has its roots in so-called human nature' and any 'unhistoric, theoretically undeveloped concept of religion consists of both knowledge and superstition.'[101] The causes of the revolt against religion were not as simple, or indeed as radical, as the Marxists would have us believe. To begin with, there is the somewhat cynical observation that, while the citizen believes passionately in the need for religion, he believes rather less passionately in its truth.[102] Second, the bourgeois revolt against religion was not so much a challenge of the idea of God, but rather a challenge of the idea of absolute authority which was contrary to the emerging bourgeois conviction that the authority of tradition as the sole legitimate source of right and truth was not compatible with the rationality of every individual.[103] If the individual is rational, he will recognise for example that there are flaws in the religious argument which cannot be glossed over. The authority of a religious tradition need not be a factor of its validity, not least because inherent in that position has been the capacity of religious tradition to accept any given attitude to social issues, irrespective of its moral content. The authority of

God over events on earth ought to be called into question, if only 'because the saint is as likely to be executed as the sinner'.[104]

In short, there is a need for a materialist view of religion, but a view which ought never to lose sight of the need for and value of religion in society. Horkheimer explained this in great detail.[105]

> It is possible to understand history without making vain attempts to interpret it into a process of salvation. Goodness, justice and wisdom which, theoretically, are always possible, are not realised as long as they remain images in the minds of men. Those who want to realise them do not need to transform the image into a god; they know full well that even goodness, once realised, has a history and will pass. The finite aims, for which fighters and pioneers of all times have accepted death, do not mean extinction, because they were not permanent aims. They differ from death in that they created a short period of happiness . . .

Yet, although materialist theory would seek to explain the concept of God from dynamic social processes, it does not thereby reject religious conceptions, but only their dogmatism, it recognises in theological concepts (e.g. resurrection, eternal life) 'man's need for never ending happiness' which stands in stark contrast to his fate on earth. Again, the materialist knows that 'the wish for eternal happiness, that religious dream of mankind, is not possible'; he is overwhelmed by 'the utter isolation of man' (grenzenlose Verlassenheit) and therefore understands the search for comfort by the religious.

What emerges from this is characteristic of Horkheimer, a simultaneous affirmation and rejection of religion, 'a materialist theology' which he himself would probably have explained from 'his Judaism' and which Friedrich Heer once described as 'the faith of the atheistic Jew'.[106] In a short fragment of 1935, Gedanken zur Religion, Horkheimer explained that, just as after Kant's critique the idea of reason survived, so, since the passing of religious longing through social practice, an idea remains which, while it can be shown to be impossible, nevertheless persists. This is the idea of complete justice. It can never be realised in history because, even if present disorder is resolved in a better society, past miseries and the cruelty of nature cannot be resolved.

That everyone is entitled to a share of happiness is a product of generalised economic principles, but[107]

> the incentive to think beyond the possible, this hopeless rebellion against reality, belongs to man as he evolved historically. It is not the rejection of this image which distinguishes the progressive person from the backward, but the recognition of the limits to which it can be realised . . . It is a vain hope that contemporary discussions of the churches will re-awaken religion as it was in the beginning; for the goodwill, the solidarity with deprivation and the aspirations for a better world have dispensed with their religious garb. The attitude of the martyrs is no longer toleration but action, their aim is no longer their own immortality in the world beyond but the happiness of men who come after them and for whom they are willing to die . . . Mankind loses its religion as it moves forward, but religion leaves its mark. Some of the drives and desires which religious beliefs have awakened and preserved are being released from their constricting frames and transformed into productive forces in social action. Even the remnants of shattered illusions acquire positive form in this process and become truths. In genuinely free thought, the concept of the infinite will be retained as an expression of the consciousness of the finality of worldly events and the unchangeable isolation of man. It will thus protect society from a vapid optimism, an arrogant assertion of science as its new religion.

Horkheimer was quite explicit about the way religion could be used, or, better, misused by ruling classes. Thus, 'the battle of the bourgeoisie against atheism demonstrates . . . the wisdom of the government. Society needs religion as a means of social control (*Herrschaftsmittel*) because the general interest does not provide enough cohesion.'[108] The analysis of religion then is not so much a rejection of the Marxian critique as an extension of it. Since Marx belonged historically to the period of transition from absolutism to liberalism, he could be expected to have missed 'the progressive elements of religion' because these were 'obscured' at that time.[109] For Marx, religion was the false consciousness of social man living in a distorted world. Once that world was put right, religion would disappear because man would have neither need of, nor use for, it. For Horkheimer, this was too broad and sweeping. It not only ignored specific historical situations, it also failed to distinguish between religion as a human manifestation and churches as social institutions. Most of all it offered no explanation for 'the longing for something quite different',[110] a concept which Marx would have repudiated as a theocentric illusion, but which for Horkheimer had two important components. The first was an idea taken from Heidegger about the centrality of death as, what in Marxian terms we might call, natural man's expression of and protest against his natural fate.[111] The second was the Judaic concept of 'complete justice', social man's expression of and protest against his own relativism in the face of an unknowable absolute, or, to paraphrase Peter Berger, the audacious attempt to conceive of the humanly significant as being universal.[112]

If Horkheimer showed much sympathy for religion *per se*, he was highly critical of Christianity, not as a religion but as a world power. In fact, the main theme of his criticism was precisely that, as a system of power, Christianity betrayed its religious mission. Accordingly, he was full of admiration for Christianity in its earliest stages as a revolutionary force, critical of Catholicism as an organised church, but most scathing about Protestantism as the moral cloak of a ruthless bourgeoise. Nevertheless, even in the betrayal of its religious principles, Christianity was the historical instrument that brought civilisation and progress to Europe. The historical sequence is clearly delineated in a brilliant paper, *Theismus-Atheismus*, which was written in 1963.[113]

Early Christians were scapegoats in Europe because they refused to place the state above everything else—'they knew of higher things than the *imperium*', but Constantine chose Christianity and raised it to the status of a world religion. Had Christians adhered to the message of their founder, they could not have achieved what they did. The first Christians followed a vision that the heavens were open to them, but as the new religion became increasingly powerful in secular matters and incorporated evil into its plans for the affairs of this world, hell assumed a correspondingly greater role in thoughts about the next world. Theology was the mediator between the Gospels and the ruling power. 'The unification of Christianity and domination, the creation of a satisfying self-consciousness for rulers and subjects to enable them to labour for an evil reality, was its outstanding achievement.' Yet, if the great theologians had taken the difference between Christendom and Christianity as seriously as Kierkegaard was to do, no monument of Christian culture would exist today. The great cultural heritage of Europe was made possible by 'the artful patchwork of scholastic theology'. Scholasticism gave a relatively static society its ideological content. It proclaimed eternal truths of the timely and the beyond time, of past and future. Of a Lord enthroned above the earth and a natural hierarchy of merit below Him. Of clergy, nobles and masters placed above citizens and serfs, and of still lower regions for the damned. There was the concept of a universe in which divine and human law, divine and human science, were united. Notwithstanding destiny and grace, the future in a world to come was largely determined by conduct here on earth. Thus the life of everyone had meaning.

Political divisions which occurred in Europe broke 'the trust in eternal concepts, in the harmony of heavenly and earthly science, the unity of theory and practice, which scholasticism shared with Marxism'. In its final stages, medieval Europe was disrupted by wars and conquests, by economic enterprise, new sciences, destitute masses, inflation and a backward clergy. It was at this point that Protestantism intervened. Not only did it acknowledge the contrast between Christianity and worldliness— it made it the core of the faith. Luther hated scholasticism, theories about eternity, philosophical systems and reason. A new theological pragmatism was the order of the day. Soldiers wading in the blood of peasants who rebelled because they were hungry could be just as Christian as the politically naive who shared their bread with them.

The only thing that mattered was that everyone must honestly believe that he is following the faith. The new interpretation paved the way for civil liberties, liberalism and merciless competition between individuals and nations. The commandment to love one's enemy remained valid, but whether one was to 'burn the heretic and the witch, make children labour before they can read, make bombs and bless them, or curse them, as the case may be', that every believer must decide for himself. One possible guide for the individual might be the interests of the fatherland. 'Over the last few centuries far more people have given their lives for the fatherland than for the forbidden love of the enemy.' In this way, belief in God had given way to belief in one's own people, a development strongly reinforced by absolute idealism from Fichte to Hegel.

Although both forms of Christianity survived in Europe, the new era also gave rise to a militant atheism and, at first, 'a metaphysical materialism', which as a Utopian-messianic theory of history was too weak to seriously threaten Christianity. 'Absolute theology was more effective in offering comfort, motivation and threat than anything that philosophical materialism could offer.' For the naturalism of the materialists was as vague as the God of the theologians. 'Naturalism, like the theological doctrine it challenges, equates the most constant and most powerful with the highest and most worthy.' In place of God, it offered only an impersonal concept unlikely to allay the fears and anxieties of men searching for salvation in the face of certain death. The materialistic belief in nature was an attempt to adapt to the new sciences without relinquishing the ancient longing for eternal truths, but traditional religion and its institutions have always been better able to cater for the irrational needs of men. In this sense, therefore, the early atheists were no more than a passing threat to Christianity. The changes of the modern era are, however, more fundamental. The growth of technology, and the extension of public administration which invaded every facet of life, destroyed the privacy of the individual, undermined his autonomy and radically altered the expectations of abilities and skills which individuals and their families had to develop in order to participate in the social system.

These changes to which theology had to adapt itself also gave rise to a new phenomenon—communism—the most powerful enemy not only of religion, but of culture generally. This is not so much the communism of Marx and Engels—who were themselves great symbols of European culture—but a dialectical materialism 'which has been converted into a mere ideology by the new masters'. The changes which this new enemy inspired in Catholicism and Protestantism are as decisive as any in the history of theology. Rome becomes both progressive and conservative. 'The new attitude seeks to improve the life of the workers to help them in a free world to share its wealth, and in backward dictatorships, to free them from brutal oppression.' The inevitability of social change is accepted and affirmed. 'In accordance with the new spirit, the church attempts to participate in the restructuring of society.' Protestantism went even further. Not only did it eliminate every vestige of conflict with science, it even challenged its own basic principles of morality. God, the holy trinity and the hereafter are relegated as myths. They survive only because they proclaim the message of the spiritual importance of every human life. The God of the Bible is reduced to 'the ultimate depth of our being'. Protestantism has gone too far. It seeks to save the importance of the individual by stipulating the concept of love. 'Love as an abstract, however, as it appears in the new writings, remains as dark as the hidden God whose place it is supposed to take.'

The real issue facing man today is no longer a subject for mere theological debate. 'Totalitarian states of whatever orientation . . . represent the real threat today', hence 'The contrast of theism and atheism is no longer acute', for 'both have their tyrants and their martyrs. Only the hope remains that in the coming period of world-blocks of controlled masses, a few human beings will be found who will resist, like the martyrs of history, among whom the founder of Christianity should be counted.'

Horkheimer writing as a philosopher of history, as a critic of religion, is well informed, persuasive and erudite. He displays profound knowledge of social and political history, of theology and psychology. He is sufficiently objective to evaluate historical events, but unashamedly demands attention for a politically inspired subjectivity which orientates his analyses towards past failures and achievements as well as future dangers and opportunities. At his most critical level he evokes the spirit of Marxian polemics, at his most prophetic level he shows a strong resemblance to Moses Hess, his real spiritual ancestor. Like Hess's, Horkheimer's early attempts to present a critique of the Jews are doctrinaire, ill informed and inspired much more by the acidic writings of Marx, by a long and painful conflict with his father[114] and by the commonly shared determination of the predominantly Jewish members of the Frankfurt School to divorce themselves from their Jewish backgrounds,[115] than by a genuine and informed interest in the subject.

Horkheimer's earliest comments on Jews, coined in classic Marxian terminology, are an attack on the Jewish capitalists who were opposed to anti-semitism simply because it posed an economic threat. 'The readiness to sacrifice life and property for belief is left behind with the material basis of the Ghetto. With the bourgeois Jew, the hierarchy of goods is neither Jewish nor Christian, but bourgeois . . . the Jewish revolutionary, like the Aryan, risks his own life for the freedom of mankind.'[116] Even in this short excerpt there are already indications of a dichotomy, originally suggested by Marx, between the Jew as a bourgeois and the Jew as either a religious or as a revolutionary phenomenon. The emphasis is on the Jew as a socioeconomic category. Where Marx spoke of 'Sabbath Jew' and 'everyday Jew', Horkheimer spoke of 'the bourgeois Jew' and 'the Jew of old'.[117] This is especially apparent in the first major essay on Jews, 'Die Juden und Europa', which was written in 1939. Although it had little enough to say about Jews and Judaism, it is a bitter polemic of a defeated and disappointed man who was, at that time, in danger of being engulfed by his experiences.[118] There were a number of reasons for this. Horkheimer had suffered all the indignities and humiliations of a refugee. He had been deprived of his position and security, had to accept the reality of seeking support as a *Jewish* rather than as a political refugee, had to face the difficult task of giving meaning to a rampant anti-semitism which was wholly indifferent to the socioeconomic rationale which had for so long been the mainstay of left-wing social analysts, and had to formulate a theory which would explain the hatred extended indiscriminately to all Jews and everything Jewish, even to those who had devoted their lives to a refutation of traditional Jewish roles in European society. Most of all, however, there was the total failure of the harbingers of the new era—the proletariat. 'The German workers,' he wrote, 'possessed the qualifications to bring a new order to the world. They were defeated.'[119] Not surprisingly, then, the paper, 'The Jews of Europe', is devoted mainly to explaining what happened in Germany, and why the German proletariat opted for National Socialism as a solution to its political and economic problems. Anti-semitism is elevated into a universalistic manifestation—'the new anti-semitism is the harbinger of a totalitarian order into which liberalism has developed'—and the Jews themselves make only a fleeting appearance towards the end of the article.

Intellectually, the problem Horkheimer appears to be trying to resolve is why the internal contradictions of German capitalism had led not to the promised proletarian revolution and socialism but to fascism. The answer he is suggesting lies not so much in the structure of capitalism but in its inseparable concomitant— bourgeois liberalism. This liberalism, with its pretentious humanitarianism, allowed capitalistic excesses to create vast numbers of unemployed across the whole spectrum of social classes who then formed an 'amorphous class' which demanded to be led 'from above'. As a result, leadership was taken over by the captains of industry, the generals of the army and the heads of the civil service, who reached an understanding among themselves and created the new order, 'the Führer-state'. In this new state, 'exploitation is no longer distributed aimlessly over the market, but carried out deliberately in the exercise of domination'.

The Jews had to become victims of such a state. From the time of the French revolution when they were first granted civil rights in Europe to Horkheimer's day (1939), this had never been a charter of inalienable rights, an altruistic programme of liberal statesmanship, but purely rational legislation: 'Not ideals but usefulness determines citizenship.' The Jews now committed a cardinal error in identifying with a political utilitarianism which was full of injustice and which tolerated them only because they happened to fulfil an economically necessary function. 'The sphere which was doubly significant for the Jews—as the source of their income and as the basis of bourgeois democracy—the

245

sphere of distribution, loses its economic importance. The famed power of money is beginning to disappear . . . The Jews as agents of distribution are deprived of power because the modern structure of the economy displaces that entire sphere. They become the first victims of the ruling dictatorship which absorbs their function.'

If Marx repudiated the idea of attacking Jews physically because they were undesirable economically, Horkheimer shared such a view even to the extent that he did not think that the fascists would do so. Instead, he predicted that they would disown (*verlumpen*) the Jews to a point where they would sink into the *Lumpenproletariat* from whence they would be unable to appeal for 'the transient support of a bourgeois class solidarity', because 'impoverished Jews do not command sympathy'. This fascist plot was not, in Horkheimer's view, restricted to the Jews of Germany. He was convinced that they would extend their plan to other European countries, and in a particularly angry passage of his article[120] which bears all the hallmarks of the tensions that arose in the 1930s between Jewish refugees from Germany and the Jews in the countries of refuge, he warned the native Jews that they were doomed to share the same fate.

> The Jews became conscious of their despair, at least those who had already been affected. Those in England and France, who can still join with non-Jews in complaining about income tax, are none too keen on their fellow-Jews who cross the border as refugees; the fascists are counting on this embarrassment. The newcomers have a foreign accent and strange habits . . . others are like Eastern Jews[121] or worse: politically suspect. They compromise those who are settled and who feel at home and who, in turn, irritate native Christians. As if cruel reality had not taught the Jews over many centuries that the concept of 'home' is a symbol of deceit and mockery, as if the Jews who are still secure somewhere do not know in their innermost being that the well-ordered systems in which they are flourishing will turn against them tomorrow. In any event, the newcomers are embarrassing. The ideological practice which seeks to denigrate the objects of social injustice . . . is Jewish as much as it is Gentile. Whoever succumbs in such a system cannot expect from those who live by it anything other than an acceptance of the verdict which has disowned them.

The danger facing the Jews is twofold. On the one hand, they have become economically redundant, surplus to the needs and functions of the social order. On the other, as redundant individuals in increasingly militaristic systems, they are likely to be exploited rather than persecuted in that the excesses of anti-semitism will act not so much as a safety-valve for frustrated groups, but as a means of intimidating the population as a whole. 'It demonstrates that the system accepts no constraints. Pogroms are really directed at the observer—to see if anyone will object.'

Horkheimer's solution to the problems of the Jew is fundamentally no different from that of any other ideologist from Paul to Luther, from Fichte to Bruno Bauer, from Marx to Trotsky— 'As human beings, [Jews] will be able to live only when men finally bring prehistory to an end.' For the Jews, like the Christians, once played a revolutionary part in history, and for Horkheimer it seems important that they should somehow recapture that role. In the final sentences of 'The Jews and Europe' he argues: 'Once the Jews were proud of their abstract monotheism, their rejection of the worship of images, their refusal to make the finite into an infinite. Their plight today directs them back to that. Lack of respect for that which is, which preens itself as divine, is the religion of those who, in a Europe under an iron heel, devote their lives to preparing us for something better.'

Five years after the publication of 'The Jews and Europe', Horkheimer, in association with Adorno and Leo Löwenthal, returned to the subject of Jews in a number of theses which were to form the theoretical basis for a series of studies in prejudice.[122] The primary concern, however, was not the Jew or Judaism but 'the authoritarian type of man' who 'seems to combine the ideas and skills which are typical of the highly industrialised society with irrational or anti-rational beliefs'.[123] In thus transferring the discussion from a socioeconomic category to a psycho-social phenomenon, the Jew again becomes abstracted from his empirical reality and, though he fares rather better in this enlarged image of victim, his essential humanity remains obscured. In much the same way the anti-semite and anti-semitism are accorded an abstract profundity which is unconvincing even if read in conjunction with the empirical studies that have been published. Let us first turn to the views expressed in the dissertation on anti-semitism before we attempt to develop these criticisms further.

As a first step it is argued that there are two kinds of anti-semitism. One type is absolute in its totality, the other an inter-action process between two social identities.[124]

> Anti-semitism today is mankind's most fateful issue for some, while for others it is a mere pretext. To the fascist, Jews are not a minority, but the anti-race, the negative principle *per se*; the happiness of the world must depend on their extermination. The other thesis, at the opposite extreme, holds Jews to be free of any national or racial characteristics and sees them exclusively as a group identified by religion and tradition . . . Both doctrines are true and false at the same time.
>
> The former is true in the sense that fascism has made it true. Today the Jews are that group which, practically and theoretically, draws the will to destroy [*Vernichtungswille*] upon itself, which a distorted social order produces from within itself. Absolute evil brands them as absolute evil. In this sense they are indeed the chosen people . . . In the innermost hearts of all potential fascists all over the world, the call to eliminate them like pests finds an echo. In the image of the Jew which the populists (*Völkische*) of the world conjure up, they express their own essence. They lust after exclusive possession, appropriation, unlimited power at any price. They burden the Jew with their guilt, mock him as ruler and crucify him, thus endlessly repeating the sacrifice, without being able to believe in its efficacy.

As far as the other thesis is concerned, it is correct 'as an idea'. The liberal principle of universal equality is supported by tolerating the Jew, yet at the same time it is denied by the Jewish refusal to submerge. 'The dual progression towards brutality and liberation, which the Jews experienced at the hands of the great heroes of the enlightenment and from popular democratic movements, shows itself also in the nature of the assimilated [Jews] themselves.' Their attempts to forget their embarrassing past, their determination to merge into the majority 'almost their second circumcision', draws them inevitably into contemporary bourgeoisie, which is itself falling back into crude oppression. Race thus becomes not the naturally particular, but the natural itself, the brutal assertion of the universality of the present. Persecution of Jews, like all persecution, is not the distortion of the social order, but a manifestation of the coercive power inherent in it.[125]

In the second thesis it is argued that anti-semitism is essentially an instrument of ruling elites who do not really hate Jews but know how to use them to pacify the economic and sexual frustrations of the masses. Hence, 'there are no genuine anti-semites, certainly no born anti-semites. The adults, whose call for Jewish blood has become second nature, know as little why they call for it as the youths who are to shed it.' This applies equally to totalitarian and to liberal regimes. The former incites to violence because violence is its creed and ritual, while the latter, by granting Jews property without power, makes them the symbol of the powerless masses who vent their fury on this self-defined projection of their own helplessness.[126]

The socioeconomic causes of anti-semitism are the themes of the third thesis. The Jew is a trader, yet 'this society—in which politics is not only a business, but business itself is nothing but politics—protests about the remnants of trading habits amongst Jews and denounces them as materialists, pedlars who must give way before the fiery spirit of those who have elevated trade to an absolute', which is why the Jew becomes 'the scapegoat not only for individual manoeuvres and machinations but, in a general sense, is burdened with the economic injustices of a whole social class'. Not that the Jews did not in some ways contribute to the disasters to which they are heir. At one level, the sheer force of being restricted for centuries to distributory trades and being hated for it was 'reflected' in their nature. At another, the hostility of bourgeois society was such that Jews were admitted to positions of power and influence only 'if by their demeanour they silently accepted and affirmed the verdict on other Jews—that is the meaning of baptism.'[127]

The next theme is the dialectic relationship between Judaism and Christianity as a source of anti-semitism. Although populist anti-semitism prefers to ignore the religious dimension and to concentrate on issues of race and nation, because 'men have long since given up worrying about eternal salvation', this is proving to be too complex, because 'a religious hostility which has led to two thousand years of Jewish persecution can be eliminated only with difficulty'. A further complication lies in the fact that for the secularists, religion has not been abolished (*aufgehoben*), but has been assimilated into the culture. There is, of course, a dynamic tension between the two religions which also plays a part. Judaism is the religion of law and rationality, Christianity the religion of love and grace. The Jew must earn his reward by serving a stern God who calls him to account for his actions, while the Christian squirms guiltily in his hunger for 'unearned salvation'. The result is that those who, in spite of a guilty conscience, 'have convinced themselves that they possessed Christianity, had to confirm their eternal salvation through the misfortune of those who would not sacrifice their reason. That is the religious origin of anti-semitism.'[128]

Anti-semitism also had a psychological dimension, the need to project what Freud might have described as the id-components of the collective consciousness. Like Otto Weininger, Horkheimer asserts: 'There is no anti-semite who does not have an inner need to be that which Jewishness means to him.' This need is exploited in fascism in that it seeks to utilise the rebellion of the oppressed in order to oppress. Thus, the deeply-rooted worker is made insecure by being presented with his opposite—the rootless Jew— whose equality and humanity are always in doubt. For 'the economic position of the Jews, the last betrayed betrayers of liberalistic ideology, offers them no protection'. Populist accusations of Jewish criminality accurately reflect the projection of unrealisable dreams of the anti-semite, especially the murder of children, poisoning of whole nations and international conspiracy. The Jews again compound the problem by characteristics which always stand in stark contrast to the psyche of the anti-semite.[129]

> [They are] the oldest surviving patriarchate, the incarnation of monotheism, who have transformed ancient taboos into civilising maxims while others remained rooted in magical thinking. They are declared guilty of that which they, as the original bourgeoisie, were

MARX AND THE SOCIOLOGISTS

the first to reject . . . Because they invented the concept of Kasher, they are persecuted as pigs. Anti-semites make them act out the Old Testament; they ensure that the Jews, because they have eaten of the tree of knowledge, become the dust of the earth.

Neither enlightenment nor emancipation was able to resolve the anti-semite's dilemma. After enlightenment, education itself became the victim of economic pressures and thereby prevented real emancipation, instigating instead 'new dimensions of paranoia of the masses', so that, even where 'the bourgeois had gone so far as to admit that the anti-semite is wrong, he wants to see at least that the victim is also guilty'. After emancipation, power which had become total had to hate Jews, no matter what the Jews themselves were really like—the only thing that mattered was how they were perceived—as 'happiness without power, reward without labour, homeland without borders, religion without myths. This hatred of Jews leads, pathetically, to uni-fication with the object in its destruction'. It is the negative of atonement. Atonement is the highest concept of Judaism and its entire sense is its expectation; because the anti-semite is incapable of it, he produces his paranoid reaction. He transforms the world into hell, the way he has always seen it. There can therefore be only one solution. Only by accepting the humanity of the Jew—the anti-race—could man restore his species-being as his true nature.[130]

In the final thesis, anti-semitism is abolished by being globalised.[131] 'There are no more anti-semites. They were, in the last resort, liberals who wanted to express their anti-liberalism.' Old conservative hostility to Jews was only reactionary. Populist abuse was no more than a distorted form of civil liberty. In any event, anti-semitism had always been based on stereotypal thinking. Since there is evidence that anti-semitism can flourish where there are no Jews, anti-semitism should not be regarded as an independent movement based on experience of Jews. It is now no more than a plank in the platform of fascism; 'whoever gives fascism a chance subscribes not only to the destruction of the trade unions and a crusade against bolshevism, but automatically also to the elimination of the Jews', even, that is, where there are none, because 'fascist anti-semitism must, so to speak, invent its object'.[132]

So much then for 'the philosophical prehistory (*Urgeschichte*) of anti-semitism'.[133] It is a *tour de force* in which perceptive insights alternate erratically with wild assertions and obtuse diagnoses, in which the dynamism of concrete ideas is constantly interrupted by dialectical disputes between words and meanings. It does not restore humanity to the Jew or logic to historical processes. It fails to meet the self-imposed task of using philosophy 'as a theoretical undertaking aimed at the objective "essence" of phenomena'.[134] Perhaps Horkheimer himself did not take this venture too seriously, at any rate in the way it was presented. A short paper published in 1946[135] uses the same headings as the theses on anti-semitism, but presents them as a typology, real and hypothetical, of anti-semites, rather than as dialectical categories. At that level both the anti-semite and the Jew remain at least what they will always be first and foremost—human beings.

Horkheimer returned once more to the subject of the Jews in a paper published in 1961, 'Über die deutschen Juden', in which reality and history are the dominant themes and the position of the Jews is given a conceptual backing which makes it clear that, unlike some other members of the Frankfurt School, he had come to terms with his own Jewishness without, however, relinquishing one iota of his philosophical radicalism or his critical stance.[136] After drawing attention to the historical background of prejudice, he argued that, from the 1920s on, the pluralistic societies of Europe began to decline as a result of the impact of technology. One consequence of this was that the periods of intense competition between individuals in the era of liberalism were being repeated globally by social collectivities. By way of preparation for this change every collectivity designated its special internal enemies. 'In National Socialism the Jews as a racial minority were selected for extermination, while in Russia, where international socialism turned into fanatic chauvinism, social minorities succumbed to mass murder.'

The real achievement of civilisation was that men learned to recognise each other with their differences. 'Difference belongs to the experience of identity, not only for individuals among themselves but also of individuals and the totalities within which they happen to exist at any given time. The diminution of the consciousness of difference, no less than that of unity, means cultural regression. Men today are too ready to talk of the "we" . . . instead of the "I"'. It seemed all wrong to Horkheimer to use the 'we' in relation not only to power, but also to guilt and remorse. Jews had a right to be accepted as citizens who were different; but wherever in Europe pluralism was in danger and injustice rampant, Jews were among the first victims. Yet the right to be different is not only a gift bestowed by society on any of its members; it is fundamental, because it is the expression of learned and partly unconscious characteristics which are transmitted by the parents. 'The more developed these attributes are, the more differentiated the individual becomes, but therein precisely lies his humanity—in that he shares with all human beings the capacity to learn the things which mark him out as different.'

Horkheimer then briefly reviewed the history of Jews in Germany and the several ways in which they adapted themselves to the experience of emancipation; from total assimilation, marked by 'an epidemic of baptism', to religious reform, orthodoxy and Zionism, which was based on Theodor Herzl's recognition that anti-semitism, no longer religious, was destined to be used as a lever in uniting nations against each other. He suggested therefore that Jewish demands should no longer be for equality at the individual, but at the national, level. Like many other German writers, he then drew attention to the affinity between Germans and Jews demonstrated by such factors as the refusal of Kant and the Jews to give God a name, similarities of approach in Hegel and the Talmud, and Hitler's insistence that there could be only one chosen people—the Germans!

The problem of the relationship between Germans and Jews then lay in the Germans' deeply hurt 'collective pride'. They had lost two wars, and 'The Jews who were the victims are associated with the thought of the catastrophe which was perpetrated by and against the Germans.' To help with this problem was the task of education, which must ensure that 'men should become sensitive not about an injustice to Jews, but against injustice as such, not against persecution of Jews, but against persecution itself, they should be outraged if an individual, whoever he may be is not respected as a rational being.'

Just as Moses Hess in his mature years proclaimed a grand synthesis of socialism, nationalism and Judaism[137] and earned the derision and contempt of the socialist world, so Horkheimer's *obiter dicta* offered a harmonised fusion of Judaism and critical theory which were presented in a series of interviews conducted by Helmut Gumnior for a television profile to celebrate his seventy-fifth birthday.[138] Like Hess, Horkheimer had attracted the hostility and contempt of some of his former revolutionary disciples,[139] and this probably contributed to the essential pessimism which pervades Horkheimer's 'last testament'. Although he was at pains during the interviews to stress the continuity of his ideas,[140] Horkheimer's attitudes displayed great inner conviction. He had fully come to terms with his Judaism, remained fundamentally critical of contemporary society, was somewhat naive on the question of women and marriage (largely as a result of his sentimentalised experiences with his mother and his wife[141]), but remained an adamant advocate of justice which he stipulated as man's greatest need. He even contemplated a secularised theology to support religion as the necessary instrument for helping man to achieve such justice or, at any rate, to overcome injustice as far as this could be achieved, but, as has been stated, he remained essentially pessimistic because he felt that the logic of history would drive man into totally bureaucratised collectivities in which 'theology will be abolished' and 'serious philosophy will come to an end'.[142]

Horkheimer's starting-point, as always, was Marx's theory. He rejected an all-pervasive concept of class solidarity and argued that real solidarity among all men would be more likely to be based on their common destiny; i.e. 'the fact that men must suffer, that they die, that they are finite beings'. This fact was also closely interwoven with the concept of God and the existence of religion. We cannot prove the existence of God, who would in any event be disqualified in view of all the suffering and injustice in this world. But man will continue to hope 'that there is a positive absolute', if only because a concept of God gives man the knowledge of his own isolation. In this dialectical position in which we cannot say anything about God except that, if we were certain of His existence, 'then the knowledge of our isolation would be a deception', Judaism and critical theory meet. Thus the religious Jew will not even write the word 'God' but, because He is 'unnameable', the Jew writes 'G'd'. Why, asks Horkheimer, 'does such a rule exist? No other religion apart from Judaism has it'. The reason he puts forward is that 'in the Jewish religion it does not matter so much what God is like, it is more important, what man is like'. Hence, Judaism has little to say about faith—all its interest is focused on action—carrying out commandments 'which prescribe the entire life of the religious Jew'. Catholicism is therefore much closer to Judaism, while Protestantism, as we have seen earlier, invented faith to enable religion to survive as an alternative to science and superstitition.

If there is religion, there must also be theology, and Horkheimer has his very own ideas about a theology which is not concerned with God. Even without a concept of divinity, man hopes that the injustice of this world is not permanent, is not the last word. Theology, then, is 'an expression of a longing—the longing that the murderer should not triumph over his victim'. Now, 'positivism knows of no authority which transcends man and which would enable him to differentiate between helpfulness and greed, goodness and cruelty, possessiveness and self-sacrifice. Logic, too, remains silent, it cannot give moral attitudes pride of place . . . Everything connected with morality must, in the last resort, fall back on theology'.

Although this theological background to morality is common to both Judaism and Christianity, they are sharply differentiated in the meaning they ascribe to suffering and the role they assign to the suffering individual. Thus the Christian martyr suffered torture in the certain knowledge that there was an eternal salvation which he, personally, would share, while the Jewish martyr sacrificed his life for the salvation of his people because he was convinced that he would live on through his people. Both attitudes, however, tend to disintegrate under the pressure of concessions which religions are continuously making to secular pressures in vain attempts to survive. For Horkheimer considers the social function of religion to have been lost, and it is interesting to observe how he analysed this function as a critical theorist, using an essentially Feuerbachian–Marxian approach, but extending the analysis well beyond the somewhat narrow anthropological-political level which the immediate experience of life in a religiously determined state had imposed on Feuerbach and Marx.

'For a long time the concept of God transmitted the idea that there are criteria of values other than those which were effectively expressed in nature and society. The recognition of a transcendental being derived its greatest strength from dissatisfaction with life on earth. In religion, the desires, aspirations and complaints of countless generations were manifested. The more Christianity aligned earthly events with the rule of God, the more this meaning of religion was distorted. In some ways God already assumes responsibility for worldly order in Catholicism, whilst Protestantism directly associates human events with a divine will. In this way, every worldly regime not only acquires an aura of divine justice, but this justice itself is reduced to the shabby conditions of reality. Christianity thus lost its cultural function of giving expression to man's idealism, to the extent that it became a partner of the state . . . Since the good will, the sense of solidarity with suffering and the efforts to create a better world have relinquished their religious garb', religion has lost its social function and cannot regain it. All that is left for it now is to help men to express their longing for complete justice—a dream that can never be realised in secular history. A more important social function, especially in a less distorted world order than the present, is reserved for critical theory, which has already reached the stage where it must carry out a dual function. It must 'clarify the things which ought to be changed, but it should also determine what should be retained. Its task therefore will be to demonstrate what price we will have to pay for this or that innovation, this or that task'. Accordingly, 'critical theory contains at least an idea of the theological, of the other', which does not mean that it negates attempts to create a more just society. It does mean that the better society will have to be paid for by a greater restriction of freedom and that this in turn will both intensify the longing for, and restrict the means of expressing, man's search for eternal salvation. This pessimism is also reflected in Horkheimer's view of the Jews and their fate. Although he accepts the need for and reality of the State of Israel, he is convinced that the persecution of the Jews will continue. 'Israel today is a harassed State, as the Jews have always been harassed.' And so, in the final analysis, the pessimistic view of man's natural evolution towards greater material justice and security needs to be tempered by a secular theology in which Horkheimer's Jewish and Marxist heritage, expressed in a somewhat privatised version of critical theory, offers some consolation for the loss of freedom which is dialectically bound up with the growth of equality. But Horkheimer does not appear to have seen the greatest flaw in his own construct —his assumption of the existence of an indivisible idea of justice was too much a product of his secularised theology, it was the great absolute of Jewish and Marxian Messianism—it was and remains contrary to 'the immanent logic of history'.

PART FOUR

Marx and the Problem
of Anti-Semitism

CHAPTER XII

Marxist Apologists

Although published in 1844, Marx's essays 'On the Jewish Question' were virtually unknown and almost forgotten until the end of the century. By this time Marxism had become a major political and intellectual movement, the deliberate use of anti-semitism as a political process had been exploited by right- and left-wing political forces, and the emergence of a strong and numerous Jewish proletarian movement, notably in Eastern Europe and England, demanded an adequate theoretical response to the earlier simplistic concepts of Judaism as a bourgeois or feudalistic manifestation in society. Friedrich Engels and Eleanor Marx were among the first to try to reconcile Marx's position with the new trends, albeit in a hesitant and somewhat uncertain manner.

The success of the anti-semitic groups, especially in Germany, had persuaded a number of socialists and Marxists to adopt this deeply ingrained prejudice and use it to their own advantage. If workers, so it was argued, could be persuaded to hate Jews as capitalists and so learn to involve themselves in class struggle to rid themselves of Jewish capitalists, then it would be but a short step from there to extend this hatred to all capitalists, gradually to drop the specifically Jewish association and thus to establish the victory of socialism because, once embarked on the class struggle, the proletariat would be carried forward by its own momentum. Thus the Council of the German Democratic Party in 1893 argued that although anti-semitism was reactionary, 'it will end by becoming revolutionary. This must necessarily happen because petit bourgeois groups in town and village, aroused by anti-semitic leaders against Jewish capitalists, will understand in the end that their enemy is not the Jewish capitalist alone but all the capitalist class and that only the victory of socialism can rescue them from their distress.'[1] This is not to say that anti-semitism was a generally accepted attitude among socialists; on the contrary, many rejected it and fought courageously against it in Germany,[2] but it did excite sufficient interest for Engels to take a strong stand against it and, at the same time, to put the youthful essays of Marx into a more 'realistic' perspective.

In a famous letter to an unknown correspondent which was published in the social democratic *Arbeiter-Zeitung* on 9 May 1890,[3] Engels wrote: 'I must ask you to consider whether you will not do more harm than good through anti-semitism.' He then set out his theory of anti-semitism, which was at the same time a theory of the role of Jews in society. The anti-semites, according to Engels, were those groups in transitional societies whose position was being eroded by developing capitalism. The extravagant low nobility, the petty bourgeoisie unable to compete against big capital, craftsmen and small businessmen, these were the people who faced ruin, who were being attacked by capital, 'Semitic or Aryan, circumcised or baptised'. It was right that they should be ruined, for only in that way could all the old social differentiations be dissolved into 'the one great conflict between capitalists and workers'. Only in those areas still close to the middle ages, where production was still in the hands of the peasants, did Jewish capital predominate and anti-semitism flourish.

Compared with the wealth of American Gentile millionaires and landed gentry like the Duke of Westminster, even compared with the great industrialists on the Rhine, Jewish wealth was modest, even beggarly. The Jew was a creature of pre-capitalist societies. Not the epitome of money and power, but a shabby little catalyst far removed from the sinister social menace presented by Marx. Engels then made two further points, both of which add to his implicit critique of the Marxian analysis. The first acknowledged the existence of a Jewish proletariat, 'the most exploited and the most miserable'. It was also a fighting proletariat, and Engels mentioned three strikes in which Jewish workers in England had been involved 'during the last twelve months'.[4] As a second point, Engels dismissed the Marxian concept of the Jew as a single, uniform entity. Not only were there Jewish capitalists and Jewish proletarians, there were also Jews who belonged to neither category and who yet contributed a great deal, such as Heine, Börne, Lassalle and Marx. 'If I had to choose,' wrote Engels, 'then rather a Jew than Herr von!'[5]

It is quite likely that the Jewish socialists in England at the end of the nineteenth century were unaware of Marx's essays and saw no difficulty in accepting the Marxist creed, especially because the focus of the Marxist movement in London was Eleanor (Tussy), Marx's youngest daughter, and 'the only one of my family who felt drawn to Jewish people, and particularly to those who are socialistically inclined. My happiest moments are when I am in the East End amidst Jewish workpeople'.[6] She called her house in London 'Jews' Den'[7] and has provided us with something of a mystery concerning the possibility of some unknown material by Marx on Jews and Judaism.

Among the young socialists around Eleanor was Morris Vinchevsky,[8] an active organiser and delegate of a number of Jewish trade unions to the Socialist Congress in Zürich in 1893. In 1918 he published a long article in *Die Zukunft*, a section of which deserves to be quoted at length.[9]

We were travelling to the International Congress in Zurich. Our delegation of English socialists and trade unionists was sixty-five strong. We occupied several rail coaches, everyone, as is usual in England, divided into a number of compartments, each compartment holding ten passengers. Either by accident or by Eleanor's design, I found myself in their [Eleanor and Aveling's] compartment, and during the journey our friendship deepened. For most of the journey Aveling[10] was busy with journalistic work; he went as the correspondent of London's most radical daily paper, the *Daily Chronicle*. Although he was working on a report of the journey, he took part in all the discussions and was lively and happy. Eleanor

263

too was not idle. She talked and laughed. If I had not known about their past I would have thought they were the happiest couple on earth.

In Zurich we more or less kept to ourselves because there were so many visiting Germans around her that she had very little time for me. One day I said to her: 'You know, I represent eight unions comprising six hundred Jewish workers. There are certainly many good socialists who cannot imagine a Jewish worker, that is to say, a Jew who is engaged in manual work, to say nothing of organised Jewish workers. Now the problem is that in our large English delegation I belong to the most extreme radicals and you can see how, at the caucus meetings, only the more moderate [get an opportunity to] speak—what can we do?' 'I will tell you what, Vinchevsky,' she said. 'Write down what you have told me, the names of your unions and the number of workers and I will translate it all and put the position to Congress.'

An hour later she announced in three languages (German, French, English) that Jewish workers, organised in eight unions have sent a delegate, Comrade V, etc. With every language the announcement was greeted by great applause. Eleanor's face shone with pride. A few days later, at the end of the Congress, she said to me, 'You know, Vinchevsky, Edward will interview you for the *Daily Chronicle*' . . . Aveling did in fact interview me at length and gave me to understand that it was Eleanor's idea. So I thought that she was still being influenced by the impact of her announcement. The strength of her Jewish feelings were described by Eduard Bernstein in 1898, after her death, in *Die neue Zeit*.[11] He quotes a letter from her, from the time of the Dreyfus trial, in which she wrote with great interest on the position of the Jews in France. He also emphasised her saying, 'I am a Jewess.'

On Saturday 11 August we marched through Zurich . . . I was looking for a place in the procession when Eleanor ran towards me in great haste. She placed me next to her, with Will Thorne on one side and Edward on the other. 'We Jews must stick together', she said,[12] and we stayed together. And we made plans. I should tell the Jewish workers who her father was. She would give me material that no one has seen. She will . . . we will. But nothing came of all these plans. When I returned I was overwhelmed with work. My health went from bad to worse. The London fog almost suffocated me. A year later I was already in America and I did not see her or him again. My personal contact was ended.

While Eleanor must have been familiar with her father's

essays on the Jews, it is unlikely that Vinchevsky would have known about them at that time.[13] Vinchevsky's account makes it quite clear how isolated he was and felt at the Congress, and how little he would have achieved without Eleanor's patronage. Eleanor, on the other hand, was clearly greatly encouraged by the interest she had aroused for Jewish workers and her promise of 'material no one had seen' might have been made in the excitement of the moment. Nevertheless, we are left with the tantalising uncertainty that Karl Marx might have returned to the subject of the Jews and that we shall never know if he changed his views.[14]

If neither Engels nor Eleanor Marx made any direct reference to Marx's analysis of the Jewish problem, Eduard Bernstein (1850–1932), the great socialist theoretician and leader of the 'revisionist' Marxists, tried to explain the Marxian essays to the Jewish workers' movement. In an article on the role of Jews in German social democracy,[15] he explained that while the fact that Marx and Lassalle were of Jewish origin influenced the SPD in favour of Jews, the things they wrote about Jews had the opposite effect. He then described the origin of the Marxian essays, and argued that 'while there is much that is deep and inspiring . . . the treatment of the main theme is unsatisfactory' because, as he summarised it, quite incorrectly, Marx 'considered the Jews a nation composed entirely of traders . . . he favoured postponement of the question of equal rights for Jews . . . until the coming socialist revolution', Marx's statement about Jews 'was not applicable to the Jews of Western Europe, still less to those of Eastern Europe', and Bernstein would probably have ignored the whole issue had it not been for the fact that what Marx had written 'was useful to the anti-semites and socialists with anti-semitic leanings'. Karl Kautsky, another great Marxist theoretician, on the other hand, preferred to pass over the Marxian essays in silence. Although he devoted an entire book to the subject of Jews,[16] he made no reference to Marx other than to use him as one of a number of examples to demonstrate his thesis that, while Judaism was reactionary, Jews were revolutionary. His solution to the Jewish problem did not differ from that which he had proposed for Christianity.[17] Since he regarded Zionism as

Utopian and 'capitalist Jews' as conservative, the future for all Jews lay in discarding Judaism and joining the class struggle. As far as Judaism was concerned, Kautsky almost repeated the Marxian prescription when he said that 'the sooner it disappears the better for society and for the Jews themselves'.

It could be argued that any reservations about Marx's views on Jews coming from Marxist or socialist sources would tend to be directed either at stressing the historical context of the essays or their unintended consequences as instruments of anti-semitism. 'Liberal-bourgeois' writers on Marx, however, tend to defend the Marxian essays on semantic grounds, both against an accusation that Marx generalised a specific situation and against the suggestion that he was anti-semitic. Thus Hook devoted a longish footnote to the question of anti-semitism though not, in this case, in relation to the essays on the Jewish question but in the context of Marx's first thesis on Feuerbach in which he used the expression 'dirty-Jewish'. 'Marx,' Hook observed, 'was free of anti-semitic prejudice' but unfortunately a little insensitive in his use of the word 'Jew', which he often used 'as an epithet of abuse'.[18] Similarly Tucker added a footnote to his discussion of Marx's essays in which he took issue with Runes's[19] edition of the Marx essays, by stating: 'Although Marx did at times express anti-Jewish feelings, his article was in no sense a plea to rid the world of Jews. It was a plea to rid the world of "Judaism" by which he meant a practical religion of money-worship. What he here called "Judaism" he later renamed "capitalism".'[20] McLellan dealt with both aspects of the essays in a brief paragraph. He rejected any suggestion that Marx might have been anti-semitic as 'inaccurate'[21] on the somewhat obscure grounds that Marx advocated Jewish emancipation. Such a defence, however, negates the whole tenor of Marx's reasoning. He did not advocate Jewish emancipation *per se*, but simply pointed out that, if society accepts the social role of the Jew (as defined by Marx) then it was senseless and illogical not to accept the Jew as well. McLellan also argued that '*Judentum*' meant both Judaism and commerce, that it was commerce that was uppermost in Marx's mind and not any religious or racial concept of Jew. Hence

'Marx's review is an extended pun at Bauer's expense.'[22] Two later writers have challenged McLellan on this interpretation. Maguire thought that McLellan had not taken the problem seriously enough. 'When Marx tells us that the "empirical essence" of Judentum/Judaism is Judentum/commerce, there is every reason to believe that he means what he says.'[23] McInnes went further and argued that McLellan involved Marx in a tautology by suggesting that he argued that 'Western society became commercialised when it was commercialised'.[24]

It would appear that attempts to 'explain' either Marx's choice of words or his motives in writing the essays are more likely to compound the problem than solve it.

CHAPTER XIII

Marxist Defenders

Basically, the apologetic approach suggested that while Marx was wrong in what he wrote about the Jews either because he did not consider the possible consequences of the way in which he wrote, or because he was too theoretical and did not take Jewish realities into account, nevertheless his *meaning* was clear, his intentions were obvious and his motives unassailable. No such reasoning is necessary or justified for those who, as Marxist theoreticians, are determined to support the Marxian analysis as being absolutely correct. They recognise the problem of anti-semitism, but see it as unrelated to Marx. To illustrate this position, we might consider three Marxists who, though agreed in their Marxism, are differentially involved in the problem of anti-semitism. Franz Mehring wrote at the beginning of this century, fully conscious of the emergence of anti-semitism as a political force. Roman Rosdolsky wrote under the immediate impact of Auschwitz and István Mészáros wrote at a time when anti-Zionism had assumed most of the burden carried for so long by the more amorphous victims of anti-semitism.

Franz Mehring (1846–1919) is important for a number of reasons. He was the first to republish Marx's essays,[1] one of the few leading Marxists to accept their content without reservation and the originator of the concept of philo-semitism to balance the assessment of anti-semitism.[2] In 1902, when he issued his *Aus dem Literarischen Nachlass von Karl Marx und Friedrich Engels*, he introduced Marx's essays on the Jewish question with a highly tendentious and very hostile account of early nineteenth-century Jewry which was intended to make Marx's and his own aversion from Jews appear both logical and rational: 'Any comment would only detract from this fundamental investigation. These few pages obviate the mountain of literature that has since appeared on the Jewish question.'[3] Mehring was entirely convinced that Judaism represented no more than 'the presuppositions of the haggler'[4] and, since capitalism is built on these presuppositions, Judaism was not, as later writers were to suggest, equivalent to capitalism, but its essential antecedent. To defend Judaism meant defending capitalism, and to demand emancipation for Jews would hinder the emancipation of the proletariat. From this sort of reasoning Mehring evolved his concept of 'philosemitism'. He was opposed to the political anti-semitism that was emerging in Germany because it is 'one thing to analyse the Jewish question as a contemporary phenomenon, under scientific, historical, psychological, social aspects; and another to make it the substance of political party strategy, of political mass agitation . . . [because] the Jewish question brings into play the three most potent sources of hatred known in history: a religious, a racial and a class conflict'.[5] It was Treitschke's 'great and unforgettable contribution' to bring out the 'objective' criticisms of 'a good many Jewish vulgarities and ill manners', and Mehring objected to 'the eternal cry for the police whenever a drastic word against the Jews was uttered'.[6]

Notwithstanding the fact that 'the fusion of Teutonic and Semitic elements' had already gone too far 'to allow a line of demarcation to be drawn that would be politically recognisable and definable by law',[7] Mehring had no problem in writing about 'hired scribblers of moneyed Jewry' and 'Jewish capital'.[8] The balance which he ultimately evolved for himself saw anti-semitism as an attack on 'Jewish capital in order the less to disturb the exploiting activity of Christian capital', while philosemitism 'claims to protect Jews by defending capitalism through thick and thin'.[9]

Mehring's famous biography of Marx was published one year

before his death and has been described by his translator as the 'culmination' of his work.[10] Mehring's treatment both of Marx's Jewish background and of his essays shows that he maintained his views on Judaism to the end. In discussing Marx's origins, he briefly described the position of Jews and the conversion of Marx's father to Christianity in a somewhat tendentious fashion. Heinrich Marx was baptised because he recognised that 'at that time the renunciation of Judaism was not merely an act of religious emancipation, but also and even more so, an act of social emancipation.'[11] Mehring then stressed a claim made earlier by Bruno Bauer that Jews had 'taken no part whatever in the great intellectual labours of the German thinkers and poets' and that 'the modest light of Moses Mendelssohn had vainly attempted to guide his "nation" into the intellectual life of Germany'. He told of the Kulturverein and how its members were 'compelled' to convert in order to contribute to the intellectual life of Germany, whereas those who did not do so had 'long since been forgotten'. Conversion was nothing other than 'an act of civilised progress' and any external pressure to do so would have been merely incidental, not causal. In a somewhat dishonest account of history, Mehring related how in the 1820s 'the breaking up of estates and farms by Jewish usurers took place' and how this led to 'a violent wave of anti-semitism in the Rheinland'.[12] 'A man of irreproachable honesty like Marx's father' had no right 'to bear any share of this hatred', since it was his duty to think of his children first. And so he converted.

However, at the time that Marx wrote his essays, the Jewish question 'had not sunk so deeply into the morass of anti-semitic and philo-semitic badgering'.[13] In a very brief summary of the Jewish position in Germany, by way of an introduction which owes more to Bruno Bauer than to Marx, Mehring described a 'class' in society which had no civil rights and only enjoyed special privileges 'as a result of its various practices'.[14] There follows a good summary of the positions of Feuerbach, Bauer and Marx, and he concluded with a final comment which interestingly enough draws more on Marx's second version of the Jewish question in the *Holy Family* than on the original essays. These are described as having achieved two things. First, to show the connection between society and the state, and second that 'the religious questions of the day had no more than a social significance'. Mehring added that in these essays, 'an outline of socialist society [is] beginning to form'.[15] Apart from one small change by way of interpretation, he accepted Marx's analysis absolutely and saw no need to adjust or reinterpret any of it. Yet the small change is interesting, because it takes Mehring beyond the position advocated by Marx. When he claimed that, according to Marx, the religious question of the day had 'no more than' a social significance, he ignored Marx's emphatic statement that in his essays 'it was by no means denied . . . that the Jewish question is also a *religious* question. It was said, on the contrary: Herr Bauer grasps *only the religious essence* of Jewry'.[16]

When Roman Rosdolsky wrote his long, meticulously researched monograph on Engels and the problem of nationalism,[17] he added a special appendix dealing with the Jews, because he wrote in 1948, very conscious of the recent mass extermination of Jews in Germany.[18] His essay is a curious, but sincere and deeply felt attempt to come to terms with a horrific reality by an uncompromising rejection of anti-semitism linked with a vigorous affirmation of his dedication to socialism and its founders, Marx and Engels. The result is a complicated argument in which he oscillates so rapidly between the two objectives that we can do justice to it only by presenting it in his own tortuous sequence.

Rosdolsky begins by noting that, while Marx's essays had attracted a substantial literature, the intense anti-Jewish references in the NRZ have been entirely ignored. Only Mehring had made reference to it when he explained the collapse of the paper due partly to the withdrawal of support by 'money-Judaism'. Would anyone, queried Rosdolsky, use a term like 'money-Christianity'? The issue was not whether the NRZ fought 'shabby money-Jews' but how it did so! It must be remembered, of course, that to the editors of the NRZ the Jews were neither a nation nor even a nationality (i.e. ethnic-linguistic community)[19] but merely an anachronistic remnant of a trading people (*Handelsvolk*) which separated itself from its host nations by its occupation, religion and mentality. In any event, Rosdolsky went on, Mehring missed the point because the *NRZ* was not really interested in 'shabby money-Judaism' but in the Jews of Posen, whom it attacked viciously and consistently, because in the struggle between Polish nationalism and Prussian imperialism, the Jews sided with Prussian power. Objectively, the *NRZ* was right, because historically the Jews as an oppressed minority had always sided with the dominant power, but in this they were no different from other minorities in similar situations. This pattern of response, which was no more than a normal consequence of nationalism, could be defended or condemned—what was certain was that it had nothing to do with Judaism as such. This was precisely what the *NRZ* was ignoring when it concentrated its attacks on Jews as Jews, as 'the dirtiest of all races'.[20] The attitudes of the Jews of Posen, while explaining the hostility of the *NRZ*, would certainly not excuse the invective used against them, but the vitriolic attacks on the Jews of Austria, in particular those in Vienna, were indefensible. Rosdolsky then devotes several pages to illustrate the purely anti-semitic excesses in reports from the Austrian correspondent of the *NRZ*, Müller-Tellering, and explains that, unforgivable as these were, they had to be seen in the context of the considerable freedom which the editors of the paper at that time allowed its correspondents.[21]

Since the *NRZ* also carried comments and insinuations by Engels in which 'the Jews' were attacked as counter-revolutionary and inferior, Rosdolsky went on to ask if it was justified to describe Marx and Engels as anti-semites. Those who did so used a simple method of extracting a number of suitable quotations from their works and letters and positing these uncritically and unhistorically against the concept of anti-semitism, thus reducing the founders of Marxism to 'spiritual comrades in arms of Julius Streicher'.[22] Such a method could add three-quarters of all thinkers, writers and politicians of the past to the ranks of anti-semites. Somewhat abruptly, in an extraordinary argument derived from Abram Léon, Rosdolsky then attacks Jewish nationalism[23] as an involuted justification for anti-semitism.While, anti-semitism posits the Jews as enemies of the whole world and thereby accords them an inordinate importance as a force in world history, Jewish nationalism, by declaring all the world— including Marx and Engels—its enemy, must give rise to the feeling that, if even Marx and Engels were against Jews, then there must be some substantive truth in anti-semitism.[24] The nationalistic-Jewish critic of Marx and Engels would at this point, said Rosdolsky, interject a psychological explanation to account for Marx's anti-semitism by reference to his 'Jewish inferiority complex' and by his status as a renegade; but apart from the inadequacy of this kind of personalisation of motives, there is also the fact that it cannot apply to Engels because he was not Jewish. Nor were any of the earlier anti-Jewish socialists such as Fourier, Proudhon or Bakunin.[25]

The correct approach would be to examine the 'anti-semitism' of Marx and Engels in its proper historical context, after the concept has been adequately defined. What then is the real difference between the views of Marx and Engels on Judaism and the Jewish question and anti-semitism proper? To Rosdolsky it is obvious. Whereas the anti-semite regards Judaism as an inborn unchanging quality of a race, or the product of a mysterious Jewish spirit or religion, Marx in his essays derived the 'Jewish national character' (*Volkscharakter*) of his time from 'the actual historic role of the Jews as the mediators of commercial and loan capital in the economies of the middle ages and modern times'. For Marx, Judaism is a social mask, a chimerical nationality of what is in fact the nationality of the merchant, the *Geldmensch*. The Jew survived only because civil society was constantly re-creating him out of its own entrails. Rosdolsky goes on to quote extensively from Marx's essay and concludes that, if this was anti-semitism, it was of a very different order from that which his critics had in mind, and that Mehring was quite right in claiming that Marx's treatment of the Jewish question stood high above that of the anti- and philo-semites of his time.

For all that, Rosdolsky concedes that legitimate objections can be raised against the Marxian thesis, particularly as it is set out in the second of the essays on the Jewish question. This applies especially to Marx's perpetual equation of Judaism and capitalism. If in capitalism, Rosdolsky reasons, Christians have indeed become Jews, if the narrowness of the Jew is only a special manifestation of the general capitalistic narrowness of civil society, in what sense then can this narrow capitalist society still be called 'Jewish'? In other words, is Marx really entitled to continue his trans-formative anti-Hegelian game and maintain that if the Jew of his own time was like the capitalist exploiter, the obverse is also true that the capitalist exploiter is like the Jew? Should it not, on the contrary, be argued that the Jew is only incidental to capitalism; and, therefore, capitalism once having emerged from feudal society, this incidental association should not have been continued? At the time that Marx wrote, the Jew *was* as he described him, and Rosdolsky quotes Mayer in support.[26] While Jewish predominance in trade and commerce created the virtual equation between the two, and the drift from Judaism of those who had left commerce and moved into other occupational fields only confirmed the earlier association. And once more Rosdolsky turned against Marx. Equating Judaism and capitalism even in his own time was false, because the emergence of capitalism changed the Jews from a trading group through the process of class differentiation into a modern nation. Hence Marx's rigid fixation of a historically limited period in Jewish evolution into a per-manent characteristic created a contradiction in his own methodology which made his analysis of the Jewish question increasingly more anachronistic and unjust.

Rosdolsky then goes on to explain this apparent Marxian aberration by using the *NRZ* and its anti-semitic character as an illustration of a concept we have already met earlier. The plight of the small man was intense and many of them associated their economic and social difficulties with Jewish exploitation and Jewish competition. The socialists of that time, unaware of the real nature of anti-semitism, thought to exploit this hostility in the interest of their cause and therefore accepted and even en-couraged it, in the hope that it would increase the revolutionary fervour of the masses. Their willingness to utilise anti-semitism is all the more comprehensible when it is remembered how readily they dismissed whole nations and their aspirations because at that time they greatly overestimated the ability of the proletariat to sacrifice national prejudices to the greater cause of proletarian solidarity. In other words, the crude anti-semitism of the *NRZ* and its editor must be seen and understood as a *childhood disease of the workers' movement*. It required the traumatic knowledge of the anti-Jewish pogroms in Russia in 1881–3, the Dreyfus affair in France and the gas chambers in Germany to teach the working-class movement the real meaning of anti-semitism, which they then fought bravely and courageously— though not without occasional backsliding under the pressure of bourgeois-ideological influences.

István Mészáros is no less opposed to 'scapegoat-hunting' anti-semitism than Mehring or Rosdolsky but, apart from that, his analysis of Marx's essays has little in common with either of the earlier writers.[27] His contribution is characterised by an absolute acceptance of Marx which is even less critical than Mehring; his own somewhat unusual view of Judaism woven into the Marxian schema; and his derivations of the Marxian essays which are very different from generally held views even amongst Marxists. Mészáros discusses the essays as a background to his analysis of the 'Economic and Philosophical Manuscripts' of 1844, which are the real focus of his study. His claims that, in the Manuscripts, Marx anticipated his later work 'by grasping in a synthetic unity the problematics of a comprehensive, praxis-centred, radical reassessment of all facets of human experience',[28] and that 'considering the monumentality of this synthesis and the depth of its insights it is almost unbelievable that they were written by a young man of twenty-six',[29] establish the way in which he approached Marx. At this level, criticism is legitimate provided it is not directed at Marx. Thus, to describe Moses Hess as a formulator of 'second-rate, provincialistic utopias',[30] who was not only 'not in the least impressed by the immense works of Marx', but who in these works 'succeeded only in arousing his narrow-minded hostility',[31] is fair comment which requires no evidence to substantiate it. However, if Daniel Bell makes equally uncomplimentary remarks about Marx, then that is simply 'personal vilification'.[32]

When Marx wrote about Judaism, he grandly took in the entire vista of Jewish history from the Pentateuch and the Talmud to the present-day Jew. For Mészáros, Judaism has three fundamental characteristics which are derived from four sentences in the Old Testament and which advocate 'a virtually endless continuation of the extension of its worldly powers'. There is first a system designed 'to soften internal class conflicts' by prescribing help for the poor (Deut. 15:11) and promising foreign labour in the future (Isa. 61:5). Second, there is the principle of 'expanding domination' through the weapon of 'usury', and third, there is the 'ethos' of Judaism, the 'God-willed superiority of the "chosen people"'. Judaism's relationship with the outside world is a prescribed 'confrontation' (Deut. 14:21 and Exod. 22:24).[33] The consequences of incorporating these principles into Jewish reality are to create a permanent particularism which only Christianity could transcend, a 'partiality' which consolidated itself into 'the Jewish narrowness of society', the real target of Marx's critique, rather than 'the mere sociological phenomenon of Jewish partiality'.[34]

Rosdolsky may have claimed that Marx was concerned only with Jews as a *Handelsvolk* at a particular time and that any concept of a mystical 'spirit of Judaism' is true anti-semitism, but Mészáros takes the opposite view. 'The issue at stake', he insists, 'is not simply the empirical reality of Jewish communities in Europe but "the spirit of Judaism"' which 'must be understood in the last analysis to mean "the spirit of capitalism".'[35]

We have earlier described how Marx derived his views on an analysis of Jews and Judaism from his philosophical predecessors, notably Bruno Bauer and Ludwig Feuerbach. Most Marx scholars accept this and have themselves described it, but Mészáros again differs fundamentally by deriving the Marxian analysis from entirely different sources. The essays 'On the Jewish Question' are seen as a direct application of the historical-materialist method and have their origin in the works of Fourier, Étienne Cabet, Pierre Leroux and Victor Considérant, i.e. the

French Utopian socialists. Their ideas, coupled with Marx's studies of the French revolution and his direct observations of German and French societies, as seen by an 'outsider', enabled him 'to tackle the Jewish question realistically'.[36]

How did Marx achieve this position of outsider? According to Mészáros, it was a result of his Jewishness. Like Spinoza, the other 'great Jewish philosopher', Marx had to come to terms with his position as outsider in the 'discriminatory and particularistic' German community and had to make himself an outsider, i.e. escape from 'the particularistic and parochial positions of Jewry'.[37] Jews who do not emancipate themselves from their 'Jewish narrowness' will remain 'second-rate and provincialistic' and that includes Moses Hess and Martin Buber.[38] It is not only the personal position of Marx which is subjected to incorrect analysis in order to establish a theoretical model which is superimposed on the Marxian position, but elements in the text of the essays are also used wrongly. Thus, according to Mészáros, Marx contrasted 'the effectively self-centred, internally cohesive, practical-empirical partiality' of Judaism with 'the theoretical universality of Christianity established as a set of "purely formal rites with which the world of self-interest encircles itself" ',[39] but this set of purely formal rites he spoke of refers to Jewish law;[40] it is that part of the Bauer–Feuerbach critique which Marx incorporated in his second essay but which, as we have seen, he later repudiated because it went beyond the 'social significance' with which he was concerned. Similarly, it is going too far to describe Marx's use of Feuerbach's 'species-being' as 'a specific socially concrete concept', when Marx himself had rejected the concept in *German Ideology* as 'philosophical phraseology'.[41]

To sum up, the 'orthodox' Marxists, however much they may differ in their views on Jews and Judaism, are agreed that the Marxian essays equate Judaism and capitalism and present an analysis which in its essentials either was or is *or* was and is correct. The fact that Marx himself did not use the term 'capitalism' in relation to Judaism *per se*, that Engels explicitly rejected the equation and that subsequent sociological researches by Max Weber and others would question such a simplistic equation did not and does not deter them. This would suggest to me that the equation as it stands can be more properly described as Marxist rather than Marxian.[42] It is, after all, important for those to whom everything that Marx wrote is binding to find meaningful principles in what to others appears to be irrational polemic.

There is yet another group of scholars who have resolved the difficulty presented by the Marxian essays by concentrating on the first essay and focusing their attention on either the state versus society issue or the emancipation question which are so brilliantly developed there, while at the same time ignoring the Jews as a subject. Thus Lukács sees the essays essentially as a critique of Bruno Bauer. He notes that Jews do not enjoy civil equality in Germany because they do not accept the 'state religion'. That, to him, is all the background required.[43] Similarly, Popitz describes Marx's 'polemical essays against Bruno Bauer' which contain a number of important formulations collating many significant ideas only hinted at so far. The Jews are not included among these important formulations.[44] In an excellent paper on 'On the Jewish Question', Scholz concentrates on the concept of 'human emancipation'. In his view Marx was not really interested in discussing the Jewish question but used it as a peg on which to hang his thoughts on the meaning of real, i.e. human, emancipation.[45] Like Lukács, but unlike Popitz, Scholz treats the two reviews as one essay. McLellan also treats the two review essays as one, and described them alternately as an essay[46] and as an article.[47] He too regarded the essays as being more important in contributing to the development of Marx's ideas on the relationship between state and civil society than as a treatment of the Jewish question *per se*. Nevertheless, clearly embarrassed by the implications of Marx's essays, he dismissed any suggestion of anti-semitism by offering three explanations. First, as we have already seen, he suggested that Marx derived his ideas on Jews from Moses Hess, an explanation which is chronologically improbable and conceptually impossible. Second, by drawing attention to Shlomo Avineri's discourse, which emphasised Marx's support of the Jewish claim for emancipation; he seemingly overlooked the fact that Avineri began his article with a simple assertion 'that Karl Marx was an inveterate anti-semite'.[48] Third, he used the well-known semantic formula that the German word '*Judentum*' ('Judaism') 'had the derivative meaning of commerce',[49] without apparently recognising the tautological nature of such an argument.

CHAPTER XIV

Jewish Responses to Marx

As a general rule we can say that the more a person knows about Jews and Judaism the less likely he is to take the Marxian analysis of Judaism seriously, no matter whether he be Jew or Gentile, even if he is himself a Marxist. It should, therefore, be of some interest to see how Marx has fared in Jewish circles. Jews who consider Marx's essays do not necessarily put their Judaism first, although they will be likely to place their knowledge of Judaism at least alongside the Marxian teaching rather than subordinate to it. They are no more subjective than, say, a Mehring or Mészáros. If specifically Jewish studies of Marx's essays are relatively few, then this is likely to be due, first, to the fact that the time between the essays reaching a wide public and the catastrophe in Germany was relatively short. A second reason may well lie in the subjective position of European Jews, for the Marxian attack is directed at them—their task must be to defend themselves against the accusing finger of Marx. No matter how untrue and unreal the Marxian image may be, the Jewish response tends to be defensive, hostile and often contemptuous. This will emerge more clearly when we come to review the work of modern Israelis who, because as nationalist Jews they no longer see themselves as the target of the Marxian polemic, can contemplate Marx and his work as critics and as disciples—able to acknowledge Marx's ideas without conceding him a place as judge and executioner of their historic identity. However, once Auschwitz had become a reality, Jewish reactions to Marx's essays were bound to be even more critical.[1] To illustrate the Jewish responses, I have selected a number of writers whose different orientations will give some indication of how they were and are seen in Jewish circles.

Very few rabbis expressed any systematic opinions on them. Quite apart from the fact that it would be difficult for them to take issue with an ideology that is committed to an anti-religious stand, the sheer force of the Marxian polemic deterred most of them from even mentioning it.[2] Chief Rabbi Joseph Carlebach examined the Marxian thesis by first comparing the nature of 'liberal capitalism' with 'the ills of existing economic systems' and then contrasting Marxian and biblical concepts of social justice:[3]

> While recognising the presumptuous self-righteousness of the existing economic system, Marx nevertheless believed in the supremacy and superiority of an economic system. Nay, further: he declared all spiritual and intellectual manifestations to be a function of the economy, even religion was no more than a superstructure of the economy for those who have, those who justify their ideology by giving their greed another—worldly—sanctity. Thus he became a preacher of hatred for and battle against religion as the protector of economic exploitation and injustice.
>
> As Jews we deeply regret this aberration of the founder of communism. We see this hatred of religion today amongst many Jews who see in Judaism, as in other religions, the assumed enemy of a just social order. Yet there can be no doubt that the holy anger with which Marx pursued and flayed social injustice, which gave him the moving words of the *Communist Manifesto*, is the heritage of Jewish prophets, those mighty adversaries of large-scale land ownership and economic self-seeking—those lofty champions of the oppressed and the disenfranchised. In Marx we see, not for the first time, the sad spectacle of those nurtured by the milk of Judaism turning the sword against the mother to whom they owe their greatness.

In a style that conceded nothing to Marx in polemic force, Carlebach claimed that 'the great social reformers have loathed Judaism, they have taken all its economic ideals and then declared war on Judaism'.

'Judaism is capitalistic? Who first pronounced a ban on interest? Who first declared labour to be the only true value, or denied money its asocial, monopolistic place?' After listing many biblical laws directed against land monopoly, capital accumulation and excess profits, which are generally intended to protect the principles of social justice, he summed up by repeating:

> Marx maintained that every ideology was only the superstructure of an economic system, that ideologies only served the ruling class to justify the *status quo*. But for which social class would Jewish law serve as a superstructure? Which group in society, which occupational interest, which economic system would have been able to see it as its exclusive law? It is, on the contrary, based on the equality of man, on the value of labour, on the protection of the economically weak, on freedom for the individual and an equality of rights. To equate Judaism with capitalism is sheer madness, because capitalism is the very antithesis of Jewish economic concepts.

Raphael Breuer, another rabbi, had even less sympathy for Marx. Although the bulk of his paper was devoted once again to showing that Judaism had its own non-materialistic philosophy of social justice, he expressed no understanding for the motives and basic interests of Marx. He began by quoting sentences from Marx's second essay and drew attention to his rabbinic ancestry. The author's anger is unmistakable when he wrote that Karl Marx, grandson of Rabbi Marx Levi of Trier, had 'an almost fanatical hatred of Judaism . . . probably motivated by his utter ignorance of all things Jewish', and that 'Marx thought and spoke of Judaism . . . as any second-rate Jew-baiter would.'[4]

Two polemicists who wrote in the early 1920s both addressed themselves directly to an analysis of Marx's essays 'On the Jewish Question'. Erwin Kohn opened on a caustic note: 'The Jew Karl Marx, socialist, philosopher of religion and anti-semite speaks here.' After some telling quotes from the second essay, Kohn argued that Marx knew nothing about Judaism, nothing of the Jewish masses, only about a tiny handful of rich Jews in Western Europe. 'Here', he proclaimed, 'it is not a case of facts convincing a man, but of a man manufacturing facts.' Marx, he explained, is using the essay to make a final break with his Jewish ancestry, which he justified by a 'dialectic *salto mortale*'. Marx saw Jewish economic function as demoniacal, but the truth is that there is no such thing as 'Jewish economics', only the economy of

Western Jewry.[5] E. J. Lesser summarised Marx's essays, from which he concluded that Marx knew nothing about Judaism and was wholly indifferent to it. These showed that he disliked the Jews of his time in a manner verging on hatred—a hatred induced by the Jews' capacity to be comfortable and at ease in bourgeois society. Nevertheless, Lesser argued, Marx's whole life style, his passion for learning, his neglect of family for the sake of study, his sharpness, his abstract 'all-knowingness'—all these made him a typical 'full-blooded Jew', an 'other-worldly talmudist' (*Jenseits-Talmudist*).[6]

An altogether different standpoint is that taken by Dagobert Runes, who claimed to have produced the first 'unexpurgated' version of Marx's essays[7] to be published in English. His book contains a bitter introduction and adds part of the 'Revised Version' from the *Holy Family* to the text of the essays. He introduced the 'embittered' Marxian reviews to demonstrate 'the Marxian type of anti-semitism', because it was still active in 'Marxist Russia' and 'Red China' and because of 'the classification of every act of religious or cultural Judaism as political Zionism and therefore a capital criminal act' by the leaders of Soviet Russia. After quoting Mao Tse-Tung's call to sweep Israel, 'the Formosa of the Mediterranean', into the sea, and a Soviet state publication of 1958[8] which called on 'all Marxists and Communists . . . to help the Asian and African people crush the reactionary Jewish forces', Runes concluded: 'It is indeed possible that these terrorist practices may succeed where the Roman Soldateska of Titus and the pyres of Torquemada failed, namely, to bring to reality the sanguinary dream of Karl Marx—a world without Jews.'[9]

Shorter and less detailed comments on Marx abound, but can be indicated here only in the briefest way.[10] Isaiah Berlin described Marx's essays as 'a dull and shallow composition' in which Marx decided 'to kill the Jewish problem once and for all'.[11] Its 'violently anti-semitic tone . . . affected the attitude of communists, particularly Jewish communists, towards the Jews and is one of the most neurotic and revolting aspects of his masterful but vulgar personality'.[12] Joel Carmichael described the essays as 'so filled with a peculiar vituperative, abusive quality that it made a curious impression of paranoid extremism . . . [Marx] never showed anything but hostility to Jewish institutions and kept himself strictly disengaged from any indication of sympathy with Jews.'[13]

The great Jewish historian Dubnow thought that 'the ideologist of social democracy, cut off as he was from the sources of Jewish culture, was unaware that he usurped a great deal of the spiritual heritage of ancient Judaism, and that he preached the social ideals of the prophets of Israel in a new terminology'. He contemptuously dismissed Marx's essays as a 'Pasquill', and argued that in his later years Marx freed himself to some extent from his 'metaphysical Jew-hatred' and instead became wholly indifferent to Jews. The only consolation for Judaism for 'the apostasy of her ablest sons' was that they became apostles of human freedom and frequently, if unconsciously, fought for the realisation of social ideas which were once proclaimed on the hills of Judea. Dubnow concluded this chapter, which dealt with the period in which Marx's essays were written, by saying that 'Judaism stood before three tribunals: The enemy of the church, Bauer, the defender of the church, [Julius] Stahl and the socialist Marx. All three sentenced it to death. Judaism heard the sentence and continued on its historic path.'[14]

For the hundredth anniversary of the birth of Karl Marx, Gustav Mayer (1871–1948), the historian of socialism, published an article in which he rejected the common practice of using Marx's essays to determine his Jewishness or his attitude to Jews.[15] In the essays Marx was solely concerned to demonstrate 'the superiority of his new materialistic mode of analysis over the ideological problematics of the Young Hegelians'. The essays also made it clear that 'no German politician of Jewish origin in the nineteenth century was so completely assimilated' as Marx. That is why he was able to label 'the ghetto Jew, crippled by external pressures, as the "real Jew" ', why he equated Judaism, which was many centuries older than Jewish peddling, as one and the same thing. In using this equation and calling for the emancipation of society from Judaism (peddling), he 'empties out the baby with the bath-water'. Compare, Mayer suggested, 'how devoid of historical understanding and psychological insight the crude antithesis "real Jew"–"Sabbath-Jew" appears in contrast to the profound synthesis with which Heine resolves the contradiction between the peddling and the Sabbath-Jew in his [poem] "Princess Sabbath".' And so because Marx, in his socioeconomic characterisation of Judaism, assumed a part to be the whole, the consequence emerged that 'no Gentile has ever condemned Judaism in a more unjust and one-sided manner'. Nevertheless, it was the very essence (*Urkraft*) of Judaism in Marx which assured him his place in the history of man. Where else but in the prophets of Judah and Israel would one find such 'rigid convictions'? Marx was first and foremost a believer, a believer in 'the immanent strength of a corrupt society to produce a better one'. Marx treated his faith as knowledge, 'the prophet dons the spectacles of the scholar', yet Marx was moved by the prophetic conviction that human emancipation would come about through the elevation of the proletariat. As Isaiah foretold doom to King Ahab, so Marx foretold the doom of early capitalism, because, like the ancient worship of Moloch, it mercilessly sacrificed its children to its greed. Because for Marx there was no God, salvation could come only from the disinherited themselves, hence Marx remains the prophet of the class struggle, his visions know of no millennium in which 'men will turn their swords into ploughshares and their spears into pruning-hooks'. Marx, though he did not know it, was in his innermost psyche a Jew cast in the mould of the prophets.

Mayer returned to the subject of Marx's essays some twenty years later, when German anti-semitism was at its height and when the Judaism–capitalism equation had acquired a sinister and more than academic significance. In this paper, Mayer was more concerned to place the Marxian essays in historical context and argued that, in his dispute with Bauer, Marx was mainly aiming to prove the limitations of politics and its dependence on social conditions. 'It was only by chance that the Jewish question became the subject whereby [Marx] advanced the proof of his theory. This also explains why Marx in his *Zur Judenfrage* does not deal with the actual position of the Jews in Prussia.' Like Bernstein's, the weight of Mayer's criticism is now directed at the effect Marx's essays have had in fostering anti-semitism. For the average German, he explained, 'Judaism and capitalism came pretty close to being synonymous. And for this they could cite Marx who, in his *Zur Judenfrage*, because of his dialectical reasoning, had set up Judaism and money power as one.'[16]

An American Jew, Solomon Bloom, in a well-known article, took issue with a number of prevailing views on Marx and sought hard to present an objective discussion on Marx and Jews. He began by arguing that Marx rejected all religion casually and without prior struggle, in fact 'he probably never believed in any religion at all'. While Marx's willingness to write a petition for Jewish emancipation[17] should not be interpreted, as Riazanov did, as a residual interest in his Jewish origins, it does preclude a conclusion of any political anti-semitism in Marx. Bloom then went on to examine Bauer's essays as the background to Marx's reviews. He thought that Bauer offered a good example of 'the application of brutal logic based on a superficial premise' and that Marx, although accepting Bauer's views on Jewish character, religion and civilisation, rejected his conclusions on emancipation. In his reply to Bauer, Marx ceased to regard the term 'Jew' as meaning a racial, religious or cultural group, but merely as an economic symbol. There were, according to Bloom, three contemporary factors which influenced Marx. One was the link between the Rothschilds and the Habsburgs and other ruling dynasties, a second was the breaking-up of large estates by Jewish financiers and the resultant animosities which affected even the radicals, and a third was the continuing impact of enlightenment literature which was often hostile to Jews and attacked the Hebrew antecedents of Christianity. In his essays, Marx was in a stage of transition from liberal idealism to socialist materialism. Here he expressed his hatred of commercial capitalism and the essays contain the germs of much of his later thought. Bloom considered that Marx changed his views on the role and economic significance of Jews and that in *Capital* he showed that he had achieved 'a certain historical perspective' on the Jewish question.

Yet there was in Marx 'an undeniable and substantial residue of anti-semitic feeling', but his call for the 'abolition' of Judaism must be explained by his general principle that problems are not solved but abolished. Bloom also rejected Otto Rühle's views that Marx suffered from 'excessive self-consciousness as a Jew' and was scornful of the frequent and, as we have seen, pervasive attempts at times to see in the pages of *Capital* 'a Hebraic spirit of righteousness'. Surprisingly, Bloom conjectured that Marx's unrelieved hostility to the trader and middleman in favour of the producer might be a reflection 'of the old, agrarian Christian and aristocratic society'. Nor would Bloom accept a crude classification of Marx as an anti-semite: 'it is fairer to say that Marx had absorbed, without much independent reflection, the prevailing prejudice of his time and environment than that he made the Jews a scapegoat of his personal disillusionments and frustrations'.[18]

Perhaps the absence of polemic, the more detached approach of Bloom, can be explained by the sheer physical distance between himself and the tragedy that was being enacted, and had to be explained, in Europe. An even more detached, though no less critical, perspective is explicit in Hans Liebeschütz's telling passage on Marx, which is characterised by the profound depth of his historical understanding. He first discussed the controversy between Bauer and Marx and then summed up the Marxian position with a succinctness that, whether one agrees with it or not, deserves to be quoted in full:[19]

Fundamentally, [Marx's] conception of Judaism is derived from the patristic interpretation of the Old Testament as a stage of revelation at which the divine law is promulgated for the sake of the people's terrestrial well-being. In Marx this concept assumed an extreme harshness by abstraction from all spiritual meaning associated with the history of salvation, and by its combination with the figure of the nineteenth century financier. The patristic account of Judaism, in contrast with the New Testament, exercised a broad influence in the modern period, traceable both in Kant and in Mendelssohn. The closest parallel and, perhaps, the key to the understanding of Marx, is Spinoza's *Tractatus theologico-politicus*. Here is worked out the theory of the superseded stage of revelation in order to establish the author's own right to be free from the Jewish law and the right of the secular state to reject any intervention based on Old Testament precedent. Spinoza's first motive seems not to have existed for Marx—neither he nor his family had any ties with the Jewish religious tradition—but Marx's *emphatic caricature* of Judaism clearly shows that he was conscious of his own social connection with Jewry. His philosophy seemed suitable to eliminate this link. It left nothing in Judaism but the motive force of a social and economic system which had to be overthrown and from which he could feel free. The new society would know no difference between Jew and Gentile. In Marx's view religious ideas influenced only the surface of human affairs. He could therefore remain unaware of the fact that the teleological outlook on history which characterised his philosophy was of Biblical origin. He could blissfully ignore this fact because the idea came to him not from any Jewish source but from the Hegelian school and he was convinced that only his materialistic, and therefore non-religious, interpretation turned it into a motive force for progress.

Michael Graetz, on the other hand, makes the influence of nineteenth-century thought on modern anti-semitism the core of his investigation into the images of Judaism and Christianity in Marx and Feuerbach. The key texts he examines are Marx's 'On the Jewish Question' and Feuerbach's *Essence of Christianity*. After a careful examination, he concludes that both writers have adopted medieval Christian and Deistic views of Judaism and reformulated them in secular terms. Marx, therefore, used traditional anti-Jewish views as a medium for propagating his revolutionary ideas. The contribution to modern anti-semitism in his view lay in the changed attitude—which Marx, perhaps inadvertently, fostered—of turning the growing willingness to co-exist which Judaism and Christianity were evolving into an intolerant demand 'to liberate mankind from Judaism'.[20]

The most recent and perhaps the most incisive critique of Marx's analysis of Judaism comes from a well-known Jewish philosopher, Emil Fackenheim, who slates the whole 'left-wing Hegelian' movement for being concerned only with 'its own ideological consistency and totally indifferent to historical fact'.[21] Fackenheim, who is equally severe with Feuerbach, Bauer and Marx, expresses amazement that the latter should not have recognised that 'any special Jewish involvement with money is both the result of, *and resistance to,* oppression in Christian society'.[22] He accuses all three critics of Judaism of not having *overcome* the otherness of the Divine but merely of *denying* it. It follows from that 'that all left-wing Hegelian atheism remains fraudulent so long as its image of Judaism is fraudulent; and that so long as even a single Jew stays freely covenanted to a God other-than-man the "criticism of religion" that Marx considers over and done with must be radically reopened.'[20] For it is not possible simply to equate Judaism with capitalism, partly because Judaism preceded capitalism by several millennia and partly because it has shown itself capable of outliving it, as in the case of orthodox Kibbutzim.

The Jews of the Diaspora, whatever their orientation, cannot accept the Marxian analysis of their own position in European society. For Marx they have no place in that society, so for them there is no alternative but to reject the Marxian view. To the Jewish nationalist in Israel, however, the challenge is a different one.

CHAPTER XV

Karl Marx in Israel

In a purely negative way, Marx may be described as a major influence on the movement which began in nineteenth-century Europe to re-establish the Jews as a nation in their ancient homeland, which culminated in the establishment of the State of Israel in 1948. It was precisely Marx's failure to deal with the question of nationalism which lay at the root of the violent fraternal struggles between Jewish-socialist groups, some of whom, as I have indicated, opted for a partial or total dissolution of Jews among national or international proletariats, while others demanded the right of the Jews to join the class struggle as a proletariat in their own right and in their own country. The conflict was not limited to Jews. Many of the great leaders of the socialist movement took a stand on this issue, notably Karl Kautsky, whose hostility to Zionism survives today in the Trotskyist movement, though many others, after an initial hostility, recognised the idea as the only 'realistic' solution to the Jewish question (e.g. Jean Longuet, Marx's grandson, Léon Blum and Harold Laski).[1] Reference has also been made to the empirical socialist tradition that was evolving in Eastern European Jewry throughout most of the nineteenth century which, in its nationalist-orientated sections, derived its inspirations more from pragmatic Jewish thinkers than from any coherent body of Marxist theory. 'Orthodox' Marxism was a product more of Central than of Eastern Europe, and the Marxism that permeated through to the young socialists who were about to make their way to Palestine was more of the Plekhanov–Lenin variety than actual Marxian teaching.[2]

Socialism came to Palestine as a social movement with the second *Aliyah* ('wave') (1904–13).[3] Although it is true that 'classical Marxism never struck roots in Palestine',[4] it is equally true that Karl Marx as a 'historic personality' was worshipped by the Jewish youth of Eastern Europe as 'liberator of the world', as 'the righteous saviour of the ghetto',[5] and that this worship, as unadulterated as it was uncritical and uninformed, was brought to Palestine by the young pioneers. To give but one example, when Melford E. Spiro carried out his research in an Israeli kibbutz he described how the kibbutz saw Marx as the true prophet, Lenin as his interpreter and the Soviet Union as the mediator of both, somewhat along the lines on which traditional Judaism venerated Torah as revelation, Talmud as interpretation and Karo's *Shulhan Arukh* as the immediate guide to correct living. To the kibbutz members, the Soviet Union was 'a combination of Vatican and heaven', a paradise on earth to be emulated. Hence they saw themselves as 'a vanguard tool of the Jewish working class' for a socialist society.[6]

Although the right of the Jewish people to a national home had been recognised in various resolutions of international socialist congresses in 1917 and 1920, this idea had never been accepted by the communists (who preferred to follow Kautsky and Otto Bauer in regarding the Jews as a 'caste'), and during the late 1920s and early 1930s communist attacks on Zionism reached a peak and went so far as to equate Zionism with the fast-rising fascism in Germany.[7] This hostility—coupled with rising demands in Palestine for more systematic teaching of Marxism, for the translation of Marx into Hebrew and a contemporary and highly significant comment that 'one can see the entire Second International strolling along the sea-shore of Tel Aviv on a beautiful Saturday'—led to the publication of the first systematic denunciation of Marx in Palestine.[8]

Moshe Glickson assured his readers that his attack on Marx 'was not written in order to criticise socialism or to turn the young Jewish generation against the socialist movement in general'. His reasons were, as he stated in a final section, that 'Marxism has been a catastrophe for socialism'; that 'real and humane socialism [is not] identical with Marxism'. His purpose was to try to explain a mystery, a contradiction:

> How could this man, with his astonishing genius, his broad and profound knowledge of life, exhibit such appalling superficiality and such audacious impertinence as to 'dissect' Judaism, so to speak, and, in total ignorance of the subject, render a verdict of 'guilty', tinged with a scorn and hatred which one usually finds only among the most rabid anti-semites? . . . Whence came these violent emotions into the heart of a man who preached redemption and brotherhood to the entire world?

For Glickson's charge against Marx was not merely that he had expressed himself in 'the basest and most venomous form' about Jews, but that Marx, 'the impassioned fighter for freedom and defender of the oppressed, did not hesitate to besmirch the traditions of the Jewish people and to place a sword in the hands of its enemies'.

Glickson then offered a brief résumé of the essays 'On the Jewish Question' and rejected their basic thesis not only as untrue but also as unoriginal—a mere repetition of Feuerbach—but 'what *is* original in Marx is his deep aggressive antipathy, his bitter grudge against Judaism, which borders on the desire to see it destroyed'. He painted Marx as a strong but cold, loveless and unloved man (excepting only his family and Engels) whose animosty towards Jews he explained at two levels. The first was self-hate, that terrible affliction of many modern Jews who can never quite free themselves from an unwanted and burdensome Jewish background. The other reason lay in the theoretical difficulties which the Jews as a social phenomenon presented in the Marxian schema: 'All of Marx's supreme, dialectical talents had to be mobilised in order to make the Jewish camel pass through the needle's eye of historical materialism.' The problem lay in the 'fanatical monism' of Marx which, while it may well have been 'a distorted reflection of Jewish monotheism', could not come to terms with Judaism, that 'irregular' phenomenon 'which denied the materialist world outlook'. Marx found it necessary, therefore, to 'correct and re-interpret' this phenomenon by using the dialectical method. He placed Judaism 'in the Procrustean bed of the system, even if this calls for breaking all the bones in the body'.

In this way, according to Glickson, the main features of Judaism are explained away 'to distort their true form and to turn them into grotesque and irritating caricatures. The God of Israel becomes money: prophecy and vision, commercialism: martyrdom—egoism: whole-hearted devotion—greed and haggling. Thus the road is paved for sermons laden with depreciation and ill will'.

Glickson's articles are a strongly felt and strongly expressed polemic against what appeared to him to be a wholly hostile, uninformed and unjustified attack on Jews by Marx. Edmund Silberner, whose approach was a complete antithesis of Glickson's, nevertheless came to essentially the same conclusion. Silberner is the best known and most scholarly analyst of Marx's essays.[9] He regarded his work as 'a contribution to the history of ideas in socialism', and examined the work of the main Western European socialists (France, Germany, Austria, Belgium and England) from 1800 to 1914. The questions he sought to examine are important. Is there a relationship between socialism and Judaism—and if so, what is it? What are Jews—a nation, a religious community, or even a caste? What attitude should socialists adopt towards anti-semitism and are the two in any way compatible? These questions are of particular interest to us here. Silberner also defined anti-semitism in the sense in which he applied it to the subjects of his investigation. 'Anti-semitism', he argued, 'is hostility towards or agitation against, Jews.'[10]

The book is scholarly and factual and Silberner takes pride in the fact that he has been accused of discrediting as well as of rehabilitating socialism, that he is a Jewish chauvinist and that he lacks Jewish patriotism. His ideal is expressed by Bayle: 'La perfection d'une histoire est d'être désagréable à toutes les sectes.' Silberner's paper on Marx is based on a systematic collection and analysis of all references to Jews and Judaism which are to be found both in Marx's works and in his voluminous letters. In the event he drew two conclusions from his research, after analysing the data on Marx and much of the literature of those who attacked and those who defended him:[11] 'If the pronouncements of Marx are not chosen at random but are examined as a whole, and if, on the other hand, by antisemitism aversion to the Jews is meant, Marx not only can, but *must* be regarded as an outspoken antisemite.'[12] Similarly, Silberner is emphatic when he argues in his final sentences that, 'willingly or not, Karl Marx contributed powerfully to provoke or to strengthen anti-Jewish prejudice among his Christian followers, and to estrange from their own people a good number of his Jewish admirers. He thus unquestionably holds one of the key positions in what may, or rather must, be designated by a new but appropriate term as the *antisemitic tradition of modern socialism.*'[13]

It was not only the Soviet-orientated kibbutzim which re-examined their position in the wake of the uncompromising Soviet hostility towards Israel—many academics in Israel were involved in similar reappraisals in the context of their respective disciplines. Nathan Rotenstreich is a philosopher who has shown particular interest in 'Anti-Judaism in Modern Thought'.[14] He is the only scholar who has attempted to analyse the Marxian essays in their intellectual context in a well-known paper in which he tried to derive the Marxian contribution both from the empirical situation of German Jewry and from the intellectual precursors of Marx, notably Hegel, Feuerbach and Bauer.[15] The focus of the paper is Bauer and the reactions to his 'Die Judenfrage', which includes, of course, the response by Marx, as well as the mostly ignored responses of Jewish writers and thinkers. Somewhat surprisingly, Rotenstreich argues for an empirical basis for Marx's view (which, whether it existed or not, was not taken into consideration by Marx), but relates the intellectual origins of the Marxian argument correctly to Feuerbach, noting that when Marx subsequently criticised him for dealing with human essence in isolation, he did not apply the same criticism to his own discussion of Jews and Judaism. This leads Rotenstreich to conclude that in the Marxian analysis, 'we have striking evidence of the infiltration of irrational, mythological elements into so rational a system as that of Marx when the subject was the problem of the Jews and their history.'[16] Shmuel Ettinger, a historian interested in the origins of anti-semitism, is non-committal on the question of Marx's personal attitude to Jews but has no doubts about the importance of the Marxian essays as the source of fundamental concepts which contribute to the stereotype of the Jew and which make some kind of opposition to Jews from socialist positions inevitable. While to the liberals of the nineteenth century Judaism was primarily an obstacle to the successful absorption of Jews into their host-nations, for Marx, 'Judaism turns Christianity and bourgeois society into Jewish entities, so that the task of humanity is to fight Judaism and all its expressions.'[17] Shlomo Avineri, a brilliant Marx scholar,[18] perhaps not surprisingly has sought to stress the positive aspects of Marx's contributions to the Jewish question in a paper which, for a thinker of his calibre, contains a number of perplexing errors.[19] Although, as has been mentioned, he is the only writer of note, apart from McLellan, to draw attention to Marx's revised version of the Jewish question in the *Holy Family*, he opens his paper with an emphatic statement: 'That Karl Marx was an inveterate anti-semite is today considered a commonplace which is hardly ever questioned.' That is, to say the least, a very doubtful assertion which is compounded by a further claim that 'Marxists feel uneasy about it', that they try to avoid discussing it, and that they, as well as non-Marxist scholars, 'are perplexed by the enormity of Marx's anti-Jewish outbursts'. Because Marx's image of Jews and Judaism is so negative in his essays, his more positive approach, particularly on the right of the Jews to emancipation, is often overlooked—as Avineri rightly stresses—and the main body of his paper is devoted to an analysis of the sections in the *Holy Family* dealing with this problem. Avineri does not, however, compare this version with the earlier one in the *DFJB*, as I have done, and therefore does not take his analysis as far as it could be taken. Nevertheless, he achieves what he had set out to do, namely to separate the 'good' in Marx from the 'bad', or 'one has to divorce Marx's acrimonious attack on the role Jews played, according to him, in history from his attitude to the question of Jewish emancipation'.

The focus of interest of Jochanan Bloch[20] and J. L. Talmon[21] was not Marx but the general question of the relationship between Judaism and socialism. They saw this problem differently from Silberner, who confined his analysis to what socialists said about Jews and Judaism. They were interested in a more explanatory type of analysis which might provide an answer to the great contradictions of the nineteenth century, in which Jews appear as the representatives both of a rising bourgeoisie and as leaders of socialist-revolutionary movements, in which capitalist societies for the first time in two thousand years offer Jews absolute social equality, while large numbers of precisely those Jews advocate the destruction of that same capitalist system. Nor is this all—the Jews who for over a century have struggled for civil emancipation also produced some of the most fervent advocates of the 'abolition' or end of Jews and Judaism; in fact the anti-semitic movement which grew out of the civil rights campaigns of nineteenth-century Europe received much of its impetus from those against whom it was directed. It is in this context that Bloch and Talmon examined Marx and his contribution to the debate on Jewish emancipation. Although substantive discussions cannot here be examined in depth, I want to note that, similar as the problematics of the two writers are, their positions and conclusions diverge fairly sharply. Bloch is primarily a Jewish nationalist with a profound commitment to Jewish spiritual values. He regarded 'socialist anti-semitism' as a concept which began with Marx,[22] and described Marx's attempt to equate Judaism with money, and the emancipation from man's self-alienation as the emancipation from Judaism, as a 'splendid joke'.[23] It does, of course, have its serious consequences too, and for Bloch these are manifested primarily in the unwavering hostility of many socialists to Jewish national aspirations, to Zionism as an atavistic, chauvinistic, bourgeois manifestation in which any attempt to synthesise Marxism and socialism is seen as 'trying to square a circle'.[24] Yet here lies the dilemma and the core of the Judaism–socialism problem: that both socialists and Jews are moved by the same inner dialectic of uniqueness and universality, of universalism and historical plurality. Bloch argues acutely the inadequacy of the Marxian model of emancipation, albeit with the wisdom of hindsight. The emancipation that the Jews were offered was predicated on their willingness to cease to be Jews, while at the same time the constantly reiterated assertion that the Jew would never cease to be Jewish, 'fixed' the Jew in his Judaism and made the entire emancipation process invalid.[25] This then is Bloch's critique of Marx. 'The most baffling aspect of Marx's anti-Jewish attitude is precisely this—that he slavishly repeated the very anti-Jewish theses of society which he sets out to demolish in the same breath', that he repeats and upholds the same prejudices which the Christianity he despised and rejected had advocated for centuries.[26] Talmon, the historian, the man who had previously assessed the Marxian contribution as 'political Messianism',[27] takes an altogether broader and calmer view. Marx's rejection of Jewish nationalism is integral to 'the relentlessly universal nature of the Messianic vision'; it is no more and no less than his 'fierce condemnation and indeed denial of any *raison d'être* to the pastoral pig-raising and pig-headed little tribal slave-nations and for that matter Denmark in 1848-49.'[28] To gain a correct perspective of Marx's comments on Jews, he posits these, together with the more positive comments of St Simonians, against the turgid, anti-Jewish polemics of 'anti-semitic socialist theoreticians and prophets', Fourier, Proudhon and Bakunin. They really loathed Jews, 'whereas Marxism was, in spite of Marx's spleen against his own race, fundamentally not anti-semitic'.[29] Talmon does not examine the Marxian essays to reach this conclusion, but bases it on an overall evaluation of the later views of Marx. Thus, while there is no evidence in Marx's second essay that he regarded the emergence of commercialism and its disruption of the feudal economy as necessarily constructive, we certainly know that once the full Marxian system had been developed, the money-based economy was seen as an essential transition towards socialism. From that perspective, the Jews assume a positive and constructive role, however transient, and to the extent that Marxism recognised that, Talmon could argue against an assumption of anti-semitism in Marxism.

The choice of dimensions within which the Marxian essays are to be judged thus plays a role in the way in which Marx's attitude is seen. This is also illustrated, perhaps even more clearly, by the next two writers to be considered, both committed Zionist-Marxists, which means that both would have to find a synthesis which would make these two ideologies compatible. We have seen how Ber Borochov adapted Marxist theory to this end and, indeed, both of the next writers follow Borochov's lead, though with very different emphases. While our first Zionist-Marxist, Jona Fink, made only casual reference to him, the second, Daniel Ben Nachum, builds his entire rationale on Borochov's Marxism. In a way, therefore, Fink is the more original, but also more controversial, contributor.

Franz Jona Fink (1906–62) was born and educated in Germany, fled to Uruguay during the Hitler era and eventually settled in Israel, where he joined Kibbutz Ma'abarot. He was an orthodox Marxist in the sense that, while he advocated a continuous 'reality-based' development of Marxist thought, he insisted that all such developments must also be based on a recognition of the founders of Marxism, by whom he meant Marx, Engels, Lenin and Stalin. No errors in theory or practice which could be attributed to any of these would obviate the need to develop Marxism along the lines they had laid down.[30] His first problem was to determine how far Marx's essays provided a solution to the Jewish question. In a short essay,[31] he argued that both Bruno Bauer and Ludwig Feuerbach were concerned only with the Jewish religion and religious emancipation: 'They make no reference at all to the national question and therefore, in this context, i.e. the critique of Bauer's analysis of the Jewish question, Marx does not consider it either.'[32] Since Marx and Marxism-Leninism are treated as a unity, Fink saw no difficulty in moving straight from Marx to Stalin's discussion of nationalism in *Marxism and the National Question* (1912), in which he discounted the idea of a Jewish nation, but in 1948, through the agency of Russia's foreign minister, Gromyko, it was established that the

Jews of the world 'came forward together' to fight and suffer in
the battle against fascism and in the war of liberation against
imperialism which led to the foundation of their State. This State
represents and achieves the 'concrete, historical conditions of our
situation through productivisation (*Chalutziut*), ingathering of
the exiles (Zionism) and the struggle against social and national
oppression (socialism).'[33] The theoretical justification for defining
Jews as a nation was thus confirmed and seen as a direct development from Marx to Fink's own days.

In his chapter on the kibbutz, Fink dealt more explicitly with
the sociohistorical position of the Jew. He began by drawing
attention to the abnormal economic, social and cultural position
of the Jews at the end of the nineteenth century when, as Pinsker
put it:[34]

> We do not count as a nation in the ranks of nations, we have no
> voice in the councils of nations, even when our own affairs are
> discussed. Our fatherland—exile, our unity—dispersion, our
> solidarity—universal animosity against us, our weapon—humility,
> our defence—flight, our originality—adaptation, our future—
> tomorrow. What a contemptuous role for a people descended from
> the Maccabees.

The Jews, Fink argued, could not survive in the Diaspora once
capitalism had given rise to modern nation-states, civil society
had removed their legal and political isolation and secularism had
deprived the religious tradition of its critical force to preserve
their identity. Even so, if the Jew could not maintain his identity,
neither could he disappear. Quoting Pinsker again, 'for the living
the Jew is a corpse, for the native, an alien, for the inhabitant a
vagrant, for the owner a beggar, for the poor an exploiter and
millionaire, for the patriot a man without a country, for all
classes a hated competitor.'[35]

The causes for this situation had to be sought in the social
structure of the Jews, the fact that they were grossly under-
represented in basic production (agriculture and heavy industry)
but over-represented in those industries and occupations 'where
their mere presence leads to friction and conflict'.[36] In addition,
the disappearance of the Jews was constantly prevented by the

pressure of anti-semitism, which was liable to manifest itself in every social crisis, thus reinforcing the communal sense among the Jews and counteracting centrifugal and assimilatory tendencies. Such an argument did not over-emphasise the Jewish question, a question which had been dominant for over one hundred years, which enabled the Nazis 'to lift the world out of its socket'—it was an international problem, but one that could be solved only by the Jews. Two solutions were current at the present time. The first was the revolution of the proletariat, which would 'deprive anti-semitism of its basis', and the second was the national revival in the ancient homeland. Neither of these solutions could succeed by itself. Fink then developed his argument against either of these two solutions being used independently of each other at some length, and I will quote him extensively, because the nature of his discussion is important:[37]

> The individual Jew can involve himself in the affairs of the pro-letariat readily enough and take part in the class struggle without regard to his ethnic origins. Yet where the individual might succeed, the mass would fail. The Jewish masses are composed mainly of a petty bourgeoisie. It is inevitable therefore that they manifest ideological tendencies which are not in accord with the interests of the proletariat . . . in the hands of the Jewish revolutionary, the weapon of the class struggle becomes a boomerang which threatens the Jewish proletarian no less than the Jewish exploiter . . . Caught up in the Jewish question, the Jew cannot have an effective role in the struggle for liberation by the oppressed classes, because the bulk of his energies will be diverted in his struggle against anti-semitism. Even in socialist societies the Jewish question remains unresolved. The attempt of the Jews to build an independent national existence among the nations of the Soviet Union failed, because it lacked the necessary assumptions, especially those concerned with a trans-formation into a normally structured social entity. A socialist but culturally and economically backward country could not deprive itself of its Jewish intelligence. Hence the conditions were lacking to create an even faster normalisation of social and occupational levels which would have made possible a national solution of the Jewish question . . . Even in the Soviet Union, assimilation was never more than a theoretical possibility . . .

Fink went on to argue that, given that anti-semitism in the Soviet

Union was illegal, that Jews there saw themselves as Russians, that they learnt to disregard the impact of anti-semitism in other countries, to accept the *Realpolitik* of Russia in collusion with Hitler's Germany, to ignore the very existence of a State of Israel—given all that, there was one thing that could not be avoided, namely:[38]

> that Jews had to be suspect on all these points merely because they were of Jewish origin. It did not and does not help them if, as proof of their loyalty, they deny the existence of a Jewish question. Precisely because they do not acknowledge the problem of the Jewish people and thereby deny its reality, the Jewish writer, civil servant, politician and physician must disavow and forget his origin, his being, to ward off suspicions of treason, of cosmopolitanism, of solidarity with a people condemned to non-existence, before these are even uttered and which may, at any time, be directed at him. He can twist and turn, assimilate and simulate as much as he likes, but he remains a Jew, his position is abnormal, his integrity called into question, his loyalty suspect, his problem unresolved.

Fink then turned to a brief account of the sources and origins of the Zionist movement for a return to the homeland, which in itself was shown to be inadequate because it could not, of itself, reverse the abnormal structure of Jewish economic life. The result then is that 'the purely national, general Zionist solution of the Jewish problem is handicapped by the unhealthy class structure of the Jewish people, while the general process of social revolution is insufficient because it cannot resolve the problem of their national existence'. Hence the only possible solution is to take the national idea of Zionism and the concept of class struggle in the socialist-revolutionary process and combine the two. 'In their own country, within the people—and only there—the social struggle for liberation must be fought, without the constraints which inhibit the Jews of the Diaspora from participating in revolutionary class struggle.'

Let us now turn to Fink's discussion of Marx's essays 'On the Jewish Question'.[39] Apart from its imaginative approach and originality in historical interpretation, this paper is outstanding not least because it is the most coherent and the most systematic critique of the Marxian analysis and at the same time a vigorous and simultaneous assertion of the Marxist approach to social analysis. After summarising the contents of the second essay of Marx, Fink posed the question which may be said to represent the core of most of the material I am discussing in this study. Marx ended his essay thus: 'The social emancipation of the Jew is the emancipation of Society from Judaism.'[40]

> The thought of how such a conception may be interpreted [wrote Fink[41]], namely as a call for the physical annihilation of the Jews by a society which thereby is provided with a scapegoat for its own corruption and, incidentally, with an opportunity to remove an unpopular competitor—this thought is the reason for our reluctance to read and analyse Marx's ideas. Discussion of a theory is at the same time the discussion of its practical consequences, even if these are not intended; how can one consider objectively, as Marx's ideas should be considered, thoughts on Judaism which (however they were meant originally) sound like a justification for the murder of Jews? What Jew could forget the mass exterminations of 1943 when he reads the death sentence of 1843?

What then is the basis of the Marxian critique? Marx equated Judaism with the evils of civil society and argued for the elimination of Judaism. Judaism is 'practical need, egoism'. This, argued Fink, is as correct as it is meaningless, for practical need and egoism is the worldly basis of everything. 'To describe practical need, egoism, as a special characteristic of Judaism is a point of view which does too much honour to Islam and Christianity.' If anything the history of feudal Christendom, with its landowner and tenant, peasant and serf, master and apprentice relationships, was more typical of the evils Marx described than the danger and fear, the patience and servitude, the lamentations and messianic dreams of the inhabitants of the ghetto. Nevertheless, Fink agreed that, factually, Jews were the representatives of a money economy in the Christian middle ages. The question is whether this predominance is related to the nature of the Jew and his religion or whether it was an inevitable consequence of the social situation in which he was functioning. Like Marx, Fink looked to history for an answer, but unlike Marx, his interpretation did not lead him towards a negation of a Jewish existence. If the Jews did turn towards a money economy, then this could be explained by the pressures generated within feudal society for flexible adaptation to growing production of agricultural and industrial goods, for diversification in production processes and the rise of urban artisanship. Just because feudal society was so rigid it could not meet the growing need for exchange in goods and commodities, while the Jew, barred as he was from the production-based dependencies in the dominant social order, could easily move into the gap it created from its own needs and inadequacies. If this explained why the Jew did what he did, how could the fact that it was the *Jew* who satisfied this social need be explained? Or, in other words, what role did the Jewish religion play in transforming Jews into a *Handelsvolk*?

Fink again moved back to basic sources for his answer. Biblical law, he noted (the law which Marx totally ignored), covered three social areas: commerce and finance, patriarchal agricultural life and nomadic shepherd life. The increasing shift in Deuteronomy to laws governing social relationships suggested to Fink that there must have been an increasing reliance on trade and commerce:[42]

> The conception of an all-mighty being, whose approval [reward] could not be obtained by sacrifice and prayer but solely by social virtues, is possible only in a social order which depends for its existence and prosperity on such social virtues. That is no longer the order of the farmer, but of the trader and merchant. Soil must be irrigated, worshipped, placated by sacrifice: to do right and love one's neighbours does not influence the quality of the harvest, the fertility of the soil, the desired climatic conditions—but they are essential in trade and commerce.

What was a trend in Deuteronomy becomes a feature of the class struggle in Jeremiah, the prophet who, for Fink, transformed the Jewish people from a land-based to a law-based nation in order to ensure their survival. Jeremiah's call to the people to submit unconditionally and simultaneously to the will of God and Babylonian overlordship[43]

> expressed the tendencies and attitudes of a rising, power-seeking, class of traders and was directed against an outdated, reactionary, doomed section of patriarchal landowners. So here, as in all great

303

revolutions, the concerns of the rising class were elevated into general concerns. Because at this time the survival of the people depended on a victory of the prophet-party and on the concentration on trade—this also meant the acceptance of a strict monotheism—and the recognition of a law which acknowledged social order in place of magical forces of nature, justice instead of sacrifice, nation instead of land.

Thus not nature but history became the God of Israel—and Israel survived because it could redefine itself as a community bound not exclusively by its land but by common origin, socio-economic ties and social order. It is simply not enough, Fink argued, to describe trade as the real basis of Jewish peculiarity and religion; it is unacceptable simply to equate Judaism with the spirit of trade. In other nations trade has produced different attitudes, and the evolution of religion has other causes beside purely economic ones. The special achievement of the Jews was to adapt and evolve the prophetic counsel to use trade as a means of survival for a national community and *not*, as in capitalism, for profit. So, unlike Marx, Fink finds much that is positive and progressive in Judaism:[44]

> An awareness of history, the unifying idea of a common humanity, the dream of eternal peace as the ultimate task of history to be expected and worked for, the concept of justice which must include all classes of men, including slaves, liberation from the forces of nature and the soil from sacrifice—these are the ideas which, springing from the special constellation of real conditions, not only exploded the restrictions of the social order of antiquity but, to the end of the period of medieval feudalism, retained their progressive, developmental function.

Fink had other criticisms of the Marxian conception. To describe Judaism as the essence of trade (capitalism) was a false assertion because real capitalism developed earliest and fastest in precisely those areas in which there were the fewest Jews (e.g. in England, France and the USA). It was also incorrect to associate peddling with the spirit of capitalism. There was no organic connection between the two. He saw the decline of the Jewish predominance in trade as linked to the decline of their religion; i.e. the shift from the grandeur of the Torah and prophets to 'narrow-minded orthodoxy' also saw the change from trade on a grand scale to petty trading and peddling. The creation of a profit-based capitalism was the product of science, technology and finance, not of the petty trade of the Jews. Marx was wrong, therefore, in proclaiming that 'the self-emancipation of our time' could be accomplished by emancipating society from Judaism, not least because the profit from real capitalism was all-consuming, while the profit from Jewish peddling and usury could offer only subsistence and protection. For the Jew needed money to survive, let alone for subsistence. Achievement or justice, work or wisdom, patience or humility—none of these mattered; only money helped against persecution, and only in that sense was money 'the worldly God of the Jews'. 'There is no link between the anxious self-defence of one's own life and the hostile exploitation of human strength and labour—they cannot be compared.'[45]

The real struggle over Jewish emancipation was fought between conservative forces fearing Jewish competition and a liberal bourgeoisie confident of its ability to contain it. For the Jew, emancipation meant a period of apeing capitalism. Because it was an imposed emancipation it did not lead to real, i.e. self, emancipation, by which Fink meant the reconstituting of the Jewish people in their homeland, productivisation and class struggle. In a final note Fink also rejected the Marxian solution to the Jewish question because Marx's efforts to bring about the socialist revolution meant only individual emancipation. Jews would remain in interstitial roles until they returned to their land to work for mankind collectively. 'Jews', said Fink, 'should not try to help the oppressed and exploited by speaking and organising *for* them but by participating in their own liberation.'

The remaining problem to be resolved was why Marx, 'who always emphasised the general social significance of every historical occurrence, should have dealt differently with the Jewish question by offering only an individual solution', and Fink resolved this by offering two reasons.[46]

First . . . Marx's circumstances and education alienated him from the Jewish collectivity from which he came; the mass of the Jewish people—especially the Jews of Eastern Europe—were unknown to him, so that he had no social relationship with concrete Judaism to which he reacted purely as an individual. Second, it was a principle of his method to pose only those problems which were immediately relevant and capable of solution. The true, communal practical solution of the Jewish question was then, at a time of prosperity— especially in the commercial world of Southern and Western German Jewry—altogether premature. This can be seen from the lack of success of the ideas which Moses Hess, Marx's contemporary and fellow-fighter, developed at that time.

While Jona Fink's critique of Marx's analysis is predominantly implicit in his alternate review of the Jewish question, which is strictly and rigidly composed within the context of Marxist historical materialism, Daniel Ben Nachum, a leading socialist writer in Israel and authority on Ber Borochov, chose a different focus for his discussion of the Marxian essays.[47] In a wide-ranging study, in which many other leading writers were also discussed, he described his aim as an 'objective-scientific' investigation into 'the effects of Marx's Jewish origins on his position in German society and the relationship between his ideological development and the situation of German Jewry as a separate social group'.[48] Ben Nachum noted the disparaging comments on Marx's 'Jewishness' which were made even by some of those who worked closely with him at some time or another, but was even more critical of Silberner's diagnosis of Marx as an anti-semite. It seemed to Ben Nachum that Silberner's 'attitude of public prosecutor on behalf of the Jewish people and its national liberation movement' was misconceived, because Zionist theory regards assimilation, with all its implications, including the symptom of Jewish 'self-hatred', as something which should not be morally censured, but which, inevitably and tragically, must be seen as part of the processes and developments of Jewish society in modern times.

In a brief review of the historical background, he pointed out that the German attempts in the mid-nineteenth century to push the Jews back into the ghetto could not stop the rapid rise of the Jewish, and particularly the baptised, bourgeoisie. This affected Marx from his early childhood and found its later expression in Marx's 'hatred of Judaism [which] was primarily a revolt against a network of sanctimonious lies woven by his Jewish environment, where human values were rejected in favour of aspirations to get rich as quickly as possible—no wonder that these distortions of an assimilated Jewish bourgeoisie, who repudiated their own people, were regarded by Marx as fundamental characteristics of Judaism'. A similar view, as Ben Nachum explains, had already been expressed by Theodor Zlocisti, the first biographer of Moses Hess, who thought that 'only a refugee from the ghetto like Marx, grandson of a rabbi, is able to curse his spiritual origins and native land like one of the medieval apostates'. Added to this background was the 'notorious anti-semitism' of the young Hegelians, notably Ludwig Feuerbach who coined the concept of Jewish egoism, and Bruno Bauer, both of whom painted Judaism as far more negative than Christianity. Although Ben Nachum noted that in his essays Marx took his first steps from 'primitive Feuerbachian materialism' to historical materialism, he also drew attention to the inconsistency in Marx, who criticised Judaism as the religion of practical need which 'found its realisation in praxis rather than in theory, because its truth is praxis', while in his *Theses on Feuerbach*, Marx himself demanded that philosophy should be based on human praxis. This led him to stipulate 'an essential kinship' between Judaism and Marxism.

Ben Nachum also rejected Avineri's suggestion that Marxian anti-semitism had its origins in traditional Christian images of Judaism. It was, on the contrary, typical of the Jewish complex of self-hatred at that time. For all that, as we shall see later, he accepted Arnold Künzli's view that Marx's comments on the Jews of Jerusalem indicated the existence of 'unconscious, pro-Jewish influences', which were also manifested in the Marxian demand that Jews be granted political emancipation.

While it is significant that Marx applied his basic ideas on historical materialism and socioeconomic as opposed to religious alienation in his analysis of the Jewish question, it is equally significant that he failed in his analysis at an empirical level. If he had investigated the Jewish reality in the way Engels investigated the position of the English working class, he would soon have found that, far from being the capitalist class, Jews were in the main poor, miserable, exploited and searching for protection. In fact, Marx's Jew is a 'metaphysical abstraction', not only because he is totally unrelated to any historical reality, but also because his argument that Judaism is 'the spirit of capitalism' contradicts his theory that capitalism is the result of the growth of the modes of production in the feudal economy.

Like Fink, Ben Nachum thought that Marx could not have seen the Jewish problem in national terms, which is why he adapted Bruno Bauer's concept of the 'chimerical' nationality of the Jew; but the application of Marxist analysis to the Jews, as in the case of Borochov, soon showed that Jews themselves had a class structure, albeit a distorted one, because they had no agriculture. Yet Marx's support for Jewish emancipation carried with it an implicit recognition of the Jews as an oppressed people and the need for and their right to liberation. This assumption, coupled with Marx's call in the *Communist Manifesto* that the worker must acquire national status in his homeland, meant that those who advocated a socialist internationalism were wrong and that Borochov was right. Ben Nachum concluded therefore that Marx's fundamental error in his essays was to confuse 'people' with 'class', and 'conditions of production' with 'relations of production'. The true resolution of the Jewish question thus lay with Borochov, who taught that all peoples must first resolve their own problems (freedom within) before they attempted to resolve external problems of political independence.

Finally, we might consider an Israeli writer who no longer questions the significance of Marx's essays because the inspiration of his general teachings have long since superseded the irritation caused by his essays on the Jews. Jewish nationalism has become a reality, largely as a result of socialists-Zionists who have infused the Jewish State with the ideals and ideology of Marxism. It only remains now to reabsorb the traditional values of Judaism to complete the aspirations of the reconstituted Jewish nation. In other words, our last example represents a return to our first, the synthesis of Judaism-socialism advocated by Moses Hess.

Yehuda Nini, like our previous two writers, came from a kibbutz background. He set out his call for a new synthesis in a recent paper which he dedicated to his father, who died for 'the love of Israel', and his rabbi, who died for 'the love of the Torah and the people of Israel'.[49] According to Nini, Israel would not have come into being without the Jewish 'left', because Herzlian, political and spiritual Zionism were too slow to have achieved anything in time to save the Jews. It was the second and third *Aliyot* which brought with them the socialist ideologies of Borochov, Syrkin and Gordon[50] who created Israel, because they combined the Zionist-national with a socialist vision. Without this leaven of revolutionary socialism, Israel would be no more than 'a ghetto with a defence army'. The socialist element in Zionism also succeeded in defeating the Jewish exile (*Galut*) culture and its traditionalism, especially in the form of Hasidism and the drift towards assimilation. It recreated Hebrew as a living language, but was temporarily seduced away from its ideology by 'right-wing Zionism and revisionism' with the slogan, 'From class to people'. This was not enough, for the slogan should be 'From class to people to a just society', and the essential ingredients for such an ideology were there but not used.

Judaism, said Nini, already embodies all the values of socialism, but traditional Judaism was no longer able to realise them. Jewish values will only be restored to their real vitality if 'we succeed in fusing the revolutionary ardour of socialism . . . with the foundations of Jewish tradition',[51] but, equally, 'it is not a New Left we need, but the renewal of the left, just as we do not need a new Judaism but a renewal of Judaism'.[52] And so, somewhat in the manner and style of a Moses Hess, Nini would like to see 'the teaching of the future' to include study and discussion of Marx and Engels, Bukharin, Rosa Luxemburg and Borochov, coupled with the study and reflection on the teachings and tradition of Judaism. Like Hess, Nini visualised a different Judaism emerging from this fusion of the old and the new, a Judaism which might, perhaps, even find a place for Marx's essays if only as a quaint historic relic of an unhappy Jewish past.

CHAPTER XVI

The Jewishness of Marx

Marx was born of Jewish parents. This much can be said without taking a position one way or the other. Almost any further comment is likely to be determined by the ideological, political, social or religious position of the commentator. It would still be reasonable to assert impartially that Marx left Judaism; i.e. he was baptised at the age of six, that he had no specific education in, or association with, Judaism and Jewish communal life, and that he freely and openly expressed a dislike for Judaism and rejected any form of identification with it as much as, if not more than, he repudiated any association with, or acceptance of, any other religious ideology. If we may judge by the number of biblical analogies which proliferate in Marx's writings, we can say that he read, and enjoyed reading, the Bible, even if many passages were treated by him with contempt and derision. We can also say that he associated with many people who were of Jewish origin or practising Jews, and that this appeared to have no bearing on whether he respected, accepted, tolerated, disliked, despised or hated them. If his own utterances and actions are to be taken at face value, Marx was utterly indifferent to all things Jewish and would probably have repudiated any suggestion that he was a Jew, or was to any extent conditioned by Jewishness. Yet, there is probably no individual, from Abraham and Moses to Herzl and Martin Buber, to whom the epithet 'Jew' has been more persistently applied than Marx, and whose teachings have more

THE JEWISHNESS OF MARX

frequently been identified with, and indeed attacked for, their Jewishness, than his revolutionary socialism. Nor has this been a temporary manifestation. It began almost as soon as he first emerged as a leading figure in nineteenth-century Europe and has continued in one form or another ever since.

We have already come across many diverse references to Marx's Jewishness, and instead of repeating these, I will look at a number of other writers who have also discussed this question. In order to make it more readily comprehensible, this subject has been divided into a number of separate issues, in line with the perspectives from which Marx's association with Jewishness has been presented. There are those who merely asked whether Marx was in fact Jewish or whether his character and behaviour indicated specifically Jewish characteristics. Some are intrigued by the parallel they thought they could draw between Old Testament prophets and Marx as champions of the oppressed. Others see in Marx's passionate devotion to the 'proletariat' a displacement of the 'chosen people' or see 'communism' as nothing other than a form of Judaism, either because 'the Jew Marx' was its prophet, or because its message is regarded as indistinguishable from the 'message' of Judaism.

'It is indeed a most ironical fact', wrote Robert Weltsch, '. . . that in the course of more than a century, most of the non-socialist, philosophical interpreters of Marx have related him in some way to Judaism', though he admits that 'it can . . . be said that his Jewish origin has been stressed more by those who regard him as a disaster for mankind than by those who see in him one of the blessed pioneers of a new era of human existence.'[1] It is not quite that simple, however, for some of the sharpest comments on Marx's Jewishness have come from those who were or had been associated with him in his radical activities. Ruge described Marx as 'an insolent Jew', while some of the most derisive remarks have come from Bakunin.[2]

> Marx is by birth a Jew. He combines within his person all the advantages and disadvantages of this gifted race. Fearful to the point of cowardice—as some maintain—he is unbelievably vicious, vain, quarrelsome, as intolerant and domineering as the God of his fathers

and like him, vengeful to the point of insanity. There is no lie, no treachery, which he would not be capable of using against those who have incurred his jealousy or his hate.

On another occasion, Bakunin wrote on Marx in equally disparaging tones:[3]

Himself a Jew, he attracts, whether in London or in France, but especially in Germany, a whole heap of Yids, more or less intelligent, intriguers, busybodies and speculators, as the Jews are likely to be, commercial and bank agents, writers . . . correspondents . . . who stand one foot in the world of finance and the other in socialism.

Similarly, Eugen Dühring thought that, in spite of Marx's 'mockery of certain Jewish authors', there were still 'elements of a persistent Judaism that remained in him'.[4] Adolf Hitler, perhaps not surprisingly, liked to refer to 'the Jew Karl Marx',[5] though he denied that Marx, or indeed any Jew, could be a German.[6] Arnold Toynbee, on the other hand, liked to combine the two epithets, e.g. 'when Lenin casts about for a creed, he borrows from a westernised German Jew, Karl Marx.'[7] Nor is the absolute assertion of Jewishness confined to hostile writers. A sober writer like Ferdinand Tönnies, commenting on the young Marx, noted: 'The young author likes to show off in brilliant antitheses. These also indicate the characteristic casuistry of Jewish thought patterns (die eigentümliche Spitzfindigkeit der jüdischen Verstandesart).'[8] To George Steiner, Marx is 'most profoundly a Jew' when he advocates a radical humanism and argues at the same time for 'a dissolution of Jewish identity'.[9] Otto Rühle was of the opinion that Marx's Jewishness was felt as a life-long handicap: 'As soon as he began to come into contact with the Gentile world and was intelligent enough to make comparisons, it was inevitable that he should feel his Jewish origin to be a disadvantage, a shackle upon his aspirations.'[10] Hence Marx's essays were explained by Rühle as Marx 'declaring himself before all the world not to be a Jew. But one who takes so much trouble to declare that he is not a Jew must have reason for being afraid of being regarded as a Jew.'[11] If a large and very diverse group of writers and scholars can be shown to regard Marx as a Jew, they do not necessarily have a uniform conception of what exactly is meant by that term. Kurt Müller, for example, argued like this. The question of whether or not Marx was a Jew depended on how that term is defined, for 'Jew' could mean beliefs, nation, race, community of interests, culture, tradition or any combination of these. The fact that Marx, in his essays, differentiated between the 'Sabbath' and the 'everyday' Jew meant that 'he recognised Judaism as a reality'. He also recognised the Jew as an economic category, while race, nation and culture did not exist for him. Marx discussed two aspects of 'Jew' which did not apply to him, i.e. religion and wealth. This suggested to Müller that Marx intended to show that he personally was not involved, hence his analysis was not 'logical but psychological'.[12] Edmund Wilson, on the other hand, appeared to have no difficulties on this score. Marx was 'the great, secular rabbi of his century' in whom 'the blood of several lines of Jewish rabbis' were concentrated. He was 'too profoundly and completely a Jew to worry much about the Jewish problem in the terms in which it was discussed during his life-time . . . the conviction of moral superiority, which gives his life its heroic dignity, seems to go back to the great days of Israel and to be unconscious of the miseries between.'[13] Some Jewish writers attempted to resolve the difficult and somewhat contradictory issue of Marx's Jewishness by introducing entirely new concepts to define the term and the man. Fritz Kahn, for example, wrote of Marx as a specifically Jewish 'cultural manifestation' along with Moses and Jesus, as Luther and Bismarck could be described as specifically German 'cultural manifestations' (*Kultur-betätigung*). In this sense, irrespective of his actual life-situation, Marx could be seen as a 'Jewish-universal genius' along with Isaiah, Amos and Spinoza. In the widest sense possible, just as Jesus was not the 'founder but the stimulus of Christianity', so Marx was the source of communism. 'In 1818 the star of Bethlehem appears for a second time. Once again it rises over the roofs of Judea: Marx.'[14] A less esoteric view was put forward by Rudolf Bienenfeld, who argued that there were some Jews who, though not recognisably associated with the Jewish people by nationality, race or religion, could yet be identified as Jews, because certain principles of the Jewish faith appeared to be relevant to their main preoccupations. He stipulated four major, universalistic tenets in Judaism. The *equality* of men as a matter of right and not of grace. *Justice* as a matter of principle and not convenience. *Reason* based on learning as a virtue and a duty, and *this-worldliness* which demanded the search for perfection on earth. These principles were opposed to the dominant (Christian) ideas of grace—poverty and riches according to God's will, subordination—men belonging to and accepting their 'station' in life, historical tradition—even if it was irrational, and a Messiah who would offer salvation in a life or world to come. If one analysed some of the more important leaders of thought who had left Judaism but who utilised one or more of its four major tenets as principles of faith, they could be shown to have retained a fundamental part of their Jewishness. Thus, in the case of Marx, his work was based on an assumption that the worker was deprived of a part of his reward. Marx did indeed 'prove' that this was so, but his argument that this was *wrong* was derived from his 'Jewish' principles of faith on equality and justice. Hence, though refuting his Judaism, Marx was still 'practising' it, and to that extent he was a Jew.[15]

In 1918, on the centenary of his birth, Hermann Glenn wrote a glowing report on Marx in which he claimed that he derived his 'being and thinking' from his Jewishness. He dismissed Marx's 'superficial and sad utterances' which identified Judaism with the worst aspects of capitalism, and insisted that 'it would be a particular impoverishment if Judaism did not have the right to claim Marx as blood of its blood, spirit of its spirit—because he was one of us (er war unser)'.[16] A few years later Hitler wrote that 'the Jew Karl Marx . . . used his keen powers of prognosis . . . [to] bring about the destruction of the independent nations on the globe . . . in the service of his race.'[17] In 1927 Riazanov observed: 'One of the questions that invariably presents itself is the extent to which Marx's subsequent fate was affected by the circumstances of his being a Jew.' After discussing how this affected Börne, Riazanov thought that, although Marx was reared under different circumstances,[18] these . . . do not warrant the disposition of some biographers to deny this Jewish influence almost entirely . . . Marx did not shun his old kin . . . he took an interest in the Jewish question and also a part in the struggle for the emancipation of the Jew. This did not prevent him from drawing a sharp line of demarcation between poor Jewry with which he felt a certain propinquity and the opulent representatives of financial Jewry.

In 1967 the East German *Biographisches Lexikon zur deutschen Geschichte* described Marx as 'the greatest son of the German people, its most important thinker, teacher and leader of the international and German worker's movement . . . the offspring of a humanist family of a lawyer',[19] and a year later Hans Lamm, president of the post-war German-Jewish community of Munich, concluded sadly, on the 150th anniversary of Marx's birth, that he 'hated Judaism' and Jews, he 'was and remained a hater of Jews'. Fifty years had passed since Glenn claimed Marx as a Jew. Lamm sadly and somewhat obscurely remarked that, if at all, then we can say only that Marx '*was* one of us'.[20]

If Marx was frequently though not invariably described as a Jew, there was at least some 'objective' basis for this assertion. The oft repeated claim that he was also a secular nineteenth-century version of an Old Testament prophet has, however, attracted some controversy. To those like Arnold Künzli and Massiczek, who in their separate ways have made the Jewishness of Marx the all-pervasive principle of their biographical studies, the issue is a foregone conclusion. Künzli, who constantly re-iterated this claim, who argued that Marx unconsciously identified himself with Moses, used an unusual approach in support of his argument. In *German Ideology* Marx made fun of 'St Bruno' and of a biblical admonition of Israel by paraphrasing Jeremiah (probably chap. 2).[21] For Künzli, the passage was remarkable not only because it demonstrated how familiar Marx was with the biblical text, but also because 'in his unbridled desire to mock the Bible, [Marx] immersed himself so completely in the language and spirit of Scripture that he forgot his intention to mock and ended up by admonishing his people with truly biblical pathos, as only a genuine prophet can do.'[22] Albert Massiczek named no less than thirty-six authors in support of the contention that Marx was like an Old Testament prophet, but also argued rightly that most of those who made this claim did not examine the concept of prophecy or explain in any detail why they described Marx in this way. His own prolonged discussion of prophecy, however, led him to much the same conclusion.[23] To Friedrich Heer, 'the ancient prophetic power emerges once again in the nineteenth century in Jews like Moses Hess and Karl Marx',[24] and 'the anger of Moses against his faithless people was heard again on Marx's lips and seen in Marx's eyes.'[25] Similarly, Max Klesse wrote of Marx as a Jew in whom, though he was no longer religious, lived 'the spirit of the great prophets of Israel who raised their voices for the poor, the widowed and the orphan 2,700 years ago.'[26] Even to Erich Fromm, Marx's socialism 'is essentially prophetic Messianism in the language of the nineteenth century'.[27]

A much more reasoned and reasonable analogy was drawn by Werner Blumenberg, who drew attention to the basic difference between prophecy and Marxian theory but thought that the fanatical commitment to his ideas, which characterised the life of Marx, and the fact that Marx's conception of a 'truly human society', which though extended beyond actual experience and scientific knowledge nevertheless became part of Marx's 'system of beliefs', allowed one to describe him as a figure in the tradition of the prophets.[28] Silberner rejected the idea altogether. He could see no justification for invoking Marx's Jewish origins to trace a line backwards from him to the prophets of the Bible. He was equally scornful of describing his 'singleness of purpose' as a Jewish quality when it was no more and no less than a general human quality, and he questioned why he should be seen as a prophet when Fourier, Owen and Lenin were not. He also argued that those who drew the analogy had yet to offer any convincing evidence for it.[29] In similar vein, Heinz Röhr rejected the imputation of elements of 'religiosity' in the early writings of Marx, as a 'backward projection'.[30]

Yet another analogy that is often made is the substitution by Marx of the 'chosen class' for the 'chosen people',[31] or his attempt to assign the role of chosen people to the proletariat. Edmund Wilson has described this in graphic terms:[32]

> Marx, on the one hand, knew nothing of the industrial proletariat and, on the other hand, refused to take Judaism seriously or to participate in current discussions of the Jewish problem, from the point of view of the special case of Jewish culture, holding that the special position of the Jew was vitally involved with his money-lending and banking and that it would be impossible for him to dissociate himself from these until the system of which they were part should be abolished. The result was that the animus and rebellion which were due to the social disabilities of the Jew as well as the moral insight and the world vision which were derived from his religious tradition were transferred in all their formidable power to an imaginary proletariat.

In rather less sympathetic fashion, Toynbee offered a similar picture:[33]

> such elements [in Marxism] as cannot be traced to Christianity, can be traced to Judaism, the 'fossilised' parent of Christianity, which had been preserved by a Jewish diaspora and volatilised through the opening of the Ghettos and the emancipation of Western Jewry in the generation of Marx's grandparents [sic!]. Marx has taken the goddess 'Historical necessity' in place of YHWH for his deity, and the internal proletariat of the Western world in place of Jewry for his chosen people, and his messianic kingdom is conceived of as a dictatorship of the proletariat; but the salient features of the Jewish apocalypse protrude through this threadbare disguise.

Künzli offered a whole chapter on 'the proletariat as the people of Israel' in which he expressed great surprise that Marx himself drew this analogy. In his assiduous search of Marxian texts, he found a reference in *The Class Struggles in France*: 'The present generation is like the Jews whom Moses led through the desert. Not only will it have to conquer a new world; it must also die out to make room for those men who will be fitted for a new world.'[34] The fact that Marx used such an analogy and that Marx's analogy would seem to extend beyond a proletariat did not shake Künzli in his conviction that here indeed was proof of Marx's inner commitment.

Marx was the man mainly—though by no means exclusively—

responsible for the recurrent association of Marxism (or communism or socialism) with Judaism. While there could be some
debate about Robert Weltsch's assertion that Marx's Jewishness
was stressed mainly by those who were opposed to him, there can
be little doubt that the communism–Judaism equation comes
mainly from those most hostile to both. Bakunin observed: 'In
that Jewish Kingdom which calls itself communist, the members
of the chosen people are liable to be in future managers of the
common treasuries of the nations and to oversee their gold, their
silver and their clothes, as they have done since their first social
undertaking in Egypt.'[35] Otto Haufer, an anti-Jewish 'anthro-
pologist', based his argument on the 'cultural manifestation'
theory of Khan (see p. 313 above), whom he quoted at length to
justify his claim that ' "Marxism" did not disintegrate Judaism, if
only because it had its origins in it, but the non-Jewish masses,
and gave Jewry an unequal advantage, by weakening its opponent.
The Jews know this full well, which is why Marx along with
Moses and Spinoza is regarded by them as a national saint
(*Volksheiliger*).' Marx admittedly attacked financial Jewry, and
Haufer quoted from the second essay on the Jewish question to
prove it, but he was nevertheless helping Jews 'to achieve even
more power'.[36] Hitler regarded Marxism and Judaism as the two
main 'perils' facing Germany,[37] although the two were in fact
fused into one and the same thing. Thus, in words somewhat
reminiscent of Feuerbach, he claimed: 'The Jewish doctrine of
Marxism repudiates the aristocratic principles of nature and
substitutes for it the eternal privilege of force and energy.'[38]
Marxism was seen as both a national and a personal threat:
'Marxism, whose final objective was and is and will continue to
be the destruction of all non-Jewish national states',[39] and
'Marxism represents the most striking phase of the Jewish
endeavour to eliminate the dominant significance of personality'.[40]

Not surprisingly, the anti-Jewish, anti-Marx polemic has spilt
over into the Arab-Israeli conflict, where comments, familiar to
the Jews of Europe, appear in a new context. An Egyptian
newspaper, *al-Tahrir*, carried a report (12 April 1959) which
argued: 'What is the role of international communism in the

318

disaster of the establishment of Israel? Karl Marx was a Jew. This is a fact. The day will come when historians will prove that communism is nothing but a Zionist plot which aims at unifying the world in order to dominate it.'[41] In September 1969 King Feisal of Saudi Arabia addressed a conference in Jedda, where he stated: 'I describe Zionism as the cause of all scandal. It is the cause of all world problems. Communism is the work of Zionism. Destructive principles are also the mark of Zionism, as is demoralisation.'[42] Another Arab writer, Aqqad, tried to set the polemic into a wider and more 'academic' framework.[43]

> It is quite impossible to understand the new schools of thought in Europe without recognising the undoubted truth that one of the fingers of the Jews is hidden behind every trend that belittles moral values and aims at undermining the foundations on which all society has been based in all ages. For the Jew Karl Marx is behind communism, which destroys the foundations of virtue and religion. The Jew Durkheim is behind sociology, which subordinates the institution of the family to artificial conditions and tries to deny its influence on the development of virtue and culture, and the Jew or half-Jew Sartre is behind existentialism.

Not all those who see a link between communism and Judaism are hostile, or see the link as a negative one. We have already made reference to Gabriele Dietrich and Friedrich Heer, who both saw communsim as a form of Messianism in the Jewish tradition. Much of what has been set out above was summarised by George Steiner:[44]

> The dream of a secular millennium, of a just city for the oppressed, relates the social Utopia of communism to the Messianic, Judaic tradition. For both, history is a drama of gradual humanisation, an immensely difficult attempt by man to become man. In both modes of feeling there is an obsession with the prophetic authority of moral or historical law, with the right reading of canonical revelations. But from Eduard Bernstein to Trotsky, from Isaac Babel to Pasternak, the involvement of the Jewish personality in Communism and the Russian revolution follows a sombre curve. Nearly invariably it ends in dissent or heresy—in that heresy which claims to be orthodox because it is seeking to restore the betrayed meaning of Marx.

What can be concluded from all these diverse views on Marx?
Let us begin with the first question—was Marx a Jew? It might
be useful for our considerations to see what aspects of this we can
firmly exclude. Marx was not a Jew in any religious, national or
cultural sense. He knew nothing about Judaism and showed no
interest in the subject. Nor did he 'inherit' any rabbinic or
talmudic qualities or properties. These are acquired skills, no
more transmitted by birth than a knowledge of philosophy or
geology would be. To treat Marx's Jewish origin as a property
would mean descending to the level of the racial obsessions of
the Nazis, who managed to dig up something like 125,000 hapless
(and loyal and faithful) Germans who, because they had Jewish
ancestors, were presumed to have Jewish qualities.[45] It is equally
false to say that Marx 'transcended' his Judaism as Isaac Deutscher
and Mészáros, for example, have claimed.[46] In the case of
Deutscher, we are faced with an almost classic confusion of
persons and meanings. He wrote of 'Jewish heretics', whose
transcendence of Jewry belonged to a 'Jewish tradition', who had
'something of the quintessence of Jewish life and Jewish intellect'
and who 'looked for ideals and fulfilment beyond the boundaries
of Jewry'. It is difficult to assign to such phrases a meaning going
beyond mere rhetoric if one looks at the names that Deutscher
mentions to illustrate his thesis: 'Spinoza, Heine, Marx, Rosa
Luxemburg, Trotsky and Freud'. Quite apart from the untenable nature of his assertion that a Jew must be a heretic to look
for ideals and fulfilments beyond Judaism,[47] how far can the
individuals he named be said to have shared a common approach?
We have had sufficient occasion to quote Heine to be able to
assert absolutely that he never did 'transcend' his Judaism, that it
was and remained an integral element of his personality and
creativity. Rosa Luxemburg, on the other hand, owed nothing to
her Jewish origins, which might never have become apparent
had her opponents not made it a target for their attacks. Similarly
Trotsky, who, although he took a much more direct interest in
the fate of the Jewish people or, perhaps better, the Jewish
proletariat, nevertheless retained an impersonal detachment;
while this demonstrated his total involvement in his own views

of international socialism, it did not suggest the slightest level of identification with, or interest in, Jews as Jews.[48] Freud was certainly a heretic. Like Marx, he saw himself as the enemy of all religion, but unlike Marx (and Trotsky and Luxemburg) he not only never 'disowned' his Jewishness,[49] he also asserted it positively when he described himself as a man 'who is completely alienated from his ancestral religion, as from any other, who cannot share nationalist ideals and yet never denies his allegiance to his people, who feels his individuality to be Jewish and does not wish it otherwise'.[50] Marx then may possibly be bracketed correctly with Rosa Luxemburg, but as far as the question of Jews and Jewishness are concerned, he had little in common with Deutscher's other examples, not only because there never was any Judaism for him to transcend, but also because there is no apparent 'quintessence of Jewish life and of the Jewish intellect' in him. It would seem that George Lichtheim came much closer to the truth when he described Marx as 'profoundly integrated within the German and European culture of his age. At the deepest level, he was at one with the social order whose doom he prophesied. There is something very revealing in his public status as a famous, learned, and somewhat irascible scholar of the late nineteenth century'.[51]

Mészáros, who follows closely in the footsteps of Deutscher, is equally wrong in describing Spinoza and Marx as 'Jewish philosophers' who could achieve 'fundamental philosophical syntheses' because, as Jews, they were 'social outcasts'. According to him, Spinoza and Marx had to overcome a double handicap. First, 'the discriminatory and particularistic national communities' which would not grant Jews emancipation and, second, 'the particularistic and parochial positions of Jewry', which differed only 'in some respects but not in substance' from the first. While one could argue over whether Spinoza suffered from discrimination (he was offered a chair in philosophy at Heidelberg in 1673), he was, as a 'heretic' Jew, much closer to Moses Hess, whom Mészáros described as 'second-rate' and 'provincial', when he wrote in his *Tractatus Theologico-Politicus* that, 'given the right circumstances, seeing that human affairs are changeable, they [the

Jews] will re-establish their state and . . . God will elect them anew',[52] than to Marx. Mészáros's comments do not apply at all to Marx. Leaving aside the description of Marx as a Jewish philosopher, it is simply not true that he was subject to any discrimination *as a Jew*, because for the Prussian authorities he was a Christian, nor did he have to free himself from any Jewish community because he never belonged to one. If Marx was a social outcast, it was as a *political radical*, not as a Jew. We need only think of Prussia's favourite theologian, Neander, and the founder of German conservatism, Julius Stahl, both of whom were baptised Jews, to appreciate that Marx chose to be an outsider. He could have been accepted within German society had he not chosen to fight the German political system. Mészáros therefore is not only objectively and factually wrong, but also makes the purely subjective assumption that a commitment to socialism means being universalistic, whereas a commitment to Judaism means not only being particularistic but of necessity makes the individual a 'second-rate' person.

What is important in determining the Jewishness of Marx is the fact that the anti-semitic world especially tends to describe him as such. In a recent study, 'Antisemitism and Socialism in Austria 1918–62', Robert Schwarz dealt with the problem of Jewishness in a telling paragraph which deserves quotation in full:[53]

> it is important to point out in what sense and by what justification committed Socialist leaders whose ancestors were Jewish but who themselves had neither a national nor a religious Jewish consciousness, could be called Jewish. While the majority of these men and women were religiously unaffiliated, philosophically atheistic or agnostic and culturally citizens of the world, and while most of them were anti-Zionist as well, they can be considered Jewish all the same, for the simple reason that non-Jews in general, and Antisemites in particular, regarded them as Jewish. Thus, for the purpose of this study, 'Jewish Socialist' means a socialist, who may or may not regard himself as Jewish by any customary definition, but who is, none the less, so regarded by the group as a whole, and especially by the enemies of the Jewish name.

In this sense, Marx too was Jewish. We conclude therefore that, while he was never what someone once called 'functionally Jewish', he was Jewish in two respects. First, by descent, and second, by common consent. It would seem that nothing much has changed since the days of Vienna's Bürgermeister Lueger, who belonged to an anti-semitic party but enjoyed the company of Jews, and who coined a famous phrase: 'I decide who is a Jew.'[54] The little evidence we possess would suggest that, while Marx would have agreed with a description of himself as a Jew by descent,[55] he would have resented the second, though it was and remains something he could not escape.[56] To some extent, his refusal to express himself clearly and unequivocally on his own Jewishness is typical of his general reluctance and even refusal to allow his personal characteristics to intrude into his life's task. Even so, it could be argued that as far as his Jewishness was concerned, there appeared to be a particular blockage, because it extended beyond the purely personal to his own social analysis of the Jewish problem. Künzli, especially, discussed Marx's relationship with his mother, and we have seen Marx's irrational response to a suggestion of prejudice in his wife's family. There is one other 'personal' manifestation which ought to be referred to. In his second essay on the Jewish question, he repeatedly attacked the Jews for their preoccupation with their needs. 'What is the profane basis of Judaism? Practical need, self-interest.' 'What was, in itself, the basis of the Jewish religion? Practical need, egoism.' 'The tenacity of the Jew is to be explained, not by his religion, but rather by the human basis of his religion—practical need and egoism.'[57] Very well then (to borrow a Marxian mode of argument), if being Jewish means being preoccupied with practical needs, then not responding to practical needs is being emancipated from being Jewish, it is the resolution of 'the conflict between the individual, sensuous existence of man and his species existence'.

In 1850 Karl Marx was thirty-two, at the peak of his physical and mental development, a refugee in London, married, with four children and no income. In that spring the family was evicted from their home. Jenny Marx went to Holland to beg Marx's uncle for help, which he refused because his business had lost too much as a result of the revolutions that swept Europe. Jenny, pregnant and in despair, returned to nurse her desperately sick little boy. All the other political refugees from Engels down went in search of work and activities to earn a living—but not Marx. In November little Edgar died. The Marxes were now living in two rooms offered by a Jewish lace-merchant. In March 1851 a little girl was born and fostered out because there was no room to nurse her. Louis Napoleon carried out his *coup d'état* at the end of 1851 and Marx immediately wrote his famous, brilliant *Eighteenth Brumaire*. The family moved to Dean Street, and the baby Franziska fell sick and died shortly afterwards, lying in the house for several days until Jenny could beg £2 to buy a coffin. 'My poor child . . . had no cradle when it was born, and even its final shelter was denied it for a long time.'[58] Was the long, painful and humiliating agony of the Marx family really as unavoidable as it appeared?[59]

All this, however, is concerned with Marx's personal situation, and the possibility of a relationship between it and his attitude to his Jewishness is purely speculative. Other factors were directly relevant to his great interest and concern to analyse and interpret the world in which he lived and the events that changed it. Here a suggestion of blockage is again supported by Marx's total silence on at least three events which were and continue to be relevant to the history of European society. The first was Moses Hess's introduction of a national concept in relation to the Jews in *Rom und Jerusalem*; the second was the emergence of a strong, active and socialist-orientated Jewish proletariat in Eastern Europe; the third were the anti-Jewish pogroms in Russia which began at a time when Marx was keenly interested in studying the social situation of Russian society. Yet none of these events drew a single comment from him. If anything, the 'abstract' Jew of Marx was totally 'reified' in the course of time, so that by 1868, in one of the rare documents he wrote about himself, he described the essays in the *DFJB* as 'directed against the ideological mysticism of Hegelian and generally all speculative philosophy'.[60]

The problem of Marx as a prophet-like figure is very different and less complex if only because he himself made reference to it and provided some evidence, both positive and negative. His remarkable and quite uncharacteristic absence of any discussion of biblical law can, I think, be seen as part of his blockage on all things Jewish; for Jewish law, the object and victim of Bruno Bauer's scathing attack, retained its centrality also in post-biblical Judaism. He preferred to remain silent on the subject, after first echoing Bauer's attack and then rejecting both it and his own. The remainder of the Old Testament, however, was sufficiently detached from any immediate Jewish reality and sufficiently integrated in general European life for Marx to enjoy reading it, to use it constantly and often sympathetically in his philosophical and historical writings, and sufficiently meaningful to serve as model, provided only that its use as such was properly circumscribed. Marx's sympathy for Hebrew prophets may be gauged from the information his daughter Eleanor conveyed to Max Beer: 'He told mother that if she wanted edification or satisfaction of her metaphysical needs, she would find them in the Jewish prophets.'[61] A more direct evaluation of the prophets is expressed in the *Eighteenth Brumaire*, in which he argued that Cromwell and the English 'borrowed the language, emotions and illusions for their bourgeois revolution' from the Old Testament and, when that had succeeded, 'Locke displaced Habakkuk'. This process was not to be seen as a simple repetition of an ancient event: 'The resurrection of the dead in those revolutions served to glorify the new struggles, not to parody the old, to enhance the present task in the imagination, not to retreat from its solution in reality, to discover the spirit of revolution, not to revive its ghost.'[62] In this sense, Marx seems to have seen the prophets as sponsors of ancient revolutionary ideas, and felt a certain kinship with their problems and their tasks. This will be even more apparent if we look a little more closely at the nature of prophecy. There are four elements which should be considered: the character of prophecy, the character of prophets, the historical background of prophecy and the task of the prophets. For the sake of a 'balanced' view, I have used Jewish and non-Jewish sources to summarise the salient points.

According to Max Weber, biblical prophecy had twenty main

characteristics, many of which had some relevance to Marx. Prophets were the first men in history to appear as demagogues, as men uttering emotional invective against political overlords. He likened their demand for freedom to prophesy with modern demands for freedom of the press. They were constantly involved in polemics against 'counter' (or false) prophets and rejected political partisanship in favour of objectively world political demagogy. Their social-ethical attitudes were not determined by political dissent. They spoke for the 'little' people and tended to attack the rich and the mighty. They were never supported by the king, nor as a rule by the ruling classes or the peasantry. They fiercely objected to impious ways of life, advocated a return to simple living, and attacked the use of religion and religious ritual as substitutes for social justice. On the other hand they were very different from Marx in that they were concerned not with man's role as a citizen but only as a religious person, and did not advocate revolution or propose means for the masses to help themselves. They offered no sociopolitical programmes, did not champion democratic ideals and often found their main support amongst pious traditionalists. They rejected world politics *per se*, worldly wisdom and aesthetic values as alien to the Jewish tradition.

As individuals, the prophets were 'ecstatic', peculiar men, who spoke only when driven by an inner compulsion. They regarded their psychopathic states as holy, never used intoxicants and always spoke spontaneously. They were misunderstood and hated by the mass of their listeners and never had the following of an ecstatic crowd, but at most a handful of faithful disciples. 'Prophetic charisma was a unique, burdensome office often experienced as a torment.'[63] Like Jeremiah, Marx might well have felt his mission to be to show humanity that 'the only way to salvation is by the steep and stony path over the recognition of reality. The feet of those who take it bleed, and there is always the threat of dizziness, but it is the one and only way.'[64] Yehezkel Kaufmann concentrated more on placing biblical prophecy into a sociohistorical context, which again shows why Marx might have been so attracted to the role of the prophet and the analogy between his own role and that of the earlier demagogues.

Kaufmann saw the distinctive feature of prophecy in its 'vehement denunciation of social corruption'. Wealthy and aristocratic classes are accused of dispossessing and impoverishing the masses whilst they lived in ease and luxury. This kind of social decay was new in Israel, and dangerous, not only because it created a sharp cleavage in society, but also because it threatened its national existence. Israel originally was an agricultural community where the land was shared by tribes and families. With the rise of monarchy, the king's right of confiscation became a new means of acquiring property, and a royal bureaucracy began to exert a new influence. A series of wars impoverished the people, while a small section amassed great wealth. War profiteers bought out the lands and houses of the poor masses. Many were forced into slavery, the rest became a miserable proletariat. War and natural disasters thus brought about the greatest evil, social dissolution. The indignation of the prophets was born out of the rift between the ideal society stipulated in Jewish law and the reality which faced them. The social crisis created the new prophets.[65]

Marx thus resembled the prophets in that he was a product of a historical situation, that he displayed a sense of dedication which suggested a mission and in his deep concern for the dispossessed and exploited. He differed from them in his exclusive interest in systems rather than in people, his philosophy of destruction before construction and his baseless assumption that a change of system would *ipso facto* bring about a change in people. The prophets on the other hand were indifferent to systems and concerned solely with the rules of justice within systems. They demanded justice as an expression of religion and refused to recognise religion *per se* as an expression of justice. While Marx's universalism ignored national boundaries, the prophets saw them as a presupposition of universalism.[66] Marx could also be said to resemble the prophets in style inasmuch as, like them, he advocated axiomatic economic laws as the pivotal structure from which social change must take its directions, just as they predicated their entire message on the absolute and binding validity of God's law. Again, like the prophets, Marx predicted doom and destruction for certain societies or sections of society, although unlike them, for whom there was always a choice, his message of doom was wholly deterministic. Yet he resembles the prophets again in his 'Messianic' concepts, though these rarely withstand the tests of either time or historical analysis.

From such an analysis we may conclude that Marx shared distinct similarities with biblical prophets, but in our context such a conclusion must be conditioned by a rider that on the whole the similarity is with the *role* of biblical prophets, it has little that is essentially *Jewish*, and there are indeed many other men from many other nations whose historical situation and modes of action cast them in a similar mould. Where in his prophetic role Marx is most Jewish, he is also most mistaken. Thus in *The Poverty of Philosophy* (1847) he proclaimed: 'The working class, in the course of its development, will substitute for the old civil society an association which will exclude classes and their antagonism, and there will be no more political power properly so called, since political power is precisely the official expression of antagonism in civil society.'[67] There is nothing 'scientific' about this prediction. In its optimism and apodictic certainty it is Jewish in the best sense of the word, but Marx did not speak as a Jewish prophet and his message lacks the realism which he valued so highly and which the Jewish prophets understood so well. In the Bible there are true prophets and false prophets, Jewish prophets and non-Jewish prophets. Whether Marx was a true or a false prophet is a matter of personal belief, but there is not enough Jewish content in his message to make him more than an admirer of the vigour and realism and perhaps also of the pain and misery of the great prophets of biblical Judaism.

The notion of a chosen class in place of a chosen people has much less substance and therefore does not require prolonged refutation. It has arisen much more because those who drew the analogy saw Marx as a Jew than because of any real conceptual similarities. We should note, however, that the idea of a proletariat existed before Marx took up its cause, that he arrived at the proletariat as the bearer of the future revolution by purely logical analysis, at a time when its real character and problems meant little enough.[68] The analogy is as false as that which Marx himself drew between Jews and money. Just as a Rothschild does not make 'the Jews' financiers, so a Marx does not make 'the proletariat' a chosen class. Rotenstreich drew attention to the fundamental difference between the two concepts for, in the case of the Jews, being chosen is essentially a volitional act of choosing, a status which is constantly threatened by ideological disloyalty, while the proletarian role in the society of the future is always seen as an inevitable process of history, the result of economic forces whose momentum neither the bourgeoisie nor the proletariat can control. To draw such an analogy is an exercise in obscuring sociological realities with mystical metaphors, as is the case with Toynbee, who tried to derive it from Marx's Jewish origins, or Mészáros, who extrapolated from it a Jewish sense of 'superiority' and desire for world domination. The reality is that any group committed to an ideology and conscious of its commitment could see itself, or be regarded as, 'chosen', in the sense that their task-orientated mission gives their existence a meaning and purpose which those who do not possess it might envy, and the absence of which often leads to existential crises.

The same criticism must be directed at even the most sympathetic attempt to equate or somehow relate communism and Judaism—and not only because the one is a religion while the other is opposed to religion. The differences between them are more fundamental, and the real or assumed Jewishness of Marx cannot bridge the gulf that separates the two conceptual systems. Where Judaism stipulates an inherent asocial drive in man which must be regulated and controlled by law, communism assumes a natural capacity for social relations in man which is distorted or possibly submerged by economic forces. It is economic forces, therefore, which, rather than man, are seen as dependent on 'laws'. Where Judaism stipulates a cultural identity as an indispensable link between natural man and social man, communism, to the extent that it follows Marx, sees a direct developmental route from natural to social man. Accordingly, where Judaism regards national-cultural groups as a presupposition of universalism, communism denies, or at most grudgingly acquiesces in, politically expedient, national groupings. Where Judaism conceives of a path to salvation prescribed for its own followers which would hopefully lead to universal salvation through Israel's example, communism prescribes a universal antagonism between classes as a *sine qua non* of salvation. Because the basis of Judaism is law, salvation is both individual and societal. It can be achieved by the individual at any time, by society at will. In communism there is no individual salvation, and societal salvation can be achieved only as a result of the resolution of social conflicts over which its participants have very little control.

By contrasting some of the underlying assumptions of communism and Judaism, I am not making any pretence at presenting the general philosophy or meaning of either, but have restricted my comments to isolating some of the assumptions which in their contradictoriness invalidate the claims of those who would see a link between them. There is no evaluation in this. By contrasting the two ideologies, I am not arguing for the superiority of one over the other, or indeed the inferiority of one in relation to the other. In this context my concern is with what I hope to be the objective observation that, whatever the merit or demerit of either system, they are incompatible. Even if it is argued that many individuals of Jewish origin have contributed to the formulation of communist concepts, and that there are similarities in the ultimate social goals and aspirations that the two systems share in their determination to improve the conditions in which men live, and in their unshakable belief in a coming millennium, these similarities are not enough to overcome the incompatibility between the two. Indeed, such similarities are in no way unique because, in one form or another, they can also be shown to exist in other ideologies and conceptual systems. Humanity, not Jewishness, is the common bond.

CHAPTER XVII

Marx and the Concept of Jewish Self-Hatred

In the extensive literature relating to the Jewishness of Marx one frequently meets references to Jewish *Selbsthass*, or what appears at first glance to be a version of Jewish anti-semitism. Thus Werner Blumenberg, in commenting on 'the contemptuous attitude towards Jews' in the Marx–Engels correspondence, thought that it was 'first and foremost a typical expression of "self-hatred" '.[1] The concept of an inwardly directed aggression, particularly in cases of depression, is of course well known, especially in psychoanalytic theory, where it has been described as the internalisation of originally external conflicts, a battle between ego and superego, and explained particularly as the result 'of severe disappointments in the parents, at a time when the child's self-esteem was regulated by "participation in the parents' omnipotence" '.[2] Accordingly, Kamenka assigned great importance to the effects of the first six (i.e. Jewish) years of Marx's life, which made him 'half-consciously dislike strongly the Jews from whom he sprang', while his use of 'Jew' as a term of abuse suggested that 'he does not so much hate the Jews for being bourgeois, as that he transfers to the bourgeois the hate he feels for the Jews.'[3] A closer look at the literature on Jewish self-hate generally and Marx's problem in particular would suggest, however, that the issue is neither as simple nor as one sided as it appears. There are in fact quite a number of manifestations and theories concerning the attitudes of those who have 'left' Judaism.

331

Historically, the problem is very old, and we have the examples of many early Christians who turned against the Judaism from which they came, notably the apostle John, whose Gospel is in many respects an anti-Jewish polemic. Throughout the years of Christian sovereignty in Europe, efforts to convert Jews and denigrate Judaism were frequently led by former Jews. The most notorious of these was probably Pfefferkorn, whose dispute with Reuchlin in the sixteenth century was a classic example of anti-Jewish activity by a former Jew. With the advent of eighteenth-century enlightenment, *religious* pressure on Jews to convert to Christianity eased, but from the beginning of the nineteenth century a new phenomenon arose, the conversion of many of them not for religious but for practical reasons;[4] in every principality of semi-feudal Germany, where access to social, political and academic advancement was closed, Jews could gain complete and immediate acceptance by becoming converted. A clear example was Eduard Gans (1798-1839), descendant of court Jews and son of a banker, who studied in Göttingen and Heidelberg, where Hegel was one of his teachers. He established himself in the academic world in 1819 by a scholarly thesis on Roman law of obligation and applied for a post in the University of Berlin, which was refused because he was a Jew. In spite of the personal intervention of Hardenberg, Karl Altenstein, the Prussian minister of education, a reformist and educational innovator, would not appoint him and he was supported in this by Friedrich Karl von Savigny, professor of law at Berlin, who expressed doubts about his scholarly abilities. In the same year, Gans founded the Verein für Kultur und Wissenschaft der Juden,[5] in which he tried to bring his Hegelian-dialectical view of Judaism to bear. Like many of his contemporaries, he was religiously and intellectually alienated from Judaism, but retained a strong emotional attachment. In 1822 the Prussian government enacted a law disqualifying professing Jews from academic teaching positions. Gans was converted to Christianity in 1825. The University of Berlin appointed him professor extraordinary in the same year, and professor ordinarius in 1828. He became one of the most popular teachers in the university and made his mark as the representative of the philosophical school of law and editor of Hegel. He, quite literally, ate himself to death and died at the height of his career. The official historian of the university, Max Lenz, described his death as 'a public disaster'.[6] Heinrich Heine was closely associated with Gans, a member of his Verein, and was also converted to Christianity in 1825. Some of Heine's letters to Moses Moser[7] give a clear impression of the effect of these conversions. When Gans went to Paris for his baptism, Heine wrote, 'Gans will return from Paris as a Christian in the wateriest sense of the word.' When, a little later, rumour had it that Gans was actually advocating Christianity, Heine commented, 'if he does it from conviction he is a fool, if hypocritically, then he is a knave'. He assured Moser that 'if the law permitted stealing silver spoons, I would not have been baptised'. Heine 'especially enjoyed' a sermon in a Hamburg synagogue by Dr Solomon, who 'attacked baptised Jews and made his special target those who in the mere expectation of obtaining a position allowed themselves to be seduced into forsaking the faith of their fathers'. Shortly after that, Heine observed bitterly: 'I am now hated by Christian and Jew alike. I deeply regret my conversion—and cannot even see that it has made me materially better off.' Highly significant in this context are comments in a letter written less than a year after his conversion. 'Forgive my annoyance—it is mainly directed against myself. I frequently get up at night, stand in front of the mirror and berate myself. Perhaps I now see the soul of the friend as such a mirror.' Returning again to reports that Gans was actively propagating Christianity, Heine wrote (alluding to Gans's Hebrew name of Eli), 'Dr Eli, Dr Eli—lama asavtani' ('why hast thou forsaken me?'—cf. Matthew 27:46 and Mark 15:34).[8]

We have noted how, in connection with the Damascus blood-libels of 1840, Heine had observed that 'amongst the baptised Jews there are many who, through cowardly hypocrisy, indulge in much more unpleasant polemics against Israel than its natural enemies. In the same way, certain writers express themselves particularly nastily about Jews, or ignore them altogether, so as not to draw attention to their own origins.'[9] An earlier similar comment was recorded in 1816 by G. Friedrich, a non-Jewish

observer: 'Among the Jews, there are many who take a particular
pride to boast of their contempt for their ceremonial laws and
who publicly indulge in just those things which their law forbids
them. Indeed, they even make the most contemptuous references
to their own people.'[10]

Not every Jew who wanted to advance in European society
was converted to Christianity, yet even some of those who were
not were sometimes given to making disparaging remarks about
Jews, such as Ferdinand Lassalle, and even among the baptised
there could be marked differences. Solomon Liptzin contrasted
the 'love–hate' attitude to Jews of Börne with the pure 'hate'
shown by Marx.[11] In the course of the nineteenth century there
were also new factors which had to be explained—religious
hostility to Jews gave way to partly economic and partly racial
opposition. Mystical concepts of a 'Jewish essence' were popularised, and Jewish nationalism emerged as a source of political
opposition. Each new factor, as it gained ground, produced not
only additional Gentile hostility but found support and adherents
amongst the Jews themselves. In 1930 Theodor Lessing (1872–
1933), physician and philosopher, himself a former convert to
Christianity who had returned to Judaism, attempted to analyse
this phenomenon in a book (Der jüdische Selbsthass) which
popularised the concept of Jewish self-hatred. He set out a number
of action-reaction patterns to explain the problem. There is,
first, a general problem in the history of man to which the Jews
particularly have given a definite answer, and this, in a sense, has
rebounded on them. It concerns the meaning of history and more
especially the meaning of suffering. There is a fundamental
principle in the Old Testament that the fate of the Jewish people
is always a consequence of their own behaviour. Suffering
therefore implies sin and guilt. Logically, the greater the suffering,
the greater the guilt. Here, for Lessing, is the root of self-hatred.
Other peoples have interpreted their misfortunes by pointing to
those who brought misfortune to them, whereas the Jews,
enmeshed in their conviction that they have brought misfortune
on themselves, can see their tormentors only as instruments of
God. The tormentor in turn can use the Jew's own view of his

guilt to explain why he ill-treats the Jew. Hence anti-semitism is not a product of ill will, national egoism or hate and jealousy in international competition. It is the Jewish conception of meaning in history. This is the action part of the pattern. The reaction is again a product emanating at least in part from the Jew. If Jews are continuously despised, hated, persecuted and discriminated against, then processes of justification, explanation and condonation will grow apace with every injustice. 'There is in history no injustice which in retrospect could not be justified or shown to have been necessary.' In the end even the victim will learn, absorb and even accept the logic of his own victimisation. 'To turn men into dogs, one need only call them "Dog" long enough.'[12] This, at any rate, was the pattern of the Christian era which acknowledged God in history and the meaning of guilt. After the enlightenment, everything changed. Jews were no longer deprived of their civil rights and no longer treated as an alien group; by the simple act of conversion they could and did join the aristocracies of Europe. They would all have 'disappeared' in due course if the simultaneous industrialisation had not created a new dimension which broke the process of absorption—class struggle. As Marx saw and described it, the Jews were no more than 'a rootless appendage of the capitalist class and its money economy', their emancipation no more than the formal choice by the Jews to join the bourgeoisie rather than the proletariat. This again was the action. The reaction came from the bourgeoisie, conscious of its struggle for ascendancy and the strength of the proletarian protest, which fastened with delight on the 'Jewish question' which allowed it to channel its own guilt over the exploitation of the working classes onto the hapless Jew who had so vigorously and hungrily fought for recognition and equality in capitalist society. Because Christianity had provided the tradition, there was no difficulty in persuading the world that that which was wrong in capitalist society was not the system itself or its abuses but the Jew who joined it, and his Jewish 'essence'. And once again there were those among the Jews, including Marx, who came to accept the indictment of the Jew as a virtue, though for others the new hatred reawakened the ancient and only genuine Jewish dream of a national revival.[13]

This is how Lessing saw the phenomenon of Jewish self-hatred. With each era in the history of man, in each dialectical process, the Jew is challenged by an I–Thou dichotomy. Without a national identity, he is for ever the personification of the subject–object conflict, the victim of his own surge towards progress caught in the toils of reaction. Lessing illustrated his thesis by an analysis of six men, all anti-semitic victims of their own anti-semitism which drove them to suicide. One of these, Otto Weininger, explained his problem shortly before he committed suicide at the age of twenty-three: 'Whoever hates Jewish being, hates it first within himself. That he persecutes it in others is only an attempt to separate himself from Jewishness in this way; he is totally in the other man . . . Hate, like love, is a projective phenomenon. A man hates only someone who reminds him too disturbingly of himself.'[14]

To H. L. Goldschmidt, the problem is rather less complex and profound. He did not think that any convert like Marx could ever escape from his status-consciousness—he would always know that his origins were Jewish, that this would always 'prove' his Jewishness and that self-hatred was thus inevitable, if only because the individual feels trapped by a past which will not release him and against which he therefore rebels.[15] Nor was the problem as complicated to Ben Nachum and Glickson, who represented the Zionist-nationalist point of view which, although it derived its main thesis from Lessing, saw the issue in very much simpler terms. The Jew in the Diaspora, precisely because he is never wholly Jew or wholly German, French, etc., is on the one hand being continuously driven towards assimilation, which from the Jewish standpoint means extinction, while there is also a more or less acute drive to maintain a Jewish identity. In the resultant conflict an element of self-hatred is inevitable. Accordingly, Ben Nachum attacked Silberner for his criticism of Marx's anti-semitism, for, as a Zionist, Silberner should know that Jewish assimilationism always includes symptoms of self-hatred.[16]

A possible explanation, free of any profound internal conflicts, has been put forward by Eduard Bernstein. It could certainly be used, though with questionable accuracy, to explain Marx's attitude. Bernstein warned 'comrades of Jewish descent who, just because they themselves are of Jewish origin, consider it their special obligation to protect the party against all suspicion of favouring Jewish interests.'[17] If not to Marx, this would certainly have applied to Victor Adler, who kept Jewish comrades out of the Deutsche Schulverein because he thought that he represented enough of Jewish membership.[18] None of these various 'theories' however could help us in understanding a fundamental distinction between three types of individuals of Jewish origin: those who do not appear to experience any psychic or social difficulties after they have left Judaism, as for example the theologian Neander; those who show some evidence of internal conflict on specifically Jewish issues but otherwise remain effective and self-fulfilling, like Marx; and those whose internal conflicts are of such overwhelming intensity that they are rendered totally ineffective and eventually destroyed by them. Such a classification suggests that psychic structures may be more significant determinants than social forces and we must therefore look at an attempt to explain Marx's self-hatred from a psychoanalytic perspective.

Arnold Künzli, in a whole chapter devoted to the problem of self-hate, presented a reasonable, if somewhat conjectural, case. He noted that whereas Marx showed a genuine ambivalence towards Germany, a 'love–hate' relationship, his utterances on Judaism suggested pure hatred. Thus, while he would have liked to have been reinstated as a German, he 'would probably have given anything not to have been born a Jew'. As we have already seen (and Künzli adds important additional sources), in spite of his early baptism and complete alienation from all things Jewish, Marx was seen, labelled and, often enough, defamed as a Jew. Yet it is a fact that Marx, the fighter, the polemicist, master of invective and controversy, never responded to this particular accusation. Even Dühring's vicious attacks were answered by Engels and not by Marx, though, as Silberner noted, Engels also did not react to the specific attacks on *Marx's* Jewishness.[19] For Künzli this could be explained only by an assumption that Marx here was hoist with his own petard—he could not reject anti-

337

semitism because he was himself possessed by 'a demonic Jewish self-hatred'. For Marx's self-hate, Künzli offered three reasons based very closely on the psychoanalytic explanation we have already described. First, Marx lived in a world in which the Jew was an object of hatred and contempt, an external conflict which he absorbed and assimilated. Second, because his father's conversion suggested a degree of 'weakness' which, from a psychoanalytic point of view, was extremely damaging for a young child, Marx was left with an 'unconscious' hatred of his father (superego). Third, Marx hated his mother, who represented everything he disliked in Judaism (and, incidentally, whose 'selfish needs' prevented Marx from collecting his 'fortune'). The resultant internal conflicts then are seen by Künzli as the source and motivation for Marx's Jewish self-hatred. Indeed he thought that the predominance of Jews in communist and psychoanalytic movements are generally to be explained by the Jewish urge to seek a 'cure' for the 'hell on earth' to which they feel they are condemned.[20]

Two types of objection have been raised against this approach. Massiczek took a particularly strong exception to the concept of Jewish self-hatred, which he saw as an offence both against Marx and against Judaism. Since Judaism and Marx in his conception are indivisible, 'devaluation, mystification and psychologisation of Marx's Judaism is at the same time an insult to Judaism and an extermination which, in the last resort, is the same as the extermination of Jews in Auschwitz'.[21] The other, more general, objection was put forward by Roman Rosdolsky, who objected to the 'quasi-psychoanalytic' explanations of Marx's 'Jewish inferiority complex' and 'renegade psychology' invoked by his 'nationalistic-Jewish' critics. Rosdolsky offered three reasons why this type of 'psychologising' was unacceptable. First, it reduced the study of the history of ideas to petty investigations into personal motives and inspirations. Second, it was meaningless because, whatever personal motives might be established for Marx's approach to Judaism, these would and could not explain why the non-Jew Engels and indeed other non-Jewish socialists such as Fourier, Proudhon and Bakunin shared the same views

Third, it was 'a servant's view of history', as Hegel called it. Every great man, every world-historical figure, is at the same time a human being possessed of all the quirks and foibles, weaknesses and idiosyncrasies that men are heir to. To ask the servant of such a man to describe him is 'to belittle the hero not because he is petty, but because the description comes from a servant'.[22] It seems to me, however, that these criticisms are not very appropriate. While Massiczek exaggerated and 'mystified' the nature of Judaism, Rosdolsky was guilty of a number of errors. He assigned 'motives' to Jewish critics although denying their right to search for motives in Marx. He ignored the fact that Engels evaluated his own anti-semitism and eventually and publicly repudiated it. His Hegelian argument is epistemologically unsound because it denies what is, in the last resort, a perfectly legitimate facet of reality. On the other hand, a substantive criticism of Künzli's approach could be made by emphasising that his 'interpretations' must, in the absence of more reliable confirmation, remain, at best, a 'backward projection'.

There can be no question that a psychopathological phenomenon of self-hate exists, and that it can have important implications for an interpretation of a particular personality in a particular setting, as well as for a proper understanding of the sociological significance of special historical problems. The difficulties that arise are concerned partly with the complexity of the phenomenon and partly with the nature of the evidence available. Let us look first at the complexity of the issue. I have shown that psychoanalytic theory has described the existence of a form of aggression which was originally directed at external objects but which, for one reason or another, was 'introjected', turned against the self. The sociological relevance of this is demonstrated by two sub-processes which are involved. First, that the 'reason' or motive for doing this may be an identification with the aggressor, an attempt to placate a hostile external world by adopting its attitudes towards the self, and second, by 'internalising' a set of values relating to an external object, i.e. through being socialised into the adoption of norms and values which are taught and seen to be of importance to significant

339

others. 'The child becomes this or that because he lives the universal as particular. This child lived, *in the particular*, the conflict between the religious ceremonies of a monarchist regime which was claiming a renascence and the irreligion of his father, a petit bourgeois intellectual and son of the French revolution.'[23] This sentence bridges not only the psychoanalytic with the sociological, but also with the more explicitly Marxist sociological analysis, although Sartre's subject was not Marx, but Flaubert. With a sociological relevance of a self-hate concept thus supported,[24] our next question must be to determine whether Jewish self-hatred would *ipso facto* mean the hatred of Jews by a Jew who hates himself, or whether there are two separate phenomena: the one a Jew who shows psychopathological symptoms of self-hate, and the other a Jew whose self-hatred assumes the form of a hatred of Jews. I have already delineated three possible types of individual who, though variously involved in expressions of hostility towards Jews, cannot simply be classified under a single heading of Jewish self-hatred. Neander, the theologian, vigorously defended the Jews against a blood-libel in 1840, but equally strongly objected to their admission to the University of Berlin seven years later. Heine could scathingly attack the Rothschilds and those who worshipped them, while glorifying the history of the Jews; Lassalle could caustically comment: 'I hate Jews and I hate journalists—unfortunately I am both.' These men displayed a level of detachment towards Jews and their own relationship to them which cannot be compared with Weininger's all-consuming hatred of Jews in general, and himself in particular, or with Marx's outright condemnation of Jews and Judaism and absolute refusal even to acknowledge (as Engels did) that, if there were many Jewish capitalists, there were also many Jewish socialists. In the cases of Neander, Heine and Lassalle, there may have been self-hatred but it was not necessarily Jewish; with Weininger there was explicitly defined Jewish self-hatred, and with Marx there may have been hatred of Jews, but there is no real evidence for self-hatred.

A concept of *Jewish* self-hatred can have meaning only if we can demonstrate, as I shall in the case of true anti-semitism, that

it must be directed at the survival of the Jew *as a Jew* or that
genuine Jewish self-hatred would logically lead to self-destruction.
It may of course be argued that Marx's prescription of an
emancipation of society from Judaism is precisely that advocacy
of Jewish self-destruction I have suggested, but Marx did not
demand the elimination of Jews, but merely predicted the disappearance of their religious consciousness[25] as a natural concomitant of the demise of capitalism, thinking that it would
'evaporate like some insipid vapour in the real, life-giving air of
society'. There remains the question of the intensity with which
Marx might have *felt* that this was desirable, as a pathological
symptom of his self-hatred. This illustrates the third main
problem involved here, the question of evidence. For an
absolutely reliable diagnosis of a condition like self-hatred one
would have to have either direct clinical evidence or at least a
frank and open 'confession' like Weininger's. Otherwise, all
other documentary evidence would have to be subjected to
interpretation which, no matter how skilled, must in the last
resort be more or less subjective. In the case of Marx, for example,
I have argued that there is evidence of a 'blockage' where Jews
and Judaism are concerned. As far as his intellectual life's work
was concerned it is difficult to understand why he remained
totally silent on Hess's challenge on Jewish nationalism, Hasselmann's[26] use of his second essay for anti-semitic purposes, the
rise of political anti-semitism generally and the emergence of a
strong Jewish proletariat. To appear not to notice such events
suggests a genuine blockage. At the emotional level, to an approach
like that of Künzli, who did interpret the call for the emancipation
of society from Judaism as Jewish self-hatred, we can respond only
by showing that if one takes account of Marx's fierce anger
against his mother at the time he wrote the second essay for
withholding his 'fortune', then one might with equal justice
interpret Marx's call as an attack on his mother, a 'wish' for her
death, so that his rightful heritage might be restored to him.
Either interpretation could be right, but must remain speculative.
Yet another factor has to be considered here which must reflect
with equal force on Künzli's as well as my own attempt at

interpretation. Marx was singularly reluctant to speak or write about himself in any context. He did not leave a systematic account of his own life, did not collect his own works and did not comment on 'the slings and arrows of outrageous fortune' as did his wife. In Marxist theory, this is an appropriate response of an individual to his own place in the dynamics of history, but not all Marxists were quite so taciturn, nor did those who were Jewish find it equally difficult to deal with that aspect either in history or in relation to their personalities.

We can now look briefly at the different 'theories' of Jewish self-hatred I have outlined. Heine's view of the Jewish 'renegade' would seem to be related more to a concept of guilt than one of self-hatred *per se*. There was the guilt of 'betraying' one's own people and the guilt of accepting the benefits of Christianity without feeling in any way committed to it. To the extent that Christianity or, more precisely, Christian circles were anti-Jewish, there must undoubtedly also have been for many converts an element of identifying with the aggressor; i.e. adopting, sharing and eventually expressing the same sentiments. In the case of Marx this may have been of less importance in terms of self-hatred, since, unlike men such as Heine, Börne and Neander, he did not actively leave Judaism, being baptised as a child. Bernstein's view that socialist leadership should not be seen to have an excessive Jewish representation is difficult to associate with Marx. From the time of the *DFJB* to his death, there is no evidence that Marx ever had the slightest interest in whether or not an associate was Jewish or of Jewish origin. He loved and hated those around him with indiscriminate fervour, and would probably have dismissed the kind of fear expressed by Bernstein and Adler. As a matter of policy, this would be more likely to have applied to non-Jewish socialists because, as Walter Laqueur pointed out in a paper referred to, although Jews did take a leading part in the formation of Russian and German socialist parties, they both ended up by having no Jews among them.

The Zionist view, which is an important aspect of Herzl's theory of anti-semitism, obviously has an element of truth, although it is weakened by the contemporary manifestation of a small number of Israelis showing exactly the same responses, in that they are expressing their criticisms of the political policies of their State in the terms of the State's external enemies; i.e. the elimination of the State as a *Jewish* State.[27] It cannot therefore be or have been the Diaspora (*Galuth*) that was the sole cause of any Jewish self-hatred to have appeared outside an autonomous national-Jewish context. Lessing's views are clearly the most profound and the most feasible, not least because they are the only ones to be developed at length and derived from systematically treated case studies. In a negative sense, his views on the Jewish philosophy of history may be an important factor. The greater the choice an individual has to escape from suffering the less likely he will be to accept it, to give it meaning, or to respect those who voluntarily assume and accept burdens which he has defined for himself as intolerable. Many young Israelis of our own day are again a good illustration of this, for to them the history of suffering which culminated in Auschwitz, and which is venerated by most Jews, is to them incomprehensible and alienating. If they despise those who stoically and silently accepted their martyrdom, then that would be an element of self-hatred to the extent that these Israelis feel themselves to be Jewish. The other important feature in Lessing is the idea of 'suggestion'. The greater the contact between the Jew and his environment, the greater must be the number of those who are likely to succumb to any constant, persistent and unvarying enumeration of Jewish faults, evils, weaknesses and wickedness. This is the theme of the anti-semite, our next subject, for even if Marx was not, or cannot be shown to have been, afflicted by Jewish self-hatred, there remains the charge, levelled by so many, that Marx was an anti-semite.

CHAPTER XVIII

The Anti-Semitism of Marx and the Use of Marx in Anti-Semitism

Anti-semitism, or hostility to Jews, is very old in historical terms, persistent, and frequently involves extremely virulent and violent modes of expression. Accordingly, several social sciences have attempted to explain it and there is a wide choice of theoretical analyses to explain the phenomenon. Some biological explanations point to the possibility of racial inferiority of Jews, or the atavistic nature of the anti-semite. Religious explanations refer to the Jews' insistence on regarding themselves as God's 'chosen people' or the 'proof' of their rejection by God as demonstrated by their suffering as a punishment. Political theorists argue that the fate of the Jews was made inevitable by their dispersion, or by the expedient of using a traditionally despised group to promote the interests of a particular ideology. Psychologically we have the 'scapegoat' theory, the concepts of a psychopathology in the anti-semite and his need to compensate or project his personal difficulties. Economically, we have the view of Jews and, *ipso facto*, anti-semitism as inevitable by-products of a capitalist system, and sociology has contributed the concepts of the Jew as 'different', alien, caught in a dual loyalty between his in-group and his out-group. Added to this must be Sartre's valuable concept of the 'imaginary Jew', the creation of a hostile model which will vary with the needs of its creator, and finally the traditionalist–rationalist argument that, if so many people have hated Jews for so long and for so many different reasons, there must be some substantive cause.

344

As far as Marx is concerned, there are those who regard him as an anti-semite, those who strongly reject such a suggestion, and yet others who treat the question itself as wholly irrelevant. It is possible to adopt such firm and contradictory attitudes if one starts with a given set of assumptions which make certain conclusions inevitable. If Silberner adds up every reference to Jews recorded by Marx, in a simple negative–positive addition, he cannot but conclude that he was anti-semitic. If Mehring, on the other hand, begins with what he regards as objectively perceived, destructive functions of Jewish commercial practices in early nineteenth-century Germany, then Marx's analysis must appear to him as both logical and correct. If our discussion is to add anything to this debate, then it can do so only if we reject the possibility of a simplistic notion of a yea or a nay. Instead we must look at the concept of anti-semitism itself and analyse our problem by reducing it to its proper constituent parts. Only in this way can we meaningfully discuss the problems of Marx and his essays in relation to anti-semitism.

Our first task, then, is to enquire into what we mean by anti-semitism when we examine the possibility that this was an attitude or a philosophy that Marx may have shared. Strictly speaking, the concept anti-semitism was not used in Germany until 1879 (i.e. four years before Marx died), when Wilhelm Marr introduced the word, and a political party predicated on the elimination of Jews from German economic and cultural life made its appearance in the Reichstag.[1] Organised German anti-semitism, which was a consequence of Jewish emancipation in 1869, was racialist, though not in a strictly scientific sense.[2] German anti-semites argued that what they objected to in the Jew were not any specific qualities or actions of particular individuals, but their 'semitic' characteristics or essence or spirit which was opposed, and always would be, to those of 'nordic' peoples.[3] Theodor Fritsch has spelt out some of the assumptions on which anti-semitism was based: 'Anti-semitism means . . . the struggle against semitism. Since the semitic race in Europe is represented almost exclusively by Jews, we are primarily concerned with Jews. In our case, therefore, anti-semite means "opponent of Jews".'[4] The 'racial' contrast is described as follows:

> The European nations belong almost entirely to the Aryan or Indo-germanic race, while the Jews are Semites. The Aryan peoples are settler peoples who practise agriculture, industry, arts and sciences; they found states, are brave and courageous; their basic characteristics are honesty, loyalty and devotion . . . Semites on the other hand are by nature nomads . . . Agriculture, technology and art are as alien to them as any honest, creative work . . . Craftiness, dishonesty and lies are the main characteristics of the Semite, as well as a boundless egoism, brutality and unbridled sexual desire. Our German concepts of loyalty, modesty, devotion and self-sacrifice for a cause are incomprehensible to the Jew and evoke his contempt.

Although set in a racialist context, the main arguments presented by the anti-semitic movement are not new.[5] Many of the points made by the racialists were mentioned by Luther,[6] by early French socialists[7] and by many church leaders. Basically, the main 'complaints' against Jews are uniform, but embellished and emphasised in varying degrees according to the standpoint of the writer. The first major source of conflict is religion. Complaints extend from what Jews do in their own religion, i.e. objectively accurate comments that dietary laws and opposition to inter-marriage imply exclusivity and in-group cohesion, to wildly fantastic claims that Jews use the blood of Christian children for ritual purposes and desecrate the host in secret ceremonies.[8] There are also many charges that Jews actively work against Christianity; accusations ranging from deicide to secret conspiracies to 'control' the world and eliminate all but their own religion.[9]

The second conflict issue concerns the social status of the Jew. That the Jew after a millennium's residence in Germany was still a visibly separate entity was used to identify him as a permanent alien, a stranger who could not be absorbed, and in anti-semitic polemic it was simple enough to invert cause and effect here to establish a fundamental causal incompatibility based on racial difference.[10] We have already seen how this issue tended to complicate the debate on Jewish emancipation. The third issue concerns the economic role of the Jew in society. Here again, their predominance in trade and moneylending, though historically conditioned, was gradually transformed from an enforced to a freely chosen to an actively preferred to a racially determined social role. To the religious anti-semite, the only acceptable solution to the 'Jewish question' was conversion. To those pre-occupied with the social status and economic role of Jews, expulsion seemed the ideal solution. This was at first, also the ambition of the racialists. It was not until the Second World War that physical annihilation was seriously contemplated, though many earlier writers had toyed with the idea.[11]

What emerges from this brief discussion is the need to differentiate between those who criticise aspects of Jewish life and activity on whatever grounds and those who convert real or imagined grievances against Jews into an absolute requirement for the elimination of Jews *per se* as the only redress for the grievance. In the former case we would be concerned with social group hostility, in the latter, with anti-semitism. Our first conclusion then is that *anti-semitism* is that view which *denies the Jews the right to an autonomous existence at any level*. Let us now turn to some of the literature that has emerged since the holocaust to explain the anti-semite. This literature, based on empirical, social scientific studies, differs from earlier discussions in that it is neither polemic nor apologetic, although the impact of the holocaust is implicit in the search for psychopathological mani-festations in those identified as anti-semites. An important difference between my approach and that of the studies to be discussed is the emphasis the latter place on anti-semitic individuals' need to criticise *any* Jew as a Jew; in other words, the move from a substantive content of a critique of Jews to the fact that they are criticised at all. It seems to me that, although this aspect is clearly important in psychological terms, it is so at a much more generic level than anything we have been discussing. It would, in fact, involve a need to move our discussion from the sociohistorical problem of German anti-semitism to a generalised psychosocial discussion of prejudice in which historical association is really quite incidental.

N. W. Ackerman and Marie Jahoda have defined anti-semitism as 'any expression of hostility, verbal or behavioral, mild or violent, against the Jews as a group or against an individual Jew because of his belonging to that group'.[12] Adorno and his colleagues have a somewhat less convincing definition in their elaborate analysis: 'stereotyped negative opinions describing the Jews as threatening, immoral and categorically different from non-Jews, and of hostile attitudes urging various forms of restriction, exclusion and suppression as a means of solving the "Jewish problem".'[13] One of the best studies of recent years offers the following definition: 'An attitude of hostility towards Jews as such, i.e. not towards a particular Jew, and not towards a number of people who, apart from having an attribute that arouses hostility, also happen to be Jewish. The hostility, to be called antisemitism, must be associated definitely with the quality of being a Jew.'[14] A similar definition was offered by C. Y. Glock and R. Stark: 'the hatred and persecution of Jews as a group; not the hatred of persons who happen to be Jews, but rather the hatred of persons *because* they are Jews.'[15] In psychological terms, these investigations see anti-semitism as functional, as fulfilling and satisfying highly specific needs of the individuals under investigation. As Robb put it: 'antisemitism is part of a complex form of reaction to experiences of deprivation extending from infancy into adult life. This reaction, though a result of psychological processes within the personality, is activated by social events and is canalised and modified by social forces.'[16] His emphasis on the non-uniqueness of anti-semitism is probably right in principle, although his explanation of it does not account for the all-pervasive obsession it was for so many Germans, coupled with their passion for studying it.

These psychological definitions are not very different from Silberner's 'hostility towards or agitation against Jews'. In their proper context they are undoubtedly valuable and relevant, but for our discussion they are wholly inadequate. There is nothing in any of these definitions which could discriminate between simple group or personal hostilities and ideological, abstractly derived, animosity. They all depend on personal pathologies or frustations to make the appearance of animosity manifest; that is to say, they assume an actual or stereotypal relationship between the hater and the hated. At this level, therefore, there would be no problem in showing that Marx was anti-semitic because he often used hostile and abusive language about Jews, that he was not anti-semitic because he mixed and associated freely with every type of Jew, and that the question is irrelevant not least because Marx is dead and any feelings and attitudes he may have had died with him, but also because the psychodynamic motivation for action in a person is, in the last resort, independent of any valuation of consequential thought or deed.[17] Another difficulty inherent in these definitions is that they do not allow us to differentiate between hostility centred on what the Jew *is* and that which is orientated towards what the Jew *does*. They assume that hostility is generalised to all Jews, but again fail to distinguish between those who hate or try to attack Jews and those who draw a fundamental conclusion from their views on Jews which rejects a Jewish existence. Finally, the psychological definitions are concerned with individuals or aggregates of individuals who manifest hostility in word or deed. Our primary interest must lie in conceptual systems, in ideologies in which the elimination of a Jewish existence is logically and functionally asserted. We are going to argue that, when Marx referred to Lassalle as 'a Jewish nigger', he was being offensive but not anti-semitic, and when he called for the emancipation of society from Judaism, he was being anti-semitic but not offensive.

What we are concerned with, then, are conceptual systems in which the exclusion of a Jewish existence is stipulated explicitly as an integral factor in the achievement of specified goals.

Two classic examples of such systems are Martin Luther and Adolf Hitler. The former argued from a religious, while the latter adopted a racial premise. Luther wanted the conversion or expulsion of Jews, Hitler argued for expulsion only. They developed complex ideologies in which Jewish being and Jewish action were separately shown to be unacceptable and evolved systems of exclusion as a preparation or an alternative to more drastic forms of elimination. If we look briefly at these conceptual systems we can then attempt to see how far Marx's analysis can be compared with them. Since there is little dispute about the anti-semitism (or better anti-Jewishness) of Luther and none about that of Hitler, a similarity of approach between Marx and the other two ought to establish an *a priori* assumption of anti-semitism in Marx.

In 1543 Martin Luther published his essay *Concerning the Jews and their Lies*, in which he asserted that Jews had characteristics and indulged in acts which made them unacceptable (as Jews) to any Christian community. As individuals Jews were stubborn, intractable, wiseacres, fanatics and full of wicked wiles. Religiously, they perverted the true meaning of scripture, blasphemed, preached false doctrine, converted Christians, worshipped idols and slandered Mary by calling her stinkpot, hag, monstrosity. The Jewish religion required Jews to break oaths, to rob, plunder and kill Gentiles, poison springs and mutilate Christian children for ritual purposes; Jewish physicians were commanded to kill Gentile patients. Socially, Jews injured people in body and property, they were usurers, drunkards and adulterers.[18] The charges, framed as they were in an appropriate medieval-demoniacal image of the Jew as devil, led Luther to propose a ten-point solution which he addressed to the princes and nobles who had Jews in their domains, in which he recommended the destruction of Jewish places of worship and homes, the collection of the Jews 'under one roof', a total ban on Jewish books of learning and worship, and the teaching or preaching of Judaism, deprivation of the right to travel, confiscation of all Jewish property and compulsory labour for all young Jews.[19]

It is not difficult to see how revolutionary and purposeful the Lutheran analysis is, once the vulgar mantle of medieval demonology is removed. Luther wanted a complete change of the social system that he felt oppressed him. He set up the Jew as the one common target for all and identified him as the source of discontent in the two areas most likely to stir the whole nation— their needs (socioeconomic) and their beliefs (religious). In precisely the same way, Hitler analysed the problem of his time and sought access to the people through their discontent and by offering them a focus for their grievances. More sophisticated and more adept than Luther, Hitler used him, as well as Marx, to prescribe and eventually to create a path to power and glory. Like Luther, he divided the problem into three parts: the characterisation of the Jew as the embodiment of the alien and unacceptable; charges that they were destroying the people's most precious possession—the Fatherland itself (beliefs); and that they were the cause of Germany's socioeconomic problems (needs). In a clever and witty address, he explained why his movement was anti-semitic.[20]

First there was the nature of the Jew, with a set of immutable qualities which made it irrelevant whether one talked about 'a good Jew or a bad Jew'. Jews hated work, had no inner peace, were restless and without art. They contaminated themselves by constant inbreeding. They were always Jews first and put Jewish interests first. They put money before family and loved only money. Just as Jews pretended to be Christian in order to destroy Rome, so now Jews were pretending to be socialists though they never became proletarians. They manipulated the world through international commercial (as opposed to good German-industrial) capital, controlled food and created hunger. They destroyed the nation's health by creating night life in the cities, destroyed the nation's art by distorting it, destroyed Christianity as a religion and destroyed the state—'the authority of reason'—by introducing democracy, 'the so-called authority of the majority'. Work for Jews consisted of exploitation and robbery, they penetrated (Judaised?) other races, undermined all authority and lived off peoples as parasites. They robbed people by using unknown trading-methods and enslaved aristocrat and commoner alike by stimulating their desire for consumption, lending money to enable them to satisfy that desire and then wielding the power of the creditor over them.

Unlike Luther, Hitler did not have to content himself with suggestions. As soon as he achieved power, he introduced a continuous programme of systematic exclusion of Jews from German social, economic and cultural life which, in the first instance at any rate, was intended to lead to expulsion.[21] As an immediate suggestion, he looked to the proletariat to save Germany, called on every German 'to remove the Jew within himself' and demanded that common needs be met before personal needs.

From this perspective, Marx's second essay on the Jewish question is cast in the same mould as those of Luther and Hitler. Like them, Marx knew little about Judaism and cared little for any empirical realities. Luther wanted to convert Jews; Marx wanted to abolish them; Hitler wanted to expel and subsequently to exterminate them. Marx is a logical and indispensable link between Luther and Hitler. He transmitted many of Luther's ideas on the Jewish religion in secular form and underwrote many of the ideas which were eventually to find their way into Hitler's conceptual system. We have already seen in detail how Marx characterised the Jews as 'a general, antisocial element' in society, that they actively promoted this negative element and that they were incapable of development because they were too limited. The Jewish religion degraded nature, art, history, man for his own sake. Jewish law was a baseless, religious caricature. Jews bartered their women, had acquired the power of money, only appeared to be oppressed while really controlling those who oppressed them. Judaism had acquired mastery over alienated man by making him a commodity. The Jews had Judaised Christian peoples. Practical need was 'the worldly basis of Judaism—the foundation of the Jewish religion—the human basis of the Jewish religion—the subjective basis of Judaism'. Peddling was the worldly cult of the Jews—the empirical essence of Judaism. The triadic pattern: essence—beliefs—socioeconomic role was too close to the other two systems to be ignored.

If we thus argue that the Marxian analysis of the Jewish question in his second essay is structured like the anti-semitic polemics of Luther and Hitler, we should be able to demonstrate its significance as an anti-semitic document. This can be done in two ways, first by looking at the semantic effect and second by looking at the essay as an instrument of anti-semitic propaganda. In 1930 Harold Laski wrote:[22]

> The English journalist who invented the word 'dole' has built into the minds of innumerable people of the comfortable classes a picture of the unemployed in England as a mass of work-shy persons,

comfortably lazy and anxious at all costs to live parasitically upon the tax-payer; the proven fact that less than a fraction of one percent really avoids the effort to work is unable to penetrate the miasma of that stereotype.

The images created in anti-semitic literature have the same effect, inasmuch as they do not allow those who follow a particular ideology to 'penetrate the miasma of [a Jewish] stereotype', because words and phrases have power—a power which often enough creates situations which need not have been intended by those who coined them; a power which can and does defy empirical realities to a point where the illusion is stronger than the experience of the senses. Alex Bein, in a profound essay, has dealt at length with this problem to show how the use of words and concepts can gradually create a form of 'knowledge' which, subliminally, becomes acceptable. In the case of Jews, a semantically created stereotype is dealt with in accordance with the analogy to which the stereotype is tied. Thus in the medieval period the Jew-devil is burnt at the stake, while in the modern situation, where the Jew is described as a parasite, he is gassed.[23] Bein quotes extensively from Klemperer, a particularly acute observer of developments in Germany, who noted that Hitler's most powerful weapons were[24]

> single words, turns of phrase and stock expressions which, imposed upon the people a million times over in continuous reiteration, were mechanically and unconsciously absorbed by them.—Words can act like tiny doses of arsenic; they are swallowed without being noticed, they appear to have no effect, but after a while the poison has done its work.—Words which formerly were used in a descriptive, logical or semantic sense are now used as magic words, destined to produce certain effects and to stir up certain emotions. Our ordinary words are charged with meanings; but these new-fangled words are charged with feelings and violent passions.

Marx did not invent the negative connotations associated with words such as 'Jews' and 'Judiasm'. He merely gave stereotypical folk-images an aura of social and philosophical respectability by giving the folklore of the Grimm brothers' *Deutsches Wörterbuch* which defined among Jewish characteristics 'slovenliness as well

353

as their greed for money and their usury ... dirt ... stink'[25] an intellectual significance which persuaded generations of his followers and admirers that, since he had defined Jews thus, they must indeed be so. In this way the prejudices, hates and pre-conceptions of centuries of Christian and German nationalist advocates became 'empirical knowledge' for Marxists. Even those who rejected 'the mystifications of anti-semitism' directed at 'the mere sociological phenomenon of Jewish partiality' nevertheless attacked and continue to attack 'the Jewish narrowness of society',[26] oblivious of the reality that so nebulous a distinction may acquire meaning in a Marxist conceptual system, but in the final analysis can lead only to the destruction of innocent Jewish lives. The same kind of semantic mysticism can be observed in the current assaults on Zionism. To give but one example: in an open letter, the Marxist candidates for president and vice-president of the United States of America in 1972 protested that because they were calling for the outright destruction of Israel they were accused of being anti-semitic. They replied: 'It is true we see the elimination [sic!] of the Zionist state of Israel as necessary. But opposition to a specifically "Jewish" state in Palestine cannot be equated with antisemitism.'[27] When Hitler made his speech on anti-semitism, he insisted that his aim was solely 'the removal of Jews from the midst of our people, not because we deny them the right to exist—we congratulate the rest of the world on their forthcoming arrival—but because we regard the existence of our own people as more important'.[28]

We have already made reference to writers such as Glickson, Silberner and Ettinger,[29] as well as Runes, Mayer and M. Graetz,[30] who have argued that Marx's polemic against the Jews has found its way into the arsenals of anti-semitism. These opinions can be illustrated by a few examples of usages. Even in Marx's life-time, as Eduard Bernstein has shown, Wilhelm Hasselmann, although strongly opposed to Marx,[31]

> couldn't resist the temptation to reprint the [second essay] in order to prove the correctness of his own opinions about Jews. Had Marx seen this article, he would have undoubtedly opposed it because his article had been written for an educated public which could be

354

trusted to see the sociological implications . . . but Hasselmann's paper was mainly circulated among poorly educated workers . . .

Massing produced an excerpt from Otto Glogau's *Der Bankerott des Nationalliberalismus und die 'Reaktion'* (1878), in which Glogau expressed himself in 'unmistakable Marxist terminology':[32]

> Jewry is applied Manchesterism in the extreme. It knows nothing any more but trade, and of that merely haggling and usury. It does not work but makes others work for it, it haggles and speculates with the manual and mental products of others. Its centre is the stock exchange . . . As an alien tribe it fastens itself on the German people and sucks their marrow. The social question is essentially the Jewish question; everything else is swindle.

In his introduction to a biographical novel on Marx, Jacob Zineman related the following:[33] 'As a convinced Marxist and enthusiastic socialist during the period of my youth, I wanted to forget the harsh, insulting expressions on Jews and Judaism which Marx had penned in his well-known article of 1844 "on the Jewish Question". I searched for all kinds of explanations and reasons to justify and excuse Marx's wholly negative attitude to Judaism', but in the summer of 1923, shortly before he left Vienna, he changed his mind when he and 'thousands of other pedestrians saw on the city walls of Vienna, bright red posters with crude anti-Jewish Nazi slogans and with authentic (unfortunately!) quotations from "what the Jew Mordechai Karl Marx had written about the God and religion of his former co-religionists". Marx's words in the context of the evil, blood-curdling swastika made a deep impression on me.' To the Nazis, of course, Marx was first and foremost a Jew, and Marxism was the embodiment of all the evils of Judaism in the Third Reich. When Karl Vorländer published his biography of Marx,[34] he tried to counter the Nazi view by emphasising Marx's own anti-Jewish statements.[35]

Hitler himself, in an unmistakable passage, referred to Marx's 'solution' to the Jewish question: 'it is quite enough that the scientific knowledge of the danger of Judaism is gradually deepened and that every individual, on the basis of this knowledge, begins to eliminate the Jew within himself and I am very much afraid that this beautiful thought originates from none other than a Jew.'[36] Nor did the use of Marx's polemic for anti-semitic purposes end with the Hitler era. One of contemporary Russia's leading Jew-baiters, whose work is modelled very closely on the style of Julius Streicher, published in 1968 a violent polemic, *Judaism and Zionism*, which also made use of Marx's essay:[37]

> The morality of Judaism [is] permeated with narrow practicality, thirst for gain and the spirit of egoism. K. Marx wrote: 'What is the foundation of the Jewish religion? Practical need, egoism . . . The god of practical need and of self interest is money. Money is the jealous god of Israel beside which no other god may exist. Money abases all the gods of mankind and changes them into commodities . . . Money is the alienated essence of man's work and existence: this essence dominates him and he worships it' . . . This is totally in accordance with the principles of Judaistic morality. Teaching others to be satisfied with little, those who serve Judaism themselves are far from renouncing all sorts of the boons of life—from luxurious villas and cars to tasty and plentiful food.

Another well-known anti-Jewish Soviet ideologist, K. Ivanov, criticised the *Great Soviet Encyclopedia* (1932) because 'there is either a passing over in silence or a tendentious treatment of the well-known work by K. Marx "On the Jewish Question".'[38] This is quite inaccurate, since the *Encyclopedia* dealt with the Jewish question at length and strictly in accordance with Marx's basic tenets.

Not surprisingly, Marx's essays on Judaism have also found their way into the anti-Zionist literature of Arabs. Thus, Naji Alush quoted Marx's analysis in support of his denunciation of Jews as the embodiment of capitalism.[39]

What conclusions can be drawn from this analysis? Was Marx an anti-semite or not? The evidence I have presented would seem to suggest, first, that it is possible to discern that Marx went through four phases in his relationship to Jews and Judaism. In the first, as a young radical, he wrote the essays 'On the Jewish Question', in which he shows himself to be aggressively hostile. The second period, in which the conception of historical materialism matured, is more balanced. The money-worshipping Jew is displaced by the Jew as an essential element in the emergence and promotion of early capitalism, as he is depicted in the *Holy Family*. The third, in which he is wholly dedicated and devoted to the analysis of and commitment to class struggle, is the period in which the Jewish bankers and financiers became the prime targets of his hostility.[40] In the final period, to the ageing, scholarly, somewhat withdrawn Marx, Jews have ceased to be of interest or consequence; the author of *Capital* has virtually nothing to say on them and the events and developments concerning them at that time evoked no response from him.

Second, I have noted that it is really neither possible nor indeed relevant to try to determine if Marx, as an individual, was anti-semitic. On the whole the evidence is against such an assumption. While it is certainly true that he found the Jewish religion 'repugnant', that he was frequently and offensively abusive about Jews as Jews, that in relation to persons who had incurred his wrath, he used coarse vulgarisms in which Jewishness and supposedly Jewish attributes were employed as insulting or derogatory attributes, the Jews were not the only ones subjected to the indignities of his vulgarity, as we know that Danes, Slavs and many others fared no better. Apart from that, there seems to be little purpose in examining the question of Marx's anti-semitism except for the professional psychologist or psychoanalyst to whom personality structure is of particular significance. For the sociologist, it can be meaningful only in the context of existing social relations, as manifestations of the dynamics of groups. The dead, according to the Psalmist, do not praise God, neither, one might add, do they preach anti-semitism. In that sense the question has ceased to be relevant, if indeed it ever was.

The problem is altogether different with Marx's essay on 'Die Fähigkeit'. This, as I have tried to demonstrate, must be regarded as an anti-semitic document. It is offensive in its language, untrue, and not only unsupported by any empirical reality but, if anything, is contrary to it. Yet it has been and indeed continues to be damaging and disparaging about a group of people who, through no fault of their own, have become the victims rather than the subject of a supposed radical mythology. I have suggested that Marx himself became sufficiently aware of this to try and reduce

357

the impact of his own radicalism. I have also quoted some evidence that his life-long friend Engels and his daughter Eleanor tried to balance the ferocious image which has nevertheless become and has remained a disproportionately important aspect of the Marxian heritage.

For all that, our comments and the purpose of our study have not been to disparage a great man, to tarnish the image of a true genius or to discredit the achievements of one of the greatest minds in the history of man. Léon Poliakov, commenting on the anti-semitism of Luther, wrote: 'Luther's character is too rich and complex, and the imprint he left on the history of his country and of our whole civilization is too profound, for us to be content with an over-simplified, unidimensional interpretation, limited to the level of individual psychology.'[41] It is in this sense and from this perspective that I have looked at the meaning and value of the Marxian contribution to the Jewish question. We have seen that, for all his emphatic assertions and confident prognosis, Marx has been proved to be wrong—factually, objectively and historically. With very few exceptions, most of those who studied his contribution on Jews rejected, corrected, reinterpreted or distorted and misused it. It has also become clear that the determinants which will induce a student of Marx to evaluate his contribution in a specific direction are more likely to lie in the socio-political and historical situations, or the personal circumstances of the student, than in the force and accuracy of the Marxian argument. Whatever the ultimate significance of Marx's contribution to human thought may be, he contributed little of importance and relevance on the Jewish question; the harm he has done and may yet do through his second essay might perhaps have been avoided had he consulted his immediate relatives on the Talmud he despised so much, but which was ahead of him in the counsel of Avtalyon, when he taught: 'Scholars, be careful with your words', for, as it is said in Proverbs (18:21): 'Death and life are in the power of the tongue.'[42]

CHAPTER XIX

Excursus: Marx and the Jews of Jerusalem

Edmund Silberner noted: 'In the whole work of Marx there is, to our knowledge, only one passage in which he speaks of a group of Jews without any derision and even with a certain friendliness.'[1] This is the passage in an article published, without a heading, in the *New York Daily Tribune* of 15 April 1854,[2] in which Marx described the plight of the Jews of Jerusalem, their poverty and misery and the hostility to which they were subjected by Moslems and Christians although, numerically, they represented even then a majority of the city's population. Silberner thought that 'this is the only text where Marx shows any sympathy for a group of Jews'[3] and accordingly described it as 'an exception to the rule', which was without 'deeper meaning'.[4] He was not alone in drawing attention to this uncharacteristic passage. S. F. Bloom, after discussing Marx's hostile comments on Jews, referred to the article 'for a more sympathetic treatment of a Jewish problem'.[5] Isaiah Berlin noted that, although Marx's attitude to Jews was 'uncompromisingly hostile', he comments 'casually and not unsympathetically on the condition of the poor Jews in Jerusalem'.[6] Arnold Künzli based the most extensive and elaborate interpretation on this passage. It seemed to him that the Jews of Jerusalem, because they were so unlike the Jews of Germany, and the place of publication for the article, because it was so far from Marx's circles of acquaintances, allowed him to give expression to his more positive feelings without running the risk of being identified with and as a Jew, in this context. Marx, said Künzli, here reveals a positive relationship to Judaism. 'Thus, even in the soul of this bitter anti-semite, this Jewish self-hater Marx, there lay buried beneath much spiritual disorder, a love for Judaism. But it remained buried throughout his life and was permitted only once to break through into the light of his consciousness.'[7] Ben Nachum, clearly influenced by the weight which Künzli attached to the passage, also based an elaborate interpretation on it. He thought it showed that Marx, like Heine and Moses Hess, was subject to an unconscious Jewish identification, that he was opposed to the persecution and forced conversion of Jews and that he shared a Jewish messianic longing for 'redemption'.[8]

A closer examination of the background of the article, and in particular of the passage on the Jews of Jerusalem, makes clear, however, not only the dubiety of such far-reaching interpretations, but also the dangers inherent in attempts to deduce a person's feelings, attitudes and expressions from such limited and un-corroborated evidence.

The articles which Marx wrote for the *New York Daily Tribune* in the early 1850s were, at the time of writing, more important to him as a source of income than as substantive material for his major intellectual concerns. He was only just emerging from the most difficult period of his life in exile,[9] and had to write a large number of articles on a wide variety of subjects. Engels is reported to have assisted, either by translating Marx's drafts into English or by writing the articles which were then published under Marx's name.[10] It is not very likely that this would apply to the article under discussion, since Marx's notes for it are available and were written *in English*.

The only source for Marx's comments on the Jews of Jerusalem was a book by César Famin: *Histoire de la rivalité et du protectorat des églises chrétiennes en orient*,[11] which he studied with great care and from which he extracted copious notes.[12] A careful study of Famin's text, Marx's notes and the published article reveals that the entire material on the Jews of Jerusalem was in fact taken from Famin, even though Marx set in quotation marks only two sentences, which he attributed to 'a French author'.[13] The actual quotation is not, however, an exact rendering of Famin's text.

It may be going too far even to suggest, as Silberner, Bloom and Berlin have done, that Marx's description implies a 'feeling of sympathy', because the description is Famin's, not Marx's. By using it, Marx conveyed an air of immediacy and familiarity to the tone of the article which, journalistically at any rate, justified the extraction of these comments. If one wishes to speculate on Marx's feelings in producing this passage, one would have to look at precise details and differences between the Famin and Marx texts for any indications of personal involvement. On balance, such an examination would be more likely to lead to a conclusion that Marx remained indifferent rather than sympathetic to the plight of the Jews of Jerusalem.

A number of factors would support an assumption that Marx, generally a meticulous and methodical scholar, was not sufficiently interested in the subject matter under discussion to concern himself with precise detail.

1 A comparison of Famin's original observations, Marx's notes on these and the text of the passage in the article in the *New York Daily Tribune* makes it apparent that some of the warmth and sympathy of Famin's description is lost in Marx's reproduction.

2 Marx wrote that Jews were attracted to Jerusalem 'by the desire of *inhabiting* the Valley of Jehoshaphat and to die on the very place where redemption is to be expected'. Yet Famin, who appeared to be more familiar with Jewish tradition in Jerusalem, wrote that Jews were attracted to Jerusalem 'by the desire to *select their place* in the valley of Jehoshaphat, to die on the very spot where the resurrection of the dead will enable them to re-emerge'.[14] The distinction between these two expressions may appear to be unimportant, but only if the subject under discussion appears unimportant.

3 In one of the sentences which Marx actually ascribed to Famin, he quoted the expression 'temple of Lebanon'. This is also quoted by Silberner, though neither he nor Avineri queried this unusual phrase.[15] Famin, however, used the correct term 'temple of Solomon' ('le temple de Salomon').[16] An examination

of Marx's notebook showed that the word 'Solomon' is quite illegible, and we may assume that Marx himself, in copying from his notes, wrote 'Lebanon' for 'Solomon' because the writing was not clear. We also know that Marx was well versed in the Bible and that he ought to have spotted this error.

4   Finally we may note that here, too, Marx could not resist the temptation to associate Jews with dirt. Famin certainly described the Jewish quarter of Jerusalem as 'the dirtiest district in the city',[17] and Marx transcribed this as 'the most filthy quarter of the town'; but where Famin referred correctly to 'the Jewish quarter', Marx preferred to speak of 'the quarter of dirt'.[18]

Famin's text[19]

p. 50: 'The Moslems who constitute approximately a quarter of the inhabitants of Jerusalem are the veritable masters in all spheres. This group composed of Turks, Arabs and Moors . . .'

p. 51: 'But of all the foreign peoples who are admitted to the holy places at the pleasure of the Moslems none is more harshly treated, nor so harassed as the Jewish people . . . the Jews in themselves constitute over half the population of the holy city.'

p. 52: 'In Jerusalem they live in a quarter which has been named after them (Hareth el Yahoud, the Jewish Quarter) lying between Mount Zion and the Temple Mount (Moriah) and they have their synagogues there. This district, the dirtiest in the city . . .'

pp. 54-5: 'There is nothing to equal the suffering of the Jews of Jerusalem, perpetually the object of the trickery and intolerance of the Moslems, insulted by the Greeks, in a state of hostility with the Latins and subsisting on the meagre alms sent with great difficulty by their European brethren. Furthermore all these Jews hail from distant lands and are attracted to Jerusalem only by the desire to select their place in the valley of Jehoshaphat, to die on the very spot where the resurrection of the dead will enable them to re-emerge. Awaiting death they suffer and they pray, they weep over the unhappy fate of Zion, over their dispersion in the world, with their eyes turned towards that same Mount Moriah on which the temple of Solomon once stood and to which they do not dare draw close; a profound pain which brings tears even to the eyes of the Christians themselves.'

Marx's notes[20]

but of all the foreign people who visit the holy places none is more — and harassed than the Jews.

The Jews form about half the population of the holy city, they ' inhabit the most filthy quarter called Harath el Yahoud between the — and the — where their synagogues are situated. Nothing is equal to the misery and the sufferings of the Jews of Jerusalem, the object of Mussulman oppression, insulted by the Greeks, in hostility with the Latins, and getting a — only from the — transmitted by their European brothers. The Jews however belong to different countries and are only attracted to Jerusalem by the desire to choose these places — the Valley of Jehoshaphat to — on the place where — the — find them — while attending[21] their death, they suffer and pray, they shed tears about the misfortune of — their dispersion throughout the world, their eyes turned to that Mountain of Moriah where once rose the Temple of — and which they dare not approach.

Excerpt from Marx's article in the New York Daily Tribune[22]

The Mussulmans forming about a fourth of the whole and consisting of Turks, Arabs and Moors are of course the masters in every respect, as they are in no way affected by the weakness of their Government at Constantinople. Nothing equals the misery and the sufferings of the Jews of Jerusalem, inhabiting the most filthy quarter of the town, called Hareth-el-yahoud, in the quarter of dirt between the Zion and the Moriah where their synagogues are situated—the constant objects of Mussulman oppression and intolerance, insulted by the Greeks, persecuted by the Latins, and living only upon the scanty alms transmitted by their European brethren. The Jews however are not natives, but from different and distant countries, and are only attracted to Jerusalem by the desire of inhabiting the Valley of Jehoshaphat; and to die on the very place where the redemption is to be expected. 'Attending their death,' says a French author,[23] 'they suffer and pray. Their regards turned to that Mountain of Moriah where once rose the temple of Lebanon, and which they dare not approach, they shed tears on the misfortune of Zion, and their dispersion over the world.'

Epilogue

A brief survey of additions to the literature on Karl Marx and the critique of religion generally, and of Judaism in particular, which have appeared since this study was completed reveals an unabated interest, but very little that is startingly new. Perhaps the most interesting material comes from publications which are only marginally relevant in that they deal with people and periods which coincide with the life and work of Marx and thereby offer some unexpected insights on our main theme.

On the subject of Marxism and religion, the most substantial study to have been published is Delos B. McKown's *The Classical Marxist Critiques of Religion: Marx, Engels, Lenin, Kautsky* (The Hague, 1975). This is a comprehensive, but in some ways rather curious, study. Marx, as we have seen, regarded it as axiomatic that religion had no content—he described it as 'inhaltlos' (*MEW*, 27, p. 412)—yet McKown presents us with an elaborate scheme of a Marxian analysis of the 'substance' (by which he means content) and function of religion (see esp. p. 47 ff.). He suggests that the best way to demonstrate the unity of the Marxian critique of religion is to start with works written after 1847 (p. 10), but also holds that Marx did not 'return to the topic of religion' after 1846 (p. 64). Again, while there is a reasonable summary of Marx's essays 'On the Jewish Question' (pp. 37–42), we are informed, somewhat dogmatically, that 'Marx identified the Jews with usury' (p. 12). However, McKown presents a clear and well argued case for separating the views of Marx and Engels on religion, the need for which was put forward above (see chapter VIII). There may, in fact, be an increasing desire for establishing an independent 'Engelsism,' a thesis argued persuasively by Norman Levine in *The Tragic Deception: Marx Contra Engels* (Oxford and Santa Barbara, 1975). In a thoughtful chapter, 'The Dutiful Disciple and the Exploitative Master', the relationship between Marx and Engels is perceptively analysed. In his comments on Marx's essays 'On the Jewish Question', however, Levine assigns too much weight to a capitalism which had not then emerged as a primary concern in Marx's thought.

Publications dealing specifically with Marx and the Jews continue to appear. The most comprehensive of these is the book by Robert S. Wistrich, *Revolutionary Jews from Marx to Trotsky* (London, 1976). A carefully researched study based on a wide literature, it is somewhat meagre in interpretation and analysis. Thus, Marx's essays on the Jews are described as 'an intensely emotional polemic' (p. 30) by a 'baptised, self-hating Jew' (p. 34). Other figures discussed in my study who are also dealt with by Wistrich include Otto Bauer and Julius Martov. A welcome reprint is the sadly neglected *Das Judentum und die Geistigen Strömungen des 19 Jahrhunderts* by Albert Lewkowitz (Hildesheim and New York, 1974), which was published originally in 1935. Lewkowitz offers a dispassionate account of the historical-materialist conception of religion, including Judaism (pp. 503–18), but rejects the Marxian critique along Weberian lines by arguing that, while Marx was right in assuming a relationship between economic conditions and religious behaviour, he was wrong in asserting this as a one-sided dependency. Owen Chadwick in his Gifford Lectures, *The Secularisation of the European Mind in the Nineteenth Century* (Cambridge, 1975), devoted a chapter to Karl Marx in which he described the 'poetic, almost wistful way' in which Marx portrayed the consoling function of religion, and concludes: 'This is, after all, a Jew speaking' (p. 49). More recently S. Levenberg has published (yet another) article on 'Karl Marx's view on the Jewish question' (*Jewish Quarterly*, 25 (1), 1977) which recounts all the basic facts, but is rather dated in its approach.

More stimulating is a brief, speculative piece in a student magazine
Manna 1977 (Cambridge University Jewish Society) in which
Daniel Hochhauser contrasts Marxism and Judaism under a title
drawn from Arnold Toynbee, 'Marxism: "the fourth Judaic
Religion"?'

Yvonne Kapp has now published the second volume of her
formidable biography, *Eleanor Marx: the Crowded Years* (London,
1976), and, as I anticipated (cf. chapter XII above), has dealt at
length with Eleanor Marx's attitude to Jews (pp. 510–26). She has
also made use of the article by Morris Vinchevsky from which I
have quoted extensively. The difficulties which she poses in
relation to that article (p. 524) appear to be based on a partial
reading of it. Other personalities appearing in my study have also
been subjects of further study. Like Marx, but regrettably unlike
Max Weber, Sombart continues to attract the attention of Jewish
scholars. A recent analysis of Sombart's 'Jew-book' is Paul R.
Mendes-Flohr's 'Werner Sombart's *The Jews and Modern Capitalism:* an analysis of its ideological premises', *LBIYB*, 22, 1976.
Tel-Aviv university's *Jahrbuch des Instituts für Deutsche Geschichte*
(5, 1976) has a rare article on the much neglected Hermann
Jellinek by Wolfgang Häusler and a major article on Moses Hess
by Shlomo Na'aman. Hess is also the subject of a highly controversial article by Shlomo Avineri, 'Socialism and nationalism in
Moses Hess' (*Midstream*, April 1976). The appearance of Ludwig
Marcuse's *Heinrich Heine* as a Diogenes paperback (1977) should
ensure a wide circulation for this provocative study in which an
analysis of the relationship between Heine and Marx is especially
important. The indefatigable Edmund Silberner has recently
completed a massive biography, *Johann Jacoby: Politiker und
Mensch* (Bonn and Bad Godesberg, 1976), which, among many
other new revelations, explains for the first time how Jacoby's
article came to be published by Marx in the *DFJB* and explores
some of the problems of the reign of Friedrich Wilhelm IV and
the situation in Prussia, which played such an important part in
the life of Marx (see chapters IV and VIII above).

Another recent book, though only very marginally related to
our main topic, graphically illustrates the complexity of any

attempt to do justice to the question of the relationships of Marx the social analyst and Marx the man to Jews and Judaism. The great Jewish historian Heinrich Graetz was quite adamant when he wrote to Mosse Hess in 1865 that Marx must be counted among the famous men who were 'enemies of the Jews' (*Tagebuch und Briefe*, ed. Reuven Michael, Tübingen, 1977, p. 253). At that time he knew him only by reputation and from his published work. The two men met in 1876 in Carlsbad (Eleanor and Graetz's son were also there) and took a great liking to each other. Marx followed up the acquaintance by sending Graetz the first volume of *Kapital* (as an 'expression of admiration and friendship'!), a copy of *The Civil War in France* and P. S. Lissagary's *L'Historie de la Commune de 1871* (Lissagary was engaged to Eleanor at that time). Graetz replied with a long letter which began: 'Even if you had committed the ultimate crime of hanging the last monarch by the entrails of the last priest, I would have forgiven you . . .' (pp. 336-7). Thus did the 'masterful but vulgar' Marx befriend the 'narrowly Jewish' historian Graetz.

It will be apparent that this must perforce be a somewhat cursory review of recent additions to the literature, and it has not been possible to discuss even the more important books in any detail. In the result this need not be regarded as a serious handicap because it has not been necessary, in the light of conclusions which subsequent research has so far produced, to revise the views and arguments put forward in this study. This is not to say, however, that the subject has been exhausted. On the contrary, there are exciting indications that the real debate about the nature of religion and its function in society is only just beginning. Perhaps we should have concentrated on the method Marx employed rather than on his subject. As we have seen, when the real target of Marx's critique was the state, he began with religion. This did not yield much information on the nature of religion, but led to a very fundamental critique of the state. In the same way, some recent sociological research on religion has bypassed religion *per se* and has focused on its supposed antithesis—secularisation. The indications are that through the critique of secularisation from the caustic assaults of a David Martin (*The Religious and the Secular*,

London, 1969) to the clinical precision of a Peter E. Glasner (*The Sociology of Secularisation: a Critique of a Concept*, London, Henley and Boston, 1977), a better understanding of one of the most profound and pervasive manifestations of 'social man' will emerge.

Finally, it would be appropriate to reiterate the point already made, when I criticised Marx for his casual and careless semantic games with artificially contrived abstractions, because, to paraphrase Marx, the critique of human behaviour is not only a question of artful manipulation of abstract categories, but also a question of the lives and fates of human beings. In our own day this problem has been greatly exacerbated, because the rapid spread of modern means of communication can circulate deliberately or casually contrived semantic atrocities across the length and breadth of the globe in a matter of hours. More serious is the sad reality that their authors, lacking the integrity and intellectual stature of a Karl Marx, are seemingly bent on displaying their hollow mediocrity by constantly refining an infinite capacity to trivialise vital and complex issues. Their inspiration is no less an authority than Humpty Dumpty, who insisted that 'when I use a word, it means just what I choose it to mean, neither more nor less' (*Through the Looking Glass*).

Judaism, or one or other facet of it, continues to be 'equated' with this or that abhorrent image, each author of each equation reserving the right to define the unknown in that equation to mean what he chooses it to mean. Nothing has changed since the days of Heine, who warned that the real victim of a process in which words are deprived of meaning and are charged instead with violent passions is mankind itself. There is, after all, no need for men to share the values by which they live, provided only that they share the meanings of the words they use, to enable them to communicate with each other about their differences.

Notes

Introduction

1 L. D. Easton and K. H. Guddat, *Writings of the Young Marx on Philosophy and Society*, New York, 1967, p. 216
2 R. C. Tucker, *Philosophy and Myth in Karl Marx*, p. 111
3 D. McLellan (ed.), *Karl Marx: the Early Texts*, Oxford, 1971, p. xxv
4 W. Post, *Kritik der Religion bei Karl Marx*, p. 147
5 R. A. Nisbet, *The Sociological Tradition*, London, 1970, p. 134
6 Franz Mehring (ed.), *Aus dem literarischen Nachlass von Karl Marx und Friedrich Engels: 1841 bis 1850*, vol. 1, p. 356
7 *Karl Marx: His Life and Environment*, p. 99
8 I. Deutscher, *The Non-Jewish Jew*, London, 1968, p. 49
9 D. Scholz argued that the title of Marx's articles was inappropriate, because 'he was not really concerned with expressing his views on the, then, acute problem of Jewish emancipation'; see 'Politische und menschliche Emanzipation: Karl Marx' Schrift "Zur Judenfrage" aus dem Jahre 1844', *Geschichte in Wissenschaft und Unterricht*, 18 (1), 1967, pp. 1–16, p. 1. Similar views were expressed by E. Andrew ('Marx and the Jews', *European Judaism*, 3 (1), 1968, pp. 9–14) and G. Mayer, 'Early German socialism and Jewish emancipation', *Jew. Soc. Stud.*, 1, 1939, pp. 409–22
10 See E. Wilson, *To the Finland Station*, p. 121, where Marx is described as 'the great secular rabbi of his century'
11 e.g. H. Liebeschütz's 'German radicalism and the formation of Jewish political attitudes', in A. Altmann (ed.), *Studies in Nineteenth Century Jewish Intellectual History*, esp. pp. 156–9
12 e.g. Nathan Weinstock, in his Introduction to A. Léon's *The Jewish Question*, rejected Marx's articles as a 'definitive analysis', although he accepts that Marx saw the problem 'in its correct perspective', pp. 30–1
13 L. Schwarzschild, *The Red Prussian: Life and Legend of Karl Marx*
14 *Ideology and Utopia*, London, 1936, p. 250
15 ibid., pp. 251–2
16 ibid., p. 247

370

17 Jean-Paul Sartre, *Search for a Method*, New York, 1968, p. 37
18 ibid., p. 39
19 ibid., pp. 43–4, 45
20 ibid., pp. 49 (Sartre's emphasis), 53
21 I have deliberately used the word 'believe' here because I recognise that men like Isaac Deutscher argued the opposite, namely that 'those who are shut in with one society, one nation or one religion, tend to imagine that their way of life and their way of thought have absolute and unchangeable validity' (*The Non-Jewish Jew*, p. 35). While I totally disagree with Deutscher, I am content to accept that he has every right to hold that view, while I subscribe to Micah 4:5
22 Max Weber, ' "Objectivity" in social science' in May Brodbeck (ed.), *Readings in the Philosophy of the Social Sciences*, London, 1968, p. 92
23 *MEW*, 1, p. 97

Chapter I   The Struggle for Jewish Emancipation

1 T. B. Bottomore, *Karl Marx: Early Writings*, London, 1963, p. 3. Bottomore's translation of the word 'begehren' as 'seek' is as accurate as Easton and Guddat's 'want' (*Writings of the Young Marx on Philosophy and Society*, New York, 1967, p. 216), though the German word has wider meanings than either of these. It is best described as conveying that German Jews 'desire, demand and covet' emancipation
2 There is a vast literature on Jewish emancipation. The great historians of Judaism: H. Graetz, *History of the Jews*, vol. 5, *1648–1870* (1895), Philadelphia, 1967; S. Dubnow, *History of the Jews*, vols 4 and 5, London, 1971, 1973; S. Baron, 'The Modern Age', in *Great Ages and Ideas of the Jewish People*, ed. L. W. Schwarz, New York, 1956, offer broad historical accounts. More specific studies: M. A. Meyer, *The Origins of the Modern Jew*, Detroit, 1967; A. Eloesser, *Vom Ghetto nach Europa*, Berlin, 1936; H. M. Graupe, *Die Entstehung des modernen Judentums*, Hamburg, 1969, deal more particularly with the intellectual developments of the emancipation period. Very little has been written from a specifically sociological standpoint. The earliest of these studies is Max Wiener's *Jüdische Religion im Zeitalter der Emanzipation*, Berlin, 1933, which contains many important insights, while Jacob Katz has written most extensively on the subject as a historical sociologist; see particularly his *Tradition and Crisis*, New York, 1971, his collection of papers published over thirty years, *Emancipation and Assimilation*, Gregg International, 1972, and the most recent *Out of the Ghetto*, Cambridge, Mass., 1973, which are, however, too broadly based to identify forces of change in particular areas. Another sociologist, Eleanore Sterling, in her *Judenhass*, Frankfurt a/M, 1969 (originally *Er ist wie du: aus der Frühgeschichte des Antisemitismus in Deutschland 1815–1850*, Munich, 1956), chose a somewhat narrow approach and obscured important developments by ignoring the chronological interactions of events and ideas. Other studies, which often give the impression that Jewish emancipation was essentially something done to the Jews but which nevertheless

are extremely important, are Ismar Freund's *Die Emanzipation der Juden in Preussen*, 2 vols, Berlin, 1912, and R. Rürup's 'Jewish emancipation and bourgeois society', *LBIYB*, 14, 1969, pp. 67–91. Essential information on which sociological analysis can be based is now becoming available; see for example Selma Stern's massive *Der preussische Staat und die Juden*, 3 vols, Tübingen, 1962, 1971, and Stefi Wenzel's *Jüdische Bürger und die kommunale Selbstverwaltung in preussischen Stadten 1808–1848*, Berlin, 1967. Here I can only attempt an outline of what I regard as the key issues in a sociological approach to Jewish emancipation

3 A. Ruppin, *Soziologie der Juden*, Berlin, 1930, vol. 1, pp. 81–2
4 A. Tartakover, 'Fundamental problems of Jewish demography today', *Hebrew Union Coll. Annual*, 13 (2), 1950–1, pp. 649–78
5 *Soziologie des jüdischen Volkes*, Hamburg, 1965, p. 18
6 R. A. Kann, 'Assimilation and anti-semitism in the German–French orbit in the nineteenth and early twentieth centuries', *LBIYB*, 14, 1969, pp. 92–115, esp. p. 108
7 Cecil Roth, *A History of the Jews in England*, Oxford, 1964, pp. 92–115, esp. p. 108; his figures are probably based on those given in Patrick Colquhoun, *Treatise on the Police of the Metropolis*, rev. ed., London, 1800
8 H. Silbergleit, *Die Bevölkerungs und Berufsverhältnisse der Juden im deutschen Reich*, vol. 1, *Freistaat Preussen*, Berlin, 1930, p. 20. Most of the statistical information I have selected was available when Marx wrote his essays, notably in the following publications: Reichsgraf Henckel von Donnersmark, *Darstellung der bürgerlichen Verhältnisse der Juden im preussischen Staate unmittelbar vor dem Edikt vom 11 März 1812*, Leipzig, 1814; Rönne and Simon, *Die früheren und gegenwärtigen Verhältnisse der Juden in den sämtlichen Landesteilen des preussischen Staates*, Breslau, 1843; Hugo Dezius, *Ueber die bürgerlichen Verhältnisse der Juden im Grossherzogtum Posen und im Kulmer Land*, Marienwerder, 1830; J. G. Hoffman, *Uebersicht der Bodenfläche und Bevölkerung des preussischen Staates*, Berlin, 1818; Hoffman, *Zur Judenfrage: statistische Erörterung*, Berlin, 1842
9 Most of the studies dealing with Jewish emancipation (e.g. Jacob Katz's *Out of the Ghetto*) deal with the subject as a whole and therefore give insufficient emphasis to specific events and personalities in specific areas
10 ibid., p. 31. We might note here that the areas of Prussia which Marx knew best (except for Berlin) had predominantly *rural* Jewish populations (see Silbergleit, op. cit., p. 11):

Local government district	Percentage of total population living in rural areas	Percentage of Jewish population living in rural areas
Trier	86.9	68.5
Aachen	75.5	68.2
Koblenz	79.5	66.5
Köln	74.8	53.7
Düsseldorf	66.8	52.8

11 The best account of Jewish internal self-government is S. W. Baron's *The Jewish Community*, 3 vols, Philadelphia, 1948; another well-known study is I. Abraham's *Jewish Life in the Middle Ages*, London, 1896. See also A. Berliner, *Aus dem Leben der Juden Deutschlands im Mittelalter*, Berlin, 1937; James Parkes, *The Jew in the Medieval Community*, London, 1938; Herman Pollack, *Jewish Folkways in Germanic Lands 1648–1806*, Cambridge, Mass., 1971. Valuable material is also to be found in Louis Finkelstein's *Jewish Self-Government in the Middle Ages*, Philadelphia, 1924 (repr. Westport, Conn., 1972)

12 L. Wirth, *The Ghetto* (1928), Chicago, 1956, p. 17

13 ibid., p. 25

14 See Freund, op. cit., p. 10

15 In a lecture at the University of Sussex, 1973

16 *The Life of Glückel of Hameln, 1646–1724* (ed. and trans. B.-Z. Abrahams), London, 1962, p. 50

17 Hermann Schwab, *Jewish Rural Communities in Germany*, London, n.d., pp. 27, 29, 35, 38

18 See S. M. Dubnow, *History of the Jews in Russia and Poland*, Philadelphia, 1916, vol. I, p. 48

19 Silbergleit, op. cit., p. 18

20 Freund, op. cit., vol. I, p. 17; W. M. Simon, *The Failure of the Prussian Reform Movement 1807–1819*, New York, 1955, p. 7. This is not to say that there was no conflict over the emancipation of peasants. The nobility fought a bitter battle to maintain their privileged position until 1848, but the conflict attracted much less attention in Prussia than the 'Jewish question'; see S. Sugenheim, *Geschichte der Aufhebung der Leibeigenschaft und Hörigkeit in Europa*, St Petersburg, 1862 (repr. Aalen, 1966), esp. pp. 464–75

21 Although I am using the term 'emancipation' throughout, it did not in fact emerge among the Jews until the 1830s, i.e. half a century after the question had emerged in public debate. See J. Katz, 'The term "Jewish emancipation": its origin and historical impact', in A. Altmann (ed.), *Studies in Nineteenth Century Jewish Intellectual History*

22 See Barrington Moore, jr., *Social Origins of Dictatorship and Democracy*, Penguin, 1969, p. 18

23 Document prepared by nobles of Prussia under the leadership of Marwitz; Simon, op. cit., p. 78

24 *Das wirtschaftliche Schicksal des deutschen Judentums*, Berlin, 1933, p. 14

25 By 1842 for instance the Jews of Prussia, while constituting about 1 per cent of the population, provided 15 per cent of its medical men (Hoffmann, *Zur Judenfrage*). On the other hand, conversions to Christianity seem to have been commonest at the highest *and lowest* social strata (see pp. 30–6)

26 See W. Freund, 'Der Judenbezirk der preussischen Gesetzgebung', in *Zur Judenfrage in Deutschland*, Berlin, 1843, pp. 31–2

27 See pp. 63–4

Chapter II   The Quiet Revolution

1   For detailed discussions see E. Zimmer, *Harmony and Discord: an Analysis of the Decline of Jewish Self-Government in Fifteenth Century Central Europe*, New York, 1970; S. W. Baron, *The Jewish Community*, esp. vol. 2

2   See J. M. Jost, *Kulturgeschichte zur neueren Geschichte der Israeliten 1815–1845*, Berlin, 1847, pp. 16, 49–51

3   *Heines Werke*, Berlin and Weimar, 1968, vol. 5, pp. 84–5. In his 'Zur Geschichte der Religion', Heine described Mendelssohn as the 'reformer of German Israelites . . . who destroyed the reverence for Talmudism and founded pure Mosaism'

4   'Jewish contributions to German philosophy', *LBIYB*, 9, 1964, pp. 161–77

5   ibid., p. 165. Heinrich Graetz (*History of the Jews*, Philadelphia, 1967, vol. 5, p. 292) described Mendelssohn in glowing terms as the rejuvenator of the Jews and leader of their 'renaissance'

6   It should be noted that, although Mendelssohn was accorded recognition by many of his greatest contemporaries—Kant, Herder, Wieland—apart from Lessing, in the context of the German little tradition he was and remained a despised Jew. His status was that of *Schutzjude* and, as Dubnow recorded (*History of the Jews*, vol. 4, London, 1971, p. 324), he was liable to be abused in the streets of Berlin as a Jew

7   See *Moses Mendelssohn's Schriften*, ed. Moritz Brasch, 2 vols, Leipzig, 1880, vol. 2. For an excellent discussion of Mendelssohn's philosophy see Julius Guttmann's *Philosophies of Judaism*, New York, 1966. His views on Judaism are carefully analysed in Max Wiener's *Jüdische Religion im Zeitalter der Emanzipation*, Berlin, 1933, pp. 34–8. A lengthy discussion of Mendelssohn, including biographical material, can be found in Graetz (op. cit.). I have also made use of A. Jospe's *Jerusalem and other Jewish Writings by Moses Mendelssohn*, New York, 1969, which contains some excellently translated passages; B. May and J. B. Levy, *Moses Mendelssohn: eine Auswahl aus seinen Schriften und Briefen*, Frankfurt a/M, 1912; chap. 7 of H. M. Graupe's *Die Enstehung des modernen Judentums*, Hamburg, 1969. Since this study was completed, Alexander Altmann has published his definitive biography, *Moses Mendelssohn*, London, 1973

8   Jospe, op. cit., p. 101

9   ibid., p. 99

10 It is quite likely that Mendelssohn recognised that his allegiance to traditional Judaism was emotional-nostalgic rather than intellectually coherent. In a letter to Sophie Becker shortly before his death, he wrote about 'the pleasant emotions' which 'popular religious notions evoke from us' and that he adhered to these because 'my reason is unable to provide a substitute for these pleasant emotions'; see ibid., p. 149

11 Quoted by M. A. Meyer, *The Origins of the Modern Jew*, Detroit, 1967, p. 61, from the *Berlinische Monatsschrift*, 1790

12 Friedländer's offer was made in an anonymous pamphlet published in 1799, 'Von einigen Hausvätern jüdischer Religion', in Franz Kobler (ed.), *Juden und Judentum in deutschen Briefen aus drei Jahrhunderten*, Vienna, 1935, pp. 122–6

13 ibid., p. 128. Teller's reply was that Jews would have to accept Christian *Grundwahrheiten* (Jesus chosen by God to give the world a better religion) but not necessarily *Grundlehren* (the Holy Trinity and Jesus as the son of God); see Mayer, op. cit., pp. 75–6

14 ibid., p. 103

15 See M. Philippson, *Neueste Geschichte des jüdischen Volkes*, Leipzig, 1907, vol. 1, pp. 101–2. For a discussion of the wider background of the riots, see Eleonore Sterling, 'Anti-Jewish riots in Germany in 1819: a displacement of social protest', *Historia Judaica*, 2, 1950, pp. 105–42

16 Quoted in Mayer, op. cit., p. 167

17 The text of Wolf's memorandum is reproduced in *LBIYB*, 2, 1957, 'On the concept of a science of Judaism', pp. 194–204 (p. 200)

18 My account of the Verein is based on Mayer's analysis (op. cit.), and H. G. Reissner, 'Rebellious dilemma: the case histories of Eduard Gans and some of his partisans', *LBIYB*, 2, 1957, pp. 179–93. My account makes it clear that I am in disagreement with scholars like S. Shazar and Gershom Scholem who saw in the Verein 'demoniac forces who contributed to the distortion and corruption of Judaism for the sake of assimilation'; see Robert Weltsch's 'Introduction' to vol. 2, *LBIYB*, p. xxv; Heine, *Confessio Judaica*, ed. H. Bieber, Berlin, 1925, p. 176

19 See, e.g. Deut. 6:7 and 20

20 e.g. for priests in biblical times, for rabbis and communal functionaries later

21 This cleavage between true (i.e. sacred) education and the acquisition of worldly skills has deep roots in Jewish tradition and is already made explicit by the Tanaim—the earliest group of rabbinic teachers. In Pirke Avoth, a brief tractate of the Mishnah which became the best known and most popular guide to daily living among Jews in the Diaspora, the message is frequently reiterated, e.g. 'he who does not study deserves to die; and he who makes worldly use of the crown of the Torah shall waste away' (1.13); 'All study of the Torah without work must in the end be futile' (2.2); 'say not . . . when I have leisure I will study; perchance thou wilt have no leisure' (2.5); 'an ignorant man [cannot] be pious, nor can a shamefaced man learn, or a passionate man teach' (2.6)

22 Classic examples of this may be found in M. Güdemann's massive *Geschichte des Erziehungswesens und der Cultur der abendländischen Juden*, 3 vols, Vienna, 1880 and his *Quellenschriften zur Geschichte des Unterichts und der Erziehung bei den deutschen Juden*, Berlin, 1891, where we find detailed discussions on size of schools, curriculum, conditions of work for teachers, management of slow-learning children, etc. Although secular education *per se* was rejected, there is a great deal of evidence that mathematics, geography, natural sciences and even fine arts often crept into a basically religious curriculum

23 Mendelssohn's friend and disciple David Friedländer, together with Daniel Itzig, established the Jüdische Freischule in Berlin in 1778. In addition to Jewish subjects it taught German, French, business studies, arithmetic, bookkeeping, writing and drawing. Other schools followed soon afterwards. In 1786, Isaac Herz Samson founded his Freischule in Wolfenbüttel and included a boarding wing (his pupils included the

historian Jost and the scholar Zunz); the Wilhelm Schule in Breslau was founded in 1791; the Jüdische Haupt und Freischule in Dessau was established in 1799 and gained almost immediate support from Prince von Anhalt. The Jacobson Schule (day and boarding) began in Seesen in 1801 and was unusual in that it catered for roughly equal numbers of Jewish and Christian boys. Two famous schools functioned until they were closed by the Nazis in the 1940s: the Real und Volksschule der Israelitischen Gemeinde in Frankfurt a/M (Philanthropin) was started in 1804 and the Talmud Torah Realschule in Hamburg in 1805

24 Mendelssohn's translation of the Pentateuch was published in 1783
25 A series of letters published in 1782. For a detailed discussion of Wessely see C. L. Ozer, 'Jewish education in the transition from ghetto to emancipation', *Historia Judaica*, 9 (1), (2), 1947, pp. 75-94, 137-58
26 ibid., p. 85
27 The *AZJ* reported the establishment of the following:

Place	Year	AZJ
Cassell	1802	1891
Prussia	1812	1882
Strasburg	1819	1840
Frankfurt a/M	1823	1845
Bavaria	1826	1888
Dresden	1829	1837
Baden	1833	1837
Schwerin	1835	1839
Saxony	1837	1837
Bonn	1841	1841
Hanover	1841	1841
Vienna	1841	1883
Mühlhausen	1843	1843

See also S. B. Weinryb, *Der Kampf um die Berufsumschichtung*, Berlin, 1936

28 Ozer, op. cit., p. 83
29 For details of Basedow (who started his Philanthropinum in Dessau, Moses Mendelssohn's home town) and the influence of other educational reformers, see K. A. Schmid (ed.), *Geschichte der Erziehung*, vol. 4, pt 2, Stuttgart, 1898, which has a special chapter on Mendelssohn and Jewish education; R. H. Quick, *Essays on Educational Reformers*, London, 1898
30 Michael Hess (brother of Mendel Hess, editor of the *Israelit des neunzehnten Jahrhunderts*), 'Kurze geschichtliche Darstellung der Real und Volksschule der Israelitischen Gemeinde zu Frankfurt am Main', *Sulamith*, 6 (2), 1822, pp. 148-62, 232-7. A complete account of the school to its closure in 1942 is A. Galliner, 'The Philanthropin in Frankfurt', *LBIYB*, 3, 1958, pp. 169-86
31 The first census of Prussian high schools to identify the religious denomination of pupils, which was carried out in 1886-7, showed that in proportion to their respective populations there were eight times as many Jews as Christians

32 See E. Troeltsch's brilliant essay, *Protestantism and Progress*, London, 1958, esp. p. 89

33 The literature on conversion is limited and often contradictory. The subject is clearly delicate, and one scholar who recently published a paper on it reported that he had been criticised for doing so (C. Cohen, *LBIYB*, 8, 1963, p. 267). Jacob Katz in his recent book (*Out of the Ghetto*, pp. 104-23) has devoted a chapter to this subject which is concerned mainly with some of the theological debates on conversion in the early nineteenth century. I believe him to be wrong when he argues that converts were mainly 'the rich and the intellectual' (ibid., p. 122). Carl Cohen, 'The road to conversion', *LBIYB*, 6, 1961, pp. 259-79, offers a useful survey. One of the most important papers is A. Menes, 'The conversion movement in Prussia during the first half of the nineteenth century', *YIVO Annual of Jewish Social Sciences*, New York, 1951, pp. 187-205. The *AZJ* republished an interesting article by M. Löwenstein, 'Ueber Judenbekehrung und Judenemanzipation' (8, 1844, pp. 665-72) which originally appeared in the *Kirchliche Vierteljahresschrift*, vol. 4, 1844. More recently the Historische Kommission zu Berlin has announced that it will shortly publish a study, *Judentaufen*, by the well-known historian Guido Kisch. I have also used a valuable article on conversion in the *Jewish Encyclopedia*, New York, 1903, vol. 4, pp. 249-53. There is also a great deal of valuable information in Hilde Spiel, *Fanny von Arnstein oder die Emanzipation*, Frankfurt a/M, 1962

34 See for example, Spiel, op. cit., pp. 81-9, though Hans Tietze (*Die Juden Wiens*, Vienna, 1933, p. 146) has suggested that it was the conversions in Berlin which influenced the Jews of Vienna

35 Carl Cohen, *LBIYB*, 6, 1961, p. 264, *Jewish Encyclopedia*, vol. 4, p. 253 and Tietze, op. cit., p. 146

36 C. Cohen, *LBIYB*, 6, 1961, p. 265

37 *Sulamith*, 1806, p. 175. For a detailed discussion of the debate, see Katz, *Out of the Ghetto*

38 There are no reliable figures on the different waves of conversions, but the extent of the disagreement among scholars may be gauged from the following. *The Jewish Encyclopedia* (vol. 4, p. 252) quotes these estimates for the whole of the nineteenth century:

De le Roi	204,540	for Europe
Heman	over 100,000	
Salmon	130,000	
Divre Emeth	250,000	

while Cohen (*LBIYB*, 6, 1961, p. 272) quotes:

Ruppin	22,520	for Germany
Nazis	224,000	for Prussia
Goldman	5,254	for Berlin, 1800-1924

Prussian statistics for 1816-48 suggest some 2,200 conversions

39 See, e.g., H. G. Reissner, 'Felix Mendelssohn, Bartholdy und Eduard Gans', *LBIYB*, 4, 1959, pp. 92-110, esp. p. 109. We will have occasion to refer to Heine as a good example of this duality later on. See also the exchange of letters on this in *AZJ*, 8, 1844, pp. 681-90

40 Löwenstein, op. cit.

41 Societies devoted to spreading the Christian gospel amongst Jews began in England and spread from there to Germany. They used particularly former Jews whose knowledge of Hebrew and Judaism was seen as a useful mode of contact; see *Jewish Encyclopedia*, vol. 4, p. 252

42 Eleonore Sterling, 'Jewish reactions to Jew-hatred', *LBIYB*, 3, 1958, pp. 103–21, esp. p. 108

43 R. A. Kann, 'Friedrich Julius Stahl', *LBIYB*, 12, 1967, pp. 55–74 (p. 68)

44 *AZJ*, 8, 1844, pp. 681–90

45 *Heines Werke*, vol. 5, p. 187

46 Löwenstein, op. cit.

47 Michael Hess, op. cit., pp. 159–60

48 H. G. Reissner, 'German–American Jews: 1800–1850', *LBIYB*, 10, 1965, p. 68

49 *AZJ*, 8, 1844, p. 670

50 Menes (op. cit., p. 200), for example, quotes an entry for Brandenburg including Berlin for 1836 on forty-three converts. Of these:

11 were university and high school students
3 were doctors
3 were tradesmen
9 were artisans
2 were a banker and his wife
4 were woman with two children and a niece
1 teacher
1 servant-girl
6 (4 girls, 2 women) occupation not stated.

Unfortunately he quotes only excerpts; more systematic research is clearly desirable

51 op. cit., p. 253. Those who were still alive when the list was compiled in 1902 were excluded

52 Hans Liebeschütz, *Das Judentum im deutschen Geschichtsbild von Hegel bis Max Weber*, Tübingen, 1967, p. 194

53 For a moving account of the inner conflicts of a 'social' convert, see Israel Zangwill's 'Diary of a Meshumad', in *They That Walk in Darkness* (*Works*, vol. 6), Globe, London, 1926, pp. 279–313

54 Nathan Glatzer, *American Judaism*, Chicago, 1957, p. 23

55 Agreement on the nature and effect of German–Jewish immigration to America in this period appears to be common. See, for example, ibid., p. 31; C. B. Sherman, *The Jew Within American Society*, Detroit, 1965, p. 63; M. Sklare, *American Jews*, New York, 1971; S. Goldstein and C. Goldscheider, *Jewish-Americans*, Englewood Cliffs, 1968, p. 24. For an interesting account of the successes of some of the poorer immigrants see Barry Supple, 'A business elite: German-Jewish financiers in nineteenth century New York', *Business Hist. Rev.*, 31 (2), 1957, pp. 143–78

56 Gabriel Riesser for instance seriously contemplated such a step but rejected it because slavery in America disgusted him. See H. G. Reissner, 'German-American Jews: 1800–1850', *LBIYB*, 10, 1965, p. 65

57 It was not until the Russian pogroms of the 1880s that Russian Jews began their mass emigration to the United States. There was also immigration

into Prussia from the East. See E. Hamburger, 'One hundred years of emancipation', *LBIYB*, 14, 1969, p. 6

58 In 1816 the Prussian ministry of finance issued a report on Jews by Councillor (*Rat*) Wolfart, whose conclusions contained the following first clause: 'It would be highly desirable if there were no Jews in the country at all' (I. Freund, *Die Emanzipation der Juden in Preussen*, Berlin, 1912, vol. 1, p. 235). During the debates of the United Landtag in Prussia in 1847, Staatsminister von Thiele declared that 'the Jew could have no fatherland other than the one indicated by his faith; Zion was the true fatherland of the Jew' (S. Bernfeld, *Juden und Judentum im neunzehnten Jahrhundert*, Berlin, 1898, p. 153). If there is no evidence that Prussian authorities did anything to stop emigration (there was also substantial non-Jewish emigration), there was considerable ambiguity among civil servants in their attitudes to Jews, as we shall show later; see also Reissner, *LBIYB*, 10, 1965, pp. 57–116

59 Jost, op. cit., p. 118

60 D. Philipson, *The Reform Movement in Judaism* (rev. ed.), New York, 1930, pp. 13–18

61 He founded the Jacobson Schule in Seesen in 1801 which enrolled an equal number of Jewish and Christian boys

62 The synagogue had always been a meeting-place as much as a place of worship, as is implied in its name, Beit Haknesset; i.e. House of Assembly rather than house of worship

63 The sermon at that time was in itself an innovation since traditional synagogues were as a rule addressed only on special occasions by their rabbis and then in Yiddish or Hebrew. For a detailed study of the evolution of the modern Jewish sermon and its roots in the Christian tradition, see A. Altmann, 'Zur Frühgeschichte der jüdischen Predigt in Deutschland', *LBIYB*, 6, 1961, pp. 3–59, and 'The new style of preaching in nineteenth century Germany', in A. Altmann (ed.), *Studies in Nineteenth Century Jewish Intellectual History*, London, 1965

64 Philipson, op. cit., pp. 24–5

65 The literal translation of *Goel* is 'redeemer', used in traditional Jewish liturgy to signify both a national and a spiritual saviour. Early reformers opted for the concept of 'redemption' partly to underline a universalist approach in Reform Judaism and partly to bypass the problem of a German national praying for national redemption in a non-German context; see Michael Leigh's essay in D. Marmur (ed.), *Reform Judaism*, London, 1973, esp. pp. 7–8

66 Max Wiener, *Jüdische Religion im Zeitalter der Emanzipation*, Berlin, 1933, p.47

67 Jost, op. cit., pp. 121, 124; see also Geiger's letters to Naftali Dernburg in Max Wiener (ed.), *Abraham Geiger and Liberal Judaism: the Challenge of the Nineteenth Century*, Philadelphia, 1962, pp. 83–96

68 *AZJ*, 7, 1843, pp. 405–7; see also Philipson, op. cit., pp. 117 ff.

69 ibid., pp. 517–20

70 ibid., pp. 405–7

71 S. R. Hirsch, *The Nineteen Letters on Judaism* (1837). I have used Jacob Breuer's edition published in Jerusalem in 1969

72 Hirsch, op. cit., p. 110
73 See Jost, op. cit., p. 129
74 Hirsch, op. cit., p. 110. He uses expressions here which are reminiscent of Bauer and Marx—indeed N. H. Rosenbloom has analysed *The Nineteen Letters* as a 'Hegelian exposition', *Historia Judaica*, 12, 1960, pp. 23–60
75 Although I have restricted my account here to the period up to Marx's publication of 'On the Jewish Question' because I am mainly concerned to show those developments which Marx *could* have looked at, the most critical events for the Reform movement in fact took place in the years 1844, 1845 and 1846, when rabbinical conferences in Brunswick, Frankfurt and Breslau were held. It was from the discussions at these that Reform evolved its programme and legitimation; see Philipson, op. cit., chap. 7
76 Jost, op. cit., pp. 132–3
77 ibid., p. 143
78 *AZJ*, 7, 1843, pp. 453–5
79 ibid., pp. 517–20
80 *Der Orient*, 4, 1843, pp. 260–4
81 Jacob Katz, 'The term "Jewish emancipation": its origin and historical impact', in A. Altmann (ed.), *Studies in Nineteenth Century Jewish Intellectual History*, p. 17
82 M. Isler (ed.), *Gabriel Riesser's gesammelte Schriften*, 4 vols, Frankfurt a/M and Leipzig, 1867 (hereafter *Riesser*); see vol. 2
83 ibid., vol. 2, pp. 12, 13
84 ibid., pp. 33, 35
85 *Mannheimer Abendzeitung*, reprinted in *Der Orient*, 3, pp. 249–50
86 *Riesser*, vol. 2, p. 83
87 Attempts to establish a Jewish press were begun by Moses Mendelssohn in 1750 with an unsuccessful publication in Hebrew, *Kohelet Mussar*, of which only two numbers appeared. In 1784 another Hebrew journal, *Hameassef*, was started by his disciples and ran for twenty-seven years. Its objective was to 'enlighten' German Jewry. The first German-Jewish newspaper was *Sulamith* (1806–48). Riesser tried his hand at a Jewish political journal, *Der Jude*, which ran for four years (1832–6) but yielded to the *Allgemeine Zeitung des Judentums*, the most successful and important paper to be published in the nineteenth century (1837–1921). Two other influential papers followed the *AZJ* for a while: *Der Israelit des neunzehnten Jahrhunderts* (1839–48), and the prestigious intellectual *Der Orient* (1840–51); see especially Margaret T. Edelheim-Mühsam, 'The Jewish press in Germany', *LBIYB*, 1, 1956, pp. 163–76
88 *Sulamith*, 1 (1), 1806, p. 164. *Sulamith* subsequently rejected the word and concept of Jews as a 'nation'
89 *AZJ*, 2 (1), 1838, p. 3
90 *Riesser*, vol. 2, p. 219

Chapter III   The Prussian State and the Jews

1 Selma Stern, *Der preussische Staat und die Juden*, vol. 3, *Die Zeit Friedrich des Grossen*, Tübingen, 1971, pp. 12–14
2 Hans Kohn, *The Idea of Nationalism* (1944), New York, 1967, pp. 358–9
3 op. cit., pp. 9–10
4 See M. Lowenthal, *The Jews of Germany*, London, 1939, p. 219
5 Hilde Spiel, *Fanny von Arnstein oder die Emanzipation*, Frankfurt a/M, 1962, p. 27
6 ibid., pp. 42, 44
7 Stern, op. cit., p. 12
8 ibid., pp. 16–17
9 ibid., p. 13
10 Lowenthal, op. cit., p. 212
11 Stern, op. cit., p. 19
12 ibid., p. 26; this report is dated 1763
13 ibid., pp. 23, 25
14 Stern, op. cit., vol. 2, pt 2, 1962, pp. 1598–9. The report is dated 26 January 1780 and headed: 'Against rigorous expulsion and suggestions for making marriages more difficult'
15 Dohm's report has become a classic and is so well known that it need not be discussed in detail here. Its importance lies not least in the term *Verbesserung*, which had a dual meaning of improvement of conditions *for* the Jews and at the same time the need for improvement *of* the Jews. The book was published in two parts in Berlin and Stettin in 1781 and 1783. The second part was a response to criticisms levelled against his first publication
16 Dohm, op. cit., vol. 1, p. 16
17 ibid., pp. 27, 34
18 Such a view remained constant in Germany even among 'liberals'. In 1912, for example, Professor F. Niebergall of Heidelberg wrote that 'a Jewish officer ... was impossible [because] the aversion of our people even in the ranks of social democrats is still so deep that the Jewish officer could not command the necessary authority in an emergency'; W. Sombart *et al.*, *Judentaufen*, Munich, 1912, p. 101
19 Lowenthal, op. cit., p. 229. Fichte's argument is remarkably similar to that employed many centuries earlier by Haman: 'There is a certain people scattered abroad and dispersed among the peoples in all the provinces of the kingdom; and their laws are diverse from those of every people; neither keep they the king's laws; therefore it profiteth not the king to suffer them. If it please the king, let it be written that they be destroyed...', Esther 3:8–9. Börne may have thought of Fichte as well as a certain Dr Holst when he wrote that 'Dr. Holst wants to kill the Jews and if they try to defend themselves, he turns to his audience saying: You see, gentlemen, how right I was when I called the Jews so incredibly insolent. They object to having their heads a little bit knocked off, and they protest'; Eleonore Sterling, 'Jewish reactions to Jew-hatred', *LBIYB*, 3, 1958, p. 105
20 For a detailed discussion of this concept see Jacob Katz, 'A state within a

state: the history of an antisemitic slogan', *Israel Academy of Sciences and Humanities*, Jerusalem, 4 (3), 1969

21 It was in the course of this conflict that Jews tried to allay German fears by adopting descriptions such as 'Israelite' for themselves instead of the tarnished word 'Jew'. Thus, *Sulamith* originally carried a subtitle to the effect that it was a journal to foster culture and humanity among 'the Jewish nation'. With the publication of vol. 3 (1810), this had been changed to 'among the Israelites'

22 Humboldt challenged the Dohm concept of 'improvement' of and for the Jews on the grounds that 'one whose hands are freed after having been shackled, only reaches the point where everyone else already is'; I. Freund, *Die Emanzipation der Juden in Preussen*, Berlin, 1912, vol. 2, p. 269

23 'Edikt . . . betreffend die bürgerlichen Verhältnisse der Juden in dem preussischen Staate', ibid., pp. 455–9

24 S. Dubnow, *History of the Jews*, vol. 4, London, 1971, p. 614

25 Robert Weltsch, 'Introduction' to *LBIYB*, vol. 7, 1962, p. ix

26 See I. Elbogen, *Geschichte der Juden in Deutschland*, Berlin, 1935, pp. 202–3

27 Freund, op. cit., vol. 1, pp. 232–3. Pensions were refused on the grounds that, since the Edict did not admit Jews to service for the state, and since war service was state service, they were not entitled to pensions since they had all joined the Prussian army as volunteers. Even those who gained the Iron Cross were refused because, as the Prussian Minister of the Interior put it, 'Courage is not the only virtue required for state service' (ibid., p. 232)

28 For a detailed analysis of the riots, see Eleonore Sterling, 'Anti-Jewish riots in Germany in 1819: a displacement of social protest', *Historia Judaica*, 2, 1950, pp. 105–42

29 Details in Freund, op. cit., vol. 1, chap. 17

30 It was a phrase used by Jews as well as by Germans; Jacob Toury 'The Jewish question: a semantic approach', *LBIYB*, 11, 1966, pp. 85–106

31 In England, for example, Moses Montefiore (see p. 71) could hold the office of High Sheriff of Kent (1837) long before the Jews there were formally emancipated

32 See for example Selma Stern, op. cit., vol. 3, p. 14; R. Koselleck, 'Staat und Gesellschaft in Preussen 1815–1848', in W. Conze (ed.), *Staat und Gesellschaft im deutschen Vormärz*, Stuttgart, 1962

33 *Class and Ideology in the Nineteenth Century*, London, 1972, esp. pp. 15–21

34 Karl Marx, *Der achtzehnte Brumaire des Louis Bonaparte*, (East) Berlin, 1971, p. 35

35 Coal production, for example, rose dramatically between 1850 and 1906 (metric tons): 1850, 1½ million; 1862, 15 million; 1871, 30 million; 1906, 136 million; see Löwenthal, op. cit., p. 235

36 Systematic research on this subject is still in its infancy

37 *Die wirtschaftliche Entwicklung des jüdischen Volkes*, Berlin, n.d.

38 'Assimilation and anti-semitism in the German–French orbit in the nineteenth and early twentieth centuries', *LBIYB*, 14, 1969, pp. 92–115 (p. 95)

39 P. Massing, *Rehearsal for Destruction*, p. 249

Chapter IV   Unexpected Developments

1   T. Ziegler, *Die geistigen und sozialen Strömungen des neunzehnten Jahr-hunderts*, Berlin, 1899, pp. 227–9
2   Apart from the vivid analysis by Ziegler, there is an excellent description of him given by Friedrich Engels in 1842 in *MEW*, 1, pp. 446–53. There is also a good account in E. J. Feuchtwanger, *Prussia: Myth and Reality*, London, pp. 153–4
3   In his *Restauration der Staatswissenschaft*, 6 vols, Winterthür, 1820–34; see W. Carr, *A History of Germany, 1815–1945*, London, 1969, pp. 29–30; see also Engels, op. cit., p. 447
4   See R. Koselleck, *Preussen zwischen Reform und Revolution*, Stuttgart, 1967, esp. p. 608
5   Carr, op. cit.; Ziegler, op. cit., p. 230
6   Bruno to Edgar Bauer, 24 July 1840, in *Bruno Bauer und Edgar Bauer: Briefwechsel während der Jahre 1839–1842 aus Bonn und Berlin*, Berlin, 1844, pp. 101–2. By the time he wrote the letter, Bauer was his usual self again: 'Sometimes', he ended, 'one has to be silly if one does not want to appear ridiculous'
7   See Heine's bitterly contemptuous poem, 'Die Audienz', *Heines Werke*, Berlin and Weimar, 1968, vol. 1, pp. 364–6
8   Ziegler, op. cit., p. 231. This was to have far-reaching effects for Bruno Bauer and indirectly for Karl Marx; see p. 126 below
9   R. Schay, *Juden in der deutschen Politik*, Berlin, 1929, pp. 139–50, esp. pp. 142–3. In 1848 Jacoby was acclaimed as one of the leaders of the democratic movement. Ziegler (op. cit., p. 232) sees this incident as the reason for the king's lifelong antipathy to Jews. See also *DFJB*, pp. 45–70
10 See Engels in *MEW*, 1, p. 493
11 J. M. Jost, *Neuere Geschichte der Israeliten 1815–1845*, Berlin, 1846, p. 294 n.
12 ibid., 293
13 This decree of 17 March, imposed on the Jews on the left of the Rhine and parts of Westphalia, was enacted for a fixed period of years and imposed severe limits on loans, debts and interest rates. The law was taken over by Prussia and continued indefinitely. It was confirmed in 1830 and remained in force until 1845; see Jost, op. cit., pp. 285–6
14 Jost (op. cit., p. 296) reported that the Prussian government were fully conscious of the drastic character of the draft law and 'leaked' it before publication to test reactions—M. Lowenthal, *The Jews of Germany*, London, 1939, p. 252, claimed that Gabriel Riesser 'unmasked the . . . project'. Neither Jost nor the Jews of the time could have known that a comprehensive law on the status of the Jews had been drafted and submitted to the Staatsrat on 2 October 1839 (under Friedrich Wilhelm III). This draft was rejected, and a review of the attitudes of the provincial authorities was called for on 20 January 1841. This rather suggests that, in 1841 at any rate, Friedrich Wilhelm IV and his senior civil servants dealing with Jews did not see eye to eye. The review of the provincial authorities' views was published in 1845; see I. Freund, *Die Emanzipation der Juden in Preussen*, Berlin, 1912, vol. 1, p. 248

15 Jost, op. cit., pp. 295–6
16 J. M. Jost, *Kulturgeschichte zur neueren Geschichte der Israeliten 1815–1845*, Berlin, 1847, p. 154
17 Jost, *Neuere Geschichte*, pp. 297, 301
18 See p. 89; 68:5 voted for removal of the decree of 1808, 54:19 for full equality
19 ibid., pp. 298–301
20 The following account of the Damascus affair is based on three main sources: H. Graetz, *History of the Jews*, Philadelphia, 1967, vol. 5, pp. 632–72; L. Wolf, *Sir Moses Montefiore*, London, 1884, pp. 80–112; S. M. Dubnow, *Neueste Geschichte des jüdischen Volkes*, Berlin, 1920, vol. 2, pp. 297–306
21 As a result of his diplomatic defeat in the Middle East, Thiers tried to abrogate the treaty of 1815 and to reoccupy the Rhineland. His actions created a tremendous war fever, especially in Prussia, and a great upsurge of German nationalism (see Carr, op. cit., pp. 28–39). He was later to become the hangman of the Paris Commune
22 See L. Stein, *The Balfour Declaration*, London, 1961, pp. 3–11. The Damascus affair sparked off a variety of projects and ideas on the resettlement of Jews in Palestine which are fully described in N. M. Gelber, *Zur Vorgeschichte des Zionismus*, Vienna, 1927. See esp. chapter IX, 'Das Jahr 1840', which includes a special section (pp. 176–201) on the reactions of the Jews of Germany
23 Throughout the Middle East the European powers were exercising influence through consuls who often had considerable freedom of action, especially in protecting their own nationals. Ratti-Menton was an Italian by birth and a man of dubious character. He had previously been expelled from Sicily and Russia; see H. Heine, 'Damaskus Briefe', in *Confessio Judaica*, Berlin, 1925, pp. 148–57
24 ibid., p. 151
25 Details of the Damascus incident began to appear in the German-Jewish press from mid-April 1840, notably in the *AZJ* and *Der Orient*
26 Wolf, op. cit., p. 99
27 Graetz, op. cit., p. 653
28 Graetz (op. cit., p. 654) claims that the Queen put her own ship at Montefiore's disposal
29 See the correspondence published by J. Ezekeil, 'Persecution of the Jews in 1840', *American Jewish Historical Society*, no. 8, 1897, pp. 141–5
30 The *AZJ* carried two odes to Montefiore composed in Hebrew (5, 1841, pp. 207–8, 214)
31 There was a strange epilogue to the Damascus story. Although the Jews had been exonerated from the charge of murdering Father Thomas, the Franciscans erected in their Church of the Capuchines at Damascus a monument to his memory, stating that he had been murdered by Jews. In spite of intervention in Rome by Montefiore, the monument remained. Twenty years later, in 1860, the Druse of southern Lebanon turned against the Catholics of Syria, and Montefiore appealed on their behalf in *The Times* (10 July), while Crémieux appealed to French Jews to aid the stricken

Christians. Montefiore's appeal raised £22,500. Order was eventually restored by French troops, but the church with its libellous monument was destroyed during the riots; see Wolf, op. cit., pp. 186-8

32 Ludwig Philippson, *AZJ*, 5, 1841, p. 23

33 The Prussian government sought Neander's advice about banning the book when Strauss published his *Life of Jesus*. He replied that 'scholarly works are to be fought with the weapons of science, not by the power of the state' (*Jewish Encyclopedia*, vol. 9, 1905, p. 198). On the other hand, he objected to the admission of unbaptised Jews to the University of Berlin in 1847; see Hans Liebeschütz, *Das Judentum im deutschen Geschichtsbild von Hegel bis Max Weber*, Tübingen, 1967, p. 68

34 op. cit., p. 149

35 ibid., p. 156

36 ibid., p. 153. For a more detailed discussion of Heine, see pp. 78-82 and 188-92 below

37 *Rome and Jerusalem* (trans. M. Waxman), New York, 1943, pp. 67-8

38 Quoted by Robert Weltsch in *LBIYB*, 4, 1959, p. xii

39 *MEW*, 2, p. 122 (English version, Moscow, 1956, p. 155). It is interesting that the meticulous scholarship of the Institute of Marxism-Leninism in Moscow has not spotted this error

40 Benoît Fould must not be confused with Achille Fould (Graetz appears to have made that mistake, see vol. 5, p. 649), who was elected only in 1847 and who, as Louis Napoleon's Minister of Finance, became Marx's 'aristocrat of finance' in *The Eighteenth Brumaire of Louis Bonaparte*

41 Zunz, *Damascus: ein Wort zur Abwehr*, Berlin, 1840. Graetz, op. cit., p. 669; Graetz was highly critical of German Jewry's part in this affair

42 S. Bernfeld, *Juden und Judentum im 19 Jahrhundert*, Berlin, 1898, p. 151

43 H. G. Adler, *Die Juden in Deutschland*, Munich, 1960, p. 76. The two professions mentioned by Geiger were among those from which Jews were excluded

44 This attitude accurately reflected the official view that, if Jews really wanted to be Prussian, they would relinquish their Jewishness. As one Prussian Minister, von Bodelschwingh, put it: 'The Jews are aliens in our country as long as they are really Jews', United Landtag Debate, 17 June 1847. There was a marked difference in the British attitude. In her citation honouring Montefiore, Queen Victoria expressed her 'desire to give to Montefiore a special mark of our royal favour in memory of his persevering efforts on behalf of his suffering and persecuted brethren in the East, and of his nation in general' (Graetz, op. cit., p. 670)

Chapter V   The Political Image of Jews

1 The Alliance Israelite Universelle was a direct result of Crémieux's efforts to improve the education of Jews in Oriental countries

2 Thus, for example, when F. W. Ghillany published a pamphlet in support of Bruno Bauer in which he made fantastic allegations that Jews wanted to kill and subject all non-Jews, a Jewish reviewer commented bitterly

that 'it is difficult to understand a censorship which excludes so much of what is right and which gives total freedom of expression to the lunatic', *Der Orient*, 4, 1843, col. 557

3 Hegel, *Lectures on the Philosophy of History* (trans. J. Sibtree, 1899), New York, 1956, pp. 39–40

4 Hegel, *Grundlinien der Philosophie des Rechts* (ed. G. Lasson), Leipzig, 1921, p. 212

5 'Civil Disabilities and Privations affecting Jews in England' (London, 1829), in H. Trevor-Roper (ed.), *Macaulay's Essays*, London, 1965, p. 117

6 There is no direct evidence that Marx had read the 'Damascus Letters' but he was certainly familiar with *Ludwig Börne*, and on a later occasion offered to defend Heine with a review of it (*MEW*, 27, p. 441). We might also note here that Jacob Toury (*Die politischen Orientierungen der Juden in Deutschland*, Tübingen, 1966) has drawn attention to certain similarities in the descriptions of Jews in Marx and Börne; see Appendix D, p. 355

7 Best summarised in Israel Zangwill's *Dreamers of the Ghetto*: 'A German Parisian, a Jewish German, a hated political exile who yearns for dear old homely Germany, a sceptical sufferer with a Christian patience, a romantic poet expressing in classic form the modern spirit, a Jew and poor'

8 'Damaskus Briefe', in *Confessio Judaica*, Berlin, 1925, p. 156

9 ibid. p. 151

10 ibid. (my italics)

11 ibid., p. 154

12 ibid., p. 152 (my italics)

13 ibid., p. 153

14 ibid., p. 155

15 This is probably a reference to the charge brought by a number of Christian clerics during the Damascus affair that only the Jews of Europe had expunged 'objectionable' passages from the Talmud (see H. Graetz, *History of the Jews*, vol. 5, Philadelphia, p. 651)

16 'Damaskus Briefe', p. 157

17 ibid. (my italics)

18 *Heines Werke*, Berlin and Weimar, 1968, vol. 5, p. 184

19 ibid., pp. 185–6

20 ibid., p. 187

21 ibid., p. 195 (my italics)

22 ibid., pp. 197–8

23 ibid., p. 197

24 ibid., p. 279

25 ibid., p. 278

26 Letter to Ruge, 9 July 1842, *MEW*, 27, p. 405

27 Letter 25 August 1842, *MEW*, 27, p. 409

28 'Karl Marx und die Bittschriften . . .', *Archiv für Sozialgeschichte*, 8, 1968, pp. 229–45

29 Bruno Bauer took this up in *Die Judenfrage*, Brunswick, 1843, pp. 14–15

30 The Landtag was not a legislative body, but merely submitted recommendations to the sovereign. In 1827 it submitted a resolution to the crown stating: 'The assessment of our loyal estates on the civil conditions of Jews

in this province will be further considered with a view to reaching a definitive conclusion'. See Appendix to part 1 of *Zur Judenfrage in Deutschland*, ed. W. Freund, vol. 1, Berlin and Breslau, 1843, pp. 81–115, in which the proceedings are recorded and from which the material for this summary has been extracted

31 A type of *rapporteur* who made the opening and closing speeches in a debate. The chamber was controlled by a Landtag Marschall who was responsible for order and for organising the vote. Members represented three groups: the *Ritterschaft* or lower nobility; *Städte*, towns; *Landgemeinden*, rural communities

32 The decree required every Jewish inhabitant to obtain a 'certificate of morality' every year. Without this certificate, all his undertakings were legally null and void. If a Jew lent money at more than 10 per cent interest, he was liable to lose the entire amount he had lent. If a Christian did the same, he was liable to lose half the capital sum. Other clauses restricted the categories of persons from whom, if they borrowed money, capital and interest could be reclaimed

33 Freund, op. cit., p. 86

34 Seven town delegates, two nobles and one rural delegate spoke in favour of emancipation, three nobles and two town delegates spoke against

35 Freund, op. cit., p. 106. This observation was also made by Max Weber, *Protestant Ethic and the Spirit of Capitalism*, London, 1968 (1930), p. 39

36 See pp. 68–9 above

37 Freund, op. cit., p. 104

38 Like the great champion of Jewish emancipation, Wilhelm von Humboldt, who once wrote to his (violently anti-Jewish) wife: 'I can appreciate your hatred of Jews ... Actually I love Jews only en masse ... en détail I avoid them' (Letter to Karoline, 30 April 1816, in F. Kobler (ed.), *Juden und Judentum in deutschen Briefen*, Vienna, 1935, p. 208)

39 An argument also used by Bruno Bauer and taken up by Marx, see p. 417n.71 below

40 A major theme in Bruno Bauer

41 *Über die Emanzipation der Juden in Preussen*, Potsdam, 1844

Part Two   Introduction

1 See particularly Hans Liebeschütz, *Das Judentum im deutschen Geschichtsbild von Hegel bis Max Weber*, Tübingen, 1967; H. M. Graupe, 'Kant und das Judentum', *Zeitschrift für Religion und Geistesgeschichte*, 13 (4), 1961, pp. 308–33; also Graupe, *Die Entstehung des modernen Judentums*, Hamburg, 1969. On Kant and Hegel, N. Rotenstreich, *The Recurring Pattern*, London, 1963; Emil Fackenheim, *The Religious Dimension in Hegel's Thought*, Bloomington, 1967, and his 'Samuel Hirsch and Hegel', in A. Altmann (ed.), *Studies in Nineteenth Century Jewish Intellectual History*, London, 1965

2 'Sur les Moeurs des nations', no. 3

3 Liebeschütz, op. cit., p. 22

4 This geographical feature of Palestine was destined to become an important

feature later for Marxist analysts of Jewish history, from which they derived the predominant trading interests of Jews. See p. 207 below

5 While it is true that, in the course of history, many 'private' laws were extended into 'public' laws, notably by the invocation of informal sanctions, this was a characteristic of highly specific social situations which were not immediately relevant; for example in Hegel's argument

6 Quoted by Liebeschütz, op. cit., p. 30

7 See the long footnote in *Grundlinien der Philosophie des Rechts*, Leipzig, 1921, p. 212. For detailed discussions of Hegel on Jewish emancipation, see S. Avineri, 'A note on Hegel's views on Jewish emancipation', *Jew. Soc. Stud.*, 25, 1963, pp. 145–51, and 'Hegel revisited', in *J. Contemp. Hist.*, 1968, pp. 133–47

8 A conception which influenced not only D. F. Strauss and Feuerbach but also Friedrich Engels, who credited Bruno Bauer with the idea and argued that Christianity did not originate in Galilee and Jerusalem but in Alexandria and Rome. It was not an abrupt creation, but one which evolved over time from various sects, the strongest of which survived in a Darwinian, evolutionary process in the same way as socialism evolved from Utopian and St Simonian forms until 'scientific' socialism or Marxism established itself as the true socialism. See Engels, 'Bruno Bauer and early Christianity', in Marx and Engels, *On Religion*, Moscow, 1955, pp. 194–204

9 Liebeschütz, op. cit., pp. 109–10. Note the similarity of views on Jewish emancipation of Gförer and D. F. Strauss

Chapter VI The Radical Image of Jews

1 Friedrich Engels, 'Ludwig Feuerbach and the end of classical German philosophy', in Marx and Engels, *On Religion*, Moscow, 1955, p. 223

2 E. L. Fackenheim, 'Samuel Hirsch and Hegel', in A. Altmann (ed.), *Studies in Nineteenth Century Jewish Intellectual History*, London, 1965, p. 180 n.

3 *Das Leben Jesu* (1835, 1836), Bonn, 1895, pp. 210–11

4 ibid., p. 213

5 ibid., p. 214

6 ibid., p. 215

7 ibid.

8 ibid., p. 219

9 ibid., p. 220; note the political parallel alluded to by Engels

10 ibid.

11 ibid.

12 ibid., p. 221; Feuerbach makes the same point, see *Essence of Christianity*, trans. George Eliot, New York and London, 1957, p. 115 (hereafter *Essence*); originally *Das Wesen des Christentums* (1841), 3rd ed., 1849, reprinted Stuttgart, 1971

13 ibid., p. 221

14 ibid.; the Essenes were represented among Alexandrian Jews as Therapeutei

15 ibid., pp. 211–12
16 ibid., p. 225
17 ibid., pp. 226–7
18 ibid., pp. 229, 232
19 ibid., p. 389
20 See Eleonore Stirling, *Judenhass*, Frankfurt a/M, 1969, pp. 95–6
21 I have not been able to trace the articles, but a full summary of them is contained in Isidor Zlocisti, 'D. F. Strauss über Judenverfolgung und Emanzipation', *Der juedische Student*, 2 (1), Berlin, 1905, pp. 10–14
22 Note that, like Max Weber, Strauss does not explain in what sense a person of Jewish origin, married to a Gentile and without a Jewish identity or religion, would still be Jewish enough to be 'accorded equal rights'
23 *Essence*, p. xii
24 ibid., p. 299. Eisenmenger (1654–1704) devoted many years to the study of the Talmud and published his *Das Entdeckte Judentum* in 1700. It became a standard work of reference for anti-Jewish polemicists. It was also used by Bruno Bauer, who derived his title, *Das entdeckte Christentum*, 1843, from it. G. F. Daumer mentioned the book in a letter of January 1842 to Feuerbach: 'Since you refer to a revision of your book, I would like to commend Eisenmenger's *Entdeckte Judentum* to you; you will find in it excellent proofs for a presentation of Judaism as the religion of egoism' (*Sämtliche Werke* with a biography by W. Bolin (1904), new ed. by H. M. Sass, Stuttgart, 1964, vol. 13, p. 89 (hereafter Bolin)). It should be noted, however, that until the first translation of Tractate Berachoth of the Talmud by E. M. Pinner in Berlin, 1842, German writers had no real access to talmudic teaching apart from Eisenmenger's distorted version
25 Bolin, op. cit., vol. 12, p. 53
26 Eugene Kamenka, *The Philosophy of Ludwig Feuerbach*, London, 1970, p. 17
27 Letter to Friedrich Kapp, 15 October 1844 (Bolin, op. cit., vol. 13, pp. 137–9). Weitling, a tailor by trade, was one of Germany's earliest communists and the first writer to come from the German 'working class'
28 G. F. Daumer, *Der Feuer- und Molochdienst der alten Hebräer als urväterlicher, legaler, orthodoxer Cultus der Nation*, Brunswick, 1842; F. W. Ghillany, *Die Menschenopfer der alten Hebräer: eine Geschichtliche Untersuchung*, Nuremberg, 1842. In an extraordinary letter to Feuerbach in April 1842 (Bolin, op. cit., vol. 13, pp. 96–8), Daumer, clearly in a state of great excitement, promised Feuerbach 'unbelievable' information about Jews slaughtering their own and Gentile children, about Hasidic rabbis being sacrificed and their remains worshipped by their followers, about human blood being drunk during the festival of Purim, about 'no one having an inkling of the cannibalism in the Talmud' and about finding under a synagogue subterranean ovens containing the remains of a great rabbi. Feuerbach appeared to have accepted this nonsense and, as stated, referred to it in *Essence* (see below) though shortly afterwards he fell out with Daumer over the latter's *Mariencultus*. In a letter to Schibich (Bolin, op.

389

cit., vol. 13, p. 189), Feuerbach wrote on 21 October 1851 that he had had no contact with Daumer since 1844, because he was 'unreliable, unfree, slave of a sick imagination, a pietistic naturalist'

29 *Essence*, pp. xli, 330–1

30 See Bolin, op. cit., vol. 12, pp. 8–9, 95. Adolph Kohut (*Ludwig Feuerbach, sein Leben und seine Werke*, Leipzig, 1909) refers to Feuerbach's enjoying the hospitality of David Friedländer, the famous disciple of Mendelssohn, and other Jewish families when he was a student in Berlin (pp. 30–1), yet he could still take Daumer seriously

31 *Essence*, p. 32

32 ibid., p. 112

33 ibid., p. 113

34 ibid.

35 ibid., p. 114

36 ibid., p. 151

37 ibid., p. 112

38 ibid., p. 113

39 ibid., p. 114

40 ibid.

41 ibid., p. 115

42 ibid., p. 117

43 ibid., p. 119

44 ibid., p. 120

45 ibid.

46 ibid., p. 121

47 ibid.

48 ibid.

49 ibid., p. 208

50 ibid., p. 209

51 ibid., p. 208

52 ibid., p. 141; this was destined to be an axiomatic principle of Jewish law for Bauer and Marx

53 ibid., p. 119

54 ibid., p. 267

55 Kamenka, op. cit., p. 172 n. 2

56 *Essence*, p. 262

57 Nathan Rotenstreich, 'The Bruno Bauer controversy', *LBIYB*, 4, 1959, pp. 3–36, deals in some detail with many issues raised in this study. The author has suggested an 'empirical' explanation ('the Jews at the time of Feuerbach and Marx were merchants', p. 25) to explain the emphasis on 'egoism'. My analysis, however, tends to show that both writers deliberately avoided arguments based on 'reality', even if Rotenstreich's assumptions were objectively true

58 He argues (op. cit., pp. 25–6) by a process of elimination that Moses Mendelssohn was the source of Feuerbach's association of Judaism and action. But the heavy emphasis in Feuerbach on Jewish ethnocentrism leads me to suggest that his source was more likely to have been Spinoza

59 First published in *Rheinische Jahrbücher zur gesellschaftlichen Reform*, ed.

H. Puttman, Darmstadt, 1845 (reprinted Leipzig, 1970), and reissued by T. Zlocisti in *Moses Hess: sozialistische Aufsätze 1841–1847*, Berlin, 1921 (hereafter *Aufsätze*). A more recent publication, Horst Lademacher's *Moses Hess: ausgewählte Schriften*, Cologne, 1962, includes an excessively abbreviated version of the essay. In an otherwise perceptive Introduction, the editor does not comment on the essay. We might note here that, because the essay was not published until 1845, both Martin Buber (*Israel und Palestina: zur Geschichte einer Idee* (1950), Munich, 1968, p. 119) and Nathan Rotenstreich (op. cit., p. 25) erroneously believed that the essay showed Marx's influence on Hess

60 Published in *DFJB*, 1844. References in this section are to Tom Bottomore's translation in *Karl Marx: Early Writings*, London, 1963

61 E. Silberner, *Moses Hess: Geschichte seines Lebens*, Leiden, 1966, pp. 184–92, esp. p. 192

62 D. McLellan, *The Young Hegelians and Karl Marx*, London, 1969, pp. 154–5 (hereafter *Young Hegelians*)

63 D. McLellan, *Marx before Marxism*, London, 1970, p. 141 (hereafter *MbM*)

64 *Philosophy and Myth in Karl Marx*, p. 112

65 Since Hess's essay is less well known than Marx's, I have also included a substantial English summary

66 6 and 30 July, 23 August 1842 (see chapter V)

67 Letter Marx to Dagobert Oppenheim, 25 August 1842, *MEW*, 27, p. 409

68 'Die Judenfrage' in *Deutsche Jahrbücher*, nos 279–82, 17–26 November 1842, pp. 1093–126. This was published as a separate book in Brunswick in 1843, from which I quote. A second article, 'Die Fähigkeit der heutigen Juden und Christen frei zu werden' ('The capacity of present-day Jews and Christians to become free'), was published in G. Herwegh (ed.), *Einundzwanzig Bogen aus der Schweiz* (*Twenty-one Pages from Switzerland*), Zürich and Winterthur, 1843, pp. 56–71

69 Letter Marx to Arnold Ruge, 13 March 1843, *MEW*, 27, p. 418

70 ibid., p. 416

71 Marx's letter to Feuerbach, October 1843, *MEW*, 27, p. 419. See below for a discussion of the precise date of that letter

72 (Trans. Edward Fitzgerald), *Karl Marx: the Story of his Life*, London, 1936, p. 56

73 *Karl Marx*, p. 50

74 *Karl Marx: the Passionate Logician*, p. 73

75 Jenny Marx, 'A short sketch of an eventful life', in *The Unknown Karl Marx*, ed. R. Payne, London, 1972. Note that she wrote in 1865, some twenty-two years after the events in question

76 *MbM*, p. 131. A. Cornu (*Karl Marx et Friedrich Engels*, vol. 2, Paris, 1958, p. 249) quotes a letter from Froebel which suggests 11 or 12 October

77 *MEW*, 1, p. 629; H. Gemkow et al., *Karl Marx: a Biography*, Dresden, 1968, p. 57

78 W. Banning, *Karl Marx: Leben, Lehre und Bedeutung*, Hamburg, 1966. This is also the view of M. Rubel in his *Karl Marx: essai de biographie intellectuelle*, Paris, 1957, p. 74

79 *MEW*, 27, pp. 419–21

NOTES TO PAGES 111-13

80   D. McLellan (ed.), *Karl Marx: the Early Texts*, Oxford, 1971, p. 83. He quotes Karl Grün (ed.), *Ludwig Feuerbachs philosophische Characterentwicklung, sein Briefwechsel und Nachlass*, 2 vols, Leipzig and Heidelberg, 1874, and Marx and Engels, *Historisch-kritische Gesamtausgabe*, ed. D. Rjazanov and A. Adoratskij (Berlin, 1927-), I i (2) as his sources

81   op. cit., vol. 13, pp. 127-8

82   Mehring, op. cit., p. 56; *MEW*, 27, pp. 422-3

83   See Marx's Preface to the *Critique of Political Economy*, *Marx-Engels Selected Works*, London, 1968, p. 182. Even so there is also some doubt about the precise period when this was written. The predominant view seems to be that it was written between March and August 1843 (J. O'Malley's Introduction to the *Critique of Hegel's Philosophy of Right*, London, 1970, pp. ix, x; *MbM*, p. 106) and we know that Marx had done some work on this subject already (letters to Ruge of 5 and 20 March 1842, *MEW*, 27, pp. 397, 401)

84   *MEW* (1, p. 629) gives the date for the composition of these essays as 'autumn 1843 to January 1844'. G. Lukács (*Der junge Marx*, Pfullingen, 1965, p. 34) thinks autumn 1843 and dates the 'Introduction' to the 'Critique' as 'early 1844'. Tucker (op. cit., p. 111) makes an unsupported suggestion that Marx's second essay was written in January 1844

85   See Marx's letters to Ruge, 9 July 1842: 'My family creates difficulties for me which, in spite of their comfortable situation, reduces me to the direst circumstances. I could not possibly burden you with accounts of these private scandals (*privat Lumpereien*) . . .' (*MEW*, 27, p. 402); 25 January 1843: 'I have . . . fallen out with my family and as long as my mother is alive I cannot claim my fortune [sic!]' (p. 414); 13 March 1843: [He complains that his fiancée has had to fight bitter battles partly with her family, and] 'partly with my own family in which a few clerics (*Pfaffen*) and others who are hostile towards me have entrenched themselves' (p. 416)

86   op. cit., p. 184; McLellan (*Young Hegelians*, p. 154) gives the end of 1843 or beginning of 1844 for the time of writing

87   McLellan (ibid.) thinks that Marx 'must have read' most of the essay, and Tucker (op. cit., p. 111) says that it is 'not certain but seems quite probable' that Marx had seen it

88   *Young Hegelians*, p. 155

89   See Hess's own statement in 'Dottore Graziano oder Dr. Arnold Ruge in Paris' quoted in ibid., p. 154

90   Mehring, op. cit., p. 52

91   *Aufsätze*, p. 186

92   *MEW*, 1, p. 344. Lenin, of course, held the opposite view. He stated quite unequivocably that the *DFJB* saw the 'final consummation' from revolutionary democracy to communism, but he does not mention Marx's letters to Ruge in *DFJB*; see V. I. Lenin, *Karl Marx* (written 1913-14), Peking, 1970, pp. 47-8

93   Marx made the decision not to publish Hess without Ruge who had not yet arrived in Paris. Marx's letter to Froebel explained his embarrassment at having to reject Hess's essay; *MEW*, 27, p. 423

94 The following summary and quotations are based on the text in *Aufsätze*, pp. 158–87

95 op. cit., pp. 191–2

96 *Young Hegelians*, pp. 154–8. The claim is repeated in *MbM*, p. 141 and in his Introduction to *Karl Marx: the Early Texts*, p. xxvi

97 op. cit., p. 112. We might also note here that none of these scholars has made reference to the fact that Hess's essay is modelled on ideas suggested in an article by Marx written in 1842 which employed similar 'animal kingdom', 'predatory animals' and '*Krämer*' concepts. See 'Debatten über das Holzdiebstahlsgesetz', *MEW*, 1, pp. 109–47, esp. pp. 115–16, 120

98 *Aufsätze*, p. 172

99 Hess drew attention to Feuerbach's failure to extend his analysis to 'the social essence of man' in 'Über die sozialistische Bewegung in Deutschland' (1845); see *Aufsätze*, pp. 115–16

100 Bottomore, op. cit., p. 22

101 ibid., pp. 22–3

102 ibid., pp. 23–6

103 ibid., p. 15

104 ibid., p. 21

105 ibid., p. 30

106 He argued that the formation of estates and corporations emphasised group needs against individual needs (p. 8)

107 *Aufsätze*, p. 178

108 *Young Hegelians*, p. 158

109 The classic example of this is one of three isolated references to Jews in vol. 1 of *Capital* (London, 1970), p. 79, where Marx refers to 'Jews in the pores of Polish society'. Some Jewish Marxists writing about East European Jews have made much of this (see A. Léon, *The Jewish Question*, p. 77; N. Weinstock's Introduction in this book, pp. 31, 60; O. Heller, *Der Untergang des Judentums*, Berlin, 1931, pp. 45, 105). Yet the original concept is not Marx's but Bruno Bauer's. In his 'Die Judenfrage', Brunswick, pp. 6–7, Bauer described the vast gap between the Polish aristocracy and peasantry and claimed that Poland's large Jewish population was explained by the Jews filling 'the pores in Polish national life'. If this appears far-fetched, let us look at Marx's full sentence and its origin in Bauer, *Capital* (p. 79): 'Trading nations, properly so called, exist in the ancient world only in the interstices, like the gods of Epicurus in the Intermundia, or like Jews in the pores of Polish society'; Bauer (op. cit., p. 9): 'As gods of Epicurus live in the interstices of the world . . . so the Jews have . . . nestled into the pores and cracks of civil society'

110 The 'Economic and Philosophical Manuscripts' of 1844 were first published in Marx and Engels, *Historisch-kritische Gesamtausgabe*, I/III, Berlin, 1932. I have consulted Easton and Guddat (eds), *Writings of the Young Marx on Philosophy and Society*, New York, 1967 and M. Milligan's translation published in Moscow in 1959. Page references here are to Bottomore, op. cit. Page references for 'Ueber das Geldwesen' are in *Aufsätze*

111 op. cit., p. 191

112 See, for example, *Rheinische Jahrbücher*, 2, 1846, pp. 158, 236, and Heine, 'Damaskus Briefe', in *Confessio Judaica*, Berlin, 1925
113 op. cit., p. 112
114 See Bottomore, op. cit., p. 39
115 *Essence*, p. 120
116 'Die Judenfrage', p. 45
117 *Young Hegelians*, esp. pp. 155, 157
118 *The Origins of Socialism*, London, 1969, p. 178
119 See *Rom und Jerusalem*, Leipzig, 1862
120 *Die Menschenopfer der alten Hebräer*. He subsequently became a strong supporter of Bruno Bauer. G. F. Daumer published his *Feuer- und Molochdienst der alten Hebräer*, in which a similar thesis was put forward in the same year
121 *Aufsätze*, pp. 37–60
122 ibid., p. 45. I am at a loss to understand Silberner's interpretation of this passage. Hess wrote about the god 'den das Justemilieu-Zeitalter des Judentums mit Geld abgefunden hat'. I understand this to mean that money became the symbol for sacrifice when the Jews had developed from a predominantly agrarian-exchange-based economy to a mainly urban bourgeois-mercantilist society; i.e. that Hess implied a historical development of the Jews which had reached its peak with the advent of Christianity. Silberner, however, maintains that in this sentence Hess described 'the present justemilieu bourgeois era as the era of Judaism' (*Sozialisten zur Judenfrage*, p. 184)
123 *Aufsätze*, p. 182
124 cf. Levit. 17: 10–14 and Deut. 12:16
125 *Young Hegelians*, p. 155
126 Lichtheim, op. cit., p. 179

Chapter VII   The Radical Challenge to Jews

1 July–August 1843 (see pp. 82–5)
2 D. McLellan (*The Young Hegelians and Karl Marx*, London, 1969, p. 50), in my view, goes too far when he describes Bauer's 'Die Judenfrage' as a treatise 'on the relation of religion to politics' in response to his dismissal from Bonn, while J. Gebhardt ('Karl Marx und Bruno Bauer', in *Politische Ordnung und menschliche Existenz*, ed. Dempf, Arendt und Jonosi, Munich, 1962, pp. 202–42, esp. p. 216) must be wrong when he describes Bauer's essay, as well as Marx's response to it, as 'a reaction of radical Hegelians to the "catastrophe" [i.e. the reimposition of censorship] of 1842–3', if only because rigid censorship was not reimposed until the end of 1842 or the beginning of 1843, whereas Bauer's first version of 'Die Judenfrage' was published in the (not as yet prohibited) *Deutsche Jahrbücher für Wissenschaft und Kunst* in November 1842. Jacob Toury ('The Jewish question: a semantic approach', *LBIYB*, 11, 1966, pp. 85–106, esp. p. 93) shows convincingly how the term 'Judenfrage' became a popular phrase as a result of the debate on the 'Corporation bill'

in 1842 when five publications bearing that phrase in their title were issued against Jewish emancipation. In the following year the Jews themselves adopted it when W. Freund began to edit and publish his *Zur Judenfrage in Deutschland*, Berlin and Breslau, 1843–4

3 e.g. 'As if oppression and persecution were not also the lot of those who go against their time', and 'Is it always only Jews who have gained and lost in history? Are there no other people who have been marked by history, who have experienced something? Always and always, only the Jews'; 'Die Judenfrage', Brunswick, 1843, pp. 23, 91

4 Hengstenberg, the forceful, anti-rationalist and anti-Hegelian, strictly orthodox Lutheran, was only twenty-six when he was appointed ordinary professor. Like Bauer's, his first publications dealt with the Old Testament and the gospel of St John

5 B. and E. Bauer, *Briefwechsel, 1839–1842*, Berlin, 1844 (hereafter *BW*), pp. 7–9

6 'I feel the more isolated since no one here represents the kind of principle that would make an exchange [of views] worth the effort'; *BW*, p. 11

7 *BW*, p. 136

8 e.g. when he received a stipend from Berlin; *BW*, p. 24

9 Thus when the Ministry suggested that Bauer might change from teaching theology to teaching church history, but would first have to give some lectures on the subject before he could be formally recognised, Bauer refused. His brother Edgar, who was his spokesman and messenger in Berlin, reported in despair that 'the civil servants think you are only concerned about your post, they have no idea that you are fighting for a principle'; *BW*, pp. 137–40. Bauer meanwhile was determined not to demean himself by formally applying to Berlin for a regular post: 'I cannot apply, I must keep myself pure'; *BW*, p. 138

10 Neither his father nor his brother understood that Bauer had broken with religion (*BW*, p. 32), and his mother failed to understand why he remained in Bonn (*BW*, p. 132)

11 cf. the unmistakable sexual symbolism of his own description of his 'method'. 'He combats theology, even in the gospels, and in the course of this combat forces his way into the sanctum of religion and when he has penetrated its theological forecourts (*propylaea*) he profanes it with relish'; *Hegel's Lehre von der Religion und Kunst*, Leipzig, 1842, p. 41 (originally published anonymously, reprinted Scientia, 1967). Marx seems to have reached a similar view; e.g. 'St Bruno would undoubtedly be a danger to the feminine sex—for he has an "irresistible personality"— did he not, "to the same extent, on the other hand", fear "sensuousness as the barrier against which man inevitably deals himself a mortal blow". Therefore, "through himself, in himself, and with himself", he will hardly pluck any flowers but rather allow them to wither in infinite longing and hysterical yearning for the "irresistible personality" who possesses this unique sex and these unique, distinct sex organs'; adapted fron *German Ideology*, Moscow, 1964, pp. 121–2

12 See S. Hook, *From Hegel to Marx*, 2nd ed., Ann Arbor, 1962, pp. 95–6; K. Löwith, *Von Hegel zu Nietzsche*, 2nd ed., Stuttgart, 1950, p. 121 (trans.

as *From Hegel to Nietzsche*, London, 1965); and the Foreword by Engels and Marx to the *Holy Family*, Moscow, 1956. In this context we might look briefly at McLellan's criticism of Hook (*Young Hegelians*, pp. 50–1 n.). McLelland complained that Hook ignored Bauer's writings of 1840–3 which were not yet obsessed with 'pure criticism', that Marx's criticisms of Bauer in the *Holy Family* were concerned 'only' with the *Allgemeine Literatur Zeitung* of 1844 and that Marx was concerned only with emphasising 'the points that divided him from Bauer, not their common ground'. On balance, however, the evidence suggests that Hook's interpretation is the correct one:

(a) Bauer's delusions about the power and significance of his 'pure criticism' are certainly evident in much of his writing of the years 1840–3 (e.g. Edgar Bauer's explanation of Bruno's *Sache* to a friend who had called Bruno 'arrogant'; 11 February 1841, *BW*, pp. 121–3; see also 'Die Judenfrage', Introduction, esp. p. 3)

(b) Marx himself denied that he was concerned 'only' with the *Allgemeine Literatur Zeitung* in the *Holy Family*—'Engels and Marx therefore know only the criticism of the *Literatur Zeitung*—a deliberate lie proving how "fluently" our saint has read a book *in which his latest works are depicted merely as the culmination of all his "work done in the past"* ', *German Ideology*, p. 116 (my italics)

(c) By the time he wrote the *Holy Family*, Marx, in my view, was no longer concerned with points of agreement and disagreement with Bauer—rather he wanted to express his total repudiation of Bauer's 'philosophical anarchism' (Hook, op. cit., p. 112), his elitist destructiveness and his theoretical terrorism

13 *BW*, p. 190
14 Welcker (1790–1869), one of the leading liberal academics in Germany, fought vigorously against political censorship and was dismissed for the second time in 1841. He was widely feted in Berlin, and Bauer was present on one occasion. In December Bauer was summoned before the *Universitätsrichter* (university judge) to account for his participation; see *BW*, pp. 160–3
15 *BW*, p. 147
16 *BW*, pp. 189–92
17 Gebhardt, op. cit., p. 209
18 e.g. Riesser, Abraham Geiger, Philippson and others. Mendel Hess, editor of the *Israelit des neunzehnten Jahrhunderts*, described Bauer as a 'highly respected, profound and truly humane' opponent, who must not be accused of being 'hostile and anti-semitic' since he had demonstrated a love of truth which made him 'resign his position rather than compromise'. Bauer's 'removal from the chair of theology which he occupied with such distinction, his excommunication by the state at the behest of church leaders, has naturally filled him with bitterness against church and state . . . yet even though he has extended his condemnation to us Jews, we should nevertheless regret that the state has seen fit to condemn him for his opinions', *Israelit des neunzehnten Jahrhunderts*, 5, 1844, pp. 113–15
19 Jellinek, a brilliant twenty-one-year-old Jewish radical, wrote some

interesting reviews for *Der Orient* (see pp. 145–6) and might have achieved great fame had it not been for his tragic fate. He wrote a number of books on religion and politics, joined the 'revolution' of 1848 in Austria and was sentenced to death for his part in it. Offered a reprieve if he would disavow his books, he refused, claiming that his ideas could not be shot, and was executed at the age of twenty-six. His radicalism did not prevent a vicious attack on 'the great literary Jew Jellinek' in the *Neue Rheinische Zeitung* (no. 101, 13 September 1848), then being edited by Karl Marx. Georg Jellinek was his nephew

20 Jellinek, *Der Orient*, 4, 1843, col. 403
21 This was Hernes's thesis; see pp. 83–5
22 'Die Judenfrage', pp. 4–5
23 ibid., p. 88
24 ibid., p. 18
25 ibid., pp. 24–8
26 ibid., pp. 97–8
27 ibid., p. 59
28 ibid., pp. 43–4
29 ibid., pp. 60–1; this is the section at which the brunt of Marx's review was directed
30 ibid., p. 93
31 ibid., p. 98
32 ibid., p. 103
33 ibid., pp. 67–8
34 ibid., p. 106
35 ibid., p. 75
36 ibid., pp. 107–9
37 ibid., p. 111
38 ibid., pp. 10–12
39 ibid., pp. 12–14
40 ibid., pp. 23, 84
41 ibid., pp. 33–4
42 ibid., pp. 79–80
43 ibid., pp. 81–2. For all his rejection of liberalism, Bauer followed the critique of Judaism by liberal protestant theologians of the 1820s very closely; e.g. 'Whereas everything is moved by time and subject to its development and transformation, the Jew alone offers defiance, standing immutable among us, a petrified living creature, as it were, of a bygone age, and his figure—like everything that runs counter to time—becomes loathsome'; quoted by R. Rürup in 'Jewish emancipation and bourgeois society', *LBIYB*, 14, 1969, p. 79
44 'Die Judenfrage', p. 45
45 ibid., p. 15
46 ibid., p. 82
47 ibid.
48 ibid., p. 83
49 ibid., p. 114
50 See J. Klausner, *From Jesus to Paul*, Boston, 1961, pp. 502, 507

51 'Die Judenfrage', pp. 26, 27
52 ibid., pp. 35–6
53 ibid., pp. 41–2
54 ibid., p. 38
55 ibid., p. 42
56 ibid., p. 36
57 ibid., p. 48
58 ibid., p. 57
59 ibid., pp. 9–10
60 ibid., p. 38
61 ibid., p. 49
62 ibid., p. 113
63 ibid., p. 115
64 'Die Fähigkeit der heutigen Juden und Christen frei zu werden', in *Einundzwanzig Bogen aus der Schweiz*, ed. G. Herwegh, Zürich and Winterthur, 1843, pp. 56–71
65 This was the principle which struck Marx, who argued that, even if one accepted a negative evaluation of Judaism, it was pure 'theology' to insist on a value-laden rank order of religions; see *Holy Family*, p. 146
66 A favourite concept of the time by which Bauer meant the practice of theologians of accepting all biblical statements as true and then interpreting contradictory and undesirable passages to align them with modern views. See *Hegel's Lehre*, pp. 41–2
67 'Die Fähigkeit', p. 61
68 ibid., p. 62
69 ibid.
70 ibid., p. 65
71 ibid., p. 69
72 Löwith, op. cit., p. 372
73 ibid., p. 373
74 ibid., p. 374
75 Apart from Marx, the main responses were a pamphlet in support of Bauer by F. W. Ghillany, *Die Judenfrage: eine Beigabe zu Bruno Bauer's Abhandlung über diesen Gegenstand*, Nuremberg, 1843, and one against Bauer by Karl Grün, *Die Judenfrage: gegen Bruno Bauer*, Darmstadt, 1844. (Grün's book was attacked by Gustav Julius in *Wigand's Vierteljahrsschrift*, I, 1844, pp. 278–86.) When Engels returned to Germany in October 1844, he wrote to Marx that, while everyone was trying to get a copy of the *DFJB*, 'one hears nothing here of the Bauers; no one knows anything about them', *MEW*, 27, p. 6
76 J. M. Jost, *Neuere Geschichte der Israeliten 1815–1845*, Berlin, 1846, p. 303
77 'For and against emancipation: the Bruno Bauer controversy', *LBIYB*, 4, 1959, pp. 3–36 (p. 12). His paper is an excellent review of the main Jewish contributions and is the only publication which deals in depth with the debate initiated by Bauer. Replies to Bauer, some of which are discussed by Rotenstreich, include G. Philippson, *Die Judenfrage von Bruno Bauer näher beleuchtet*, Dessau, 1843; S. Hirsch, *Das Judentum, der Christliche Staat und die moderne Kritik: Briefe zur Beleuchtung der Juden-*

frage von Bruno Bauer, Leipzig, 1843; G. Salomon, *Bruno Bauer und seine gehaltlose Kritik über die Judenfrage*, Hamburg, 1843; A. Geiger, 'Bruno Bauer und die Juden', *Wissenschaftliche Zeitung für jüdische Theologie*, 5, 1844, pp. 199–234, 325–71; G. Riesser, 'Die Judenfrage: gegen Bruno Bauer', *Konstitutionelle Jahrbücher*, pt 2, 1843, pp. 1–42, pt 3, 1843, pp. 14–57, pt 2, 1844, pp. 172–236; H. Jellinek, 'Die Judenfrage' *Der Orient*, 4, 1843, cols 385–90, 423–30; and W. Freund, *Zur Judenfrage in Deutschland*, vol. 2, 1844, pp. 211–30. Of these, Philippson and Salomon offered a straight counter-polemic. Hirsch and Jellinek offered a 'Hegelian critique' while Riesser particularly defended the idea of civil rights. Since Rotenstreich has discussed the major responses, I shall concentrate on the reaction to Bauer in the German-Jewish press

78 Mendel Hess (1807–71), one of the first German rabbis with a university education, was Chief Rabbi of the Grand Duchy of Weimar and an extreme reformer. He enforced a government decree to hold services in German, had to report to the government Jews who failed to attend services, and officiated at mixed marriages where the Christian upbringing of children was a condition. He edited his paper 1839–48 (with S. Holdheim as co-editor in 1847) and played a leading role in the Reform movement

79 4 January 1843, p. 13; excerpts from Bauer are on pp. 13–14, 25–6, 29–30
80 ibid.
81 ibid., pp. 33–4 and 37–8; note how Hess's dispute with Bauer illustrates the intellectual foundations of the Reform movement
82 ibid., p. 37
83 ibid., p. 38
84 ibid.
85 ibid.
86 4, June–July 1843, pp. 99–100, 103–4, 107–9
87 *Israelit des neunzehnten Jahrhunderts*, 4, 1843, pp. 99–100
88 Löwith (op. cit., p. 366) described it as an old stable Bauer had converted for his use
89 ibid., p. 109
90 Salomon (1784–1862) was a famous Jewish preacher, an editor of the first German-Jewish newspaper, *Sulamith*, and a defender of Jews against attacks from intellectuals. In *Bruno Bauer und seine gehaltlose Kritik über die Judenfrage*, he concentrated on a point-by-point refutation of Bauer's arguments against Jews, and accused him of anti-Jewish prejudice
91 *Israelit des neunzehnten Jahrhunderts*, 5, 1844, pp. 89, 92, 97, 101. 105–8, 113–15; the following summary is based on the introduction to the review on pp. 89–92
92 Philippson wrote in November 1842, i.e. the same month that Bauer's first version was published; see *AZJ*, 6, 1842, pp. 697–8
93 *AZJ*, 7, 1843, pp. 265–7 and 290–2. Further reviews of K. Grün and G. Salomon were published in 8, 1844, pp. 294–6, 339–40. G. Riesser was reviewed on pp. 445–9 in the same year
94 Edited by Julius Fürst (1805–73), an academic Hebraist and orientalist who studied under Hegel, Neander and Gesenius. He was *Privatdozent*

in Leipzig for twenty-five years, until the government of Saxony awarded him the title of professor. He founded *Der Orient* in 1840 as the most learned and scholarly of the German-Jewish papers

95 See nn. 19, 77

96 See n. 77

97 *Der Orient*, 4, April 1843, cols 257–64; this is, of course, what Marx eventually did

98 See D. Philipson, *The Reform Movement in Germany*, rev. ed., New York, 1930; M. Wiener, *Jüdische Religion in Zeitalter der Emanzipation*, Berlin, 1933

99 *AZJ*, 7, 1843, p. 26. See also J. M. Jost, *Neuere Geschichte*, p. 305, and M. Isler (ed.), *Gabriel Riesser's gesammelte Schriften*, Frankfurt a/M and Leipzig, 1867, vol. 1, p. 366

100 B. Bauer, *Das Judentum in der Fremde*, Berlin, 1863, p. 29

101 After Bauer died on 13 April 1882, Engels wrote 'Bruno Bauer and early Christianity' (in Marx and Engels, *On Religion*, Moscow, 1955, pp. 194–204) in which he referred to the fact that Bauer had been largely forgotten. Engels paid a generous tribute to Bauer's achievements, but nevertheless presented his own view on early Christianity because, in Bauer, 'phrases often replace substance' (ibid., p. 198), a view echoed by H. Steinthal in his long and detailed critique of Bauer's later theological work (*Über Juden und Judentum*, Berlin, 1906, pp. 148–95). I can find no evidence for Gebhardt's statement, in an otherwise meticulously supported paper, that Marx and Bauer retained a sentimental regard for each other. His reference to Engels's article would, if anything, suggest the contrary; Gebhardt, op. cit., p. 212

102 Gebhardt, op. cit., pp. 238–9, described Bauer as the *spiritus rector* of the *Internationale Monatsschrift*, which, after his death, was renamed *Antisemitische Blätter*

103 *AZJ*, 46, 1882, p. 282

Chapter VIII   The Marxian Response

1 *MEW*, 1, pp. 12, 15

2 Werner Post, for example, in a book of 300 closely printed pages (*Kritik der Religion bei Karl Marx*, Munich, 1969), takes the problem not much further than Alasdair MacIntyre in eleven casual pages (*Marxism and Christianity*, London, 1969, pp. 103–16), for both agree that Marx had correctly identified the failure of Christianity to resist the social injustices of the early nineteenth century. N. Lobkowicz's article, 'Karl Marx's attitude towards religion' (*Review of Politics*, University of Notre Dame, 26 (3), 1964, pp. 319–52), devotes most of its discussion to the attitudes of Hegel and Feuerbach and has but little to say on Marx. The interchangeability of religion and Christianity appears to be taken for granted by a number of writers in addition to those already mentioned, e.g. H. Gollwitzer, *Die Marxistische Religionskritik und der Christiche Glaube*, Munich and Hamburg, 1967 and H. Bosse *Marx–Weber–Troeltsch Religionssoziologie und marxistische Ideologiekritik*, Munich, 1970

3   Thus, one of the ablest analysts of Marx described his critique of religion as the exclusive product of Hegelian and post-Hegelian philosophy; see K. Löwith, *Von Hegel zu Nietzsche*, Stuttgart, 1950. Löwith set out to demonstrate a direct development from Hegel—via Strauss, Feuerbach, Ruge and Bauer—to Marx

4   See for example Lenin's uncompromising attack on 'all and every religious organisation' in his essay, 'On the Relationship of the Workers' Party to Religion' of May 1909, in which he repeatedly appeals to the authority of Marx to explain his position. V. I. Lenin, *Marx–Engels–Marxismus*, Moscow, n.d., pp. 325–42 (p. 326), or B. Bonpane and T. Edwards, *Marxism and Christianity: Are They Compatible?*, New York, 1970

5   e.g. Post, op. cit., esp. his final chapter. See also Marcel Reding, 'Der Sinn des Marxschen Atheismus', *Universitas: Zeitschrift für Wissenschaft, Kunst und Literatur*, 16 (5), May 1961, pp. 517–25

6   See Bosse, op. cit., pp. 108–15

7   e.g. A. Künzli, *Karl Marx: Eine Psychographie*, p. 302, quotes Eleanor Marx's report that Marx had said: 'we can forgive Christianity much, because it has taught us to love children'

8   J. P. Sartre, *Search for a Method*, New York, 1968, p. 3

9   See 'Economic and Philosophical Manuscripts', T. B. Bottomore, *Karl Marx: Early Writings*, London, 1963, p. 167; *Holy Family*, Moscow, 1956, p. 148

10 'Contribution to the Critique of Hegel's Philosophy of Right', Bottomore, op. cit., p. 43

11 Marx was probably using Hermes's claim, that the Christian state needed its religion to improve the moral conduct of its citizens, as the most glaring application of this contradiction (see pp. 83–5 above), which he had refuted in detail in his article on Prussian censorship; see *MEW*, I, esp. pp. 12–13

12 In Prussia the onus of definition was placed on the Jew. 'The state must regard him, who claims to be a Jew, as a Jew', wrote Hermes (*Kölnische Zeitung*, 6 July 1842), though it was not quite that simple. Heine converted to Protestantism not to gain 'an entrance-ticket to European culture', as he once jokingly remarked, but rather because, although he would have preferred not to belong to any religion, the Prussian authorities in Berlin insisted that every individual belong to a recognised religion. Failure to comply led to expulsion not only from Berlin but from the whole of Prussia; see *Heines Werke*, Berlin and Weimar, 1968, vol. 5, pp. 355–6

13 It is noteworthy that whereas most of Marx's works are peppered with examples and analogies drawn from the Bible, the essays 'On the Jewish Question' contain none. As far as I know Marx referred to only one single biblical law and that is in *Capital*, vol. I (London, 1970), p. 375 ('Thou shalt not muzzle the ox when he treadeth out the corn', Deut. 25:4). This deliberate omission of any reference to biblical law, which is often very close to Marx's own position, is sometimes quite striking. One example will suffice. In the 1842 article, 'Debates on the Thefts of

Timber' (*MEW*, 1, pp. 109-47), he is concerned with the problem of legal rights and common usage rights in relation to rich and poor members of society. The Landtag debate Marx is discussing dealt with wood-gathering, but he extended this to gleaning after harvests generally (op. cit., p. 119). The biblical laws concerning gleaning instantly come to mind (Deut. 24:19-22), but he does not mention them. Yet a few pages on he is able to construct a sentence effectively by using a passage from the book of Ruth (1:16-17) to make his point (*MEW*, 1, p. 126)

14   A full development of this problem will be found in Hans Liebeschütz's outstanding book, *Das Judentum im deutschen Geschichtsbild von Hegel bis Max Weber*, Tübingen, 1967

15   In his *Anthropologie in pragmatischer Hinsicht* (*Werke*, Berlin, 1917, vol. 7)

16   See Liebeschütz, op. cit., p. 32

17   Marx did not apparently see the contradiction in his two contentions that by becoming 'Judaised' man was being made greedy and yet 'religion does not make man', since he accepted that, in addition to being a 'social' element, Judaism was 'also a religious' element

18   See J. O'Malley's Introduction, Cambridge, 1970, pp. xxvii-xxviii

19   Bottomore, op. cit., pp. 43-4

20   In Marx's own conception of the meaning of 'empirical analysis' which he espoused at that time. Thus in the Preface to the 'Economic and Philosophical Manuscripts' of 1844, Marx claimed that his critique of political economy was based 'entirely on empirical analysis based on careful critical study'. His critique of Judaism shows no evidence of such preparation; see Bottomore, op. cit., p. 63

21   For a detailed discussion see Gabriele Dietrich, 'Das jüdisch-prophetische Erbe in den neueren revolutionären Bewegungen', in *Jüdische Hoffnungskraft und Christlicher Glaube*, Freiburg, 1971

22   I have translated from a photostatic reproduction of the *DFJB* published by the Wissenschaftliche Buchgesellschaft-Darmstadt in 1973

23   Nevertheless Marx certainly did much of the groundwork on it, including the difficult task of turning down some contributions, such as Moses Hess's article 'Ueber das Geldwesen' (letter to Julius Fröbel, 21 November 1843, *MEW*, 27, pp. 422-3)

24   Reproduced in *MEW*, 1, pp. 337-46

25   Ferdinand Coelestin Bernays (1815-79), wrongly referred to in *MEW* (vol. 1, pp. 617, 710) as Karl Ludwig Bernays. According to D. McLellan (*Marx before Marxism*, London, 1970, pp. 131, 157), he was editor of the Bavarian *Mannheimer Abend-Zeitung* but was expelled from there and went to Paris. He contributed to the *DFJB* (which is not mentioned in *MEW*) and subsequently became co-editor with Heinrich Börnstein of *Vorwärts*, the famous radical German-language newspaper in Paris. Bernays, who was almost certainly of Jewish origin (he also sported the name of Lazarus), was closely associated with Marx and Engels in Paris, but fell out with Marx in 1847 and with Engels in 1848. After the revolution of 1848 he emigrated to America but does not appear to have become involved with the socialist movement there (see M. Hillquit, *History of Socialism in the United States*, 5th ed., New York, 1971). He appears to

have been a witty, able, but very unstable character, somewhat manic-depressive and only moderately serious in his politics; see Engels's description of him in *MEW*, 27, pp. 78–9, and Boris Nicolaievsky and Otto Maenchen-Helfen, *Karl Marx: Man and Fighter*, pp. 76, 88, 90, 91

26   Feuerbach's letter dated June 1843 is of interest only because he discussed the problem of Theory and Praxis in one short paragraph (in a way, the famous Thesis XI of Marx's *Theses on Feuerbach* is a reply to this letter). Feuerbach adopted a position here which is not unlike that of Bruno Bauer when he argued that Theory is that which 'is only in my head' while Praxis is that which 'occupies many heads'. Hence Praxis involved no more than spreading awareness among the masses

27   For details see *Karl Marx: Man and Fighter*, p. 76

28   See also chapter V above

29   These were republished in T. Zlocisti (ed.), *Moses Hess: sozialistische Aufsätze 1841–1847*, Berlin, 1921, pp. 87–97

30   See esp. p. 121. Both Hess and Engels heavily relied on and referred to Feuerbach in their respective attacks on religion

31   Engels wrote to Marx in October 1844 that, while his Carlyle essay had made him famous amongst the 'masses', his article on political economy had been read by very few people (see *MEW*, 27, p. 6). This essay was intended to be the first of a series to be published in the *DFJB*. Subsequent instalments were published in *Vorwärts* between August and October 1844 (see *MEW*, 1, pp. 550–92)

32   These reviews were also published in *MEW*, 1, pp. 347–77

33   See Marx's 'Programmentwurf' for the first issue (preserved in MS. form as Document A6 of the Marx Nachlass in the Institute for Social History in Amsterdam) in which he recorded his plans for reviewing 'literature on French and German politics'. There is no mention of Bauer's 'Die Judenfrage'

34   Note again the similarity with Hess's views on political economy

35   F. Mehring, *Karl Marx*, London, 1936, p. 82

36   *DFJB*, p. 33. For the sake of brevity, I have summarised the two stories

37   See W. Fischer, 'Staat und Gesellschaft Badens in Vormärz', in W. Conze (ed.), *Staat und Gesellschaft im deutschen Vormärz*, 2nd ed., Stuttgart, 1970, pp. 143–71. Trefurt, according to Fischer, was known only for the frequency with which he changed his mind; Itzstein was a leading advocate of a free economy without any form of state intervention. The names in italics are mentioned in Bernays's account

38   Many of these details are hinted at in Bernay's polemic. They are incomprehensible to a modern reader without the background information which I have added

39   See K. Grünwald, 'Europe's railways and Jewish enterprise'; Rahel Liebeschütz, 'The wind of change: letters of two generations', *LBIYB*, 12, 1967, pp. 163–209 (esp. pp. 207–8), 227–56 (esp. p. 243) respectively; A. Kohut, *Berühmte Israelitische Männer und Frauen*, Leipzig, 1901, vol. 2, pp. 387–8

40   See E. Andrew, 'Marx and the Jews', *European Judaism*, 3 (1), 1968, pp. 9–14; G. Mayer, 'Early German socialism and Jewish emancipation',

Jew. Soc. Stud., 1, 1939, pp. 409–22; D. Scholz, 'Politische und menschliche Emanzipation', *Geschichte in Wissenschaft und Unterricht*, 18 (1), 1967, pp. 1–16

41 'Contribution to the Critique of Hegel's Philosophy of Right', Bottomore, op. cit., p. 43

42 Bottomore, op. cit., p. 7

43 ibid., p. 8

44 ibid., p. 9. For a full discussion of Marx's use of these three writers, see H. Hirsch, 'Marxiana judaica', *Cahiers de l'Institut de Science Économique Appliquée*, série 7, 1963, pp. 5–52, esp. pp. 6–19

45 Bottomore, op. cit., p. 9

46 ibid., p. 10

47 ibid.

48 ibid., pp. 15–16

49 Shlomo Avineri, 'Marx and Jewish emancipation', *Journal of the History of Ideas*, 25 (3), 1964, pp. 445–50; McLellan, *MbM*, p. 141

50 Bottomore, op. cit., p. 16

51 ibid., p. 17

52 ibid., pp. 19–20; note how all the characteristics of a Christian state as described here demonstrate the integration of religion into the formal social control functions of the state

53 ibid., p. 8

54 ibid., p. 29

55 Marx uses this issue differently and more effectively in the *Holy Family*; see pp. 180–1 below. S. Avineri ('Marx and Jewish emancipation', p. 449) rather gives the impression that Marx had selected this issue to support his arguments for Jewish political emancipation. In fact, however, he dealt with it because both Hermes and Bauer had quoted it in support of their arguments *against* Jewish emancipation

56 Bottomore, op. cit., pp. 9–10

57 ibid., pp. 10–11

58 ibid., p. 12

59 Bottomore, op. cit., p. 13. Apart from the obvious Feuerbachian source of this conception, it is tempting to speculate that Marx might also have been influenced by Moses Mendelssohn's 'Morgenstunden' (esp. chap. 10), in which a sequence 'Idealist-Egoist-Gemeinsinn' is discussed; see *Moses Mendelssohn's Schriften*, ed. Moritz Brasch, Leipzig, 1880, vol. 1, esp. pp. 370–4

60 Bottomore, op. cit., p. 14

61 ibid., p. 15

62 ibid., p. 22

63 ibid., p. 26

64 ibid., pp. 26–7

65 ibid., p. 28

66 ibid., pp. 29–30

67 ibid., p. 31

68 The second essay, a review of 'Die Fähigkeit der heutigen Juden und Christen frei zu werden' (Bottomore, op. cit., pp. 32–40), is so short that

page references will not be given. In this section, I have used the translations of Bottomore, of Easton and Guddat (eds), *Writings of the Young Marx on Philosophy and Society*, New York, 1967, as well as my own, to convey Marx's style as effectively as possible

69 The concept of commerce as an informal means of social control and, therefore, as an instrument of power, is made explicit here

70 McLellan, *MbM*, p. 142

71 Trans. George Eliot, New York and London, 1957, p. 32

72 See S. Avineri, 'Marx and Jewish emancipation'; McLellan, *MbM*, pp. 141–2. Avineri described the version in the *Holy Family* as evidence that Marx, though anti-Jewish, nevertheless strongly defended the demand for Jewish emancipation. McLellan quotes this version in support of his assertion that, since Marx supported the demand for Jewish emancipation, it would be 'incorrect' to describe him as anti-semitic

73 Both Lenin and Plekhanov stressed this, and it has become the accepted view of the Marxist-Leninist Institute in Moscow: see N. I. Lapin, *Der junge Marx im Spiegel der Literatur*, Berlin, 1965, pp. 23–9, 46–7 (originally published in Russian in Moscow in 1962) and *MEW*, 1, Introduction and p. 604. Lenin and Plekhanov might possibly have assigned less importance to the *DFJB* had Marx's 'Economic and Philosophical Manuscripts' of 1844 been available to them

74 In view of Heinrich Heine's later criticisms of the approaches to Judaism suggested by Marx, it seems very probable to me that he exerted some influence on Marx, while they were in contact in Paris, to reconsider the intemperate tone of his essays in the *DFJB*; see p. 189 below

75 References are to the English translation, *Holy Family*, Moscow, 1956. The 'first campaign' is on pp. 117–21, the second on pp. 127–33 and the third on pp. 143–59

76 ibid., p. 118

77 ibid., p. 119

78 ibid., p. 128. That Marx was concerned about this can be seen also from recurrence of this issue in *German Ideology*, Moscow, 1964, pp. 118, 677

79 *Holy Family*, pp. 130–1

80 While Bauer's essay provoked a large number of newspaper articles and books, especially from Jewish critics, Marx's essays, because very few of them reached Germany, produced only one single anonymous review in the *Israelit des neunzehnten Jahrhunderts*, 5, 1844, pp. 258–9. For discussion of this review see p. 188 below

81 *Holy Family*, esp. p. 139

82 ibid., p. 144

83 ibid., p. 146

84 See, e.g., D. Runes (ed.), *Karl Marx: a World without Jews*

85 *German Ideology*, p. 224

86 It is precisely because his first essays can easily be interpreted as a call to eliminate *Jews* that I believe Marx wanted to correct that impression in this version

87 *Holy Family*, p. 146

88 Bruno Bauer, 'Die Judenfrage', Brunswick, 1843, p. 42; 'Die Fähigkeit',

in *Einundzwanzig Bogen aus der Schweiz*, ed. G. Herwegh, Zürich and Winterthur, 1843, p. 57

89 Bottomore, op. cit., p. 38
90 ibid., p. 29 (my italics)
91 *German Ideology*, p. 195
92 *Holy Family*, p. 148
93 Bottomore, op. cit., p. 34
94 *Holy Family*, p. 147
95 Bottomore, op. cit., p. 34
96 *Holy Family*, p. 148
97 ibid.
98 ibid., p. 149
99 ibid., p. 150
100 ibid., p. 153
101 Bottomore, op. cit., p. 6
102 *Holy Family*, p. 154
103 ibid., p. 156
104 ibid.
105 ibid.
106 ibid., p. 157
107 ibid., p. 158
108 *German Ideology*, p. 259
109 Bottomore, op. cit., p. 20

Chapter IX   The Quest for a Jewish-Socialist Synthesis

1 Although Engels wrote to Marx from Germany in October 1844 (i.e. eight months after publication of the *DJFB*) that 'the *Jahrbücher* are still being snatched up', *MEW*, 27, p. 6
2 *Israelit des neunzehnten Jahrhunderts*, 5, 1844, pp. 258–9
3 Early in April 1844, i.e. within a few weeks of the publication of the *DFJB*, *Der Orient* carried two items in its 'Personal and Miscellany' (5, 1844, p. 120). The first, which listed publications for and against Jews, included, 'against non-talmudic Jews, Marx in Vol. 1 of *DFJB*'. The second item reported: 'Dr. Marx, former member of the *Rheinische Zeitung*, is said to have expressed himself on the Jews in *DFJB* (Vol. 1, Paris, 1844) in the manner of B. Bauer'. The same column in the following year (6, 1845, p. 144), reported on recent publications: 'Dr. Marx on the Jewish Question (previously in *DFJB* by Ruge and Marx, Strassburg and Zürich [?], 1844) and *The Holy Family or Critique of Critical Critique: Against Bruno Bauer and Associates* by F. Engels and Karl Marx. 22 sheets. 1 RThlr. (Frankfurt am Main Literatur Anstalt 1845)'
4 Letter to Löwenthal, 9 May 1845, *MEW*, 27, p. 436
5 *Confessio Judaica*, Berlin, 1925, p. 181
6 *Heines Werke*, Berlin and Weimar, 1968, vol. 5, p. 354
7 ibid., p. 340
8 ibid., p. 352

9 ibid., pp. 10, 352; this preface was written in 1852
10 ibid., p. 355
11 ibid., p. 360; note Heine's emphasis on Moses in marked contrast to Marx's refusal to discuss him
12 ibid., p. 361
13 Exod. 2:15–6
14 Hebrew version of 'Moses, our teacher', the traditional manner in which Moses is referred to in religious Judaism
15 *Heines Werke*, pp. 361–2
16 ibid., p. 357
17 ibid., pp. 354–5
18 ibid., p. 359
19 ibid., pp. 359–60
20 ibid., pp. 358–9
21 When he wrote his *Confessions*, Heine had of course the additional advantage of having read the *Communist Manifesto* and subsequent publications
22 ibid., p. 357
23 A reference to an attempt by the ruling clergy of Cologne in 1510 CE to destroy the Talmud and other Hebrew books, which was prevented by Reuchlin
24 ibid., pp. 357–8
25 Hess belongs to that group of socialists who offered a positive solution to the Jewish question
26 The main targets of the attack against 'German' or 'true' socialism were Moses Hess and Karl Grün (*Manifesto of the Communist Party*, Moscow, 1952 ed., repr. 1969, pp. 82–6). Even Franz Mehring thought that the attack was 'exaggerated in point of fact and quite unjust as far as the persons were concerned', see *Karl Marx: the Story of his Life*, London, 1936, pp. 112, 114, 135
27 *Rom und Jerusalem: die letzte Nationalitätsfrage* was published in 1862 in Leipzig by Eugen Wangler. I have used the text in H. Lademacher's *Moses Hess: ausgewählte Schriften*, Cologne, 1962, pp. 223–63, and M. Waxman's translation, originally published in 1918 and reissued in New York in 1943. References will be to this translation, which I have adapted occasionally to bring it closer to Hess's style (hereafter *RJ*). As a matter of interest, Hess called his study *Rom und Jerusalem* because he was inspired by Garibaldi's fight to free Rome from papal government, He may possibly have been aware of a call for a Protestant attack on Rome coupled with a restoration of the Jews to Palestine which was made ten years earlier; see A. Capadose, *Rome en Jeruzalem*, Utrecht, 1851
28 A notable exception is Jochanan Bloch, 'Moses Hess: Rom und Jerusalem: jüdische und menschliche emanzipation', *Kölner Zeitschrift für Soziologie und sozial Psychologie*, 16 (2), 1964, pp. 288–313. This was subsequently published as chapter 2 in Bloch's *Judentum in der Krise*, Göttingen, 1966. Bloch writes from the standpoint of a Jewish nationalist and deals specifically with some aspects of Hess's response to Marx's essays 'On the Jewish Question'

29 See E. Silberner, *Moses Hess*, Leiden, 1966, p. 441
30 I. Berlin, *The Life and Opinions of Moses Hess*, p. 47. Although Marx was somewhat contemptuous towards Hess (as he was towards most of the men he knew), Hess appears to be one of the very few figures in Marx's life for whom he retained a lifelong affection, even though they fell out in 1848 and Hess subsequently irritated Marx on a number of occasions. Silberner has suggested (*Sozialisten zur Judenfrage*, pp. 135–6) that Marx had probably seen *Rom und Jerusalem*, although he would have rejected its main thesis partly because he felt that he had 'solved' the Jewish question and partly because he felt a general contempt for the national aspirations of all small nations. Yet, even when Marx is most irascible and vulgar, he is almost courteous towards Hess. Thus in a letter to Engels (3 February 1865, *Marx–Engels: Selected Correspondence*, Moscow, 1965, pp. 160–1), in which Lassalle is referred to as 'Baron Itzig', the Countess of Hatzfeldt as 'the old bitch', Bismarck as 'Pissmark' and Eduard Einhorn as 'Rabbi Ein-horn', and even though Hess was the immediate cause of Marx's irritation, he remained 'Moses Hess' or 'Moses' in the letter. In what were, for Marx, unusually warm letters to Sibylle Hess after Moses's death, Marx spoke of him as 'our deceased friend' and 'our immortal friend' (*verstorben-verewigt*); see letters of 25 October and 29 November 1877, *Moses Hess: Briefwechsel*, The Hague, 1959, pp. 642, 643, Whatever Marx's views, therefore, he appears to have retained his regard for Hess
31 *RJ*, p. 40. Although the biological concept of race, which ultimately led to Hitler's extreme concepts, were beginning to be asserted at the time that *Rom und Jerusalem* was published (e.g. J. A. de Gobineau published his *Essai sur l'inégalité des races humaines* in Paris between 1853 and 1855), Hess used the concept very differently. He clearly visualised an ethno-cultural grouping which was important not because it established superior-inferior gradations, but because it highlighted differences in custom and tradition; in fact he explicitly rejected the 'blood' concept of race; see *RJ*, p. 116
32 ibid., p. 226
33 Berlin, op. cit., p. 32. See also Helmut Hirsch, 'Tribun und Prophet', *International Review of Social History*, 2 (2), 1957. Lenin once wrote, albeit in another context: 'Nowadays, no one, thank God, believes in miracles. Prophecies are fairy-tales. But it is a fact that there are scientific predictions'; V. I. Lenin, *Marx–Engels–Marxismus*, Moscow, n.d., p. 519. Hence, if Hess's predictions have been proved to be correct, this would be an argument that he was 'scientific'
34 *RJ*, p. 80
35 ibid., p. 225
36 T. B. Bottomore, *Karl Marx: Early Writings*, London, 1963, p. 34
37 *RJ*, p. 55
38 ibid., p. 126
39 ibid., p. 162
40 ibid., p. 172; as did Heine
41 Bottomore, op. cit., p. 36
42 *RJ*, p. 48

43 Bottomore, op. cit., p. 36
44 *RJ*, p. 48
45 ibid., p. 52
46 Bottomore, op. cit., p. 36
47 *Holy Family*, Moscow, 1956, p. 147
48 *RJ*, p. 116
49 ibid., p. 125
50 ibid., p. 131
51 ibid., p. 165
52 ibid.
53 ibid., p. 91
54 *Manifesto*, p. 86
55 *RJ*, p. 120. This exchange was also noted by Bloch, op. cit., p. 313 (in the 1966 book, p. 74 n.). Although Hess was critical of some of Marx's work, he retained his high regard for him and for Marxian theory. Disputes between the two, as far as Hess was concerned, arose more from the activities of Marx's circle than from any theoretical disagreements; see *Hess: Briefwechsel*, esp. p. 157: 'I would like to keep as much contact as possible with you personally, but I do not want to have any further dealings with your party' (Hess to Marx, May 1846). There is no justification for I. Meszaros's contemptuous comments that 'Marx's immense works . . . not only did not in the least impress . . . Moses Hess but succeeded only in arousing his narrow-minded hostility' (*Marx's Theory of Alienation*, London, 1970, p. 76)
56 It is unlikely to be coincidental that much of the literature on Marxism/ socialism and nationality is by Jewish authors: e.g. Ber Borochov, 'The national question and the class struggle' (1905), in A. G. Duker (ed.), *Nationalism and the Class Struggle*, New York, 1937; Otto Bauer, *Die Nationalitätenfrage und die Sozialdemokratie*, Vienna, 1907; C. Zhitlowsky, *Der Sotzialism un di Natzionale Frage*, Warsaw, 1935; Solomon F. Bloom, *The World of Nations: a Study of the National Implications in the Work of Karl Marx*, New York, 1941. Lenin's articles on the subject are almost devoid of theoretical content and are concerned mainly with practical political questions of the day; see *Lenin on the National and Colonial Questions*, Peking, 1967. As a general problem, the subject of nationality in relation to Marxism lies beyond the scope of this book
57 A. L. Patkin, *The Origins of the Russian-Jewish Labor Movement*, Melbourne and London, 1947, p. 231. This meant less direct knowledge of Marx's original work and more of Plekhanov–Axelrod–Lenin interpretations (ibid., p. 112)
58 *Essays on Nationalism, Class Struggle and the Jewish People*, London, 1971, p. 4
59 In *The Poverty of Philosophy*
60 Borochov, *Essays*, p. 6
61 ibid., p. 10
62 ibid., p. 7
63 ibid., p. 63
64 'The national question and the class struggle', p. 83

65 ibid., p. 77. In addition to common cultural values, Borochov also stipulated a common historic past and used both these factors to argue against generalised territorialism (i.e., settling Jews 'somewhere, anywhere'), and for Jewish resettlement in Palestine

66 See the Introduction by A. G. Duker to *Nationalism and the Class Struggle*, p. 33

Chapter X Marxist Solutions to the Jewish Problem

1 *Die Nationalitätenfrage und die Sozialdemokratie*, Vienna, 1907, pp. 366–81. For a fuller discussion of Bauer on the Jews, see E. Silberner, *Sozialisten zur Judenfrage*, pp. 240–5

2 Bauer, op. cit., p. 368

3 ibid., p. 373

4 ibid., p. 376

5 Borochov, 'The national question and the class struggle', in A. G. Duker (ed.), *Nationalism and the Class Struggle*, New York, 1937, pp. 75–83

6 Bauer, op. cit., p. 378

7 *Lenin on the National and Colonial Questions*, Peking, 1967, p. 6

8 A. L. Patkin, *The Origins of the Russian-Jewish Labor Movement*, Melbourne and London, 1947, p. 44

9 Patkin, op. cit., pp. 43–4. The name of the associations has a distinctly bourgeois flavour, because the social conflict between employer and employee was free of the class concept that later Marxist theory was to add to it

10 T. B. Bottomore, *Karl Marx: Early Writings*, London, 1963, p. 43

11 Short for the General Jewish Workers' Union in Lithuania, Poland and Russia. The history of the Bund is too vast and complex to be dealt with here in any detail. It has its own very substantial literature, only some of which need be mentioned, especially since most of it is in Yiddish. An excellent short account is contained in H. M. Sachar's *The Course of Modern Jewish History*, London, 1958, chap. 14, esp. pp. 289–96. Patkin, op. cit., contains much important data on the relationship of the Bund to Marxism. E. Mendelsohn's *Class Struggle in the Pale*, London, 1970, also contains much important background material. Vol. 5 of Dubnow's *History of the Jews*, London, 1973, has a great deal of detail, esp. from p. 702 onwards, and his *Nationalism and History*, Philadelphia, 1958, is important in relation to the 'cultural autonomy' concept which influenced the Bund. Yiddish publications I have consulted include G. Aaronson et al., *Die Geschichte fun Bund*, 2 vols, New York, 1962, and J. S. Hertz (ed.), *Doires Bundistn*, 2 vols, New York, 1956. A more recent study is H. J. Tobias, *The Jewish Bund in Russia: from its Origins to 1905*, Stanford, 1972

12 Mendelsohn has explained the predominance of Jews amongst Russian radical intellectuals by their inability to obtain academic or civil service posts after graduation; op. cit., p. 29

13 ibid., p. 33

14 For a detailed account of the disintegration of the Bund in Russia, see Z. Y. Gitelman, *Jewish Nationality and Soviet Politics*, Princeton, 1972
15 Quoted by Walter Laqueur, 'Zionism, the Marxist critique and the left', in I. Howe and C. Gershman (eds), *Israel, the Arabs and the Middle East*, p. 19
16 Quoted by J. L. Talmon, *Israel Among the Nations*, London, 1970, pp. 45–6
17 See Israel Getzler, *Martov: a Political Biography of a Russian Social Democrat*, Melbourne and London, 1967, esp. pp. 26–8, 46–8, 59–61
18 J. S. Hertz (compiler), *The Jewish Labor Bund: a Pictorial History 1897–1957* (English and Yiddish), New York, 1959, p. 183
19 Otto Heller, *Der Untergang des Judentums*, p. 16
20 Abram Léon, *The Jewish Question: a Marxist Interpretation*, p. 66
21 Trotsky does not appear to have been interested in the Jewish question, which in his view would be solved, along with all other social questions, by the revolution of the international proletariat. Although opposed to Zionism, he may have become somewhat less hostile to Jewish nationalism after the rise of Hitler. See *Leon Trotsky on the Jewish Question*, New York, 1970, esp. pp. 22, 18; I. Deutscher, *The Prophet Outcast*, London, 1970, p. 369. For a detailed discussion of Trotsky's views and attitudes to Jews, see Joseph Nedava's *Trotsky and the Jews*, Philadelphia, 1972
22 Laqueur, 'Zionism, the Marxist critique and the left', p. 33. W. F. Albright (*From the Stone Age to Christianity*, 2nd ed., Baltimore, 1957) described another Marxist attempt to deduce the existence of capitalism in the biblical period of the Judges by M. Lurje (1927), based on a distorted philological analysis of a single Hebrew word and also records the subsequent liquidation of Lurje after the Zinoviev trial in 1936 (p. 91). Nevertheless Heller represented what was, in his time, the recognised Soviet view on the Jewish question; see J. Miller's excellent paper, 'Soviet theory on the Jew', in L. Kochan (ed.), *The Jews in Soviet Russia since 1917*, 2nd ed., London, 1972, esp. pp. 51–3
23 op. cit., p. 16
24 ibid., pp. 16–17
25 ibid., pp. 23–9
26 ibid., p. 36
27 ibid., p. 36; Léon, op. cit., p. 89
28 Heller, op. cit., p. 48
29 ibid., pp. 54–7
30 ibid., p. 77
31 ibid., p. 103
32 ibid., p. 22
33 Heller devoted half his book to a description of the Russian experiment
34 Heller, op. cit., p. 83
35 ibid., p. 125
36 ibid., p. 150
37 ibid., p. 147; a lengthy 'reply' to Heller's book was published by Eli Strauss, *Geht das Judentum unter?*, Vienna, 1933
38 *Are the Jews a Race?*, London, 1926, though Heller does not apparently share his view that Jews are revolutionary whilst Judaism is reactionary

39 *The Jews and Modern Capitalism*, New York, 1962. For a discussion of Sombart, see p. 227 f. below
40 Léon, op. cit., pp. 180–1
41 *The Origins of Totalitarianism*, 3rd ed., London, 1967, p. 15; she argued that wealth and power can be maintained and will be accepted—only wealth without power, i.e. a socially non-functional wealth, is threatened
42 op. cit., p. 66
43 ibid., p. 69
44 ibid., p. 74
45 ibid., p. 75; this may possibly be a reply to Moses Hess's thesis that race struggle is primary to class struggle
46 ibid., p. 81
47 ibid., p. 87
48 ibid., p. 117
49 ibid., pp. 118–19
50 ibid., p. 121
51 ibid., p. 122
52 ibid., p. 137
53 ibid., p. 141
54 ibid., esp. pp. 152–3; he does not explain why Jews were readmitted
55 ibid., pp. 195–209
56 ibid., p. 210; Léon was probably unaware that Bruno Bauer and Marx would have characterised this kind of reasoning as pure 'Jesuitism'
57 ibid., p. 224
58 'capitalism has managed to channelise the anti-capitalist consciousness of the masses into a form that antedates capitalism'; ibid., p. 237
59 'Capitalist decay [is the] basis for the growth of Zionism', ibid., p. 249
60 ibid., p. 255; this is the classic Trotskyist thesis
61 ibid., p. 256; Léon completes a full circle here, for Zionism is also regarded as 'an ideological excrescence' by the extreme right in Judaism (e.g. the Neturei Karta in Jerusalem), because it re-established the Jewish State without waiting for the Messiah
62 ibid., p. 257
63 ibid., pp. 259, 261
64 ibid., p. 263
65 For an account of Biro-Bidjan see C. Abramsky, 'The Biro-Bidzhan project, 1927–1959', in L. Kochan (ed.), op. cit.

Chapter XI Marx and the Sociologists

1 Max Weber, *Ancient Judaism* (hereafter *AJ*), Chicago, 1952, p. 425 n. 1
2 e.g. Abram Léon, *The Jewish Question*; Otto Heller, *Der Untergang des Judentums*
3 A. Giddens, *Capitalism and Modern Social Theory*, Cambridge, 1971, p. 185; N. Birnbaum, 'Conflicting interpretations of the rise of capitalism: Marx and Weber', *Brit. J. Sociol.*, 4, 1953, pp. 125–41, esp. p. 127
4 *AJ*, loc. cit.

5   *The Protestant Ethic and the Spirit of Capitalism* (hereafter *PE*), London, 1930, p. 39
6   *PE*, p. 57
7   The literature on the subject is seemingly endless. See for example S. N. Eisenstadt (ed.), *The Protestant Ethic and Modernisation*, New York, 1968 (especially the editor's introductory essay and those of S. Andreski and E. Fischoff); R. W. Green (ed.), *Protestantism and Capitalism*, Lexington, 1959; M. J. Kitch (ed.), *Capitalism and the Reformation*, London, 1967
8   'The status of the Jews in the middle ages considered from the standpoint of commercial policy', *Historia Judaica*, 6, 1944, pp. 13–26; the paper was originally published in 1875
9   Marcus Arkin has put forward a substantially similar thesis in a more recent paper, 'West European Jewry in the age of mercantilism', *Historia Judaica*, 22, 1960, pp. 85–104
10 *PE*, p. 165; 'Modern capitalism', in S. N. Eisenstadt (ed.), *Max Weber on Charisma and Institution Building* (hereafter *C&I*), Chicago, 1968, pp. 156–7
11 *AJ*, chap. 13
12 H. H. Gerth and C. Wright Mills (eds), *From Max Weber: Essays in Sociology* (hereafter *FMW*), London, 1948, p. 267
13 *PE*, p. 187
14 Max Weber, *The Sociology of Religion* (1922) (hereafter *SR*), London, 1966, pp. 259, 261. This is of course a problem inherent in a great deal of the literature on Jews and would not require special comment here did it not stand in such marked contrast to Weber's otherwise methodical and meticulous habit of defining and clarifying his terms. The difficulty lies precisely in the underlying assumptions of any given writer. For example, René König argued that 'Jude ist wer sich als Jude weiss' ('a Jew is he who knows himself to be a Jew'), *Studien zur Soziologie*, Fischer, Frankfurt a/M, 1971, p. 127, yet on p. 129 he describes Karl Marx—the man who denied his Jewishness all his life—as 'a Jewish social philosopher'
15 I am not suggesting that this is necessarily intended to be derogatory on Weber's part. In a well-known speech about his greatly admired friend and colleague in Heidelberg, Georg Jellinek, who, though the son of a famous rabbi, was himself baptised, Weber referred to his 'legacy of oriental wisdom from his forebears'; Marianne Weber, *Max Weber: ein Lebensbild*, Tübingen, 1926, p. 520
16 *SR*, p. 261. A similar comment occurs in *PE*, p. 270, where Weber talked of the leaders of the Educational Alliance in the United States americanising Jewish immigrants 'on a grand scale and with astonishing success' by 'emancipation from the second commandment' (of the decalogue). This statement, which is again alluded to in *SR*, seems to me to be quite nonsensical. There is also no evidence that Reform Jews in America received preferential treatment at any level over religious Jews
17 R. König and J. Winckelmann (eds), *Max Weber zum Gedächtnis*, Cologne, 1964, esp. pt 1, section 6
18 See H. H. Gerth's and D. Martindale's Introduction to *AJ*, pp. xxiii–xxv; S. W. Baron, *A Social and Religious History of the Jews*, vol. 1, New York,

1952, p. 297. On the whole, Weber has not attracted a great deal of interest from Jewish scholars (unlike Sombart). Ignaz Schipper has sharply attacked his *Ancient Judaism*, in which he finds value only in the analysis of the covenant and the concept of the Israel confederacy; 'Max Weber on the sociological basis of the Jewish religion', *Jew. J. Sociol.*, 1, 1959, pp. 250–61. Toni Oelsner, in an exceptionally well documented but highly critical paper, has discussed Roscher, Weber and Sombart, though he seems to me to be excessively severe in his strictures of Weber; see 'The place of the Jews in economic history as viewed by German scholars', *LBIYB*, 7, 1962, pp. 183–212. A more sympathetic review of Weber is Hans Liebeschütz's 'Max Weber's historical interpretation of Judaism', *LBIYB*, 9, 1964, pp. 41–68. This paper also forms chap. 10 of Liebeschütz's *Das Judentum im deutschen Geschichtsbild von Hegel bis Max Weber*, Tübingen, 1967. Only Christian scholars have adopted the Weberian approach to early Jewish history; see H. Tadmor, in H. H. Ben Sasson and S. Ettinger, *Jewish Society through the Ages*, London, 1969, p. 48

19 *FMW*, p. 134 ('abandon all hope . . .'). As in the case of 'assimilated' Jews in Germany, Weber expressed no opinion on these issues, though in this instance he may have had in mind Georg Simmel, who, notwithstanding his renown as a scholar and direct intervention by Weber, was refused a professorship for thirty years because he was a Jew. Simmel died in the year that these comments were made by Weber

20 ibid., p. 156. The issue of Jewish exclusiveness in Weber's work becomes even more confused when we look at his assertion: 'In the case of the Jews . . . communal relationships [exist] only to a relatively small extent; indeed Jews often repudiate the existence of a Jewish "community"', *The Theory of Social and Economic Organisation* (1947), Chicago, 1964, p. 138

21 The main formulation is in *AJ*, pp. 336–45. It is also referred to in *PE*, p. 271, *C&I*, p. 157, *SR*, p. 250, and in a discussion of Jewish sacred law which, for Weber, is remarkably superficial; see M. Rheinstein (ed.), *Max Weber on Law in Economy and Society*, Cambridge, Mass., 1966, p. 244

22 See J. Katz, *Exclusiveness and Tolerance*, Oxford, 1961, p. 56, and the important studies by S. Stein: 'The laws on interest in the Old Testament', *J. Theol. Stud.*, n.s., 4, 1953, pp. 161–70; 'The development of the Jewish law on interest from the biblical period to the expulsion of the Jews from England', *Historia Judaica*, 17, 1955, pp. 3–40; 'Interest taken by Jews from Gentiles', *J. Semit. Stud.*, 1, 1956, pp. 141–63; Léon Poliakov, *Jewish Bankers and the Holy See*, London, 1978, esp. chap. II

23 We need only look at the remarkable way in which Jewish activity reflected the dominant interests of their *environment* to recognise this. For example Arab Spain's interest in mathematics, medicine and poetry, medieval Germany's preoccupation with moralistic books, and nineteenth-century Germany's fascination for philosophy were all faithfully reflected among their Jewish communities, no matter how thick the walls of the ghetto; see M. Lowenthal, *The Jews of Germany*, London, 1939, pp. 102–7

24 Benjamin Nelson's devotion to Weber does not really obscure the fact

that his book underlines how ideal-typical Jewish ethic was posited against a somewhat idealised-typical Puritanism; see *The Idea of Usury*, 2nd ed., Chicago, 1969

25 See C. B. Sherman, *The Jew within American Society*, Detroit, 1965, p. 6. Puritans were hostile to other Christian sects as well as to Jews; L. Wirth, *The Ghetto*, Chicago, 1956, pp. 133 ff.

26 *AJ*, p. 343

27 This attitude is closely mirrored by some Christian scholars. The Church Father Ambrosius of the fourth century for example held that the Jew should be burdened by usury so severely that it would compel him to adopt the 'true' faith; see S. Stein, *Historica Judaica*, 1955, p. 33

28 For details, see the papers by S. Stein in n. 22

29 Tractate Baba Metziah, 71a

30 Tractate Makkoth

31 S. Stein, *Historia Judaica*, 17, 1955, p. 19

32 ibid., p. 22

33 Quoted in ibid., p. 24; see also M. Hoffmann, *Der Geldhandel der deutschen Juden während des Mittelalters*, Leipzig, 1910, esp. p. 83

34 J. J. Rabinowitz (ed.), *The Code of Maimonides. Book 13: The Book of Civil Laws*, New Haven, 1949, p. 93

35 Stein, *Historia Judaica*, 17, 1955, p. 27, and e.g. Lowenthal, op. cit., p. 116

36 Stein, *Historia Judaica*, 17, 1955, p. 30. The need for fairness and reciprocity rather than exclusiveness is also conveyed by an interesting comment on Deut. 23:20 in *Sefer Hachinuch* (*Book of Education*—a thirteenth-century commentary on all biblical laws, in Hebrew): 'If a heathen borrows money on interest from an Israelite—even if he then converts to Judaism, he must pay the interest up to the time of his conversion, so that it should not be said that he converted to avoid paying the interest'. The ruling is based on Tractate Baba Metziah, 72a

37 S. Stein, *J. Semit. Stud.*, 1, 1965, pp. 148–9

38 ibid., pp. 153–4

39 ibid., p. 157

40 Lowenthal, op. cit., p. 169

41 Leon da Modena (1571–1648), though the authorship is under dispute; see Stein, *J. Theol. Stud.*, 4, 1953, pp. 162–4. Stein takes the view that this revolutionary approach, which in its way is as radical as Calvin's interpretation of the Deuteronomic text, could not be published among Jews until the nineteenth century, but it seems to me that it is no more than an attempt to make explicit what had in fact been happening to Jewish approaches in a continuous development

42 *AJ*, p. 343

43 Lowenthal, op. cit., p. 212 (see also p. 54 above)

44 James Parkes, *The Jew in the Medieval Community*, London, 1938, pp. 387, 382

45 *AJ*, p. 344

46 Karl Marx, *Capital*, London, 1970, vol. 1, p. 753

47 *AJ*, p. 345

48 In the Talmud, the Roman emperor Hadrian is the typical anti-semite—

he executed a Jew for daring to salute him and another subsequently for passing him without saluting him

49 SR, p. 259
50 Karl Löwith in a 'Nachwort' to Feuerbach's Das Wesen des Christentums, 3rd ed., 1849, reprinted Stuttgart, 1971, p. 527
51 AJ, p. 426
52 (Hereafter J &MC). The text I have used is the translation by M. Epstein, New York, 1962
53 ibid., p. 187
54 See Sombart's contribution in A. Landsberger (ed.), Judentaufen, Munich, 1912, p. 12
55 Although he loved quoting figures, Sombart saw no difficulty if these were not available. Thus 'millions' of Jews were forced to become wanderers (J &MC, p. 52), and while there were no figures to show the proportion of Jews in America, 'there must always have been a large number there' (p. 65). Again, although it was impossible to determine the true numbers of Jews in commerce and industry, this was of no consequence, because 'mere numbers are no criterion of the extent of influence' (p. 121). By 'genetic', Sombart meant the genesis of—i.e. historical—origins (pp. 28–9)
56 ibid., pp. 30–1
57 ibid., p. 199
58 ibid., p. 241
59 Even Ernst Troeltsch, who was indifferent to the subject of Jews, rejected Sombart's thesis because he overestimated the role of the Jews in the development of capitalism, ignored the influence of persecution of and on the Jews and oversimplified the whole issue by identifying Puritanism and Judaism; see his Protestantism and Progress (1912), Boston, 1958, p. 142. Jewish scholars are somewhat ambivalent towards Sombart. While recognising his 'complimentary' statements about Jews, they naturally reject his racial thesis; see H. M. Sachar, The Course of Modern Jewish History, London, 1958, p. 39; M. I. Dimont, Jews, God and History, New York, 1962, esp. p. 255
60 J &MC, p. 36. The idea was not of course new. Bruno Bauer refuted it in his 'Die Judenfrage' (Brunswick, 1843, pp. 5–6), where he rejected the suggestion that Spain declined because it expelled the Jews (as Sombart suggests), by arguing that the expulsion of the Jews was symptomatic of the steady decline of Spain
61 J &MC, p. 42
62 ibid., p. 52
63 ibid., pp. 57–8
64 ibid., p. 62
65 ibid., p. 77
66 ibid., p. 139
67 ibid., pp. 127–37. There is some confusion about the Jewish pariah status in Sombart. Later in the book (pp. 227–9) he argued like Weber that Jews created the ghetto because they wanted to live separately from others

68 ibid., pp. 144–5
69 ibid., pp. 153–6
70 ibid., p. 176
71 ibid., p. 316; cf. Bruno Bauer: 'in theory the Jew is deprived of political rights, while in practice he enjoys enormous power' (op. cit., p. 114), and Marx: 'The Jew has emancipated himself in a Jewish manner not only by acquiring the power of money, but also because money had become through him and also apart from him, a world power' (T. B. Bottomore, *Karl Marx: Early Writings*, London, 1963, p. 35)
72 *J&MC*, pp. 200–1; cf. Heine's remarks that Jews 'always presented the most marked contrast to neighbouring countries and peoples, who, with their sensuous, varied and fervent modes of worship, devoted their lives to a Bacchantic feast of the senses' (*Werke*, Berlin and Weimar, 1968, vol. 5, pp. 359–60)
73 Bottomore, op. cit., p. 43
74 ibid., p. 34, but see Sombart's reversal of his position (p. 231 below)
75 *J&MC*, p. 215
76 ibid., pp. 223–4
77 ibid., pp. 235–6
78 ibid., p. 243
79 ibid., pp. 242–52
80 ibid., p. 271
81 ibid., p. 279
82 ibid., p. 298
83 ibid., p. 299. Bauer described in similar vein how 'Christianity emerged when the manly spirit of Greek philosophy and classic culture in a weak moment mated with randy Judaism'; 'Die Fähigkeit', in G. Herwegh (ed.), *Einundzwanzig Bogen aus der Schweiz*, Zürich and Winterthur, 1843, p. 62
84 *J&MC*, pp. 303, 308
85 In a biographical note to *J&MC*, p. 386
86 'From Marx to Hitler', *AJR Information*, January 1963, p. 6
87 See the excerpt from the book in *Protestantism and Capitalism*, ed. R. W. Green, pp. 34, 38. In his 'Erinnerungen an Max Weber', Paul Honigsheim expressed himself quite explicitly about Sombart, whom he described as 'the Proteus of German social scientists', his ingratitude to Weber and his multiplicity of *Weltanschauungen*, in R. König and J. Winckelmann (eds), *Max Weber zum Gedächtnis*, Cologne, 1964, esp. p. 169
88 W. J. Cahnman and R. Heberle (eds), *Ferdinand Tönnies on Sociology*, Chicago, 1971, p. 310 (the paper was originally published in 1913)
89 The leading academics of the Institute of Social Research, established in association with the University of Frankfurt a/M in 1923, subsequently became famous as the Frankfurt School. For its history, see Martin Jay, *The Dialectical Imagination*, London, 1973, although it deals only with the period 1922–50. It therefore leaves open many important questions on which Horkheimer expressed himself more explicitly in later years. Since it is also concerned with all the members of the 'Institute' it does not make Horkheimer's position as explicit as one might wish. For an

excellent biographical study of Horkheimer, see H. Gumnior and R. Ringguth, *Max Horkheimer in Selbstzeugnissen und Bilddokumenten*, Reinbek b. Hamburg, 1973

90 As we shall see, the failure of the German proletariat in the 1930s, the experience of being a refugee, the conflict with the father, the role of the mother and the wife—all these are incorporated into theory. Thus Horkheimer criticised the use of the contraceptive pill because he thought it would destroy 'erotic love', which he regarded as valuable because of his experience of marriage; see *Die Sehnsucht nach dem ganz Anderen*, Hamburg, 1970, p. 73

91 ibid., p. 54

92 See for example R. König's scathing attack (in this case mainly on Adorno) on the 'actionless praxis', the 'notorious practical sterility' of the critical theorists whose work he described as *Vulgärmarxismus* and 'uncritical critique' in *Studien zur Soziologie*, p. 8. Jay (op. cit., p. 36) also notes that members of the Frankfurt School might have been 'more intimately involved in practical politics'

93 In 1960 Horkheimer wrote a bitter and incisive denunciation of the arrest and trial of Adolf Eichmann in Israel. In that article he sharply contrasts the action role of the politician (i.e. the government of Israel) with 'the philosopher who is not a practitioner' (i.e. himself); A. Schmidt (ed.), *Zur Kritik der instrumentellen Vernunft*, Frankfurt a/M, 1974, p. 320. It is also significant that Horkheimer did not publish the article until 1967 (see *Die Sehnsucht*, p. 47)

94 See especially Jay's detailed comments on the attitudes to their Jewish background of most of the Frankfurt School, op. cit., pp. 32-5

95 Max Horkheimer, *Kritische Theorie* (ed. A. Schmidt), 2nd ed., Frankfurt a/M, 1969, vol. I, p. 264

96 ibid., p. 234

97 ibid., p. 289

98 ibid., p. 292

99 ibid., p. 295

100 ibid., p. 294

101 ibid., pp. 297, 301

102 ibid., p. 365

103 ibid., pp. 303-4

104 ibid., pp. 366-7

105 ibid., pp. 370 ff.

106 Friedrich Heer, 'Jüdische Messianismen im 20 Jahrhundert: Probleme des jüdischen Marxismus', in *Die geistige Gestalt des heutigen Judentums*, Munich, 1969, p. 88

107 *Kritische Theorie*, vol. I, pp. 374-6

108 ibid., vol. 2, p. 58

109 ibid., p. 227

110 The well-known idea of the *ganz Anderes* of the Frankfurt School members is translated by Jay as 'entirely other'. Peter Berger also uses this concept as 'totally other' (*The Social Reality of Religion*, Penguin, 1973, p. 81), but in a more specifically theological sense. I have tried to express

the generalised nature of Horkheimer's use of this *Sehnsucht nach dem
ganz Anderen* by translating it freely, but I think more appropriately,
as 'the longing for something quite different' (after A. Otto's 'the
numinous')

111 Martin Heidegger, *Being and Time*, London, 1962. Peter Berger has also
stressed the influence of death as a source of religion, op. cit., esp. pp. 60,
87

112 op. cit., p. 37

113 *Zur Kritik der instrumentellen Vernunft*, pp. 216–28

114 Gumnior and Ringguth, op. cit., esp. pp. 13, 18

115 Jay, op. cit., esp. pp. 32, 35

116 Quoted by Jay, op. cit., p. 32, from *Dämmerung* which was published
under the pseudonym 'Heinrich Regius' in 1934 in Zürich

117 See for example M. Horkheimer and T. Adorno, *Dialektik der Aufklärung*,
Frankfurt a/M, 1969, pp. 226, 250, 262

118 See *Zeitschrift für Sozialforschung*, 8 (1–2), 1939, pp. 115–37. Jay (op. cit.,
p. 133) has described this essay as one of Horkheimer's 'most despairing'.
According to Ernst L. Ehrlich, Horkheimer refused to include this article
in the reissues published in the 1960s because of the harsh comments on
Jews in it; see *Allgemeine jüdische Wochenzeitung*, 29 (6), 8 February 1974,
p. 11

119 'Die Juden und Europa', p. 121

120 ibid., p. 131

121 *Ostjuden*: Horkheimer is here referring to the long-standing tension in
Germany between German Jews and those who migrated into Germany
from Russia and Poland. These Eastern Jews, the first victims of Nazi
hostility, were often described in German anti-semitic literature as the
real threat to Germany, not because they tended to be more religious
than German Jews, but because, numerically, they were thought to have
the potential to 'engulf' the Germanic spirit. In addition, they were also
often the bearers of socialist ideologies

122 'Elemente des Antisemitismus-Grenzen der Aufklärung', in *Dialektik der
Aufklärung*, pp. 128–217. There are seven theses. Löwenthal co-operated
in writing the first three. The final one was added in 1947. The main
parts were written in conjunction with the empirical studies of the
Institute. The main co-author is, of course, Adorno and it is impossible
to say to what extent each author was responsible for the views expressed
here. As Horkheimer himself described it: 'No outsider can imagine to
what extent we are jointly responsible for every sentence. Whole
sections were dictated together'; see Preface to the 1969 edition, p. ix.
I am, therefore, ascribing the views expressed to Horkheimer, even
though, in this instance, he may not necessarily have originated them

123 From Horkheimer's Preface to T. Adorno *et al.*, *The Authoritarian
Personality*, New York, 1964, vol. 1, p. ix

124 *Dialektik der Aufklärung*, p. 177

125 ibid., p. 178

126 ibid., pp. 179–81

127 ibid., pp. 182–3

NOTES TO PAGES 250-63
NOTES TO PAGES 250-63

128 ibid., pp. 185–8
129 ibid., pp. 188–96
130 ibid., pp. 196–209
131 See the Preface to the 2nd edition of *Dialektik der Aufklärung*, written in 1949, i.e. three years after the completion of the earlier texts
132 ibid., pp. 209–17
133 ibid., p. 7
134 A. Schmidt, *Zur Idee der kritischen Theorie: Elemente der Philosophie Max Horkheimers*, Munich, 1974, p. 52
135 'Sociological background of the psychoanalytic approach', in E. Simmel (ed.), *Anti-Semitism: a Social Disease*, New York, 1946, pp. 1–10, esp. pp. 4–5
136 In *Zur Kritik der instrumentellen Vernunft*, pp. 302–16
137 In his *Rom und Jerusalem*, 1862
138 The interviews were published with a long introduction by Gumnior in August 1970 after earlier excerpts had appeared in *Der Spiegel* in January 1970; see *Die Sehnsucht*
139 According to Gumnior (op. cit., p. 5), radical students and orthodox Marxists described the interviews as 'the confessions of a heretic on his deathbed'. This was not, of course, the first clash between Horkheimer and young activists. A. Schmidt (*Zur Idee der kritischen Theorie*, pp. 62–3) has drawn attention to the conflict which arose, particularly in 1968, over 'the careless instrumentalisation' of Horkheimer's theories by student activists. Horkheimer himself commented on this in 1968 when his early articles were reissued (see *Kritische Theorie*, vol. 1, New Preface, pp. xii–xiii) when he wrote: 'I am in sympathy with the young in their longing for something better, the right society, their reluctant adjustment to the *status quo*. I also share their reservations on schools and higher education. But I differ in the attitude to force—questionable democracies are always preferable to dictatorship, which any violent change must bring about'
140 *Die Sehnsucht*, pp. 60, 69–70
141 ibid., pp. 73, 80
142 ibid., pp. 88–9

Chapter XII   Marxist Apologists

1 Quoted by S. Ettinger, 'The origins of modern antisemitism', *Dispersion and Unity*, Jerusalem, no. 9, 1969, pp. 17–37, esp. p. 28; see also R. Rosdolsky, *Archiv für Sozialgeschichte*, 4, 1964, pp. 259–67, which is discussed on p. 271 f. below
2 See the sympathetic chapters 10 and 11 in Massing's brilliant book *Rehearsal for Destruction*
3 For the text of the letter, see Massing, op. cit., pp. 311–12. Note that in this letter the role of the Jew is equivalent to what Engels in his 'Umrisse' had called 'unscientific peddling'; *DFJB*, p. 86
4 Probably even Engels did not know that if Marx had been as aware of

NOTES TO PAGES 263-5

social realities as he was, he would have known that in 1843 when Marx wrote his essays, some Jewish workers were already protesting against their working conditions. See E. Mendelsohn, *Class Struggle in the Pale*, London, 1970, p. 27

5   For a fuller discussion of Engels's relationship with Jews and Judaism, see E. Silberner, 'Friedrich Engels and the Jews', *Jew. Soc. Stud.*, 11 (4), 1949, pp. 323-42. A slightly altered version of this paper forms Chap. 9 of *Sozialisten zur Judenfrage*. Silberner quotes Gustav Mayer, Engels's biographer, who stated that the Marx–Engels Institute in Moscow has a manuscript note of Engels 'on the Jew in Germany', which has not yet been released

6   Max Beer, *50 Years of International Socialism*, London, 1935, p. 72. The two main biographers of Eleanor do not devote much attention to her 'Jewishness': C. Tsuzuki, *The Life of Eleanor Marx, 1855-1898*, Oxford, 1967, and Y. Kapp, *Eleanor Marx: Family Life, 1855-1883*, London, 1972, though Miss Kapp may, of course, do so in her second volume. Some interesting aspects are discussed by L. Feuer in 'Marxian tragedians', *Encounter*, November 1962, pp. 23-32

7   Beer, op. cit., pp. 73-4

8   Vinchevsky (1856-1932) was born in Yanova, Lithuania, and went to Germany in 1877, but had to leave a year later owing to Bismarck's anti-socialist laws. He came to London and became involved in the socialist movement, but emigrated to the USA in 1894. There he wrote mainly on literary and socialist topics and translated many European writers into Yiddish. He edited, amongst other papers, a well-known socialist monthly, *Die Zukunft*

9   'Eleanor Marx: her love life and her tragic death'; the article is reproduced in his *Gezamelte Verke*, vol. 8, 1927-30, pp. 181-221, from which I have taken the passage quoted (pp. 197-201). Since this article is available only in Yiddish, I thought it worth while to quote at length. Silberner, *Jew. Soc. Stud.*, 11 (4), 1949, refers to it (pp. 339-40) but does not quote extensively, though he agrees that Vinchevsky's failure to follow up Eleanor's offer may be an 'irreparable' loss

10 Edward Aveling (1849-98) was gifted but unstable, trained in the natural sciences, a radical socialist and a philanderer. He formed a stormy and passionate association with Eleanor in 1883. His plan to leave her to live with an actress is generally considered to have been the immediate cause of her suicide

11 Bernstein published two articles in *Die neue Zeit* after Eleanor's suicide: 'Eleanor Marx' and 'Was Eleanor Marx in den Tod trieb', vol. 16, pt 2 (1897-8), pp. 118-23, 481-91

12 This sentence is quoted by Vinchevsky in English, op. cit., p. 200

13 Vinchevsky's primary languages in Lithuania were Hebrew and Yiddish. Marx's essays might have been available in German but were not available until 1905-7 in Russian, when some 160,000 copies were distributed (N. I. Lapin, *Der junge Marx im Spiegel der Weltliteratur*, (East) Berlin, 1965, pp. 41-2), and not until the 1920s in English (see Bibliography in Franz Mehring, *Karl Marx: the Story of his Life*, London, 1936, pp. 557-9)

421

14 Arthur Prinz for example has argued a case for assuming that in his later years Marx might have become 'reconciled to his own Jewish background'; see 'New perspectives on Marx as a Jew', *LBIYB*, 15, 1970, pp. 107–24

15 'Jews and German social democracy', *Die Zukunft*, 26 March 1921, reproduced in Massing, op. cit., pp. 322–30 (quotations from pp. 322–3)

16 *Rasse und Judentum*, Berlin, 1914, esp. p. 94, English translation *Are the Jews a Race?*, London, 1926

17 His earlier book, *Foundations of Christianity*, originally published in 1908, which provided so much material for later Jewish Marxists like Heller and Léon, is interesting in our context only because it uses a quotation from Marx to explain the emergence of monotheism and a priestly caste, but the source is Marx's 'Introduction to the Critique of Political Economy' and not his essays on Judaism

18 S. Hook, *From Hegel to Marx*, 2nd ed., Ann Arbor, 1962, pp. 278–9 n.

19 D. D. Runes (ed.), *Karl Marx: A World Without Jews*

20 R. C. Tucker, *Philosophy and Myths in Karl Marx*, p. 112

21 *Marx before Marxism*, London, 1970, p. 141

22 ibid., p. 142

23 J. Maguire, *Marx's Paris Writings: an Analysis*, Dublin, 1972, p. 30

24 N. McInnes, *The Western Marxists*, pp. 193, 227

Chapter XIII   Marxist Defenders

1 G. Mayer, 'Early German socialism and Jewish emancipation', *Jew. Soc. Stud.*, 1, 1939, pp. 409–22, on Mehring, see esp. pp. 420–2

2 The concept of philo-semitism as used by Mehring was recognised as dangerous by E. Bernstein (Massing, op. cit., p. 188) and did not come into general use. In recent years I have seen it used only once. It does not appear to have lost its nonsensical character over time. Thus, in their Preface to Max Weber's *Ancient Judaism*, H. H. Gerth and D. Martindale (Chicago, 1952, p. xiv) wrote that 'Weber was neither an antisemite nor an equally dangerous [sic!] philosemite'

3 Vol. 1, pp. 352–6 (p. 356)

4 Mayer, op. cit., p. 422

5 Quoted by Massing, op. cit., pp. 315–16

6 ibid., pp. 314–15

7 ibid., p. 316

8 ibid., pp. 317, 319

9 Mayer, op. cit., p. 421

10 Edward Fitzgerald's Preface to Franz Mehring, *Karl Marx: the Story of his Life*, London, 1936, p. ix

11 Mehring, op. cit., p. 3. Heinrich Marx's motives in converting have long been subject of dispute. For the most recent discussion, see L. S. Feuer, 'The conversion of Karl Marx's father', *Jew. J. Sociol.*, 14 (2), 1972, pp. 149–66

12 I have described this as somewhat dishonest, (a) because the anti-Jewish

riots took place *before* the 1820s, particularly in 1819; (b) it is a highly distorted version of what happened (see Eleanore Sterling, 'Anti-Jewish riots in Germany in 1819: a displacement of social protest', *Historia Judaica*, 2, 1950, pp. 105–42); (c) Mehring 'forgot' to place this situation into its proper 'historical materialist' context as he had done in his earlier (1910) *Deutsche Geschichte*, (East) Berlin, 1947, esp. pp. 86–99, and as Marx did in the 1844 Manuscripts; see T. B. Bottomore, *Karl Marx: Early Writings*, London, 1963, pp. 113–14

13 Mehring, op. cit., p. 68
14 ibid., p. 69
15 ibid., p. 73
16 *Holy Family*, Moscow, 1956, pp. 146–7; the italics are Marx's
17 Roman Rosdolsky, 'Friedrich Engels und das Problem der "Geschichtslosen" Völker', *Archiv für Sozialgeschichte*, 4, 1964, pp. 87–282
18 '*Die neue Rheinische Zeitung und die Juden*', ibid., pp. 251–67, in which he stated (p. 266): 'In dieser Beziehung hat uns die Geschichte der deutschen Judenvergasungen hellhörig gemacht' ('In this respect, the history of the extermination of Jews by Germans has made us particularly sensitive')
19 I do not think that Rosdolsky is quite correct here. In a series of articles, 'The Frankfurt Assembly Debates the Polish Question', Engels made a particular issue precisely of the 'ethno-linguistic' character of the Jew. See the recent (highly censored) Marx and Engels, *Articles from the 'Neue Rheinische Zeitung', 1848–49*, London, 1972, pp. 82–101, esp. pp. 86–7
20 An expression used by Engels, see Rosdolsky, op. cit., p. 253
21 Rosdolsky rejected the claim of Nicolaievsky and Maenchen-Helfen that Marx as editor made 'every word of the NRZ his own' (*Karl Marx: Man and Fighter*, p. 178), but he ignored an earlier remark of Engels that the paper was run on 'a simple dictatorship of Marx' which was 'undisputed and gladly acknowledged by us all' (ibid., p. 177), which rather undermines Rosdolsky's suggestion of the freedom of correspondents. Rosdolsky does, however, report that in 1850, i.e. within a year of the closing of the NRZ, *Marx himself* became the subject of one of Tellering's antisemitic attacks; Rosdolsky, op. cit., p. 258
22 ibid., p. 259; Rosdolsky is clearly directing his criticism mainly at Edmund Silberner
23 Presumably because many attacks on anti-semitism stemmed from them
24 Rosdolsky's confused position is well illustrated here, since he treats Léon's polemic as 'objective' truth
25 Again note that Rosdolsky includes here Bakunin, who made many particularly virulent attacks on *Marx as a Jew*
26 Mayer, op. cit., p. 419; but again Rosdolsky ignores his emphatic statement in that paper that Marx did *not* 'deal with the actual position of the Jews of Prussia' (p. 417)
27 *Marx's Theory of Alienation*, London, 1970
28 ibid., p. 20
29 ibid., p. 76
30 ibid., p. 72
31 ibid., p. 76

32 ibid., p. 229; see also Bell, *The End of Ideology*, New York, 1961, p. 364
33 ibid., p. 29. It is difficult to take this 'summary' of Judaism seriously, even if it were treated as a polemic, which is not Mészáros's intention. It is not our purpose here to 'defend' Judaism but merely to point out that this conceptual system has nothing to do with Marx's. Mészáros here does exactly what he accuses others of doing with Marx, i.e. using 'the narrow "literal" reading of isolated passages . . . [and] ideologically motivated misreadings of similarly isolated . . . passages' (p. 11)
34 ibid., p. 32. Mészáros does not mention that Marx took the concept of 'Jewish narrowness' from Bruno Bauer
35 ibid., p. 30
36 ibid., p. 72
37 ibid., p. 71. It should be pointed out here that Mészáros in this argument is following Isaac Deutscher (*The Non-Jewish Jew*, London, 1968, esp. pp. 26–34) very closely, which does not however prevent him from being *objectively* wrong; see p. 310 f. below for a fuller discussion of the 'Jewishness' of Marx
38 I would not dispute an *opinion* that Hess and Buber may have been second-rate, etc. To base such a claim on the single fact that they were and remained Jewish seems to me to be grotesque; see op. cit., p. 72
39 ibid., p. 30
40 Bottomore, op. cit., p. 38
41 Moscow, 1964, p. 259
42 My objections to the plausibility of Mészáros's analysis could be set against the fact that his book was awarded the Isaac Deutscher Memorial Prize in 1970 by an impressive panel of judges including E. H. Carr, Tamara Deutscher, E. Hobsbawm and R. Miliband
43 Georg Lukács, 'Zur philosophischen Entwicklung des jungen Marx', *Deutsche Zeitschrift für Philosophie*, 2 (2), 1955 (reprinted as *Der junge Marx: seine philosophische Entwicklung von 1840 bis 1844*, Pfullingen, 1965), p. 42
44 H. Popitz, *Der entfremdete Mensch*, Frankfurt a/M, 1968, esp. p. 87
45 Dietmar Scholz, 'Politische und menschliche Emanzipation: Karl Marx' Schrift "Zur Judenfrage" aus dem Jahre 1844', *Geschichte in Wissenschaft und Unterricht*, 18 (1), 1967, pp. 1–16
46 *Marx before Marxism*, London, 1970, p. 132
47 *Karl Marx: the Early Texts* (trans. and ed., D. McLellan), Oxford, 1971, p. xxv
48 S. Avineri, 'Marx and Jewish emancipation', *J. History of Ideas*, 25 (3), 1964, p. 445
49 *Marx before Marxism*, p. 142

Chapter XIV Jewish Responses to Marx

1 It is interesting to observe that the great *Jewish Encyclopedia* which was published in New York at the turn of the century, and which contains a substantial entry for Karl Marx, makes no mention of his essays on the Jewish question. The German *Encyclopaedia Judaica*, which was published

in Berlin in 1928 and only got as far as 'Ki', has a long essay on anti-
semitism in which, again, Marx's essays are not mentioned, even though,
by that time, they were being used by the Nazis for propaganda purposes
2 Two points might be added here. 1. When I discussed the research for this
study with several rabbis, most of them responded by asking why I wanted
'to waste my time' and 'stir up hatred by discussing that which is best
forgotten'. 2. The concept of a 'dialogue' between religion and Marxism
is relatively new, though by now quite extensive. See for example Garaudy-
Metz-Rahner, *Der Dialog: oder ändert sich das Verhältnis zwischen Katholizismus und Marxismus?*, Reinbeck b. Hamburg, 1966; H. Gollwitzer, *Die
marxistiche Religionskritik und der Christliche Glaube*, Munich and Hamburg,
1967; 'Judaism and Marxism, first European dialogue', *European Judaism*,
3 (1), 1968, pp. 30–41; W. Post, *Kritik der Religion bei Karl Marx*; B.
Bonpane and T. Edwards, *Marxism and Christianity: Are They Compatible?*,
New York, 1970
3 *Religion und Wirtschaft*, esp. pp. 10–14
4 'Marxism and Judaism', in J. Breuer (ed.), *Fundamentals of Judaism*, pp.
232–40 (p. 233)
5 'Jüdische Volkswirtschaft im Westen', *Der Jude*, 5, 1920–1, pp. 425–8
6 'Karl Marx als Jude', *Der Jude*, 8 (3), 1924, pp. 173–81 (p. 177)
7 *Karl Marx: a World without Jews*; this is the best-known anti-Marxian
version (see D. McLellan, *Marx before Marxism*, London, 1970, p. 141),
but I have not been able to ascertain to what extent Runes's translation of
the Marxian essays differs from those of Stenning and Fitzgerald (see
Bibliography)
8 K. Ivanov and Z. Sheinis, *The State of Israel: its Position and Policies*,
Moscow, 1958
9 Quotations are from Runes, op. cit., Introduction, pp. v–xi
10 For further details see my annotated bibliography
11 *Karl Marx: his Life and Environment*, pp. 99–100
12 Berlin, *The Life and Opinion of Moses Hess*, pp. 17–18
13 *Karl Marx: the Passionate Logician*, p. 75
14 Simon Dubnow, *Die neueste Geschichte des jüdischen Volkes*, vol. 2, pt 2,
pp. 116–17. For a fuller discussion of Marx in the tradition of Jewish
prophets, see the excellent article by Gabriele Dietrich, 'Das jüdisch-
prophetische Erbe in den neueren revolutionären Bewegungen', in W.
Strolz (ed.), *Jüdische Hoffnungskraft und Christlicher Glaube*, pp. 191–243.
See also following section on Gustav Mayer
15 Gustav Mayer, 'Der Jude in Karl Marx', *Neue jüdische Monatshefte*, April
1918
16 Gustav Mayer, 'Early German socialism and Jewish emancipation',
Jew. Soc. Stud., 1, 1939, pp. 409–22 (pp. 417, 420). We might note here
that Mayer, in this article, confused Moses Hess with Mendel Hess,
editor of the *Israelit des neunzehnten Jahrhunderts* (see pp. 414, 416). He
claimed that Moses Hess had replied to Bruno Bauer, which is incorrect
17 *MEW*, 27, p. 418
18 Solomon F. Bloom, 'Karl Marx and the Jews', *Jew. Soc. Stud.*, 4 (1),
1942, pp. 3–16

19 'German radicalism and the formation of Jewish political attitudes during the earlier part of the 19th century', in A. Altmann (ed.), *Studies in Nineteenth Century Jewish Intellectual History*, pp. 141–70 (pp. 158–9) (my italics)
20 Michael Graetz, 'Judentum und Christentum bei Karl Marx und Ludwig Feuerbach', *Das Neue Israel* (Zürich), 5, 1968, pp. 374–7; 8, 1969, pp. 603–4
21 *Encounters Between Judaism and Modern Philosophy*, New York, 1973, esp. pp. 145–53. It is not possible here to do full justice to this major work, which reaches many conclusions similar to my own
22 ibid., p. 146 (his italics)
23 ibid., p. 151

Chapter XV   Karl Marx in Israel

1 For details see Walter Laqueur's interesting article, 'Zionism, the Marxist critique and the left', in I. Howe and C. Gershman (eds), *Israel, the Arabs and the Middle East*
2 A. L. Patkin, *The Origins of the Russian-Jewish Labor Movement*, Melbourne and London, 1947, esp. p. 112
3 S. N. Eisenstadt, *Israeli Society*, London, 1967, pp. 16–18. The settlement of Palestine by the Zionist movement from its beginning to the foundation of the State is usually described as five 'waves' which began in 1882–1903 and ended in 1939 with the British Mandatory White Paper which ended immigration until 1948
4 V. D. Segre, *Israel: a Society in Transition*, London, 1971, p. 42
5 'Karl Marx ist der Zaddik der Judengasse'; see A. Boehm, *Die zionistiche Bewegung*, Berlin, 1920, vol. 2, p. 73
6 *Kibbutz: Venture in Utopia*, New York, 1955, pp. 183 ff. Spiro returned to the kibbutz later, and described the change that had taken place in the second edition of his book (1963, pp. xi ff.). Russia's changed attitude after the Suez war and Khrushchev's anti-Stalinist revelations at the 20th Communist Congress 'de-Sovietised' the kibbutz, which thereafter redefined its task in terms of solving its own problems and looking after its members, rather than as 'a cell in an international revolutionary movement'
7 See Otto Heller's book which was discussed on p. 206 f. above
8 In a series of articles by Moshe Glickson (1878–1939) in the liberal democratic daily *Haaretz* on 6, 10 and 17 April 1936. *Haaretz*, which was edited by Glickson 1922–37, was the only paper not affiliated to a political party. The articles were published in English as a pamphlet under the title *The Jewish Complex of Karl Marx*
9 'Was Marx an anti-semite?', *Historia Judaica*, 11 (1), 1949, pp. 3–52. This paper forms chapter 8 of his 1962 book, *Sozialisten zur Judenfrage*, the most important publication in this field. I am discussing him as an Israeli. He was born in Poland (1910), educated at Geneva and taught at Princeton (USA), where most of the book was written, though the chapter on Marx was written in Geneva. He has taught at the Hebrew University, Jerusalem,

since 1951, and his book was first published in Hebrew in 1955. It is of some interest that, although the book was written in English, it has been published only in Hebrew and German. Because Silberner's article on Marx is so well known, I shall not deal at length with it but rather with the context in which it was presented

10   Silberner, 1962, p. 6
11   ibid., p. 9
12   Silberner, 1949, p. 50
13   ibid., p. 52 (his italics)
14   This is the subtitle of his book, *The Recurring Pattern*, London, 1963, which examines the treatment of Jews and Judaism in the philosophical systems of Kant, Hegel and Toynbee
15   'For and against emancipation: the Bruno Bauer controversy', *LBIYB*, 4, 1959, pp. 3–36
16   ibid., p. 26
17   'The origins of modern antisemitism', *Dispersion and Unity*, 9, 1969, pp. 17–37 (p. 26)
18   See, for example, his deservedly esteemed *The Social and Political Thought of Karl Marx*, Cambridge, 1968
19   'Marx and Jewish emancipation', *J. Hist. Ideas*, 25 (3), 1964, pp. 445–50. Thus Hook and Tucker (see p. 266 above) are described as being 'perplexed' by Marx's anti-Jewish attitude, which is incorrect, and there is a reference to Rotenstreich's book, when his paper in *LBIYB* is meant (see p. 139 above). Marx's reference to Jewish writers as 'triste' in the *Holy Family* refers to their political positions, not to their polemic skills, as Avineri suggests, and he repeats Marx's error of quoting Crémieux instead of Fould
20   *Judentum in der Krise*, Göttingen, 1966. The chapter we are concerned with here was also published as 'Sozialismus und Judentum', *Neue deutsche Hefte*, 93, 1963, pp. 86–113
21   *Israel Among the Nations*, London, 1970. We are concerned with the first essay, 'Jews between Revolution and Counter-revolution'
22   Bloch, 1966, p. 23
23   ibid., p. 26
24   ibid., p. 29
25   ibid., p. 37. If this argument sounds a little far-fetched, we need to point only to Marx, who, though 'the most assimilated', never did escape from his Jewishness
26   ibid., p. 40
27   *Political Messianism*, London, 1960, described Marx's 'Kritik der Hegelschen Rechtsphilosophie' as 'a Messianic document *par excellence*' (p. 211) and noted Marx's lack of 'any genuine feeling for the mythology of nationhood' (p. 282)
28   *Israel Among the Nations*, pp. 20–1
29   ibid., p. 13
30   Although I shall be concerned mainly with three published papers of Fink, I have been very fortunate in securing, through the good offices of the members of Kibbutz Ma'abarot and his literary executor, Dr A.

Maimon, a number of unpublished manuscripts which have been most useful in determining Fink's theoretical position in relation to Marxism. In particular, there is a long, incomplete MS., 'Das Problem des Menschen in der Marxistischen Philosophie', which was probably written in the early 1950s and revised after the 20th Communist Party Congress in Russia. (The MS. is in the Jewish National and University Library of the Hebrew University, Jerusalem, MS. Var. 398/8.) It deals with general Marxist theory, but chapter 6, 'Ideal and Reality in the Kibbutz Community', which was published as an article in *Be-Shaar*, 36, 1960, pp. 19–28 (Hebrew), deals specifically with the 'Jewish question'. My references will be to the text of the MS. (hereafter F2). We cannot deal here with Fink's general views on Marxism, but must confine ourselves to the subject under discussion

31 'Ein Feuerbach-Zitat bei Marx (Zur Judenfrage)' (MS. Var. 398/12.9) (hereafter F1); this essay was published in Hebrew in *Al Hamishmar*, 4 July 1955

32 F1, p. 4

33 ibid., p. 5

34 Fink's quotation is from Leo Pinsker's *Autoemanzipation* (Berlin, 1882, pp. 18–19)—a stirring challenge addressed to the Jewish people, in the wake of pogroms in Russia, calling for the restoration of Jewish national consciousness. He rejected civil emancipation as a solution on the grounds that 'anyone who needs to be *placed* on an equal footing is bound to be weak on his feet'

35 op. cit., p. 15

36 This was Borochov's basic argument

37 F2, pp. 153–5

38 F2, p. 156. For a remarkable account of this process, exactly as Fink anticipated it, see Z. Bauman, 'The end of Polish Jewry: a sociological review', *Bulletin on Soviet and East European Jewish Affairs*, January 1966, pp. 3–8

39 'Die Judenfrage bei Marx und bei uns', *Periodikum für wissenschaftlichen Sozialismus*, 23, 1964, pp. 31–44. The article was published posthumously (hereafter F3)

40 T. B. Bottomore, *Karl Marx: Early Writings*, London, 1963, p. 40

41 F3, p. 32

42 ibid., p. 35

43 F3; note the affinity of this interpretation with Weber

44 ibid., p. 39

45 ibid., p. 42

46 ibid., p. 44

47 'Marx on the Jewish question and the national problem', *Be-Shaar*, 11 (6), (88), 1968, pp. 449–56

48 Ben Nachum was clearly deeply impressed by Künzli's *Karl Marx: eine Psychographie* and followed his general approach, if not all his specific interpretations

49 'Socialist Zionism', in *Dispersion and Unity*, 15–16, 1972, pp. 64–73

50 Nachman Syrkin (1868–1924), an influential labour-Zionist leader who

argued that there could be no Zionism except socialist Zionism. His book, *The Jewish Problem and the Socialist Jewish State* (Berlin, 1898), provided the programme for the Jewish labour organisations. Aharon David Gordon (1856–1922) was the ideological leader of the Jewish workers' movement and is best known for his ideas on 'the religion of labour'

51 Nini, op. cit., p. 70
52 ibid., p. 71

Chapter XVI   The Jewishness of Marx

1 Introduction to *LBIYB*, 4, 1959, p. x
2 Quoted by Kurt Müller in 'Karl Marx' Schrift "Zur Judenfrage" ', *Judaica*, 25, 3–4 November 1969, pp. 185–98
3 Quoted by Adam B. Ulam, *Lenin and the Bolsheviks*, London, Fontana, 1969, p. 54
4 *Kritische Geschichte der Nationalekonomie und des Sozialismus*, Berlin, 1875, p. 574
5 *Mein Kampf* (trans. J. Murphy), London, 1939, pp. 184, 320, 328
6 ibid., p. 63
7 *A Study of History*, p. 204, also p. 368
8 *Marx: Leben und Lehre*, p. 14
9 'One definition of a Jew', *Cambridge Opinion*, 39, 1964, pp. 16–22
10 *Karl Marx: His Life and Work*, p. 13
11 ibid., p. 377
12 op. cit.
13 *To the Finland Station*, pp. 115, 121
14 *Die Juden als Rasse und Kulturvolk*, 3rd ed., Berlin, 1922, pp. 198–200
15 *Die Religion der religionlosen Juden*, Vienna, 1938
16 'Karl Marx: zu seinem hundertsten Geburtstag', *Der Jude*, 3, 1918, pp. 62–8
17 *Mein Kampf*, pp. 320–1
18 D. Riazanov, *Karl Marx and Friedrich Engels*, pp. 32–5
19 Quoted in Hans Lamm, *Karl Marx und das Judentum*, Munich, 1969, p. 12
20 ibid., pp. 59–61
21 Moscow, 1964, p. 112
22 *Karl Marx: eine Psychographie*, p. 801. It would be neither possible nor fair to do justice to this massive study by extracting some selected references, and as far as possible I have avoided this. This also applies to the more diffuse study of Massiczek
23 *Der menschliche Mensch*, pp. 476 ff.
24 'Jüdische Messianismen im 20 Jahrhundert: Probleme des jüdischen Marxismus', in *Die geistige Gestalt des heutigen Judentums*, Munich, 1969, pp. 74, 84
25 *God's First Love*, London, 1967, p. 188
26 *Vom alten zum neuen Israel*, Frankfurt a/M, 1965, p. 213
27 *Marx's Concept of Man*, New York, 1961, p. 5
28 *Karl Marx*, pp. 77–81
29 *Sozialisten zur Judenfrage*, p. 114

30 *Pseudoreligiöse Motive in den Frühschriften von Karl Marx*, Tübingen, 1962
31 Karl Popper, *The Open Society and its Enemies*, 5th ed., London, 1966, vol. 1, p. 9
32 op. cit., p. 149
33 op. cit., p. 400. It is both surprising and somewhat incomprehensible to find Popper observing that 'there is certainly not much in this brilliantly phrased passage with which I do not agree', even though he regards it as only an 'interesting analogy'. Quite apart from the fact that, even as an analogy, this passage embodies purely subjective and wholly unsubstantiated implications, it contains factual errors and makes unsupported assumptions (e.g. Marx's grandparents were not emancipated, and 'fossilised' Judaism is a favourite and entirely personal view of Toynbee). See Popper, op. cit., vol. 2, p. 253. For a critique of Toynbee's 'conceptual clarity', and indeed of the whole chosen people–chosen class association, see N. Rotenstreich, *The Recurring Pattern*, London, 1963, p. 82
34 Künzli, op. cit., pp. 634 ff., 640
35 Quoted by S. Ettinger, 'The origins of modern antisemitism', *Dispersion and Unity*, 9, 1969, p. 27
36 *Geschichte des Judentums* (Anthropologische Geschichtsauffassung), Weimar, 1921, pp. 458–9
37 *Mein Kampf*, p. 31
38 ibid., p. 65
39 ibid., p. 150
40 ibid., p. 373
41 Quoted by Y. Harkabi, *Arab Attitudes to Israel*, London, 1972, p. 239
42 Reported in *Jewish Chronicle*, 26 September 1969
43 Quoted by Harkabi, op. cit., p. 251
44 op. cit., p. 20
45 Paul Hilberg, *The Destruction of the European Jews*, London, 1961, pp. 53, 267
46 See Deutscher, *The Non-Jewish Jew*, London, 1968, p. 26; István Mészáros, *Marx's Theory of Alienation*, London, 1970, pp. 70–1
47 Would he for instance argue that a Talmon is a lesser historian, Menuhin a lesser violinist, Sholem Aleichem a lesser writer, etc., because they remained within the Jewish community? Then again, are not the very individuals he and Marx hated so much, the great Jewish bankers and financiers, equally people who have chosen the world, rather than the confines of their community, to seek fulfilment?
48 Compare for example the vicious anti-Zionist/Israel polemic in Peter Buch's introduction to *Leon Trotsky on the Jewish Question*, New York, 1970, with the sympathetic but impersonal comments of Trotsky himself
49 Ernest Jones, *Sigmund Freud: Life and Work*, London, 1957, vol. 3, p. 131. Note also on p. 236 of the same volume Freud's analogy between himself and a famous figure in Jewish history when he had to flee from Austria in 1938
50 Quoted by Selma Spier, 'Jewish history as we see it', *LBIYB*, 1, 1956, p. 11
51 'Reflections on Trotsky', *Commentary*, January 1964
52 Franz Kobler (ed.), *Juden und Judentum in deutschen Briefen aus drei Jahrhunderten*, Vienna, 1935, pp. 28–9

53   in Josef Fraenkel (ed.), *The Jews of Austria*, London, 1967, esp. p. 447
54   Max Brod, *Heinrich Heine*, Leipzig and Vienna, 1934, p. 337
55   In a letter to Lion Phillips dated 29 November 1864, Marx referred to
     Benjamin Disraeli as 'unser Stammgenosse', i.e. someone who shared the
     same descent (*MEW*, 31, p. 342)
56   Blumenberg in his biography (p. 59) related how, when Marx's son-in-law
     Longuet spoke of 'racial prejudice' in Jenny Marx's family because of
     Marx's Jewish origins, Marx turned furiously to his daughter, denied that
     there had been any prejudice and demanded that henceforth Longuet was
     not to mention Marx again in anything he wrote
57   T. B. Bottomore, *Karl Marx: Early Writings*, London, 1963, pp. 34, 36, 39
58   See the moving 'Kurze Umrisse eines bewegten Lebens' ('Short Sketch
     of a Busy Life') by Jenny Marx in *Mohr und General: Erinnerungen an Marx
     und Engels*, (East) Berlin, 1970, esp. pp. 213–18. It is difficult in reading
     this account by a loyal and devoted wife, not to think of Heine's 'Grenad-
     iere' (*Werke*, Berlin and Weimar, 1968, 1, p. 15):
          'Was schert mich Weib, was schert mich Kind
          Ich trage weit besseres Verlangen
          Lass sie betteln gehen wenn sie hungrig sind'
59   For a detailed discussion of this tragic aspect of Marx's life, see Walter
     Blumenberg's searching but essentially sympathetic chapter, 'Die Misere
     des Lebens', in op. cit.
60   In a letter to N. F. Danielson (7 October 1868) in *Erinnerungen an Karl
     Marx*, (East) Berlin, 1953, p. 249
61   Max Beer, *Fifty Years of International Socialism*, London, 1935, p. 72
62   Karl Marx, *Der achtzehnte Brumaire des Louis Bonaparte*, (East) Berlin, 4th
     ed., 1971, p. 17. I have translated this short passage because the Moscow
     translation (Marx and Engels, *Selected Works*, London, 1968, p. 98) seems
     to me to miss the real meaning of it
63   Max Weber, *Ancient Judaism*, Chicago, 1952, pp. 267–306 (p. 294)
64   Martin Buber, *Israel and the World*, London, 1963, p. 116
65   *The Religion of Israel*, London, 1961, p. 347
66   Ernst Simon, *Brücken*, Heidelberg, 1965, p. 23
67   New York, 1963, p. 174. For a full discussion of the 'Messianic' passages
     in Marx, see Martin Buber, *Paths in Utopia*, London, 1958, pp. 80–98
68   See for example S. Avineri's chapter 'The Proletariat: the Universal Class'
     (in his *The Social and Political Thought of Karl Marx*, London, 1968) in
     which he shows the derivation of Marx's concept of a proletariat from
     Hegel's 'universal class'

Chapter XVII   Marx and Jewish Self-Hatred

1   *Karl Marx*, p. 58
2   Otto Fenichel, *The Psychoanalytic Theory of Neurosis*, London, 1946, pp.
    393, 405
3   'The baptism of Karl Marx', *Hibbert Journal*, 56, 1958, pp. 340–51 (pp.
    350–1)
4   Although this was a specific feature of the emancipation period, it was not

entirely new. The Rabbis of the Talmud (cf. Tractate Avodah Zarah) had differentiated between those who apostatised from personal motives and those motivated by malice

5 See chapter II

6 See H. G. Reissner, 'Rebellious dilemma: the case histories of Eduard Gans and some of his partisans', *LBIYB*, 2, 1957, pp. 179–93; Ernest Hamburger, 'Jews in public service under the German Monarchy', *LBIYB*, 9, 1964, pp. 206–38, esp. p. 212; M. A. Meyer, *The Origins of the Modern Jew*, Detroit, 1967, pp. 162–8

7 Moser (1796–1838), a founder member of the Verein, was a great friend of Heine, who described him as 'a living appendix to Nathan der Weise'

8 *Confessio Judaica*, Berlin, 1925, pp. 63, 64, 68, 73. For details of Heine's conversion, see Max Brod, *Heinrich Heine*, Leipzig and Vienna, 1934, pp. 342–3

9 *Confessio Judaica*, p. 153

10 *Die Juden und Ihre Gegner: ein Wort der Beherzigung für Wahrheitsfreunde gegen Fanatiker*, Frankfurt a/M, 1816, p. 10

11 *Germany's Stepchildren*, Philadelphia, 1961, p. 48

12 *Der jüdische Selbsthass*, Berlin, 1930, p. 17

13 ibid., pp. 9–37

14 *Geschlecht und Charakter*, Vienna and Leipzig, 1903, pp. 403–4. This extraordinary book had reached eighteen reprints by 1919. It should be added that Weininger strongly repudiated any attempt to use his anti-semitism as a justification for the persecution of Jews; ibid., p. 414

15 *Das Vermächtnis des deutschen Judentums*, Frankfurt a/M, 1957, pp. 122–3

16 D. Ben Nachum, 'Marx on the Jewish question and the national problem', *Be-Shaar*, 11 (6) (88), 1968, pp. 449–56; M. Glickson, *The Jewish Complex of Karl Marx*, pp. 9–13

17 Quoted in P. W. Massing, *Rehearsal for Destruction*, p. 188

18 E. Silberner, *Sozialisten zur Judenfrage*, p. 234; see also p. 359 for further references on 'self-hatred'

19 'Friedrich Engels and the Jews', *Jew. Soc. Stud.*, 11 (4), 1949, pp. 323–42, esp. pp. 332–3

20 See the chapter on 'Jewish Self-Hatred' in *Karl Marx: eine Psychographie*, pp. 195–203

21 Massiczek, *Der menschliche Mensch*, p. 184; he wrote specifically in answer to Künzli

22 Roman Rosdolsky, '*Die neue Rheinische Zeitung* und die Juden', *Archiv fur Sozialgeschichte*, 4, 1964, pp. 259–60

23 J. P. Sartre, *Search for a Method*, New York, 1968, p. 58

24 Kurt Lewin considered self-hatred to be a 'social-psychological' problem characteristic of individuals of underprivileged minority groups and strongly advocated the strengthening of group loyalties to overcome it. This clearly has no relevance to our discussion of Marx. See 'Self-hatred among Jews', *Contemp. Jew. Record*, 4 (3), 1941, pp. 219–32

25 T. B. Bottomore, *Karl Marx: Early Writings*, London, 1963, p. 34. Marx never recognised that there was more to Jewish consciousness than socio-economic function and religious 'superstructure'

26 Wilhelm Hasselmann (b. 1844), one-time leader of the Lassallean German Workers' Party. He was a vociferous anti-semite and was expelled from the Party in 1880 because of his anarchist views. He edited *Der Sozial-demokrat*

27 There is, for example, an Israeli socialist group, Matzpen, who, like the Trotskyite International Socialists, are calling for 'the elimination of the Zionist State of Israel'

Chapter XVIII   Marx and Anti-Semitism

1   For details see P. W. Massing, *Rehearsal for Destruction*. Uriel Tal has argued that Marx's anti-semitism had its roots in Voltaire, Feuerbach, Bruno Bauer and Daumer; see *Religious and Anti-religious Roots of Modern Antisemitism*, New York, 1971, pp. 5–6

2   R. Hilberg, *The Destruction of European Jews*, Chicago, 1961, p. 45

3   Fritsch, a theoretician of anti-semitism, at first strongly rejected any suggestion that his movement was in any way opposed to the Jewish religion. In his early speeches, Hitler also argued on these lines; see H. Coudenhove-Kalergi, *Das Wesen des Antisemitismus*, Vienna and Zürich, 1935, p. 101; R. H. Phelps (ed.), 'Hitler's "Grundlegende" Rede ueber den Antisemitismus', *Vierteljahrshefte für Zeitgeschichte*, 16 (4), 1968, pp. 390–420, esp. p. 414

4   *Das Wesen des Antisemitismus*, pp. 102 ff.

5   The literature on anti-semitism is too vast to be dealt with here either historically or analytically. Useful summaries are contained in James Parkes's books, *The Jew and his Neighbour*, 2nd ed., London, 1938, and *Antisemitism*, London, 1963. Excellent articles are to be found in *Jewish Encyclopedia*, vol. 1, New York, 1901, pp. 641–9 (G. Deutsch); *Encyclopaedia of Religion and Ethics*, vol. 1, Edinburgh, 1908, pp. 593–9 (H. L. Strack); *Encyclopaedia Judaica*, vol. 2, Berlin, 1928, cols 956–1104 (various); ibid., vol. 3, Jerusalem, 1971, cols 87–160 (various)

6   See quotations in Hilberg, op. cit., p. 9

7   e.g. E. Silberner, *Sozialisten zur Judenfrage*; G. Lichtheim, 'Socialism and the Jews', *Dissent*, July–August 1968, pp. 314–42

8   For details of the more extreme charges against Jews, see Joshua Trachtenberg, *The Devil and the Jews*, New York, 1943; J. R. Marcus, *The Jew in the Medieval World 315–1791*, New York, 1969. For a detailed analysis of the 'blood-libel', see H. L. Strack, *Das Blut im Glauben und Aberglauben der Menschheit*, Munich, 1900

9   cf. N. Cohn, *Warrant for Genocide*, Pelican, 1970

10 The ultimate logic of racial anti-semitism also saw no difficulty in reversing this issue in the Hitler era, when a major concern was the racial penetration of the Aryan German race by Jews. If it were not for its tragic consequences, German deliberations on racial purity and the problems of the *Mischlinge* would be pure comic opera; see Hilberg, op. cit., esp. pp. 268 ff. He also reported that SS officers had to *prove* pure German descent back to 1750 (ibid., p. 49)

433

11 As we shall see, this had been advocated by Mohammed and Luther. Later, in 1816, Herr Rat Wolfart presented an evaluation to the Prussian administration in which he argued that if the Jews were as bad as some claimed, the only answer would be to eliminate them (*ausrotten*). See I. Freund, *Die Emanzipation der Juden in Preussen*, Berlin, 1912, vol. 1, p. 235. H. Ahlwardt (an anti-semitic member of the Reichstag in the 1890s) wrote: 'No reform of a social or religious kind is possible until Judaism has been totally eliminated', *Judenflinten*, 10th ed., Dresden, 1892, p. 34

12 *Antisemitism and Emotional Disorder*, New York, 1950. They deal with the point I made earlier by arguing that social forces determine the nature of the Jewish stereotype. This may be of interest in the USA where religion plays very little part in the anti-semitic picture, but in nineteenth-century Germany other facets of conflict were involved

13 *The Authoritarian Personality*, vol. I, New York, 1964, p. 71

14 J. H. Robb, *Working Class Antisemite*, London, 1954, p. 11. Robb has the best and most lucid review of the social-scientific literature, but does not devote much attention to the complex German *Judenfrage*, which was never as superficial as the anti-semitism he investigated

15 *Christian Beliefs and Anti-Semitism*, New York, 1966, p. 102

16 op. cit., p. 173

17 At its crudest level we might say that evidence of sadistic tendencies in a surgeon are irrelevant to an evaluation of a contribution to surgery he may have made

18 See Saul S. Friedman, 'Luther and Muhammad', *Patterns of Prejudice*, 5 (2), 1971, pp. 6–11. Friedman draws a comparison between the two religious leaders in relation to anti-semitism which is of great interest, but would take us too far here. See also Jacob R. Marcus, *The Jew in the Medieval World: a Source Book 315–1791*, New York, 1938, pp. 167–9

19 Marcus, op. cit., pp. 167–9; see also Léon Poliakov, *The History of Anti-Semitism*, vol. 1, London, 1974, esp. chap. 7; Joshua Trachtenberg, *The Devil and the Jews*, New York, 1943, for discussions of Luther and the devil-image

20 Phelps, op. cit., contains a verbatim report of the speech, which was delivered in August 1920

21 For details see L. Poliakov, *Harvest of Hate*, London, 1956, esp. pp. 1–9. I share Poliakov's view that expulsion was the original aim, not mass extermination

22 *Liberty in the Modern State*, Penguin, 1938, p. 162

23 'The Jewish parasite: notes on the semantics of the Jewish problem with special reference to Germany', *LBIYB*, 9, 1964, pp. 3–40. Victor Klemperer, a baptised Jew who was allowed to remain in Nazi Germany because of his Aryan wife, published *LIT* (*Lingua Imperii Tertii*): *Notizbuch eines Philologen* (2nd ed., Berlin, 1949), based on a study of the way the Nazis used words

24 op. cit., pp. 4–5

25 Quoted by Poliakov, *History of Anti-Semitism*, vol. 1, pp. 239–40

26 I. Mészáros, *Marx's Theory of Alienation*, London, 1970, p. 32

27 P. Seidman (ed.), *Socialists and the Fight Against Antisemitism*, New York, 1973, p. 4
28 Phelps, op. cit., p. 417
29 See chapter XV
30 See chapter XIV
31 E. Bernstein, 'Jews and German social democracy', *Die Zukunft*, 26, 1921; also reproduced in Massing, op. cit., pp. 322–30 (p. 323). Bernstein's attempt to rationalise Marx's polemic is tragi-comic, since it was precisely the 'educated public' that was the main carrier of German anti-semitism. According to M. Rubel, parts of Marx's essays were reprinted in *Der Sozialdemocrat*, Zürich, 30 June and 7 July 1881. See *Bibliographie des oeuvres de Karl Marx*, Paris, 1956, p. 52. As far as I can ascertain, there is no real evidence that Marx did *not* see Hasselmann's excerpts. For further details see Silberner, op. cit., pp. 199 ff.; he also assumed that Marx did know of the publication
32 op. cit., p. 11
33 *In Rabonischn Schotn* (Yiddish), Paris, 1954, p. 9. The *Encyclopaedia Judaica* (vol. 3, Jerusalem, 1971, p. 146) reproduced a typical Nazi anti-semitic cartoon which uses Marxian phraseology
34 *Karl Marx: sein Leben und sein Werk*, Leipzig, 1929
35 See also W. Blumenberg, *Karl Marx*, p. 58
36 Phelps, op. cit., p. 415
37 T. K. Kichko, *Judaism and Zionism*, Kiev, 1968, p. 39. The original is in Ukrainian. I have used an anonymous mimeographed translation except for the quotation from Marx which is taken from Bottomore, *Karl Marx: Early Writings*, p. 37
38 Quotation from *Jews in Eastern Europe*, 4 (3), 1970, p. 59. For a detailed discussion of the entry in the Soviet *Encyclopedia*, see J. Miller, 'Soviet theory on the Jews' in L. Kochan (ed.), *Jews in Soviet Russia since 1917*, London, 1972
39 Y. Harkabi, *Arab Attitudes to Israel*, London, 1972, pp. 301–2
40 Especially in Marx's articles, notably in the *New York Daily Tribune*
41 *History of Anti-Semitism*, vol. 1, p. 221
42 Pirke Avoth, 1.11; Bein, op. cit., p. 37 ends his article on semantics with the same quotation

Chapter XIX   Marx and the Jews of Jerusalem

1 *Sozialisten zur Judenfrage*, p. 134
2 Silberner gave a heading, 'The States of Europe', for the article, as some earlier editors of Marx had done. S. Avineri, who included it in his *Karl Marx on Colonialism and Modernization* (New York, 1968, pp. 134–43), headed it 'The Outbreak of the Crimean War: Moslems, Christians and Jews in the Ottoman Empire', because, in the absence of a heading by Marx, this was 'more in tune with the content of the article' (personal communication from Avineri, 11 February 1973). I have used the text in Avineri's book, where the relevant passage is on p. 142

3   op. cit., p. 135
4   ibid., pp. 134 5
5   'Karl Marx and the Jews', *Jew. Soc. Stud.*, 4 (1), 1942, p. 11
6   'Benjamin Disraeli, Karl Marx and the search for identity', *Midstream*, 16 (7), 1970, pp. 43–4
7   *Karl Marx: eine Psychographie*, pp. 218–20 (pp. 219–20)
8   Daniel Ben Nachum, 'Marx on the Jewish question and the national problem,' *Be-Shaar*, 11 (6) (88), 1968, p. 452
9   H. Gemkow *et al.*, *Karl Marx: a Biography*, Dresden, 1968, pp. 212–17; see also Jenny Marx, 'Kurze Umrisse eines bewegten Lebens', in *Mohr und General*, (East) Berlin, 1970, pp. 204–36, esp. pp. 214–20
10 Gemkow, op. cit., p. 214; see also Gustav Mayer, *Friedrich Engels: a Biography*, New York, 1969, pp. 144 and 155
11 Paris (Librairie de Firmin Didot Frères), 1853
12 I am indebted to Professor de Jong Edz of the International Institute of Social History, Amsterdam, for giving me access to the notebooks in the Marx *Nachlass* which contain the notes on Famin's book. (Classified as B 69, notebook pp. 11–17, esp. pp. 13–14 on Jerusalem)
13 Avineri, op. cit., p. 142
14 Famin, op. cit., p. 54. 'attirés à Jérusalem que par le désir d'y choisir leurs places dans la vallée de Josaphat, et d'y mourir sur les lieux mêmes où la résurrection doit les retrouver'. Marx's term 'inhabit' does not make sense in this context. The valley of Jehoshaphat separates Jerusalem from the Mount of Olives. Its significance is obscure. Though referred to in the Bible (Joel 4:2) as the place where God would judge all nations (hence the name Jehoshaphat—God will judge), the Midrash Tehillim declared quite unequivocally that 'there is no valley by the name of Jehoshaphat'. Joel's prophecy has nevertheless taken root in Jewish legend (see *The Holy City: Jews and Jerusalem*, ed. A. Holtz, New York, 1971, p. 175). Famin's observations may equally well apply to the Mount of Olives, which from ancient times (e.g. Absalom) to the present day has been the most sacred Jewish burial-ground, the place where every pious Jew would like to be laid to rest (*Jewish Encyclopedia*, vol. 7, New York, 1904, and *Encyclopedia of Zionism and Israel*, vol. 2, New York, 1971)
15 Avineri in fact is under the impression that Marx took the term from Famin and thought that it might have been based on '*Mikdash Halvanon*', a Hebrew expression which is used occasionally in traditional literature (personal communication, 2 February 1971)
16 op. cit., p. 55
17 ibid., p. 52
18 Avineri has suggested that the connection between the Jewish quarter and 'dirt' may be due to the fact that the Jewish quarter was adjacent to the 'Dung-Gate' (Sha'ar Ha-Aspoth), since we have no reason to think that the Jewish quarter was, during the nineteenth century, more of a slum than any other area of the Old City of Jerusalem; there is evidence to the contrary (personal communication, 11 February 1973)
19 Only those comments which eventually receive a mention in Marx's article are given here

20 B 69, p. 14 (the page numbers have been pencilled in). Dashes in the text represent words I have not been able to decipher
21 Meaning 'awaiting'; Avineri called this 'an obvious gallicism' arising from Marx's poor English (personal communication, 2 December 1971)
22 Reproduced in Avineri, op. cit., p. 142
23 Original quotation marks

Annotated Bibliography

References here are mainly to books and articles which deal with Marx's essays on, and his associations with, Jews. I have also included publications whose authors or contents have made them particularly influential in determining contemporary views on Marx as a Jew and Marx on the Jews, including materials which adopt frankly ideological stances either in support of or in refutation of Marx. Items marked with an asterisk are those I have not been able to consult. The letters in brackets refer to the language in which the item was published: E—English; F—French; G—German; H—Hebrew; P—Polish; Y—Yiddish.

Adams, H. P., *Karl Marx in his Earlier Writings*, London, 1965 (E)
    'Marx had no love for the religion of his forefathers'. He regarded Jewish law 'as an arbitrary regulation of material concerns without reference to the true nature of man'. The earthly reality of the Jews corresponded to their 'sordid heaven', they had emancipated themselves in the money-market, and Christians had followed suit (p. 95)

Andrew, Edward, 'Marx and the Jews', *European Judaism*, 3 (1), 1968, pp. 9–14 (E)
    Marx's essays are 'emphatically not about Judaism'. His simple, Feuerbachian views on religion 'prevented him from saying anything very interesting on the subject'. He was anti-semitic, but his essays were an assault on capitalism rather than on Jews. His views on Jews are 'inaccurate, inadequate and ridiculous'. He expressed qualified approval of the Jewish role in history, 'strongly' advocated the Jews' right to emancipation, and would have disapproved of the treatment of Jews in present-day Eastern Europe

[Anonymous], *Israelit des neunzehnten Jahrhunderts*, 5, 1844, pp. 258–9 (G)
    A brilliant summary of Marx's first essay 'On the Jewish Question', in which he is described as the man who 'saved religion'

Avineri, Shlomo, 'Marx and Jewish emancipation', *Journal of the History of Ideas*, 25 (3), 1964, pp. 445–50 (E)
    No one today questions that Marx was an 'inveterate antisemite', but a distinction must be drawn between his slating of the role of the Jews in

438

society and his defence of the right of the Jews to emancipation. This is shown by concentrating on the sections in the *Holy Family*. This paper contains a number of factual errors

Behncke, Claus, 'Karl Marx: ein Psychopath?', *Merkur (Deutsche Zeitschrift für europäisches Denken)*, 11 (6), 1967, pp. 586–92 (G)
A strong attack on Künzli's (q.v.) book on Marx in which Künzli is accused of confusing the social pathology of Marx's time with his personal pathology

Ben Nachum, Daniel, 'Hanekeidah hayehudit vehashe-elah haleumith etzel Marx' ('Marx on the Jewish question and the national problem'), *Be-Shaar (Social and Cultural Review)*, 11 (6) (88), 1968, pp. 449–56 (H)
One of the best and most comprehensive articles on the subject. Looks at Marx's personal and intellectual background, also discusses Moses Hess, Ber Borochov and Otto Bauer. Main conclusion is that Marx confused 'people' and 'class' in his analysis of the Jewish question

Berlin, Isaiah, *The Life and Opinions of Moses Hess*, Cambridge, 1959 (E)
The violently anti-semitic tone of Marx's essays affected the attitude of communists towards Jews, and 'is one of the most neurotic and revolting aspects of his masterful but vulgar personality' (pp. 17–18)

Berlin, Isaiah, *Karl Marx: his Life and Environment*, London, 3rd ed., 1963 (E)
Marx's hostility to everything connected with religion, particularly Judaism, may have been due to his 'embarrassed situation' as a convert (p. 27). His essays on Jews are a 'dull and shallow composition' in which he decided to 'kill the Jewish problem once and for all' (pp. 99–100)

Berlin, Isaiah, 'Benjamin Disraeli, Karl Marx and the search for identity', *Midstream*, 16 (7), 1970, pp. 29–49 (E)
Marx's attitude to Jews is 'uncompromisingly hostile', yet he invites comparison with the 'ancient Hebrew prophets'—he failed to consider the problem of nationalism

*Berneri, Camillo, 'Karl Marx the antisemite', in Berneri, C., *Le Juif antisémite*, Paris, 1935, pp. 62–78 (F)

Bernstein, Eduard, 'Jews and German social democracy', *Die Zukunft*, 26, 1921 (Y); an English translation appears in P. W. Massing, *Rehearsal for Destruction*, New York, 1967, pp. 332–30
Marx's essays are unsatisfactory and have been used for anti-semitic purposes. Bernstein shows a remarkable lack of either knowledge or understanding of some of his points

Bienenfeld, Rudolf, *Die Religion der religionlosen Juden*, Vienna, 1938 (G)
Marx's idea of justice showed that he adhered to one of the four major tenets of Judaism, viz. he 'proved' that the worker is being deprived of part of his reward, but argued a principle of faith that this was wrong

Bloch, Jochanan, 'Sozialismus und Judentum', *Neue deutsche Hefte*, 93, 1963, pp. 86–113; also published as chapter 1 in Bloch, *Judentum in der Krise*, Göttingen, 1966 (G)
A discussion of the apparent contradiction that socialism, which counts so many Jews amongst its founders, should have shown a persistent trend towards anti-semitism, not only in the Marxian view of Judaism but also in the attitude to Jewish nationalism which is given particular emphasis here

Bloch, Jochanan, 'Moses Hess: Rom und Jerusalem: jüdische und menschliche Emanzipation', *Kölner Zeitschrift für Soziologie und sozial Psycholgie*, 16 (2), 1964, pp. 228–313; also published as chapter 2 in Bloch, *Judentum in der Krise* (G)
Includes some comparisons on Hess's and Marx's views on the Jewish question
Bloom, Solomon F., 'Karl Marx and the Jews', *Jewish Social Studies*, 4 (1), 1942, pp. 3–16 (E)
A wide review of Marx's background, the essays of Bruno Bauer and Marx's response. Saw Marx as a fighter for social justice in the 'Hebraic' tradition but subject to prevailing anti-semitic prejudices which he accepted
Blumenberg, Werner, *Karl Marx in Selbstzeugnissen und Bilddokumenten*, Reinbek b. Hamburg, 1962 (G) (trans. D. Scott, *Karl Marx*, London, 1972); I have translated from the German edition.
Marx's essays are important because they pose the question of his anti-semitism. He suffered from Jewish self-hatred. He was particularly vicious to those who called him a Jew. His anti-Jewish remarks were quoted by Karl Vorländer to refute Nazi charges that Marx was a Jew (pp. 57–8). He behaved in the tradition of O.T. prophets (p. 78)
*von Boenigk, Freiherr Otto, 'Marx and the Jewish problem', *Die Gegenwart*, 45, 1894, pp. 180–2
According to Silberner, he advocates merely a 'fusion' of Germans and Jews
Braun, S., 'Die Vorfahren von Karl Marx', *Mitteilungs Blatt* (Leo Baeck Institute, Tel-Aviv), 44, 10 November 1967, p. 5 (G)
About the ancestors of Marx
Breuer, Raphael (Rabbi), 'Marxism and Judaism', in Jacob Breuer (ed.), *Fundamentals of Judaism*, New York, 1949, pp. 232–40 (E)
Marx, grandson of a rabbi, had an 'almost fanatical hatred of Jews' based on total ignorance of Judaism (p. 233). Marxism and Judaism are incompatiable. Judaism has its own, non-materialist philosophy of social justice
Brilling, Bernhard, 'Beiträge zur Geschichte der Juden in Trier', *Trierisches Jahrbuch*, 9, 1958, pp. 46–50 (G)
Deals with Marx's rabbinic ancestors
Carlebach, Joseph (Rabbi), *Religion und Wirtschaft*, Frankfurt a/M, 1933 (G)
Marx was right in castigating the faults of liberal capitalism but his attacks on religion are an 'aberration', especially since his 'holy anger' over social injustice is a heritage of Jewish prophets. In Marx, 'we see the sad spectacle of those nurtured by the milk of Judaism turning the sword against the mother'. His economic theories were 'looted from Judaism'
Carlebach, Julius, 'Karl Marx and the Jews of Jerusalem', *Soviet Jewish Affairs*, 2 (2), 1972, pp. 71–4 (E)
See chapter XIX in the present book
Carmichael, Joel, *Karl Marx: the Passionate Logician*, London, 1968 (E)
Marx never showed anything but hostility to all Jewish institutions. In his essays he declared the Jewish problem to be 'simply fictitious' (p. 75)
Dietrich, Gabriele, 'Das jüdisch—prophetische Erbe in den neueren revolutionären Bewegungen', in W. Strolz (ed.), *Jüdische Hoffnungskraft und Christlicher Glaube*, Freiburg, 1971, pp. 191–243 (G)
An original and exceptionally interesting discussion of a prophetic-revolu-

tionary Jewish tradition into which the Marxian critique of Judaism is placed. By seeking to uncover a Jewish 'essence', Marx failed to see the link between historical conditions and Jewish reality

Dubnow, Simon, *Neueste Geschichte des jüdischen Volkes*, vol. 2, pt 2, *Zeitalter der ersten Reaktion, 1815–1848*, Berlin, 1920 (G) (trans. M. Spiegel, *History of the Jews*, vol. 5, London, 1973); I have translated from the German edition. The essays are a 'Pasquill' (p. 116). Marx had usurped a great deal of the spiritual heritage of ancient Judaism. 'Judaism stood before three tribunals. The enemy of the church, Bauer; the defender of the church, Stahl; and the socialist, Marx. All three sentenced it to death. Judaism heard the sentence and continued its historic path' (p. 117)

Feuer, Lewis S., 'The conversion of Karl Marx's father', *Jewish Journal of Sociology*, 14 (2), 1972, pp. 149–66 (E)
Deals mainly with the controversy over the conversion of Marx's father. Was it for personal advantage or an act of social emancipation? While Karl wrote an essay attacking the Jews, his father wrote a petition in their defence. Karl's essay 'was meant to conceal his own Jewish descent' (p. 157)

Feuer, Lewis S., 'Karl Marx and the Promethean complex', *Encounter*, December 1968, pp. 15–32 (E)
Marx's 'hysterical hatred of Jews' (p. 26) was a reaction to his mother and her ways

Fink, Jona, 'Die Judenfrage bei Marx und bei uns', *Periodikum für wissenschaftlichen Sozialismus*, 23, 1964, pp. 31–44 (G)
A brilliant, materialist interpretation of Judaism, which rejects the Marxian version as offering a solution only for the individual Jew, where Fink wants a collective solution along Zionist Marxist lines

Glenn, Hermann, 'Karl Marx: zu seinem hundertsten Geburtstag', *Der Jude*, 3, 1918, pp. 62–8 (G)
A laudatory article which claimed that Marx unconsciously derived his being and thinking from his Jewishness. Marx's 'superficial and sad utterances' on Jews were brushed aside, and Judaism should claim for Marx: 'Er war unser' (cf. Lamm)

Glickson, Moshe, *The Jewish Complex of Karl Marx*, New York, 1961 (first published in Hebrew in *Haaretz* in April 1936) (E)
A bitter polemic against Jews, whose 'self-hate' led them to attack Judaism, notably Karl Marx, 'the virtuoso of hatred'. The author intends to show that the tenets of socialism do not require an acceptance of Marx's ignorant comments on Jews and Judaism.

Graetz, Michael, 'Judentum und Christentum bei Karl Marx und Ludwig Feurbach', *Das neue Israel* (Zürich), 5, 1968, pp. 374–7; 8, 1969, pp. 603–4 (G)
Both men adapted medieval Christian and Deistic views of Judaism and restated them in secular terms. Marx used traditional anti-Jewish views as a vehicle for propagating his revolutionary ideas

Heller, Otto, *Der Untergang des Judentums: die Judenfrage, ihre Kritik, ihre Lösung, durch den Sozialismus*, Vienna and Berlin, 1931 (G)
A Leninist-Stalinist analysis of the Jewish question which starts from Marx's 'correct but incomplete' view of Judaism and offers a threefold solution: (a) The disappearance of Jews in capitalist societies; (b) the salvation of a

Jewish proletariat in the Russian province of Biro-Bidjan; (c) the reactionary character of Zionism, which must be eliminated

Hirsch, Helmut, 'Marxiana Judaica', *Cahiers de l'Institut de Science Economique Appliquée*, 1963, pp. 5–52 (F)

A broad review of Marx's relationship to Jews and Judaism considered under a number of headings: e.g. Marx's American sources, aspects of Bauer's views, the influence of Hess, Heine and Hegel, and anti-Jewish views current in Marx's youth, particularly those of Arnold Ruge. He concludes that Marx's attitudes vary from outright anti-semitism to mild philo-semitism

Hirsch, Helmut, 'Karl Marx und die Bittschriften für die Gleichberechtigung der Juden', *Archiv für Sozialgeschichte*, 8, 1968, pp. 229–45 (G)

Deals mainly with background and supplementary materials of the Cologne and Trier petitions for Jewish emancipation

*Hoffmann, Benzion, 'Marx and the Jewish problem', in B. Hoffmann (ed.), *Karl Marx*, New York, 1918, pp. 153–76 (Y)

Kamenka, Eugene, 'The baptism of Karl Marx', *Hibbert Journal*, 56, 1958, pp. 340–51 (E)

Argues for the importance of the first six years of Marx's life, i.e. the period before his conversion. His use of the term 'Jew' suggests that he does not hate Jews for being bourgeois, but that he transfers his hate of Jews to the bourgeoisie

Kohn, Erwin, 'Jüdische Volkswirtschaft im Westen', *Der Jude*, 5, 1920–1, pp. 425–8 (G)

A review of a re-issue of Marx's essays in 1919. Argues that Marx knew nothing about Jews and that he wrote as a socialist, philosopher and anti-semite. 'Here it is not a case of facts convincing a man, but of a man manufacturing facts'

Köllner, Lutz, 'Hoffnung auf eine vaterlose Welt: Karl Marx psychoanalytisch betrachtet', *Der Monat*, 17 (206), 1965, pp. 31–9 (G)

About the love-hungry, father (i.e. state) -dominated genius who seeks salvation in a mystical youth, i.e. the youngest human (Jewish) group, the proletariat

Künzli, Arnold, *Karl Marx: Eine Psychographie*, Vienna, 1966 (G)

A formidable (870 pp.) biographical study of Marx based on a meticulous psychoanalytically orientated discussion of his life and work. Though somewhat one-sided, the book contains a great deal of new and original material, but some of the interpretations are inaccurate and wide of the mark. Marx's Jewishness and Jewish self-hatred are central themes of the book. Künzli defined 'Psychographie' as a critique of ideology based on an assumption that non-social interests influence ideological awareness

Lamm, Hans, *Karl Marx und das Judentum* (first published in *Karl Marx 1818–1968: neue Studien zu Person und Lehre*, Mainz, 1968, then separately, Munich, 1969) (G)

A review of the literature on Marx and his attitude to Jews and Judaism which relies heavily on the work of Silberner (q.v.) and Künzli (q.v.). Unlike Glenn (q.v.), who, writing for the hundredth anniversary of Marx's birth, concluded that Marx was 'one of us', Lamm, writing fifty years later, concludes that he was not one of us

442

Laqueur, Walter, 'Zionism, the Marxist critique and the left', in Howe, I. and Gershman, C. (eds), *Israel, the Arabs and the Middle East*, Bantam Books, 1972 (E)
A scholarly survey of Marxist and neo-Marxist attitudes to Jewish nationalism, beginning with Marx's 'totally negative' approach (p. 18)

Léon, Abram, *The Jewish Question: a Marxist Interpretation*, New York, 1970 (first published in French as *La Conception materialiste de la question juive*, Paris, 1946, 1968) (E)
A Trotskyist approach beginning with Marx's 'brilliant' analysis. It calls for the formation of a Jewish proletariat which would resolve its problem through international revolution and class struggle and by rejecting Zionism

Lesser, E. J., 'Karl Marx als Jude', *Der Jude*, 8 (3), 1924, pp. 173–81; also reproduced in A. Massiczek, *Der menschliche Mensch* (q.v.), pp. 613–25 (G)
Marx's essays show his indifference to, and ignorance of, Judaism, but his life and characteristics expose him as a 'full-blooded Jew', an 'other-world talmudist'

Lichtheim, George, 'Socialism and the Jews', *Dissent*, July–August 1968, pp. 314–42 (E)
This interesting paper contains only brief references to Marx. It is pointed out that Marx's position in Western European eyes as a German Jew had an important bearing on his views and on his 'paradoxical and rather self-contradictory utterances on the Jewish question' (p. 340). He also notes Marx's failure 'to work out a satisfactory doctrine of citizenship'

Liebeschütz, Hans, 'German radicalism and the formation of Jewish political attitudes during the earlier part of the nineteenth century', in Alexander Altmann (ed.), *Studies in Nineteenth Century Jewish Intellectual History*, London, 1965 (E)
Marx's conception of Judaism was 'patristic', and can best be understood in relation to Spinoza's *Tractatus Theologico-politicus*. Though the personal association was absent in Marx, his 'emphatic caricature of Judaism clearly shows that he was conscious of his own social connection with Jewry' (p. 158). He could remain unaware of the biblical origin of his teleological outlook on history because he took it over from the Hegelian school

Lipset, Seymour Martin, 'The return of anti-semitism as a political force', in Howe, I. and Gershman, C. (eds), *Israel, the Arabs and the Middle East*, Bantam Books, 1972 (E)
A review of post Second World War left-wing anti-semitism, which is shown to have begun with Marx's 'anti-semitic comments' (p. 419)

Löwenstein, Julius I., 'Karl Marx' jüdischer Humanismus', *Mitteilungs Blatt* (Leo Baeck Institute, Tel-Aviv), 24, 11 June 1971, p. 7 (G)
A critique of Massiczek's book (q.v.). While 'it should not be denied that Judaism manifested itself unconsciously in Marx's teaching', Massiczek claims too much for Marx's Jewish origins and fails to substantiate his rejection of the Kant–Hegel–Feuerbach influences

McInnes, Neil, *The Western Marxists*, London, 1972 (E)
Marx's second essay on the Jewish question expresses his horror of economic rationalism—which he identified with Judaism, rather than with anti-semitic feelings towards Jews (pp. 192–6)

Marcuse, Ludwig, 'Heine und Marx', *Der Monat*, 6 (64), 1954, pp. 407–16 (G)
Argues that there was little real friendship between the two—it was more a case of each using the other

Marx, Hugo, 'Das Verhältnis von Heinrich Heine und Karl Marx zum Judentum', *Rhein-Neckar Zeitung*. 15, 16, 17 August 1969 (G)
While Heine remained a Jew in spirit ('I was baptised but not converted'), Marx 'pushed Jews into the dirt' in a manner unequalled until the advent of the Nazis. It is possible that Marx was less hostile about his Jewish origins with his family

Massiczek, Albert (ed.), *Der menschliche Mensch: Karl Marx' jüdischer Humanismus*, Vienna, 1968 (G)
A cultural anthropological study of Marx (cf. A. Kardiner, *The Psychological Frontiers of Society*, New York and London, 1945) in which his life and work are described as emanating directly from his Jewishness. For all its profound analyses of Jewish thought in the post-emancipation era, it treats Jewishness as a 'mystery'; this detracts from the author's essentially scholarly approach

Massing, Paul W., *Rehearsal for Destruction: a Study of Political Anti-semitism in Germany*, New York, 1967 (E)
This book contains a great deal of relevant material. Marx's essays on the Jewish question are discussed on pp. 159, 253

Mayer, Gustav, 'Early German socialism and Jewish emancipation', *Jewish Social Studies*, I, 1939, pp. 409–22 (E)
Marx's essays on the Jewish question do 'not deal with the actual position of the Jews in Prussia' (p. 417); they represent and go beyond Feuerbach's analysis of Judaism. Marx's dialectical reasoning had equated Judaism and money power

Mayer, Gustav, 'Der Jude in Karl Marx', *Neue jüdische Monatshefte*, April 1918, reprinted in Massiczek (q.v.), pp. 599–604 (G)
In his essays, Marx was neither interested in nor concerned with Jews or Judaism. He merely used the topic to demonstrate 'the superiority of his new materialistic analysis over the ideological problematics of the Young Hegelians' (p. 600). In his analysis, Marx 'pours out the baby with the bath-water'. No Gentile has ever been more unjust and one-sided in writing about Jews. Nevertheless, Marx was a Jew in his innermost being, cast in the mould of the prophets

Mehring, Franz, *Aus dem literarischen Nachlass von Karl Marx und Friedrich Engels: 1841 bis 1850*, 3 vols, Stuttgart, 3rd ed., 1920, vol. 1, *Einleitung zu der Judenfrage*, pp. 352–6 (G)
The 'murderous role of Jewish usury' and the refusal of the Jews 'to participate in the renowned work of [Germany's] great thinkers and poets' were the basis of the Marxian critique

Monz, Heinz, *Karl Marx und Trier*, Trier, 1964 (G)
The most substantial study of Marx's background

*Monz, Heinz, 'Die soziale Lage der elterlichen Familie von Karl Marx', in *Karl Marx 1818–1968: neue Studien zu Person und Lehre*, Mainz, 1968 (G)

Monz, Heinz, 'Die jüdische Herkunft von Karl Marx', in *Jahrbuch des Instituts für deutsche Geschichte*, vol. 2, Tel-Aviv, 1973, pp. 173–97 (G)

An interesting paper containing a great deal of detail about the social situation of the Jews of Trier and particularly the family of Marx

Müller, Kurt, 'Karl Marx' Schrift "Zur Judenfrage" ', *Judaica* (*Beiträge zum Verständnis des jüdischen Schicksals in Vergangenheit und Gegenwart*), 25, 3–4 November 1969, pp. 185–98 (G)

A stimulating essay which argues that Marx tried to present himself as an 'outsider' by discussing Judaism only in the context of religion and wealth, neither of which applied to him. The author implies that Marx may have based his analysis of Judaism on the social legislation of the Bible, i.e. if the Jews had laws against land ownership, usury, exploitation etc., they must have developed them because they were intended to deal with typically Jewish behaviour

Nicolaievsky, Boris, and Maenchen-Helfen, Otto, *Karl Marx: Man and Fighter* (trans. G. David and E. Mesbacher), London, 1973 (E)

The new edition contains a special Appendix (whose author is not identified) on 'Marx's antecedents and his attitude to Judaism' (pp. 408–11), which records some of the more recent literature on Marx and the Jews, rejecting the idea that Marx was anti-semitic, and suggesting that 'he was aiming through the Jewish religion at a certain way of living'

Payne, Robert, *Marx*, London, 1968 (E)

Marx's essays are 'laboured attempts to invalidate Judaism' and their arguments are pursued 'with a bitter hatred of Judaism' (p. 93). Although it was not uncommon for Jews of Marx's time to profess a defiant anti-semitism, Marx's anti-semitism 'had a virulent quality lacking among his contemporaries', and was motivated by a 'deeply personal hatred' of Jews (p. 94). In much the same way as Marx, 'Hitler would later pass sentence of death on "the empirical nature of Judaism" ' (p. 95)

Post, Werner, *Kritik der Religion bei Karl Marx*, Munich, 1969 (G)

This is probably the most extensive and elaborate analysis of the Marxian critique of religion. The essays on the Jewish question are discussed in 11 out of 320 pages for their particular political character. But the author declines to discuss either Judaism or the question of Marx's attitude to it

Prinz, Arthur, 'New perspectives on Marx as a Jew', *LBIYB*, 15, 1970, pp. 107–24 (E)

Using some new material on Marx's relationship with his Dutch relatives, the correspondence with Graetz and Marx's later lifestyle, the author argues that there are indications that Marx's attitude to Jews became friendlier towards the end of his life

Prinz, Arthur, 'Myths, facts and riddles about the literary estate of Karl Marx', in *Der Friede: Idee und Verwirklichung-Festgabe für A. Leschnitzer*, Heidelberg, 1961, pp. 405–22 (E)

A paper of general interest, which includes a passage that Bernstein eliminated 'several extremely caustic remarks by Marx about his mother' and that Marx's aversion to his mother 'may assume special significance in connection with his anti-semitism' (pp. 417–18)

Rennap, I., *Anti-Semitism and the Jewish Question*, London, 1942 (E)

A Marxist-Stalinist but gently written analysis of the Jewish question. A section on Marx's essays describes how Marx foretold that Jews could achieve human emancipation only through communism. The author related how this had already been achieved in the USSR and how dangerous Jewish nationalism was

Riazanov, D., *Karl Marx and Friedrich Engels*, London, 1927 (E)
The influence of Marx's Jewish origins must not be overlooked. Marx 'took an interest in the Jewish question and also a part in the struggle for . . . emancipation . . . This did not prevent him from drawing a sharp line of demarcation between poor Jewry with which he felt a certain propinquity and the opulent representatives of financial Jewry' (pp. 34–5)

Rosdolsky, Roman, 'Friedrich Engels und das Problem der "geschichtslosen" Völker', appendix 1, 'Die neue Rheinische Zeitung und die Juden', *Archiv für Sozialgeschichte*, 4, 1964, pp. 251–67 (G)
After a résumé of some viciously anti-semitic reports in the NRZ, the author turns to a long and detailed discussion of Marx 'On the Jewish Question', in which he is both critical of the anti-semitic implications while at the same time defending the Marxian position. The article was written in 1948, and conveys the impression of an attempt to come to terms with a Marxist approach to Judaism in the wake of the holocaust. The author describes early socialist anti-semitism as a 'childhood disease' of the movement

Rosenbaum, Eduard, 'Ferdinand Lassalle: a historiographical meditation', *LBIYB*, 9, 1964, pp. 122–30
Discusses the likely reason for the fact that only Marx and Engels uttered a 'constant stream of anti-semitic vilification' against Lassalle. Agrees with Isaiah Berlin (*Karl Marx: his Life and Environment*, q.v.) that Marx's essays 'On the Jewish Question' are 'dull and shallow'

Rosenberg, Leo, 'Karl Marx', reproduced in Massiczek (q.v.), pp. 605–12, probably written in 1918 (G)
'He was not Jewish and was not consciously Jewish in any way', is the main argument of this paper. Even if Marx had known anything about Jews he would have been incapable of writing about them in a balanced way. Nevertheless he was, and was seen by the world as, a Jew, an O.T.-type prophet

Rubaschow (Shazar), Salman, 'Marx wegen Judentum un Judentum in Marx', in *Oif der Schwell*, Berlin, 1918, pp. 26–41 (Y).
Also published in German in *An der Schwelle*, Berlin, 1918, and republished in Schneir Zalman Shazar, *Orei Dorot* (*Light of Past Generations*), Jerusalem, 1971 (H)
The author, President of the State of Israel 1963–73, wrote as a socialist-Zionist. He argued that Marx's views of Judaism were 'typical' of his time and that his concepts related to a 'dream world' which had nothing in common with the Jewish reality

Rühle, Otto, *Karl Marx: his Life and Work* (trans. Eden and Cedar Paul), London, 1929 (E)
Marx suffered from three handicaps—disorder of the liver, being the first-born, and 'all the odium attaching to his race'. By 'ostentatiously showing his opposition to Judaism, [Marx] is demonstrably severing himself from his own race . . . One who takes so much trouble to declare that he is not a

Jew must have reason for being afraid of being regarded as a Jew' (p. 377)

Runes, Dagobert D. (ed.), *Karl Marx: a World without Jews*, New York, 1959; 4th ed., 1960 (E)
One of the best known but least valuable editions of Marx's essays, which are represented as purely anti-semitic. The presentation is less than scholarly, part of Marx's passages from the *Holy Family* being added to the essays but not identified, and the editor's comments are highly polemical. As a translation, it is, however, accurate

Sanders, Ronald, 'Moses Hess: the Hegelian Zionist', *Midstream*, 8 (1), 1962, pp. 57–69 (E)
Marx's essays are 'disturbingly harsh in tone towards the Jews', but the author claimed that 'Marx had often shown concern for the Jewish problem'

Schay, Rudolf, *Juden in der deutschen Politik*, Berlin, 1929 (G)
A series of biographical studies, the first of which deals with Karl Marx, whom the author describes as a Jew cast in the mould of the ancient prophets —'the greatest Jew of his century' (p. 19). Marx's essays 'On the Jewish Question' are discussed with some embarrassment. Schay explains that Marx knew 'only' Rhineland Jews, who were traders and moneylenders (p. 44), and concludes that Marx's passionate attempt to identify Judaism as the immoral element in history and society was an expression of a radical break with his own past (p. 49)

Schmidt, H. D., 'The terms of emancipation, 1781–1812', *LBIYB*, 1, 1956, pp. 28–47 (E)
Marx 'rationalised his self-hatred into an economic theory when he called upon the world to emancipate itself from Judaism. There was in that call a pathetic fight against his own shadow and past' (p. 40)

Scholz, Dietmar, 'Politische und menschliche Emanzipation: Karl Marx' Schrift "Zur Judenfrage" aus dem Jahre 1844', *Geschichte in Wissenschaft und Unterricht (Zeitschrift des Verbandes der Geschichtslehrer Deutschlands)*, 18 (1), 1967, pp. 1–16 (G)
A very able summary of Marx's essays, which concentrates on the concept of human emancipation. The author takes the view that the question of *Jewish* emancipation was only a peg on which Marx developed his thoughts on 'real' emancipation. Scholz makes no reference to the *Holy Family*

Schwarzschild, Leopold, *The Red Prussian: Life and Legend of Karl Marx*, London, 1948 (E)
The method used by Marx of singling out one facet of Jewish activity, i.e. bargaining, from a manifold complex of occupations, was rejected even as early as the Romans. His analysis of the Jewish question is of interest only because 'dispersed throughout these two unread and unreadable articles were the first socialist formulae of their author' (p. 82)

Silberner, Edmund, *Sozialisten zur Judenfrage*, Berlin, 1962 (G)
By far the most comprehensive and scholarly contribution to the subject. Silberner finds the evidence for arguing that Marx was anti-semitic overwhelming. His chapter on Marx was originally published in English in *Historia Judaica*, 11 (1), 1949, pp. 3–52, under the title 'Was Marx an anti-semite?'

*Stein, Hans, 'Der Übertritt der Familie Heinrich Marx zum evangelischen

Christentum', in *Jahrbuch des Kölnischen Geschichtsvereins*, vol. 14, Cologne, 1932

Steiner, George, 'One definition of a Jew', *Cambridge Opinion*, 39, 1964, pp. 16–22 (E)
'But if the poison [of the chosen people concept] is, in ancient past, Jewish, so is the antidote, the radical humanism which sees man on the road to becoming man. This is where Marx is most profoundly a Jew (while at the same time arguing the dissolution of Jewish identity)' (p. 22)

Sterling, Eleonore, 'Jewish reactions to Jew-hatred in the first half of the nineteenth century', *LBIYB*, 3, 1958, pp. 103–21 (E)
Marx attacked Judaism as a general historical and theoretical manifestation, not Jews as human beings of flesh and blood. He used Judaism to demonstrate man's self-alienation in capitalist society (p. 109)

*Tartakower, Arje, 'Marx and Judaism', *Miesiecznik Zydowski*, 3, 1933, pp. 224–38 (P)

Tönnies, Ferdinand, *Marx: Leben und Lehre*, Jena, 1921 (G)
Marx's essays 'On the Jewish Question' are not important for what he has to say about Jews and Judaism, but for his anlaysis of the relation between state and religion and state, society and the individual. Marx's style is characteristically 'Jewish sharp-witted reasoning' ('*Spitzfindigkeit der jüdischen Verstandesart*') (p. 14)

Toynbee, Arnold, *A Study of History*, abridged ed., London, 1960 (E)
Insists that Marx was Jewish: e.g. 'when Lenin casts about for a creed, he borrows from a westernised German Jew, Karl Marx' (p. 204); 'the German Jew Karl Marx' (p. 368). Marx chose 'historical necessity' in place of the Jewish God, and the proletariat in place of Jewry as the chosen people, 'but the salient features of the Jewish apocalypse protrude through this threadbare disguise' (p. 400)

Tucker, Robert, *Philosophy and Myth in Karl Marx*, Cambridge, 1969 (E)
Tucker discusses Marx's essays in an abstract way and deals with their possible anti-semitic implications in a footnote attack on Runes (q.v.): 'Although Marx did at times express anti-Jewish feelings . . . he meant a practical religion of money-worship' (p. 112)

*Wachstein, Bernard, 'Die Abstammung von Karl Marx', in *Festskrift . . . Professor David Simonsen*, Copenhagen, 1923 (G)
Deals with both paternal and maternal ancestors of Marx

*Weinstein, Marcos, 'Marx and the Jewish question', *Judaica*, 5, 1933 (Spanish)

Weltsch, Robert, 'Introduction', *LBIYB*, 4, 1959, pp. ix–xxvi (E)
Although Marx 'killed' the Jewish problem for himself, a hostile world branded his ideas as Jewish. Those who insist on regarding Marx as a Jew are more likely to consider his ideas as a disaster for mankind than as the mark of a great pioneer. It is ironical that most non-socialist interpreters of the history of ideas relate Marx's thought in some way to Judaism (p. x)

Wilson, Edmund, *To the Finland Station* (1940), Fontana, London, Collins, 1968 (E)
Described Marx as 'the great secular rabbi of his century . . . a teacher in the Jewish tradition but . . . quite free of the Judaic system'. Yet 'Marx was too profoundly and completely a Jew to worry much about the Jewish

problem in the terms in which it was discussed in his lifetime' (p. 121). Because of that, Marx transferred the animus and rebellion associated with Jewish disabilities 'to an imaginary proletariat' (p. 149)

Wistrich, Robert S., 'Karl Marx, German socialists and the Jewish question, 1880–1914', *Soviet Jewish Affairs*, 3 (1), 1973, pp. 92–7 (E)

A short paper which discusses the reactions of Mehring, Bebel, Kautsky and Eduard Bernstein to Marx's essays, and argues that, with the exception of Bernstein, they were all typical of the 'socialist ambivalence' towards Jews

Wistrich, Robert S., 'Karl Marx and the Jewish question', *Soviet Jewish Affairs*, 4 (1), 1974, pp. 53–60 (E)

A brief review of the subject, which relies heavily on a number of sources I have also used. The author follows McLellan in assuming that Marx based his analysis of Judaism on the work of Moses Hess. He regards the essays as products of Marx's philosophical background and of his 'desire to dissociate himself from his Jewish origins' (p. 54)

Zineman, Jacob, *In Rabonischen Schotn* (*In the Shadow of the Rabbis*), (biographical novel), Paris, 1954 (Y)

A fictionalised account of Marx's stay in Paris, dealing particularly with his Jewish origin and his attitude to Jews. Although a serious attempt is made to use reliable information, the book contains many errors of fact and romanticises such individuals as Heine and Moses Hess. The author claims to have been a Marxist before the use of Marxian material by the Nazis showed him the true significance of Marx's essays. The author reports that he published an article, 'Karl Marx and the Jewish Question', in 1930, in which he 'sharply and ruthlessly attacked Marx's essays'

General Bibliography

MARX

Essays 'On the Jewish Question'
These essays were first published in English in H. J. Stenning's *Selected Essays* (London, 1926, 1929), though only selected passages and summaries were produced. A full translation was published by Edward Fitzgerald in *The Jewish Question* (London, 1935). Dagobert Runes's polemical version, *Karl Marx: a World without Jews*, was issued in New York in 1959, and a fourth enlarged edition in 1960. Tom Bottomore published his translation in *Karl Marx: Early Writings* (London, 1963) and Lloyd D. Easton and Kurt H. Guddat produced another good translation in *Writings of the Young Marx on Philosophy and Society* (New York, 1967).

More recently, David McLellan has published a somewhat tendentious and at times inaccurate translation in *Karl Marx: the Early Texts* (Oxford, 1971). A translation by Gregor Benton was issued in *Karl Marx: Early Writings* (Pelican Marx Library, 1975) and Clemens Dutt has contributed a further translation in *Karl Marx—Friedrich Engels—Collected Works*, vol. 3: *Marx and Engels 1843-44* (London, 1975). Both these latest translations adhere closely to the approach of the Marxist-Leninist Institute in Moscow by treating the essays as Marx's 'materialist' analysis of the Jewish question.

Collected Works
F. Mehring (ed.), *Aus dem literarischen Nachlass von Karl Marx und Friedrich Engels 1841-1850*, 3 vols, 3rd ed., Stuttgart, 1920
Karl Marx—Friedrich Engels—Werke, 42 vols to date, (East) Berlin, 1956-68
Karl Marx and Frederick Engels: Selected Works in one Volume, London, 1968
Karl Marx and Frederick Engels: Selected Correspondence, 2nd revised ed., Moscow, 1965

Single Editions
Karl Marx: Critique of Hegel's Philosophy of Right (ed. J. O'Malley), Cambridge, 1970

Deutsch-Französische Jahrbücher (ed. Arnold Ruge and Karl Marx), pts 1 and 2, Paris, 1844
Economic and Philosophic Manuscripts of 1844 (trans. Martin Milligan), Moscow, 1959
Friedrich Engels and Karl Marx, *Die heilige Familie: oder Kritik der kritischen Kritik: gegen Bruno Bauer und Konsorten*, (East) Berlin, 1971
Karl Marx and Friedrich Engels, *The Holy Family: or Critique of Critical Critique* (trans. R. Dixon), Moscow, 1956
The Poverty of Philosophy (with Introduction by Engels), New York, 1963
Karl Marx and Friedrich Engels, *The Communist Manifesto* (with Introduction by A. J. P. Taylor), Penguin, 1967
Karl Marx and Frederick Engels, *Articles from the 'Neue Rheinische Zeitung' 1848–49*, London, 1972
Karl Marx and Frederick Engels, *The German Ideology*, Moscow, 1964
Der achtzehnte Brumaire des Louis Bonaparte, 4th ed., (East) Berlin, 1971
Karl Marx and Friedrich Engels, *On Religion*, Moscow, 1955
Karl Marx on Colonialism and Modernization (ed. S. Avineri), New York, 1968
Capital: a Critique of Political Economy (trans. S. Moore and E. Aveling; ed. Frederick Engels), London, 1970

Biographies
Cornu, Auguste, *Karl Marx et Friedrich Engels: leur vie et leur oeuvre*, vol. 2: *1842–1844*, Paris, 1958
Erinnerungen an Karl Marx, 2nd ed., (East) Berlin, 1953
Gemkow, Heinrich *et al.*, *Karl Marx: a Biography*, Dresden, 1968
Korsch, Karl, *Karl Marx*, New York, 1963 (first pub. 1938)
Lafargue, Paul, *Das Recht der Faulheit und persönliche Erinnerungen an Karl Marx*, Frankfurt a/M, 1966
McLellan, David, *Marx before Marxism*, London, 1970
McLellan, David, *Marx*, Glasgow (Fontana Modern Masters), 1975
Mehring, Franz, *Karl Marx: the Story of his Life* (trans. E. Fitzgerald), London, 1936
Mohr und General: Erinnerungen an Marx und Engels, (East) Berlin, 1970
Payne, Robert, *The Unknown Karl Marx*, London, 1972
Rubel, Maximilien, *Karl Marx: Essai de biographie intellectuelle*, Paris, 1957
Schlesinger, Rudolf, *Marx: his Time and ours*, New York, 1950
Sombart, Werner, *Das Lebenswerk von Karl Marx*, Jena, 1909
Vorländer, Karl, *Karl Marx: sein Leben und sein Werk*, Leipzig, 1929

Bibliographies
Lachs, John, *Marxist Philosophy: a Bibliographical Guide*, Chapel Hill, N.C., 1967
Lapin, N. I., *Der junge Marx im Spiegel der Literatur*, (East) Berlin, 1965
Rubel, Maximilien, *Bibliographie des oeuvres de Karl Marx*, Paris, 1956

Studies on Marx
Althusser, Louis, *For Marx* (trans. B. Brewster), Penguin, 1969

Avineri, Shlomo, *The Social and Political Thought of Karl Marx*, London, 1968

Avineri, Shlomo, *Hegel's Theory of the Modern State*, London, 1972

Avineri, Shlomo (ed.), *Marx's Socialism*, New York, 1973

Banning, Willem, *Karl Marx: Leben, Lehre und Bedeutung* (trans. B. Toet-Kahlert), Munich and Hamburg, 1966

Bloch, Ernst, *Über Karl Marx*, Frankfurt a/M, 1968

Bloch, Ernst, *Karl Marx und die Menschlichkeit: Utopische Phantasie und Weltveränderung*, Munich, 1969

Bober, M. M., *Karl Marx's Interpretation of History*, 2nd revised ed., New York, 1965

Delfgaauw, Bernard, *Der junge Marx: eine Einführung in sein Denken* (trans. M. Fuhrmann), Munich, 1962 (*The Young Marx*, London, 1967)

Fleischer, Helmut, *Marx und Engels: die philosophischen Grundlinien ihres Denkens*, Freiburg and Munich, 1970

Friedrich, Manfred, *Philosophie und Ökonomie beim jungen Marx*, Berlin, 1960

Fromm, Erich, *Marx's Concept of Man*, New York, 1966

Gebhardt, J., 'Karl Marx und Bruno Bauer', in A. Dempf, H. Arendt and F. Engel-Janos (eds), *Politische Ordnung und menschliche Existenz*, Munich, 1962

Hook, Sidney, *From Hegel to Marx: Studies in the Intellectual Development of Karl Marx*, Ann Arbor, 1962

Kamenka, Eugene, *Marxism and Ethics*, London, 1969

Karl Marx 1818–1968: neue Studien zu Person und Lehre, Mainz, 1968

Lefebvre, Henri, *The Sociology of Marx*, Penguin, 1968

Leff, Gordon, *The Tyranny of Concepts: a Critique of Marxism*, London, 1961

Lenin, V. I., *Collected Works*, vol. 38: *Philosophical Notebooks*, London, 1963

Lenin, V. I., *On the National and Colonial Questions*, Peking, 1967

Lenin, V. I., *Karl Marx* (a brief biographical sketch with an exposition of Marxism), Peking, 1970

Lenin, [V. I.], *Marx-Engels-Marxismus*, Moscow, n.d.

Lichtheim, George, *Marxism: an Historical and Critical Study*, 2nd revised ed., London, 1964

Lichtheim, George, *The Origins of Socialism*, London, 1969

Löwith, Karl, *Von Hegel zu Nietzsche der revolutionäre Bruch im Denken des neunzehnten Jahrhunderts: Marx und Kierkegaard*, 2nd ed., Stuttgart, 1949

Lukács, Georg, *Der junge Marx: seine philosophische Entwicklung 1840–1844*, Pfullingen, 1965

McLellan, David, *The Young Hegelians and Karl Marx*, London, 1969

Maguire, John, *Marx's Paris Writings: an Analysis* (with Introduction by D. McLellan), Dublin, 1972

Marcuse, Herbert, *Reason and Revolution: Hegel and the Rise of Social Theory*, 2nd ed., London, 1955

Mészáros, István, *Marx's Theory of Alienation*, London, 1970

Meyer, Alfred G., *Marxism: the Unity of Theory and Practice*, Ann Arbor, 1963

Mitrany, David, *Marx against the Peasant: a Study in Social Dogmatism*, London, 1951

Plekhanov, George V., *Fundamental Problems of Marxism*, London, 1969

Popitz, Heinrich, *Der entfremdete Mensch: Zeitkritik und Geschichtsphilosophie des jungen Marx*, Frankfurt a/M, 1968

Talmon, J. L., *Political Messianism: the Romantic Phase*, London, 1960
Thier, Erich, *Das Menschenbild des jungen Marx*, 2nd ed., Göttingen, 1961

Marx/Marxism and Religion
Garaudy, R., Metz, J. B. and Rahner, K., *Der Dialog: oder andert sich des Verhaltinis zwischen Katholizismus und Marxismus?*, Hamburg, 1966
Gollwitzer, Helmut, *Die Marxistische Religionskritik und der Christliche Glaube*, Munich and Hamburg, 1967
Kautsky, Karl, *Foundations of Christianity: a Study in Christian Origins* (trans. from 13th German ed.), London, n.d.
van Leeuwen, Arend T., *Critique of Heaven*, London, 1972 (Gifford Lectures, 1970)
Link, Christian, *Theologische Perspektiven nach Marx und Freud*, Stuttgart, 1971
MacIntyre, Alasdair, *Marxism and Christianity*, London, 1969
Röhr, Heinz, *Pseudoreligiöse Motive in den Frühschriften von Karl Marx*, Tübingen, 1962

General
Beer, Max, *Allgemeine Geschichte des Sozialismus und der sozialen Kämpfe*, 8th ed. (with additions by H. Duncker), Berlin, 1932
Beer, Max, *50 Years of International Socialism*, London, 1935
Braunthal, Julius, *History of the International 1864–1914*, London, 1966
Feuer, Lewis S., 'Marxian tragedians: a death in the family', *Encounter*, November 1962, pp. 23–32
Kapp, Y., *Eleanor Marx: Family Life 1855–1883*, London, 1972
Mayer, Gustav, *Friedrich Engels: a Biography*, New York, 1969 (first pub. 1936)
Tsuzuki, Chusichi, *The Life of Eleanor Marx 1855–1898: a Socialist Tragedy*, Oxford, 1967

BAUER

Die evangelische Landeskirche Preussens und die Wissenschaft, 2nd ed., Leipzig, 1840
Hegel's Lehre von der Religion und Kunst von dem Standpunkte des Glaubens aus beurtheilt, Leipzig, 1842 (originally anon.)
Die gute Sache der Freiheit und meine eigne Angelegenheit, Zürich and Winterthur, 1842
Die Judenfrage, Brunswick, 1843
'Die Fähigkeit der heutigen Juden und Christen frei zu werden', in G. Herwegh (ed.), *Einundzwanzig Bogen aus der Schweiz*, Zürich and Winterthur, 1843
Briefwechsel zwischen Bruno Bauer und Edgar Bauer während der Jahre 1839–1842 aus Bonn und Berlin, Berlin, 1844
Kegel, M., *Bruno Bauer's Übergang von der Hegelschen Rechten zum Radikalismus*, Leipzig, 1908

FEUERBACH

Sämtliche Werke (ed. with biography by W. Bolin, 1904; new ed. by H. M. Sass, Stuttgart, 1964)

Das Wesen des Christentums (with *Nachwort* by Karl Löwith), Stuttgart, 1971
Essence of Christianity (trans. G. Eliot; Introduction by Karl Barth; Foreword by
  R. H. Niebuhr), New York and London, 1957
Kamenka, Eugene, *The Philosophy of Ludwig Feuerbach*, London, 1970
Kohut, Adolph, *Ludwig Feuerbach: sein Leben und seine Werke*, Leipzig, 1909

HEINE

Buch der Lieder, 33rd ed., Hamburg, 1872
Confessio Judaica (ed. Hugo Biber), Berlin, 1925
Heines Werke (ed. Helmut Holzhauser), 5 vols, (East) Berlin and Weimar, 1968
Brod, Max, *Heinrich Heine*, Leipzig and Vienna, 1934
Karpeles, Gustav, *Heinrich Heine und das Judentum*, Breslau, 1868
Sammons, Jeffrey L., *Heinrich Heine: the Elusive Poet*, New Haven and London,
  1969
Victor, Walther, *Marx und Heine: Tatsache und Spekulation in der Darstellung
  ihrer Beziehungen*, (East) Berlin, 1970

HESS

Jüdische Schriften (ed. Theodor Zlocisti), Berlin, 1903
'Ueber das Geldwesen', in *Rheinische Jahrbücher zur gesellschaftlichen Reform* (ed.
  H. Puttman), Darmstadt, 1845; reprinted, Leipzig, 1970
Rom und Jerusalem, Leipzig, 1862
Rome and Jerusalem: a Study in Jewish Nationalism, New York, 1943
Sozialistische Aufsätze 1841–1847 (ed. T. Zlocisti), Berlin, 1921
Briefwechsel (ed. Edmund Silberner), The Hague, 1959
Ausgewählte Schriften (ed. Horst Lademacher), Cologne, 1962
Frankel, Jonathan, ' "The communist rabbi": Moses Hess', *Commentary*, June
  1966, pp. 77–80
Lademacher, Horst, 'Die politische und soziale Theorie bei Moses Hess', *Archiv
  für Kulturgeschichte*, Cologne and Graz, 42 (2), 1960, pp. 194–230
Schulman, Mary, *Moses Hess: Prophet of Zionism*, New York and London, 1963
Silberner, E., 'Zur Hess Bibliographie', *Archiv für Sozialgeschichte*, Hanover,
  6–7, 1966–7, pp. 241–314
Silberner, E., *Moses Hess: Geschichte seines Lebens*, Leiden, 1966
Zlocisti, Theodor, *Moses Hess: der Vorkämpfer des Sozialismus und Zionismus
  1812–1875: eine Biographie*, 2nd revised ed., Berlin, 1921

HORKHEIMER

'Die Juden und Europa', *Zeitschrift für Sozialforschung*, 8 (1–2), 1939, pp. 115–37
Kritische Theorie (ed. Alfred Schmidt), 2 vols, 2nd ed., Frankfurt a/M, 1969
*Die Sensucht nach dem ganz Anderen: ein Interview mit Kommentar von Helmut
  Gumnior*, Hamburg, 1970
Zur Kritik der instrumentellen Vernuft: aus den Vorträgen und Aufzeichnungen seit

Kriegsende (ed. A. Schmidt), Frankfurt a/M, 1974 (part 1 is a trans. by Schmidt of *Eclipse of Reason*, New York, 1947)

Horkheimer, Max and Adorno, Theodor, *Dialektik der Aufklärung*, Frankfurt a/M, 1969

Adorno, T. W. *et al.*, *The Authoritarian Personality*, 2 vols, New York, 1964

Gumnior, Helmut and Ringguth, Rudolf, *Max Horkheimer in Selbstzeugnissen und Bilddokumenten*, Hamburg, 1973

Jay, Martin, *The Dialectical Imagination: a History of the Frankfurt School and the Institute of Social Research 1923–1950*, London, 1973

Koch, Thilo (ed.), *Porträts deutsch-jüdischer Geistesgeschichte* (with *Nachwort* on Germans and Jews by Horkheimer, pp. 255–72), Cologne, 1961

Schmidt, Alfred, *Zur Idee der kritischen Theorie-Elemente der Philosophie Max Horkheimers*, Munich, 1974

Simmel, E. (ed.), *Anti-Semitism: a Social Disease*, New York, 1964

MENDELSSOHN

Schriften zur Metaphysik und Ethik sowie Religionsphilosophie (ed. Moritz Brasch), 2 vols, Leipzig, 1880

Die Familie Mendelssohn 1729 bis 1847 nach Briefen und Tagebüchern (ed. Sebastian Hensel), 2 vols in 1, 2nd ed., Leipzig, 1880

Jerusalem and other Jewish Writings (ed. Alfred Jospe), New York, 1969

Denkmäler jüdischen Geistes (ed. B. May and J. B. Levy). Vol. 1: *Moses Mendelssohn: eine Auswahl aus seinen Schriften und Briefen*, Frankfurt a/M, 1912

Altmann, Alexander, *Moses Mendelssohn: a Biographical Study*, London, 1973

Rotenstreich, Nathan, 'On Mendelssohn's political philosophy', *LBIYB*, 11, 1966, pp. 28–41

RIESSER

Gesammelte Schriften (ed. M. Isler), 4 vols, Frankfurt a/M and Leipzig, 1867

Denkmäler jüdischen Geistes (ed. B. May and J. B. Levy). Vol. 2: *Gabriel Riesser: eine Auswahl aus seinen Schriften und Briefen*, Frankfurt a/M, 1913

Feiner, J., *Gabriel Riessers Leben und Wirken*, Hamburg, 1906

Isler, M., *Gabriel Riesser's Leben nebst Mitteilungen aus seinen Briefen* (vol. 1 of Isler's ed. of *Gesammelte Schriften*)

Rinott, Moshe, 'Gabriel Riesser: fighter for Jewish emancipation', *LBIYB*, 7, 1962, pp. 11–38

Veit, M., 'Dem Andenken G. Riessers', *Preussische Jahrbücher*, vol. 11, Berlin, 1863, pp. 516–32

Studies on the Times of Mendelssohn and Riesser

Glatzer, Nahum, 'The dynamics of emancipation', part 3 of *The Judaic Tradition*, Boston, 1969

Graupe, Heinz Moshe, *Die Entstehung des modernen Judentums: Geistesgeschichte der deutschen Juden 1650–1942*, Hamburg, 1969

Kampmann, Wanda, *Deutsche und Juden: Studien zur Geschichtes des deutschen Judentums*, Heidelberg, 1963

Katz, Jacob, *Out of the Ghetto: the Social Background of Jewish Emancipation 1770–1870*, Cambridge, Mass., 1973

Mayer, Michael A., *The Origins of the Modern Jew: Jewish Identity and European Culture in Germany 1749–1824*, Detroit, 1967

Rotenstreich, Nathan, *Jewish Philosophy in Modern Times: from Mendelssohn to Rosenzweig*, New York, 1968

Stern-Taeubler, Selma, 'The first generation of emancipated Jews', *LBIYB*, 15, 1970, pp. 3–40

Toury, Jacob, *Die politischen Orientierung der Juden in Deutschland: von Jena bis Weimar*, Tübingen, 1966

Wiener, Max, *Jüdische Religion im Zeitalter der Emanzipation*, Berlin, 1933

SOMBART

The Jews and Modern Capitalism (trans. M. Epstein; Introduction by B. F. Moselitz), New York, 1962 (first pub. 1911)

Die Zukunft der Juden, Leipzig, 1912

Deutscher Sozialismus, Berlin, 1934

Sombart, Werner *et al.*, *Judentaufen* (ed. A. Landsberger), Munich, 1912

Friedlander, Fritz, 'From Marx to Hitler: centenary of Werner Sombart's birth', *AJR Information*, 18 (1), 1963

STRAUSS

Das Leben Jesu für das deutsche Volk bearbeitet, 9th–11th ed., Bonn, 1895

WEBER

The Protestant Ethic and the Spirit of Capitalism (trans. Talcott Parsons), London, 1930

Ancient Judaism (trans. and ed. H. H. Gerth and D. Martindale), New York and London, 1952

The Sociology of Religion (trans. E. Fischoff; Introduction by T. Parsons), London, 1965

On Charisma and Institution Building (ed. S. N. Eisenstadt), Chicago and London, 1968

The Interpretation of Social Reality (ed. J. E. T. Eldridge), London, 1971

Arkin, Marcus, 'West European Jewry in the age of mercantilism', *Historia Judaica*, 22 (2), 1960, pp. 85–104

Bendix, Reinhard, *Max Weber: an Intellectual Portrait*, London, 1966

Birnbaum, N., 'Conflicting interpretations of the rise of capitalism: Marx and Weber', *Brit. J. Sociology*, 4, 1953, pp. 125–41

Bosse, Hans, *Marx-Weber-Troeltsch: Religionssoziologie und marxistische Ideologiekritik*, Munich, 1970

Eisenstadt, S. N. (ed.), *The Protestant Ethic and Modernization*, New York, 1968
Freud, Julien, *The Sociology of Max Weber* (trans. M. Ilford), London, 1968
Green, Robert W. (ed.), *Protestantism and Capitalism: the Weber Thesis and its Critics*, Lexington, Mass., 1959.
Hoffmann, Moses, *Der Geldhandel der deutschen Juden während des Mittelalters bis zum Jahre 1350*, Leipzig, 1910
Kitch, M. J., *Capitalism and the Reformation*, London, 1967
König, R. and Winckelmann, J. (eds), *Max Weber zum Gedächtnis*, Cologne, n.d.
Liebeschütz, Hans, 'Max Weber's historical interpretation of Judaism', *LBIYB*, 9, 1964, pp. 41–68
Nelson, Benjamin, *The Idea of Usury: from Tribal Brotherhood to Universal Otherhood*, 2nd ed., Chicago and London, 1969
Oelsner, Toni, 'The place of the Jews in economic history as viewed by German scholars', *LBIYB*, 7, 1962, pp. 183–212
Rabinowitz, J. J. (ed.), *The Code of Maimonides: the Book of Civil Law*, New Haven and London, 1949
Roscher, Wilhelm, 'The status of the Jews in the middle ages considered from the standpoint of commercial policy', *Historia Judaica*, 6, 1944, pp. 13–26
Schiper, I., 'Max Weber and the sociological basis of the Jewish religion', *Jewish J. Sociol.*, 1, 1959, pp. 250–60
Stein, Siegfried, 'The development of the Jewish law on interest from the biblical period to the expulsion of the Jews from England', *Historia Judaica*, 17 (1), 1955, pp. 3–40
Stein, Siegfried, 'Interest taken by Jews from Gentiles: an evaluation of source material (14th–17th centuries)', *J. Semitic Hist.*, 1 (1), 1956, pp. 141–64
Tawney, R. H., *Religion and the Rise of Capitalism*, Penguin, 1938
Troeltsch, Ernst, *The Social Teaching of the Christian Churches*, 2 vols, London, 1956 (first pub. 1911; first English trans. 1931)
Troeltsch, Ernst, *Protestantism and Progress*, Boston, 1958 (first pub. 1912)
Troeltsch, Ernst, *Aufsätze zur Geistesgeschichte und Religionssoziologie* (ed. H. Baron), Tübingen, 1925

JEWS, SOCIALISTS AND JEWISH SOCIALISTS

Buber, Martin, *Paths in Utopia* (trans. R. F. C. Hull; Introduction by E. Fischoff), Boston, 1958
Deutscher, Isaac, *The Non-Jewish Jew and other essays*, London, 1968
Duker, A. G. (ed.), *Nationalism and the Class Struggle: a Marxian Approach to the Jewish Problem: Selected Writings by Ber Borochov*, Westport, Conn., 1972
Epstein, Melech, *The Jew and Communism: the Story of Early Communist Victories and Ultimate Defeats in the Jewish Community U.S.A. 1919–1941*, New York, 1959
Getzler, Israel, *Martov: a Political Biography of a Russian Social Democrat*, Melbourne and London, 1967
Gitelman, Zvi Y., *Jewish Nationality and Soviet Politics: the Jewish Sections of the CPSU 1917–1930*, Princeton, N.J., 1972

Heller, Otto, *Der Untergang des Judentums: die Judenfrage—ihre Kritik, ihre Lösung durch den Sozialismus*, Vienna and Berlin, 1931

Hirsch, Helmut, *Rosa Luxemburg in Selbstzeugnissen und Bilddokumenten*, Hamburg, 1969

Kautsky, Karl, *Are the Jews a Race?*, London, 1926

Kochan, Lionel (ed.), *The Jews in Soviet Russia since 1917*, 2nd ed., London, 1972

Licththeim, George, 'Socialism and the Jews', *Dissent*, July-August 1968, pp. 314–42

Lipset, Seymour M., ' "The socialism of fools": the left, the Jews and Israel', *Encounter*, December 1969, pp. 1–11

Marxist Zionists—Young Mapam, *Ber Borochov: Essays on 'Nationalism, Class Struggle and the Jewish People'*, London, 1971

Mayer, Gustav, 'Early German socialism and Jewish emancipation', *Jew. Soc. Stud.*, 1, 1939, pp. 409–22

Mendelsohn, Ezra, *Class Struggle in the Pale: the Formative Years of the Jewish Workers' Movement in Tsarist Russia*, London, 1940

Merchav, Peretz, *Die Israelische Linke: Zionismus und Arbeiterbewegung in der Geschichte Israels*, Frankfurt a/M, 1972

Nedava, Joseph, *Trotsky and the Jews*, Philadelphia, 1972

Nettl, Peter, *Rosa Luxemburg*, abridged ed., London, 1969

Patkin, A. L., *The Origins of the Russian-Jewish Labor Movement*, Melbourne and London, 1947

Perlmutter, Amos, 'Dov Ber Borochov: a Marxist-Zionist ideologist', *Middle Eastern Studies*, 1, 1969, pp. 32–43

Strauss, Eli, *Geht das Judentum unter? Erwiderung auf Otto Heller*, Vienna, 1933

Szajkowski, Zosa, 'The Jewish Saint-Simonians and socialist antisemites in France', *Jew. Soc. Stud.*, 9, 1947, pp. 33–60

Tobias, Henry J., *The Jewish Bund in Russia: from its Origins to 1905*, Stanford, 1972

Uexküll, Gösta v., *Ferdinand Lassalle in Selbstzeugnissen und Bilddokumenten*, Hamburg, 1974

459

Index

(Titles not of periodicals are works by Marx)

Abarbanel, Don, 223, 225
Ackerman, N. W., 347
Adler, Victor, 205, 337, 342
Adorno, Theodor, 247, 348
Alexander the Great, 100
Allgemeine Zeitung des Judentums
  (*AZJ*), 45, 50, 68, 82, 125, 145
Altenstein, Karl, 66, 126–7, 332
Alush, Naji, 356
Arendt, Hannah, 210
Arndt, E. M., 66
Aveling, Edward, 263–4, 421
Avineri, Shlomo, 165, 175, 278–9,
  295, 307, 361, 367, 427

Bakunin, Mikhail, 273, 297, 311–12,
  318, 338
Banning, W., 111
Baron, S. W., 219
Basedow, J. B., 30
Bauer, Bruno, 1, 6, 9–10, 16, 46, 60,
  66, 68, 74, 80, 82, 97, 103–4, 108–9,
  111, 118–20, 122, 125–47, 150,
  152–3, 158–9, 163–8, 170, 172–3,
  176–82, 188, 190, 192, 207, 213,
  215–16, 227–8, 230–2, 247, 267,
  270–1, 276–8, 284–8, 294, 298,
  307–8, 315, 325, 383, 395
Bauer, Edgar, 147
Bauer, Otto, 200–2, 205, 291, 366

Baur, F., 65
Beaumont, Gustave de, 164
Bebel, August, 209
Beer, Max, 325
Bein, Alex, 353
Bell, Daniel, 275–6
Ben Nachum, Daniel, 298, 306–8,
  336, 369
Berger, Peter, 240
Berlin, Isaiah, 2, 283, 359, 361
Bernays, Ferdinand Coelestin, 157–9,
  161–2, 163, 402
Bernstein, Eduard, 264–5, 286, 319,
  336–7, 342, 354
Bienenfeld, Rudolf, 313
Bismarck, 313
Blittersdorf, F. K., 162
Bloch, Jochanan, 296–7
Bloom, Solomon F., 286–7, 359, 361
Blum, Léon, 290
Blumenberg, Werner, 111, 316, 331
Bograd, Rosalia, 204
Bolin, W., 111
Börne, Ludwig, 32–3, 151, 263, 314,
  334, 342
Borochov, Ber, 63–4, 197–9, 201,
  206, 208, 298, 306, 308–9
Bottomore, T., 371
Breuer, Raphael, 282
Buber, Martin, 277
Bukharin, N. I., 309

461

Glasner, Peter E., 369
Glenn, Hermann, 314
Glickson, Moshe, 291–3, 336, 354
Glock, C. Y. and Stark, R., 348
Glogau, Otto, 355
Glückel of Hameln, 14
Göhler, Baron Julius von, 162–3
Goldschmidt, H. L., 336
Graetz, Heinrich, 29, 368
Graetz, Michael, 288, 354
Grimm brothers, 353
Gumnior, Helmut, 254

Haber, Baron Moritz von, 162–3
Haller, Karl Ludwig von, 66
Hamilton, Thomas, 164
Hardenberg, Karl, 15, 23, 31, 58, 332
Hasselmann, Wilhelm, 341, 354–5
Haufer, Otto, 318
Häusler, Wolfgang, 367
Heer, Friedrich, 238, 316, 319
Hegel, G. W. F., 6, 24–5, 76–7,
    80–1, 94–5, 99, 103, 109, 112,
    132–3, 140, 143–7, 148–50, 152–3,
    158, 167, 189, 215, 227, 242, 253,
    288–9, 294, 332–3, 339
Heidegger, Martin, 240
Heine, Heinrich, 20, 26, 32–3, 35,
    37, 73, 78–82, 152, 157, 188–92,
    228, 230, 263, 285, 321, 333, 340,
    342, 360, 367, 369, 401
Heinemann, F. H., 20
Heller, Otto, 5, 206–11, 213
Hengstenberg, E. W., 125–6, 395
Hermes, Carl H., 68, 74, 83–5, 89,
    111, 125, 130, 153, 165–8, 180
Herwegh, Georg, 66, 158
Herz, Henrietta, 23
Herz, Jakob, 105
Herzl, Theodor, 253, 309, 342
Hess, Mendel, 139–41, 396, 399, 425
Hess, Michael, 30, 34–5
Hess, Moses, 73, 98, 109–24, 152,
    157, 160, 193–7, 199, 202, 206,
    243, 254, 275, 277–8, 306–9, 316,
    321, 324, 341, 360, 367–8, 408
Hirsch, Helmut, 83

Hirsch, Samson Raphael, 43–4
Hirsch, Samuel, 145
Hitler, Adolf, 187, 204, 253, 312,
    314, 318, 349–52, 354–6
Hochhauser, Daniel, 367
Hoffmann, J. G., 33
Holy Family, The, 2, 74, 138, 174,
    176, 178, 188, 270, 283, 295, 357
Hook, Sidney, 266
Horkheimer, Max, 234–57, 417–18,
    420
Hoselitz, Bert, 232
Humboldt, K. W., 58, 382

Institute for Marxism-Leninism
    (Moscow), 111, 405, 421
Itzig, Daniel, 53, 375
Itzstein, Johann Adam von, 162
Ivanov, K., 356

Jacobson, Israel, 39–41
Jacoby, Johann, 67, 157–9, 367
Jahn, 'Turnvater', 66
Jahoda, Marie, 347
Jellinek, Hermann, 127, 145–6, 367,
    396
Jeremiah, 303, 315, 326
Jesus, 81, 94, 102, 109, 132–3, 143,
    313
John, St, 332
Josel of Rosheim, 223, 225
Joseph, Rabbi, 220–1
Josephus, 99
Jost, J. M., 26, 44

Kahn, Fritz, 313, 318
Kamenka, Eugene, 331
Kann, R. A., 63–4
Kant, Immanuel, 37, 93–4, 108, 143,
    146, 148, 152–3, 238, 253, 287
Kapp, Yvonne, 367
Kapsali, Rabbi, 222
Karl Ludwig Friedrich, Grand Duke,
    162
Katz, J., 371, 377

Modena, Leon da, 223, 225
Mohammed, Sultan, 69
Montefiore, Moses, 71–2, 74, 86
Moser, Moses, 25, 35, 333
Moses, 81, 88, 93, 129, 133, 140, 190,
    195, 313, 315, 317–18
Müller, Kurt, 313
Müller-Tellering, E. von, 272, 423

Na'aman, Shlomo, 367
Nachmanides, Rabbi, 221–2
Napoleon, 58, 130, 193
Neale, R. S., 61
Neander, J. A. W., 73, 96, 322, 337,
    340, 342, 385
Neue Rheinische Zeitung (NRZ),
    271–2, 274–5
New York Daily Tribune, 359–61, 363
News Chronicle, 201
Nini, Yehuda, 308–9

O'Connell, Daniel, 71–2
'On the Jewish Question', 9, 74, 110,
    112, 118, 121, 150, 165, 174–5,
    177–8, 182, 197, 261, 269, 273,
    276–8, 282, 285–6, 288, 292, 297,
    301, 323, 341, 352, 355–6, 365–6
Oppenheim, Dagobert, 82, 152
Oppenheimer, H. B., 49
Orient, Der, 145
Owen, Robert, 316

Palmerston, Lord, 70–1
Parkes, James, 226
Paul, St, 79, 133, 247
Paulus, H. E. G., 48
Peel, Robert, 71
Pfefferkorn, Johannes, 332
Philippson, Gustav, 145–6
Philippson, Ludwig, 45–6, 69, 82–4,
    145, 147
Philo Judaeus, 96, 99, 104, 107
Picciotto, Isaac Levi, 70
Pinsker, Leo, 299
Plekhanov, G. V., 204–5, 291

Plessner, Solomon, 43
Poliakov, Léon, 358, 414
Popitz, H., 278
Popper, K., 430
Poverty of Philosophy, 328
Proudhon, P.-J., 273, 297, 338

Rabenu Tam, 221
Rashi, 221–2
Ratti-Menton, Count, 70–1, 78
Reuchlin, Johannes, 332
Riazanov, David, 286, 314
Richelieu, Cardinal, 80
Riesser, Gabriel, 46–50, 71, 74, 97,
    135, 177
Robb, J. H., 348
Röhr, Heinz, 316
Roscher, Wilhelm, 216–17, 229
Rosdolsky, Roman, 268, 271–6,
    338–9, 423
Rotenstreich, Nathan, 109, 139, 294,
    329, 390
Roth, Cecil, 11
Rothschild, Baron James, 79–80, 87
Rothschild family, 80, 286, 340
Rudy, Z., 10
Ruge, Arnold, 111–13, 127, 136,
    157, 161, 163, 188, 190, 311
Rühle, Otto, 287, 312
Runes, Dagobert, 266, 354
Ruppin, A., 10
Russian Social Democratic Labour
    Party, 203–4

Salomon, Gotthold, 143, 399
Sartre, Jean-Paul, 4, 149, 319, 340,
    344
Savigny, Friedrich Karl von, 332
Schleiermacher, Friedrich, 22, 96
Scholem, G., 375
Scholz, Dietmar, 278, 370
Schrötter, Friedrich L. von, 31
Schwarz, Robert, 322
Shazar, S., 375
Silberner, Edmund, 110, 112, 118,
    122, 293–4, 296, 306, 316, 336–7,
    345, 348, 354, 359, 361, 367, 394